Politics and War

POLITICS AND WAR

European Conflict from Philip II to Hitler

ENLARGED EDITION

David Kaiser

Harvard University Press
Cambridge, Massachusetts
London, England
2000

This book was prepared in part under a one-month grant from the
Woodrow Wilson International Center for Scholars, Washington, D.C.

Cataloging-in-publication data is available from the Library of Congress.

Politics is much harder than physics.

—Albert Einstein

We are much beholden to Machiavelli and other writers of that class, who openly and unfeignedly declare or describe what men do, and not what they ought to do.

—Francis Bacon

Contents

Preface, 2000

This book first appeared in 1990, not long after Paul Kennedy had published *The Rise and Fall of the Great Powers*, a very different general survey of European and world history that concluded with some tentative and qualified predictions about the future. Since then, the collapse of Communism and the disintegration of the Soviet Union, Yugoslavia, and Czechoslovakia have utterly transformed European international politics. Meanwhile, two other large-scale historical theories of international politics have appeared. One, put forth most notably in Spencer Weart's *Never at War* and Michael Doyle's *Ways of War and Peace*, argues that peace and democracy go hand in hand, and that the spread of democracy will inevitably reduce or eliminate war as an element of international politics. The other theory, advocated by the political scientist Samuel Huntington in *The Clash of Civilizations*, predicts that differences among civilizations—defined mainly by common religion or philosophy—will now become the major sources of international conflict. As a millennium ends, metahistory and large-scale analysis are enjoying a revival.

This book had a different premise, namely, that war in any era of European history was closely related to politics, and that its purposes, scope, and duration could only be understood in the context of European politics as a whole. Each era of general war in Europe grew out of specific political developments: the uncontrolled power of aristocracies in the late sixteenth and early seventeenth centuries, the consolidation of monarchies in the late seventeenth, the expansion of state power and the new spirit of rationalism in the late eighteenth, and the twin problems of imperialism and the rights of nationalities in the twentieth. In each case, in contrast to many earlier treatments that saw most of the nations of Europe uniting to defeat a single aggressor, I argued that the common features of European politics far overshadowed the differences among the various states.

The reissue of this book is doubly timely. On the one hand, the end of the Cold War allows for the statement of some broader conclusions than I was originally able to reach about the years 1945–1991—not, of course, another era of general European war, but an era that showed some similarities to the first half of the century. On the other hand, Europe clearly entered into a new era in the 1990s, and as the century ends, its own particular threats to the peace and their close resemblance to earlier periods have become fairly clear. I address both these issues in a new epilogue.

The first edition of this book referred more than once to Carl von Clausewitz, the greatest of all theorists of war. In the last nine years, while teaching in the Strategy and Policy Department of the Naval War College in Newport, Rhode Island, I have come to realize that *Politics and War* complements his classic book *On War*, because it systematically addresses key issues to which he paid very little attention. Clausewitz emphasized, of course, that war must serve politics (or "policy," which in his language is the same word), but he paid much less attention to the nature of policy in different eras—that is, to the changing objectives for which war was fought. I have argued, in contrast, that the nature of policy in different eras, and above all the extent to which military power allows governments to secure the objectives they seek, determine the character of war in different periods of European history. Of the four eras this book treats in detail, the first and the last were the most violent and the most destructive precisely because European states sought ends beyond their capacity to achieve. The same kind of analysis must now be applied to the new problems facing the states of Eastern Europe and the former Soviet Union—a region once again in crisis—and to the responses that Western Europe and the United States, now united within NATO, make to them.

I also wrote this book to show how the vast body of monographic literature that the historical profession has generated during the last one hundred years or more might be used to draw general conclusions about the past while taking full account of the individual characteristics of every period. In so doing, I seem to have gone well beyond the boundaries of the interests of nearly any other

professional historian. I still believe that every individual mono-
graph should have a broader application, and that the critical
characteristics of any particular period in history emerge only
when compared with another. Thus I welcome the opportunity to
reintroduce *Politics and War.*

Politics and War

Introduction

This book treats an old topic from a new perspective. The study of European war has occupied historians at least since the time of Leopold von Ranke, and although the focus of professional historians has largely shifted away from politics and diplomacy in recent decades, general treatments of European war in the modern era have continued to appear. The overwhelming majority of such treatments have taken a broadly similar approach. They generally treat every era of European war as an attempt by one power or coalition of powers to conquer most or all of Europe, and focus upon the reasons for the failure of such attempts. They pay relatively little detailed attention to the sources of European international conflict, implicitly considering war a normal phenomenon or assuming that states naturally try to expand. For all these reasons, most discussions of different eras of European war from the sixteenth through the twentieth centuries have an essential similarity.[1]

Here I argue instead that the sources and consequences of European international conflict differ radically from one era to another, and that they can be understood only in the context of contemporary European domestic and international politics. In four distinct periods of European history—1559–1659, 1661–1713, 1792–1815, and 1914–1945—war became a natural function of politics, an inevitable result of contemporary political behavior. The wars of these eras must be understood within their political, eco-

1. The most recent example of this tendency is Paul Kennedy, *The Rise and Fall of the Great Powers: Economic Change and Military Conflict from 1500 to 2000* (New York, 1987).

nomic, social, and intellectual context. Each period of general war reflects a distinct stage in the political development of modern Europe—a stage in which states fought wars for particular ends, with specific means, and with particular consequences. While many historians have traced the origins of each era of general European war to the ambitions of one particular power—Spain in the sixteenth century, France and England from the late seventeenth through the early nineteenth centuries, and Germany in the twentieth[2]—I argue instead that general war in Europe does not normally grow out of the ambitions of one power or coalition, but reflects a common set of European political developments among all the major European powers. Even if one power bears more responsibility for beginning a conflict, the conduct of all involved powers usually becomes almost indistinguishable. Within such an analysis, the issue of winners and losers—the focus of so much previous discussion—retreats into relative insignificance. In each of these eras the similarities among states—in economic strength and military tactics, as well as in political systems and social structure—generally outweigh the differences. Their similarities are reflected in the generally indecisive outcomes of the wars they fought. Of these four eras, only one, the last, ended with a decisive victory, and that victory was won mainly by one partially non-European power, the Soviet Union, and by the United States of America.

Thus, during the years 1559–1659, the almost continuous wars which plagued Europe revolved around the unsuccessful attempts of European monarchs to impose their authority upon great aristocrats and to impose religious uniformity throughout their domains—tasks which they lacked the necessary resources to accomplish. War in that period was the very essence of aristocratic politics, as well as one of the means by which the aristocracy drew resources from the rest of society, and the so-called general crisis of the 1640s was just one episode in a whole century of crisis. Then, during the rule of Louis XIV (1661–1715), the Sun King and his fellow monarchs largely brought European violence under their control, and changed the pattern of international conflict in ways which not only strengthened their own authority but made

2. For a classic treatment along these lines, see Ludwig Dehio, *The Precarious Balance: Four Centuries of European Struggle* (New York, 1962). Kennedy, *Rise and Fall of the Great Powers*, also frequently takes this approach.

war much less destructive to European society as a whole. By the time of the revolutionary and Napoleonic period, war was accepted not only as a right but as a duty of European states, who used it to consolidate central authority at the expense of surviving feudal institutions and to reorder the map of Europe along theoretically more rational lines. War also became a channel of social and political mobility and an outlet for the ambition of rising social groups. The course and consequences of the two world wars, whose human and material effects rivaled those of the wars of 1559–1659, reflected the gap between contemporary beliefs and contemporary European social and economic reality. They were fought partly for the purpose of establishing economically self-sufficient empires—a goal which the development of the world economy had rendered obsolete—and partly in an attempt to apply the principle of nationality to a Europe composed of mixed populations.

Indeed, in each era the relationship between idea and reality largely determined the extent and the effects of general war. Thus, the politics of the twentieth century required European governments to seek the total defeat of their opponents, even though they not only lacked the resources to achieve this but also had no prospect of any gain that would compensate for the cost of victory. The political logic of the late sixteenth and early seventeenth centuries encouraged monarchs forcibly to impose their authority upon their nobility and to enforce religious uniformity upon their subjects, despite their lack of the resources which would enable them to do so. In the era of Louis XIV and in the revolutionary and Napoleonic period, contemporary political logic also required rulers frequently to undertake war, but it did not so frequently require them to attempt the impossible. As a result, the wars of those eras destroyed far less than the struggles of the years 1559–1659 or 1914–1945. Politics has a logic of its own, and the logic which governs political behavior need not seem reasonable or sensible when evaluated according to its consequences.

The organization of this book reflects its emphasis on politics as the source of war. Each of its four main chapters begins with a brief survey of the politics of the era and the ways in which contemporary politics promoted international conflict. Because the sources, nature, and consequences of war vary enormously from era to era, however, I have not adopted a single organizational scheme for all four periods but have rather tried to organize each analysis in the way best calculated to bring out the particular period's features. Each era is characterized by certain special political problems and by contemporary rulers' specific responses to them—responses which involved the sustained use of military power. In each case, politics operated within its own autonomous sphere, but nonetheless reflected and powerfully affected contemporary social, economic, and intellectual life. The work as a whole provides a comparative treatment of European politics in the modern era, as well as of European war.

Narrative plays an important role in my presentation, but always within a well-defined analytical framework. One cannot show how certain common patterns of behavior characterized each of these periods of European history without discussing key events in some detail. Comprehensive arguments require a comprehensive demonstration. While presenting new analyses of different periods of European war, my book will acquaint the reader with the essential facts of the last four centuries of European conflict—and rare indeed is the contemporary reader who already knows them, even within the professional historical community.

Individuals also play an important role in my analysis, but their role must always be understood within a broader political framework. Although political leaders make the decisions that lead to war and peace, they can only exercise power according to the rules of contemporary politics. In the short run, their effectiveness depends upon the manipulation of contemporary beliefs and institutions, while in the long run it often depends upon their understanding of the need to reconcile existing beliefs with inescapable realities. Every age includes men like Wallenstein, Olivares, Louis XIV, Napoleon, Bethmann-Hollweg, Lloyd George, and Hitler, who exemplify particular aspects of contemporary political behavior, and whose careers therefore reflect in striking detail the politics of their age. Each era also includes politicians such as Henry IV of France, Elizabeth I of England, Lord Salisbury, or German Imperial Chancellor Bernhard von Bülow, who understand the problems inherent in the illogic of contemporary political wisdom, and who therefore manage to avoid certain critical pitfalls. Precisely because of their unusual perspicacity, however, individuals of the latter type generally exercise only a limited influence upon the course of European politics. Most politicians share, or at least respect, the illusions of their age, and therefore suffer the consequences of these illusions along with their peoples. Even Napoleon and Hitler, who initially took advantage of contemporary circumstances to achieve spectacular conquests or wreak enormous destruction, ultimately encountered the limits imposed by their circumstances.

This book differs from many earlier treatments in another way as well. Since Ranke, the historiography of European warfare has tended to idealize the state and its works, including warfare. While some historians have chosen simply to champion the claims of one state against the rest of Europe, others, like Ranke, have seen states as embodiments of the individual genius of nations, or as independent entities pursuing a higher good. Either approach bathes the doings of soldiers and statesmen in an aura of majesty. Such an attitude can produce inspiring writing but does not in my view promote historical understanding. This book tells a very different story. Here the history of European international conflict emerges not as a triumphant story of human progress, or of the victories and defeats of particular European states, but rather as a series of tragedies. War, though frequently a critical aspect of politics, has been a largely sterile pursuit. European society has survived and prospered, but the great economic and intellectual advances of modern civilization have generally taken place during periods of peace. Europe's eras of general war testify to the enormous latent emotional power of war and politics in Western civilization, if not indeed in mankind as a whole. They reveal war as a recurring form of political behavior, one which in these periods became the essence of politics—often, and especially in the twentieth century, with terrible consequences. War and politics are not humanity's highest callings, but their enormous consequences touch upon virtually every other aspect of life.

1 The General Crisis of the Sixteenth and Seventeenth Centuries

The wisest philosophers have for long taught us that it is impossible to avoid sedition in a kingdom, if persons of worth see themselves rejected and lose hope of achieving the dignities they think they have merited by their birth and virtue.

—Pomponne de Bellièvre to King Henry IV of France, 1598

The Nature of Early Modern Politics

The armed conflicts which took place all over Europe between 1559 and 1659 grew out of three fundamental elements of European political life: the power and values of the aristocracy; the attempts by various European monarchs to assert more power and authority than their resources could command; and the spread of religious differences, which intensified these political conflicts. These problems lay behind all the major conflicts of this century of crisis—the revolts against Spanish rule in the Netherlands, Catalonia, and Portugal; the civil wars in France; the Thirty Years' War in Germany; and the civil wars in the British Isles in the 1640s and 1650s. While some of the conflicts of the era have customarily been regarded as civil wars or rebellions and others as wars between states, the political structure of Europe in the late sixteenth and early seventeenth centuries actually blurs the distinction between domestic and international conflict. All formed a part of a general struggle among the European aristocracy for economic and political power. To understand these wars, we must look first at the aristocracy and the nature of aristocratic politics; second, at the goals of contemporary monarchs; and last, at the nature of early modern armies, and the ways in which they affected the course of armed conflict. We shall then look in more detail at the politics of the Spanish empire, France, the Holy Roman Empire, and England, to see how each of them reflected the same underlying social and political problems.

The Politics of the European Aristocracy

Although by the sixteenth century the European nobility had to contend with interlopers from other ranks of society, its values still reigned supreme. The lesser nobility in particular seems to have been losing power and influence to other classes. The increasing importance of education favored the bourgeoisie in the competition for administrative and judicial positions, and at the infrequent meetings of the French Estates General in the latter half of the sixteenth century the nobility protested its loss of government offices.[1] But noble values still dominated society. In Spain, rising bourgeois aspired to a noble way of life and regarded their own class as something to escape from. Even in the Netherlands, where the urban bourgeoisie played a major political role, it frequently invested in land, seigneurial rights, and titles of nobility, both for reasons of prestige and as a hedge against endemic inflation.[2] Virtually all available evidence suggests that the rising official class wanted to join, rather than to supplant, the aristocracy.

The values of the nobility varied relatively little across the aristocratic spectrum. From the king of Aragon and Castile to the impoverished *gentilhommes* of rural France, nobles sought to preserve and extend the holdings of their house, to increase their own power and influence at the expense of their neighbors, to accumulate marks of wealth and status such as books, new edifices, and works of art, and to establish useful ties with others who could help them. Monarchs like Philip II, clerics like Richelieu, bureaucrats like Antonio Perez, and military entrepreneurs like Wallenstein all followed such strategies. And while their business was frequently the business of the state, none of these men recognized any real distinction between the public welfare and their own.

Aristocratic networks of influence and patronage were the basic units of early modern politics. In seeking his fortune each noble

---

1. Lucien Romier, *Le royaume de Cathérine de Medici: La France à la veille des guerres de religion* (Paris, 1922), pp. 168–181.

2. Fernand Braudel, *The Mediterranean and the Mediterranean World in the Age of Philip II*, 2 vols. (New York, 1972), II, 725–734; D. J. Roorda, "The Ruling Classes in Holland in the Seventeenth Century," in J. S. Bromley and E. H. Kossmann, eds., *Britain and the Netherlands*, vol. 2 (Utrecht, 1964), pp. 109–132.

possessed one critical asset: his personal allegiance, which he could assign to a more powerful patron in exchange for money, favor, and support. Although pure feudalism based upon grants of land in exchange for military service had disappeared, clientage and patronage still held the upper layers of society together.[3] Patrons and clients pledged mutual support and assistance, and clients could expect to share in their patron's good fortune. The importance of patronage was reflected in dress. Most nobles wore livery which marked them as adherents of a particular grandee. Clients sought favor, and patrons granted it, for any number of reasons: kinship, a long-standing connection between families, sexual favors granted by the client's daughter or wife (though these, of course, could estrange men as easily as unite them), or a particular skill of which the patron could make use. Some evidence suggests that great men regarded their willingness to take in *anyone* who would pledge his loyalty as a basic attribute of lordship. One common instrument of patronage was the noble household, which obviously varied greatly in size from the bottom of the aristocratic scale to the top, but which always provided places to fill with youths from the immediately inferior noble stratum—youths who would grow up to become reliable clients.

The stability of the political order depended upon the strength of the client-patron ties that held it together. And while for a few nobles the client-patron tie seems to have been virtually unbreakable, many others seem to have regarded their allegiance as a conditional grant, easily withdrawn from an unrewarding patron. The strength of ties of patronage and clientage seems to have varied inversely with the stature of patrons and clients, and ties between monarchs and great aristocrats often proved to be the weakest of all. Men of distinction quickly broke off connections that had lost their utility. Richelieu, who rose under the patronage of Marie de Medici, became her bitter enemy as soon as he had won Louis XIII's confidence, and royal favorites like Essex in England and Cinq-Mars in France rebelled or conspired against their monarchs as soon as they felt they had been slighted.

Armed conflict played a continual role in politics because aristocrats customarily resorted to violence as well as influence to ad-

3. This is a major theme of Roland Mousnier, *Les institutions de la France sous la monarchie absolue*, 2 vols. (Paris, 1974), and Lawrence Stone, *The Crisis of the Aristocracy, 1558–1641* (Oxford, 1965), as well as several important recent works on Bourbon France.

vance their aims.[4] The right to bear arms was a key noble prerogative, jealously guarded and frequently exercised. Whereas in
modern society the poorest and weakest often settle disputes violently, in the early modern period the richest and most powerful
did so. Great men relied on their retainers for armed support,
while their followers eagerly turned real or imagined insults into
occasions for fighting and murder. English monarchs made no serious attempt to control clashes between rival factions. Leading
Spanish political figures routinely included notorious murderers
among their retainers.[5] Even in the late seventeenth century Louis
XIV vainly tried to stop dueling and to assert a royal right to settle
disputes among his nobles, who regarded personal violence as a
prerogative of their status.[6]

Both domestic and international politics revolved around a few
great families—families whose networks of clients often extended
to every corner of their kingdoms, and who frequently offered
their allegiance to foreign princes against their own. While theoretically the vassals of their monarchs, in practice they were often a
law unto themselves. In late sixteenth-century France noble clienteles were divided among the Guise, Bourbon, and Montmorency
factions.[7] In England the great families included the Howards, the
Seymours, the Dudleys, and, under Elizabeth I, the Cecils. In
Spain the duke of Alba and the prince of Eboli led rival factions at
mid-century, while power and patronage in the Netherlands belonged to Orange, Egmont, Horn, and Aerschot. In the Holy Roman Empire princely families divided into parties based mostly,
though not exclusively, upon religion. The pervasiveness of faction
in early modern Europe can hardly be exaggerated. In the early
seventeenth century virtually the entire population of Catalonia
was divided into two factions, the *nyerros* and the *cadells*.[8] Conflicts
among factions never ceased, largely because they fought for intangible, irrational stakes. Great aristocrats, like many other espe-

4. For an interesting discussion of aristocratic violence, see J. R. Hale, *War and Society in Renaissance Europe, 1450–1620* (New York, 1985), pp. 90–99.

5. Stone, *Crisis of the Aristocracy*; Gregorio Marañon, *Antonio Perez* (English edition, London, 1954), pp. 23–38; Geoffrey Parker, *Philip II* (Boston, 1978), pp. 173–174. My thanks to Geoffrey Parker for his criticisms of Chapter 1 of this work.

6. Roger Mettam, *Power and Faction in Louis XIV's France* (New York, 1988), pp. 76–77.

7. For a detailed description, see Romier, *Le royaume de Cathérine de Medici*, pp. 223–230.

8. J. H. Elliott, *The Revolt of the Catalans* (Cambridge, 1963), pp. 64–77.

cially favored individuals, generally measured rewards and satisfactions relatively rather than absolutely, and no amount of prestige or money was adequate if a rival seemed to possess more.

The struggle between factions took various forms. In an age of increasing literacy, a continual flow of pamphlet literature spread the more scurrilous and extraordinary accusations. Many great magnate's clients included spies who infiltrated his rival's household to collect intelligence and, occasionally, to commit murder.[9] Local factions resorted to uncontrolled banditry in remote regions of Spain, France, and England. Behind every political or even social conflict between aristocrats lay the threat that one party might take up arms, and we shall see how often this threat was carried out even by nobles quarreling with their own kings.

Aristocratic rivalry was not the only source of violent conflict in early modern Europe. The spirit of direct action was not confined to the nobility, but the aristocracy generally managed to keep other practitioners of violence under its control. Lower-class resentment of the rich frequently broke out into the open in times of crisis. Urban artisans sometimes took up arms, particularly when moved by a combination of religious and political motives, and peasants intermittently revolted when seigneurial or governmental exactions became intolerable. Rarely, however, did the lower orders threaten the social order, and at no time did the aristocracy allow such threats to become serious. Democratic factions emerged within the revolutionary Holy League in France, the Calvinist resistance in Holland, and the Parliamentary faction in the English civil wars, but their aristocratic allies dealt with them severely as soon as circumstances permitted.[10] Conflict between classes never dominated early modern politics; conflict among the aristocracy did.[11]

At the highest level factional struggles became international. Leading magnates sought the favor of foreign sovereigns as soon

9. Francis, duke of Guise, and William of Orange were murdered by men infiltrated into their households by Gaspard de Coligny and by the duke of Parma.

10. On France and the Netherlands, see H. L. Koenigsberger, "The Organization of Revolutionary Parties in France and the Netherlands during the Sixteenth Century," in Koenigsberger, *Estates and Revolutions: Essays in Early Modern History* (Ithaca, 1971), pp. 244–252.

11. J. H. Elliott, "Revolution and Continuity in Early Modern Europe," *Past and Present*, 42 (February 1969): 35–56, makes some trenchant observations on views of sixteenth- and seventeenth-century rebellions as class conflicts.

as they became dissatisfied with their own, while monarchs regarded ties with their enemies' vassals as useful assets. During the French civil wars, leaders of the Guise and Bourbon factions continually entered into relations with foreign sovereigns. In the Bohemian civil war in 1618, both Protestant and Catholic factions enlisted foreign help, and when in 1630 Emperor Ferdinand II dismissed his general Wallenstein, Wallenstein opened talks with the emperor's enemy the king of Sweden. Such connections, examples of which could be multiplied almost indefinitely, gave international relations their almost anarchic character.

In the almost complete independence of the great lords of much of Europe lies the key to both the domestic and international politics of the century beginning in 1559. Indeed, the line between princes and magnates was not clearly drawn. Several magnates, such as Anthony of Bourbon, king of Navarre, and William, prince of Orange, ruled sovereign principalities, while others, such as the Guises, had married into royal houses and dared to aspire to thrones themselves. They seem to have seen their allegiance to their princes as entirely conditional, and they negotiated freely with foreign princes. Marriage linked many of them across frontiers. Both Count Egmont and William of Orange were linked by marriage to the French Montmorencys, and at one time William had been a suitor for the hand of Mary Stuart, a granddaughter of the duke of Guise, who instead married Francis, dauphin of France, and later became Mary, Queen of Scots. Nor is it coincidental that so many of them—including two dukes of Guise, Condé, Coligny, Egmont, Horn, and Orange—met violent deaths. Their execution or assassination reflected the importance of their persons.

The religious divisions of the late sixteenth and early seventeenth centuries accentuated the tendency toward anarchy in European politics. While the power and factiousness of the aristocracy created chaos even in areas of religious homogeneity, competing religious factions—almost invariably led by great aristocrats—fought one another with even greater tenacity and bitterness and showed even less willingness to compromise. In France, Huguenots and Catholics waged a continual struggle from 1560 through 1598; in the Netherlands, the rise of Calvinism became a key issue of the revolt against Philip II; and religious conflict played a central role in the outbreak and course of the Thirty Years' War in Germany and the civil war in England. None would deny the extreme religious fervor of the age, especially among the common people. Yet in politics, religion tended to reinforce the preeminence of the aristocracy, especially when monarchs tried to impose religious uniformity. In France and the Netherlands, the religious conflicts of the late sixteenth century tended both to intensify existing conflicts among aristocratic factions and to create a new series of links between great lords and other social elements. In France leading members of the Montmorency and Bourbon families adopted Calvinism with an eye upon church lands, then almost entirely at the disposal of the Guises. Both the Huguenot organizations of consistories and synods and the subsequent Catholic leagues ultimately depended upon aristocratic patrons.[12] In the Netherlands Calvinist fervor also reinforced the power of the rebellious nobility. As in Germany in the 1520s, religious revolution eventually became linked to social revolution, but in neither case did the aristocratic leadership allow the lower orders to gain the upper hand.[13] Religious change did not undermine the social order; it generally reinforced it.

Religious differences made factional conflicts more bitter and compromise more difficult. In France the exile of Huguenot notables like Coligny and Condé from court, where they were forbidden to exercise their religion, encouraged their plots in the countryside, while the attempt to bring all parties together again for the marriage of Henry of Navarre in 1572 led to the massacre of St. Bartholomew. The Huguenots in turn painted the Catholic faction as entirely subversive of the public welfare, and thereby worthy of elimination. The frequency of assassination during the late sixteenth century testifies both to the importance of the victims and the heightened bitterness of political conflict in an era of religious struggle. Religious differences also undermined the legitimacy of monarchs. Elizabeth I's Protestantism enabled the Guises to dream of putting their own Mary, Queen of Scots, on the English throne, and the Protestantism of King Henry IV enabled Philip II to put forth his own candidate for the French throne.

The violent, uncontrollable ethos of the aristocracy guaranteed a high level of violence in European society during the late six-

12. Robert R. Harding, *Anatomy of a Power Elite* (New Haven, 1978), pp. 46–68.
13. Koenigsberger, "Organization of Revolutionary Parties," pp. 244–252.

teenth and early seventeenth centuries. Attempts by monarchs to increase their authority over the aristocracy led to further conflicts.

The Pretensions and Resources of European Monarchy, 1559–1659

European monarchs—themselves generally representatives of the prevailing aristocratic ethos—bore the responsibility of maintaining public order despite aristocratic factionalism and religious diversity. They could do so only by exercising extraordinary political skill, since attempts to *impose* order, as we shall see, generally produced more chaos. Sixteenth-century monarchs governed successfully only by acknowledging and working within the existing framework of their society and state. Kings had first of all to satisfy their own families, a task which could have far-reaching consequences. Thus, Francis I of France undertook his wars in Italy partly to find a kingdom for his favored youngest son,[14] and Philip II chose four of his viceroys in the Netherlands—probably the most important post he had to fill—from among his family.[15] Beyond that, successful government depended upon a never-ending balancing act among several great families. In Spain the continuing struggle between the Alba and Eboli factions—factions which originated in the great *comunero* revolt of the 1520s—dominated politics, and Charles V and Philip II carefully maintained the balance between them. In the Netherlands Charles shared his favors among several great families, taking care to visit the territory at regular intervals and distribute them in person. To bestow favor exclusively upon any single faction risked armed rebellion among the others, as the Guises discovered when they monopolized state power after Henry II's death in 1559. Henry VIII of England, who customarily did allow one favorite—Wolsey, More, Cromwell, or Norfolk—to monopolize a great deal of royal patronage, periodically swept the slate clean by disgracing the favorite himself. Henry also used judicial terror against those who displeased him—a technique later employed by Cardinal Richelieu. Effective

14. Lucien Romier, *Les origines politiques des guerres de religion*, vol. 1 (Paris, 1913), pp. 1–2.

15. Margaret of Parma was Charles V's illegitimate daughter; Don Juan of Austria was his illegitimate son; Alexander Farnese, duke of Parma, was Margaret's daughter; and the Infanta Isabella, wife of Archduke Albert of Austria, was Philip II's daughter. The interest of the family sometimes transcended that of its individual members, as shown by Philip II's treatment of Don Carlos.

government required the careful distribution of favors to balance contending parties, good intelligence to head off conspiracies, the avoidance of costly foreign adventures and, when possible, intimidation through draconian punishments. Only a few monarchs or favorites such as Elizabeth I, Henry IV of France, and Richelieu proved capable of it, and even they often faced tremendous problems.

At the same time, several other monarchs and royal ministers claimed vast new religious and political powers and tried to impose them by force. The gap between monarchical pretensions and real monarchical authority lies behind much of the chaos of the years 1559–1659. Much of the historiography of early modern Europe focuses upon the supposed rise of the state, and most of it has exaggerated the pace at which state authority increased. Charles Tilly, for example, recently listed the distinguishing features of the kind of state which, he argues, "became dominant in Europe after 1500": its control of "a well-defined, contiguous territory," its relative centralization, its differentiation from other organizations, and its "tendency to acquire a monopoly over the concentrated means of political coercion within its territory."[16] This definition implies that at least some sixteenth-century monarchs disposed of financial resources sufficient to command unchallengeable military force and to maintain an independent, centralized, and loyal bureaucracy. Such, indeed, was the *aim* of numerous monarchs, and their pursuit of this aim lay behind much of the conflict of the years 1559–1659. Philip II, Charles I of England, Emperor Ferdinand II, Olivares, Richelieu, and Mazarin all tried to establish much stronger monarchies based upon a secure and independent revenue, a reliable and effective armed force, and a homogeneous, reliable national church. What historians have tended to ignore, however, is their failure to achieve any of these aims. More than anything else, the tension between the pretensions of European monarchs and the power of European aristocracies created a century of destructive chaos.

Although on the surface monarchs seemed to be securing more control over the church and expanding their civil service in the early sixteenth century, in practice recent institutional changes had tended to benefit the aristocracy. The new national churches were

16. Charles Tilly, "Reflections on the History of European State-Making," in Tilly, ed., *The Formation of National States in Western Europe* (Princeton, 1975), p. 27.

not staffed with clerics primarily loyal to the monarchy. Thus, after securing the patronage of the French church in the Concordat of Bologna in 1516, Francis I handed it over to leading families in return for annual money payments. Monasteries also fell under the patronage system, and great lords distributed benefices without regard to qualifications.[17] The Dutch revolt broke out partly as a result of Philip II's attempt to take monastic patronage out of the hands of the Netherlands' magnates. In England Henry VIII distributed monastic lands to his favorites—often forcing them to cede their own estates in exchange to tighten his grip upon them—while Elizabeth forced bishops to lease their lands to favored nobles at artificially low rates.[18] The Spanish crown did reserve some high church positions for lowborn clerics and had managed to secure large shares of ecclesiastical revenues for its own purposes, but much church patronage went to great families. In Germany Protestant princes diverted church lands to their own purposes, while the ecclesiastical states furnished places for the younger sons of the Catholic princely families.

Nor was the new civil service independent of the aristocracy. All over Europe the rising class of lawyers and other officials sought aristocratic patrons as a matter of course, and when they had amassed enough wealth and power they established factions of their own. In Paris or in the French provinces, no one could expect a position who had not secured the ear of one of the great lords around the king, and the royal governors provided the link between their office-seeking clients and their own patrons at court. Francis I sold more offices than any other previous monarch but established no independent officer class. He preferred to give the offices to aristocratic favorites in return for services and they in turn resold them.[19] The situation was not much different in the Spanish empire, where provincial governors continually sought rewards for their friends—a major theme of the correspondence of Charles V and Philip II—and where the councils that dominated

17. One classic example, Montmorency's nephew the cardinal of Châtillon, had never even taken orders. J. M. H. Salmon, *Society in Crisis: France in the Sixteenth Century* (New York, 1975), pp. 79–92.

18. Stone, *Crisis of the Aristocracy*, pp. 404–408.

19. Martin Wolfe, *The Fiscal System of Renaissance France* (New Haven, 1972), pp. 67–136; see also Roland Mousnier, *La vénalité des offices sous Henri IV et Louis XIII* (Rouen, 1945), pp. 20–28; Harding, *Anatomy of a Power Elite*, pp. 21–45.

the Spanish government constantly struggled over patronage. Even so distinguished a bureaucrat as Antonio Perez, Philip's secretary of state and a major political power in his own right, was known first of all as a client of Ruy Gomez, prince of Eboli.[20] The increasing centralization of patronage in England worked to the advantage of great lords as much as to that of the crown. "It was not merely those who aspired to posts in the central government who had to lobby in the Court," writes Lawrence Stone, "but also those content with a rural life, to whom it was essential to obtain the rangership of a forest, a stewardship, the lease of a manor, the insertion or omission of a name on a commission."[21] On the whole, indeed, officers seem to have divided their allegiance between their patron and their own pocketbook. Office was a mark of favor or, in countries where venality predominated, an investment, and office holders exploited their official and unofficial prerogatives shamelessly.

Life at court revolved around a continuing exchange of gifts and bribes, each calculated to a specific end. The nature of court life found clever expression in a Spanish game, *The Courtier's Philosophy*, first published in 1587 and recently described by Geoffrey Parker.

> The game was played on a board with dice and tokens, and it combined elements from Monopoly and Snakes and Ladders. The board was divided into sixty-three squares, to represent the years of a man's life, some of the squares representing hazards to his progress, others bonuses. Those who landed on square 15, entitled "the step of hope," paid the "bank" and advanced to square 26, "the house of the favorite." By contrast, those who landed on square 32, "the well of forgetfulness," lost a turn and had to pay all the other players to remind the favorite of their existence. Those who landed on square 40, "change of ministers," were sent back to square 10, "the house of adulation"; and those who landed on square 43, "your patron dies," had to go back to the start.[22]

Similarly, the recently published Lisle correspondence shows beyond question that the idea of a bureaucratic Tudor government is a myth, and that exotic and expensive presents did far more to

20. H. G. Koenigsberger, "Patronage and Bribery in the Reign of Charles V," in Koenigsberger, *Estates and Revolutions*, pp. 166–175; see also Marañon, *Antonio Perez*. Perez may actually have been Gomez's son.

21. Stone, *Crisis of the Aristocracy*, p. 402.

22. Parker, *Philip II*, p. 170.

determine the standing of English noblemen than their administrative ability.[23]

Local government rested firmly in aristocratic hands. In France,
royal governors—great aristocrats who customarily rode about
with fifty to five hundred retainers—supervised the entire administration. Lesser officials like *baillis*, *sénéchaux*, and town councillors fell within the governors' patronage, and they supervised the
gendarmerie, responsible for keeping order, and filled it with their
dependents.[24] In England local lords used their retainers to intimidate magistrates and juries, and in Wales and the north ancient
feuds knew no authority but armed force.[25] In Spain only Castile
came under the effective authority of the monarchy at all, and even
in Castile about 70 percent of the territory was ruled independently by magnates, the church, and military orders. Even the *cor-
regidores* whom the king appointed as proxies in the remainder of
Castile frequently succeeded in turning their posts into hereditary
livings.[26]

In practice, the political power of the prince depended upon his
relationships with the great men of his realm. Indeed, the history
of these relationships frequently raises the question of who
needed whom. The great families showed extraordinary independence of mind and deed. Economically they were often more secure than the king. Most royal domains had been substantially
alienated by the mid-sixteenth century, but aristocrats still disposed of enormous estates, together with the clientage that went
with them. Kings flattered and courted them not only with offices
and honor, but with gifts of hard cash. The leading French magnates received large pensions in the reigns of Francis I and Henry
II, and the Guises enraged their Bourbon and Montmorency rivals
after 1559 by sharply reducing their share.[27] Frugal Elizabeth I
never gave money away, but the export licenses she farmed to
Leicester were worth thousands of pounds a year.[28] In 1565 Count

23. See Lawrence Stone, "Terrible Times," *New Republic*, 186, no. 8 (May 5, 1982): 24–
28.

24. Robert Harding, *Anatomy of a Power Elite* (New Haven, 1978), pp. 21–45.

25. Stone, *Crisis of the Aristocracy*, pp. 199–234.

26. I. A. A. Thompson, *War and Government in Hapsburg Spain, 1560–1620* (London,
1976), pp. 60–67; see also Antonio Dominguez Ortiz, *The Golden Age of Spain, 1516–1659*
(New York, 1971), pp. 130–161.

27. Wolfe, *Fiscal System*, pp. 137–140. Francis I even paid the dowries of the nobility's
daughters and ransomed them during the Italian wars.

28. Stone, *Crisis of the Aristocracy*, p. 430.

Egmont visited Madrid to discuss the religious situation in the Netherlands with Philip II. Philip distrusted the count and expected little to come of his talk but still began their conversation by bestowing upon him presents amounting to 50,000 ducats.[29] No matter how rich the magnates, they seem to have regarded such rewards as a matter of course. They were far more willing to take risks to secure the loyalty of their clients than to help the crown carry out the monarch's will.

"No government in seventeenth-century Europe," J. H. Elliott wrote more than twenty years ago, "was capable of maintaining order solely through the efforts of its own officials. Ultimately, its success depended on the co-operation of the aristocracy and on the acquiescence, if not the positive assistance, of the mass of the population."[30] Had monarchs been able to count upon the loyalty of other powerful men within their societies their financial weakness would have been a less critical problem, but such was most definitely not the case. The problem of disloyalty was most critical in France, where both magnates like the Guises and the prince of Condé and members of the royal family like the duke of Anjou and Gaston d'Orléans, brother of Louis XIII, took the field against the monarchy again and again. The Spanish monarchy in the years 1559–1659 faced revolts in the Netherlands, Aragon, Catalonia, Portugal, Naples, and Sicily, although Castile itself was quiet. Neither Protestant nor Catholic German princes showed consistent loyalty to the emperor, even when allied with him during the Thirty Years' War. And while the English aristocracy was generally less violent during this period, violence dominated politics in the rest of the British Isles, and civil war eventually broke out in England in the 1640s.

Despite all this, monarchs and ministers such as Philip II, Olivares, Richelieu, Mazarin, Ferdinand II of Bohemia, and Charles I of England made enormous efforts to impose greater political authority over their subjects, to enforce religious uniformity in their domains, and to increase their authority vis-à-vis other monarchs. Religious controversies posed particularly difficult problems for monarchs, since most of them—like most of their contemporaries—rejected toleration on principle but lacked the means to impose uniformity. A few leading political figures, such as Henry IV

29. Geoffrey Parker, *Philip II*, pp. 60–65.
30. Elliott, *Revolt of the Catalans*, pp. 102–103.

of France, Wallenstein, and, in a less explicit fashion, Elizabeth I, favored the less costly policy of toleration, but such policies tended to antagonize all the warring parties.[31] Attempts to increase monarchical authority generally failed, as we shall see later on in more detail, because of the inadequacy of royal material resources, and because of the nature of early modern armies. Such evidence as we have suggests that most monarchs' revenues were *not* increasing significantly during the late sixteenth century, if inflation is taken into account. Under Francis I royal revenue increased from 5 million livres in 1515 to only 9 million in 1546; by 1610 it had reached 33 million. Since however an average inflation of about 3 percent per year doubled European prices every twenty-five years during the sixteenth century, these figures show an overall decrease in real income.[32] The ordinary revenues of Charles V's vast domains in Spain, Italy, and the Netherlands totaled roughly 4 million ducats (equivalent to about 8 million livres), almost all of which was swallowed up by the costs of administration.[33] Under Philip II Castilian revenues rose from 1.5 million ducats upon his accession to about 11 million in the 1590s, but inflation reduced even this huge increase to about 50 percent.[34]

In and of themselves, these revenues could not finance wars. Not only were they too low, but they also dribbled in in small amounts throughout the year and could not therefore provide the large sums needed to put an army in the field. Only by securing loans on future revenues from the great German and Italian banking houses of the era could kings amass and transfer the huge sums necessary to raise armies. In exchange, they signed away both the yield and the administration of these revenues for years on end. Wars invariably left them in a much weaker financial position, and their borrowing periodically led them to bankruptcies and to a rescheduling of their obligations.[35] In addition, the alien-

31. In Henry IV's case, toleration initially established his authority but subsequently led to his assassination. See Roland Mousnier, *The Assassination of Henry IV* (London, 1973), pp. 138–158.

32. Wolfe, *Fiscal System*, pp. 90–103; on prices, see Braudel, *The Mediterranean*, I, 517–536.

33. Leopold von Ranke, *The Ottoman and the Spanish Empires in the Sixteenth and Seventeenth Centuries* (New York, 1975), pp. 55ff.

34. These figures are from J. H. Elliott, *Imperial Spain, 1469–1716* (New York, 1963), pp. 203, 282–283.

35. The tendency of war to *reduce* rather than increase the scope of the central power is the theme of Thompson's excellent book, *War and Government*.

ation of revenues to financiers angered not only the taxpayers, who protested the enrichment of both domestic and foreign financial interests, but also the nobility and officer class, who coveted the royal revenues themselves.[36]

The nature of available instruments of armed force also militated against the growth of royal power.[37] As we shall see in numerous specific cases, European armies of the late sixteenth and early seventeenth centuries were joint-stock companies designed to serve the interests of their aristocratic officers. War remained an important outlet for noble ambition, especially for younger sons of noble houses whose families could not bequeath them an adequate estate. The nature, function, and consequences of sixteenth- and early seventeenth-century international conflict reflect the goals of the nobles who raised and led the armies of the time.[38]

European society in the sixteenth and seventeenth centuries included thousands of nobles and commoners eager to sign up to fight for almost any cause. The pool was international: Walloons, Italians, Germans, Englishmen, and Scotsmen could be found in virtually every European army. More significantly, because of the poverty of the monarchs who required armies, the generals, colonels and captains who commanded armies, regiments, and companies retained considerable independence even in the midst of war. Royal commissioners acting directly on behalf of their princes raised only a minority of troops. Warring princes and magnates customarily enlisted the services of military entrepreneurs, usually colonels or captains who undertook to provide companies or regiments at a given place and time. Sometimes the prince ad-

36. The best single source for the workings of European public finance is still Richard Ehrenberg, *Capital and Finance in the Age of the Renaissance* (New York, n.d.). See also Geoffrey Parker, "The Emergence of Modern Finance in Europe, 1500–1730," in Carlo Cipolla, ed., *The Fontana Economic History of Europe: The Sixteenth and Seventeenth Centuries* (Glasgow, 1974), pp. 527–594.

37. On armies in this period generally, see Hale, *War and Society in Renaissance Europe*.

38. Our knowledge of European armies during these years varies enormously. By far the most important work on the subject is Fritz Redlich, *The German Military Enterpriser and His Work Force: A Study in European Economic and Social History*, 2 vols. (Wiesbaden, 1964–1965), a much-neglected study filled with important data and theoretical contributions on the German armies of the Thirty Years' War. Another extremely useful work on the same period is Theodor Lorentzen, *Die Schwedische Armee im Dreissigjährigen Kriege und ihre Abdankung* (Leipzig, 1894); Geoffrey Parker, *The Army of Flanders and the Spanish Road, 1567–1659* (Cambridge, 1972), deals with the most important Spanish army. We know little, however, about the French armies during the wars of religion and virtually nothing about the French army under Richelieu and Mazarin.

vanced the recruiting money necessary to raise the troops; sometimes the entrepreneur put up the money, becoming a creditor of the prince's almost at once. In either case, the prince remained liable for the payment of relatively high salaries to both the officers and men for as long as the troops remained in the field. Since monarchs could seldom if ever make such payments, officers built up claims which could be satisfied only by large future payments or by grants of land. Wallenstein is only the most spectacular example of a soldier who enriched himself in this fashion. And while in actual fact war seems to have impoverished its practitioners as often as it rewarded them,[39] much of the European nobility regarded war as a source of fortune.

A monarch or magnate who commissioned military entrepreneurs to raise an army had to try to pay it until victory had been won. When as frequently happened, he could not do so, armies had two ways of defending their interests. On the one hand, they could try to extract their means of subsistence and the salaries they were owed from the surrounding territory—with or without the consent of their employer or the local territorial prince. On the other hand, when their patience was exhausted, they could mutiny or sell themselves to the enemy—a frequent practice in the Spanish-Dutch wars, as Geoffrey Parker has shown.[40] Mutinous troops could wreak havoc upon friend and foe alike. The need to find a way to pay off troops, indeed, prolonged many wars, since campaigns had to be continued until the troops had been satisfied. During the French wars of religion rebellious nobles almost always refused to lay down their arms until the king paid off their armies. In the Thirty Years' War the demands of the Swedish army, which for prestige reasons the Swedish government was determined to meet, became a critical issue in peace negotiations and prolonged the war for several years. In England the Commonwealth fell when it could no longer maintain its army. War, in short, was waged by men of independent disposition who insisted upon handsome compensation—compensation which monarchs could not consistently provide.

Contemporary military technology also made war an ineffective

39. The war in the Netherlands, to cite only one example, seems to have exhausted three of the greatest private fortunes in Europe—those of the duke of Alba, William of Orange, and the earl of Leicester.

40. Parker, *Army of Flanders*, pp. 185–206.

means of settling political conflict. Early modern armies were cumbersome instruments, and decisive victories were rare. In addition, because fortifications were temporarily superior to artillery, many strong points could be reduced only by lengthy sieges that put tremendous financial pressure on besieging armies.[41] The difficulty of indefinitely maintaining an army in the field tended to create a kind of natural balance of power, most notably in the Thirty Years' War. The emperor, the elector of Bavaria, the Swedes, and the French all seemed to be on the point of total victory at one time or another, only to see the situation transformed by the disintegration of much of their armies.

The combination of these interrelated structural problems within European society—the strength of an ambitious and violent aristocracy, the weakness of territorial princes, and the autonomy of noble-dominated armies—led inevitably to almost continuous internal and international conflict in the years 1559–1659. Several historians have already analyzed *parts* of this period within a more general framework. Over thirty years ago, Hugh Trevor-Roper, noting the coincidence of several major revolts during the 1640s, including the Fronde in France, the Catalan, Neapolitan, and Portuguese rebellions, and the English revolution, argued that they reflected a European-wide "crisis in the relations between society and the State," and suggested that these upheavals were rebellions against the Renaissance court and the Renaissance state which had come to dominate Europe.[42] In 1969, J. H. Elliott, who had already questioned some aspects of Trevor-Roper's argument, noted that the decade of the 1560s could as easily be selected as a candidate for "general crisis" as that of the 1640s.[43] T. K. Rabb subsequently argued that a crisis regarding "the location of political authority" took place shortly before the middle of the seven-

---

41. Ibid., pp. 3–21.

42. Hugh Trevor-Roper, "The General Crisis of the Seventeenth Century," *Past and Present*, 16 (1959), reprinted in Trevor Aston, ed., *Crisis in Europe, 1560–1660* (New York, 1965), pp. 59–96. A few years earlier E. J. Hobsbawm had identified a general European economic crisis during the seventeenth century; see Hobsbawm, "The Crisis of the Seventeenth Century," in Aston, ed., *Crisis in Europe*, pp. 5–58.

43. Elliott, "Revolution and Continuity in Early Modern Europe"; earlier Elliott suggested that Trevor-Roper's model would not satisfactorily explain the revolts within the Iberian peninsula and argued that war, rather than expensive courts, had created the unreasonable financial demands which in turn had provoked revolutions on the Continent. See Aston, ed., *Crisis in Europe*, pp. 97–110.

teenth century, leading to a strengthening of European monarchies and of a new international European order symbolized by the Peace of Westphalia.[44]

Expanding upon these foundations, and especially upon Elliott's 1969 remarks, we may note that one can find armed conflict in much of Europe not merely in the 1560s, *but in almost any decade from 1559 through 1659,* save perhaps the 1610s. This leads to a further conclusion: that the persistence of conflict over this chaotic century does not reflect a "crisis," in the sense of a temporary breakdown of European political or institutional arrangements, but was rather the *natural consequence* of the key social, political, economic, and religious aspects of European society, which made conflict inevitable and its lasting resolution almost impossible.[45] European politics in the late sixteenth and early seventeenth centuries closely resemble John. H. Kautsky's paradigm of "aristocratic empires." In such empires, Kautsky argues, one class dominates the economy and politics, and politics as a struggle among different classes hardly exists. The aristocracy insists upon its social and in some cases racial separateness,[46] monopolizes military functions, and struggles continually for "honor and glory, prestige and respect." The monarch's status is essentially that of another aristocrat, civil and foreign wars are endemic, and "family feuds, civil wars, and wars may be difficult to distinguish as forms of aristocratic politics."[47] Kautsky argues that commercial influence had by the late Middle Ages turned the western European states into something other than aristocratic empires, but his description fits them very well, particularly with respect to the blurring of the distinction between civil and foreign war.

To show how a combination of aristocratic power, religious strife, and ambitious but ineffective monarchs brought about the continual domestic and international conflicts of the years 1559–1659, we must look successively at developments within the Span-

44. T. K. Rabb, *The Struggle for Stability in Early Modern Europe* (Oxford, 1975).

45. This point was hinted at but not developed by H. L. Koenigsberger, "Early Modern Revolutions: An Exchange," *Journal of Modern History,* 46, no. 1 (March 1974): 99–106.

46. This was true especially in sixteenth-century Spain, where the Inquisition certified the purity of noble blood—that is, nobles' freedom from Jewish or Moorish ancestry. Henry Kamen, *The Spanish Inquisition* (New York, 1965), pp. 121–139.

47. John H. Kautsky, *The Politics of Aristocratic Empires* (Chapel Hill, 1982), esp. pp. 341–346.

ish empire, France, Germany, and the British Isles. We shall then turn to the consequences of these conflicts for European economy and society, before seeing how European monarchs led by Louis XIV finally brought violence under more effective control in the second half of the seventeenth century.

The Spanish Imperial Experience

Historians have frequently so exaggerated the power of the Spanish crown between 1559 and 1659—especially during the reign of Philip II (1555–1598)—that they have regarded the wars of the late sixteenth and early seventeenth centuries as Spanish (or Hapsburg) attempts to rule all Europe.[1] Certainly the Spanish empire was vast. In 1584 Philip II added Portugal to the crowns of Aragon and Castile and ruled over the whole of the Iberian peninsula. The empire in 1559 also included the Netherlands, Franche-Comté, the duchy of Milan, Naples, Sicily, and the West Indies. In addition, Spain between 1559 and 1659 found itself at one time or another at war with most of Europe's major powers, including France, England, Sweden, and the Ottoman empire, and waged an almost continuous struggle against the Dutch in the Netherlands.[2] The reality of early modern politics, however, contradicts any interpretation which treats Philip II as a modern conqueror of the type of Napoleon or Hitler.

In fact, these wars illustrate the essential features of early modern politics, including the independence of the aristocracy, the limitations of monarchical resources, and the problems of contemporary armies. Thus, the strength of the Spanish monarchy came largely from its alliance with the Castilian nobility, with whom it jointly sought to exploit the rest of the Spanish empire. The crown never challenged the Castilian nobility's prerogatives, and the nobility relied upon the crown both for patronage and for important economic favors. Yet perhaps because the resources of Castile could not in themselves satisfy the ambitions of the Castilian no-

1. This is the view of Dehio, *Precarious Balance*, pp. 43–62, and more recently of Kennedy, *Rise and Fall of the Great Powers*, p. 35. A more restrained view is H. G. Koenigsberger, *The Hapsburgs and Europe, 1516–1660* (Ithaca, 1971).

2. A convenient summary is Geoffrey Parker, "Spain, Her Enemies and the Revolt of the Netherlands, 1559–1648," in Parker, *Spain and the Netherlands, 1559–1659* (London, 1979), pp. 18–44.

bility—led by the king—the crown during this period repeatedly tried to strengthen its authority over other parts of its empire, including the Netherlands, the realms of the crown of Aragon, and Portugal. The men who undertook these ambitious plans—especially Philip II and the count duke of Olivares, the favorite of Philip IV—were frequently trying to implement a recognizably more modern concept of royal authority, but one which they lacked the resources to realize. Because of the limitations of royal political, economic, and military power, these attempts led to a series of rebellions which the crown could not put down. Because foreign monarchs—following contemporary custom—assisted some of the rebellions against the crown, or threatened the strategic unity of the empire, the Spanish crown also found itself embroiled in wars with England, France, and Sweden. The Spaniards also failed to bring these wars to successful conclusions, both because of a lack of resources and because of the inability of contemporary armies to win decisive victories.

During most of the period 1559–1659 the Spanish crown maintained its authority over the Castilian nobility very effectively. Like their counterparts in the rest of western Europe, the Spanish nobles—particularly at the highest levels—were violent, ambitious, extravagant, and shot through with factional struggles. But although Philip II, his son, and his grandson never dealt successfully with resistance to their authority in the periphery of their empire, they retained the loyalty of the nobility of Castile to a far higher degree than the king of France, the Holy Roman Emperor, or even the king of England in their respective domains. The Castilian nobility and the crown jointly exploited both the other regions and the other classes of the Spanish empire for their mutual benefit.

The rise of the Castilian nobility began in the late fifteenth century, when civil wars enabled the victors to accumulate huge entailed estates. The reconquest of Granada allowed them to expand their holdings further, and Ferdinand and Isabella often borrowed money from them and repaid it with grants of new seigneuries. By the time of Ferdinand's death in 1516 the grandees firmly controlled the army in Italy, the royal guard, and a great deal of the royal revenue. At home they used private armies to intimidate villages and towns and add to their domains, defying royal judicial edicts against them.[3] During the sixteenth century the emerging *letrado* class, composed initially of middle-class officials trained in universities, supplanted the nobility in many offices of state. But *letrados* frequently entered into client-patron relations with leading nobles, and before long the aristocracy was both educating its own sons in universities and intermarrying with *letrado* families.[4]

After the *comunero* revolt of 1520–21 Charles V took some steps to restore the balance between the nobility and the towns, but the power of the Castilian nobility within the empire as a whole continued to grow. During the sixteenth century Castilians increasingly monopolized favor and office throughout most of the Spanish empire. Thus, although Naples and Sicily had originally belonged to the crown of Aragon, the king in 1555 created the Council of Italy to handle Italian business and staffed it largely with Castilians. Opportunities for settlement and for government office in the New World were also reserved for Castilians.[5] The system of councils that ruled Spain enabled the aristocracy to control much of the imperial patronage and provided numerous opportunities for corruption.[6] Historians since Ranke have frequently noted that most of the empire's territories yielded no net revenue for the crown because the costs of administration used up everything collected in taxes. Politically, however, the Castilian monarchs drew enormous benefits from the overseas territories, which provided places for the magnates whose support they could not do without.

The crown also helped protect the aristocracy's social and economic status. Beginning in the late fifteenth century the Inquisition functioned as a class weapon on behalf of the aristocracy, using "purity of blood" statutes to break the power of the partly Jewish urban middle class and inculcate aristocratic values throughout Spanish society.[7] Through the Council of the Indies the nobility exercised ultimate authority over trade with the New

---

3. Stephen Haliczer, *The Comuneros of Castile: The Forging of a Revolution, 1475–1521* (Madison, 1981), pp. 66–93.

4. Richard L. Kagan, *Students and Society in Early Modern Spain* (Baltimore, 1974), pp. 78–105.

5. Elliott, *Revolt of the Catalans*, pp. 1–21.

6. Elliott, *Imperial Spain*, p. 177.

7. Kamen, *Spanish Inquisition*, *passim*.

World and assured themselves of a healthy cut of the profits.[8] Spanish politics under the Hapsburgs show no fundamental split between aristocrats and trading and colonial interests, but rather occasional fights between those grandees who had an interest in the trade of the New World and those who did not.

Despite their advantages however, it seems clear that many Castilian nobles were heavily in debt by the 1580s, and their situation became much worse in the seventeenth century. Like the greatest aristocrat of all, the king, the nobility were notoriously poor credit risks. By law they could not be imprisoned for debt, and laws of entail forbade them from mortgaging their properties. To make it possible for them to borrow from bankers or the bourgeoisie, Philip II began issuing licenses which allowed them to mortgage individual properties. Later, when individual nobles could not make their mortgage payments, Philip III and Philip IV frequently granted them the right to suspend payment of the principal— much in the way that the monarchs themselves converted short-term obligations into annuities during their periodic bankruptcies. Thus the aristocracy continued to live in the style to which it believed itself entitled, while the kings acquired a lever that enabled them to draw upon private fortunes to help finance their court expenditures and foreign wars.[9]

During the years 1559–1659 the politics of the Spanish empire and Spain's international role centered upon the attempts of the monarchy and the Castilian nobility to continue and increase their exploitation of the rest of the empire. This is not to say that unity prevailed in the upper reaches of the Spanish government. The court was beset by factionalism, especially in the first half of the reign of Philip II. The leading nobles and secretaries—the duke of Alba, the prince of Eboli, Francisco de Eraso, Gonzalvo Perez and his son Antonio, Gabriel de Zayas, and Mateo Vazquez de Leca— continually slandered and spied upon one another, forcing Philip II to perform a complicated balancing act that consumed huge amounts of his time and energy.[10] Although nobles and secretaries

8. Ibid., p. 20.

9. See the very interesting article by Charles Jago, "The Influence of Debt on the Relations between Crown and Aristocracy in Sixteenth-Century Castile," *Economic History Review,* 26, no. 1 (February 1973): 218–236.

10. The best sources for the atmosphere of the Spanish court are Marañon, *Antonio Perez;* William S. Maltby, *Alba: A Biography of Fernando Alvarez de Toledo, Third Duke of*

rose to favor at court by different routes, they behaved in a remarkably similar fashion once they had risen to the top. All of them built lavish homes, acquired large retinues, infiltrated one another's households, and plotted their rivals' disgrace.

The Reign of Philip II

An examination of the source of the wars that began in the 1560s with the revolt of the Netherlands and lasted, with one interruption, until 1659, must begin with a look at Philip II, his sense of his own authority, and his attempts to extend it in the Low Countries.[11] Philip's approach to government shows both late medieval and modern features. On the one hand, he was concerned above all with the welfare of his family and the safety of his possessions. No less than any great lord, he had a responsibility to provide for his nearest relatives, both legitimate and illegitimate. Three of his five viceroys in the Netherlands—the single most important appointment he had to make—were his illegitimate half-sister, Margaret of Parma, his illegitimate half-brother Don Juan of Austria, and Margaret's son Alexander Farnese, duke of Parma. Like any aristocrat, he eagerly sought new titles whenever they became available, including the crown of Portugal, which he successfully seized after 1580, and the crown of France, which he unsuccessfully claimed for his daughter after 1588. He was also passionately interested in architecture, gardening, and books; concerned with the welfare of the church; and well aware, within Castile at least, of the need to balance off the leading aristocratic factions.

On the other hand, and in a more modern vein, Philip preferred doing business on paper rather than face-to-face, and he expected more unquestioned obedience from his subjects than sixteenth-century monarchs generally enjoyed. More important, Philip began his reign by attempting to put the royal finances on a more sound footing and to substitute a paid royal administration for the system of contracting, or *asiento*, that dominated Spanish public finances. His own reign began with a state bankruptcy which forced him to make peace with France in 1559, and during the early

---

Alba, 1507–1582 (Berkeley, 1983); and, above all, J. H. Elliott, *The Count-Duke of Olivares: The Statesman in an Age of Decline* (New Haven, 1986).

11. Parker, *Philip II*, provides an excellent introduction to Philip and his reign.

1560s he tried to put the construction of the Mediterranean fleet and the custody of important fortresses in the hands of royal officials, rather than letting them out by contract (*asiento*) to private parties who would thereby secure large claims on the crown. He also tried to professionalize the Council of War, by appointing more military officers and secretaries, and to centralize recruiting within Spain.[12]

Philip treated religion in the same way as most contemporary monarchs: as a source of authority and patronage. Philip's religious attitudes have often been misunderstood. Although undoubtedly more personally religious than many contemporary European monarchs, he was no fanatic. On the whole he approached religious questions from the point of view of their political significance, and he never regarded himself simply as a soldier of the Counter-Reformation. In his frequent negotiations with the popes regarding Mediterranean campaigns he consistently remained the judge of "what is required for Christendom in general and for the good of my . . . states in particular,"[13] and he intermittently courted foreign Protestants such as Elizabeth I and Henry of Navarre. Within his own domains, however, he regarded the church as an indispensable bulwark of royal power. In Spain the church was an important source of revenue and patronage, and his policies toward the Moriscos at home and the Calvinists in the Netherlands reflect his belief that heretical subjects could not in the nature of things be loyal subjects.[14]

The revolt of the Netherlands—in many ways the key to Philip's reign—began when he decided to use the church to increase his personal authority at the expense of the local aristocracy.[15] Under Philip's father Charles V, the Netherlands had been virtually the center of the Hapsburg empire. Extraordinarily wealthy and industrious, they had provided more annual income than Castile.[16] The leading Netherlands nobles—Prince William of Orange, Count Egmont, and Count Horn—had been the leading luminar-

12. Thompson, *War and Government*, pp. 4–72.

13. Braudel, *The Mediterranean*, II, 1117, 1143.

14. Parker, *Philip II*, pp. 38–61.

15. The best accounts of the origins of the Dutch revolt are Geoffrey Parker, *The Dutch Revolt* (Ithaca, 1977); Pieter Geyl, *The Revolt of the Netherlands, 1559–1609* (London, 1958); and Maltby, *Alba*, pp. 110–137.

16. Ranke, *Ottoman and Spanish Empires*, pp. 84ff.

ies of Charles's court and the commanders of his armies. They had willingly contributed from their private fortunes to the common cause. As members of the Netherlands Council of State and governors of various provinces, they controlled civil and ecclesiastical patronage and received many gratuities from the powerful provincial estates.[17] As Knights of the Golden Fleece, the leading nobles had the right and duty to assist their sovereign with completely frank advice.

Although Philip II had worked closely with the Netherlands magnates during the 1550s, by the time he left the Netherlands for Spain in 1559 he had apparently decided to reduce the nobles' patronage and power and increase his own. Naming his half-sister Margaret of Parma as regent, he left Cardinal Granvelle to keep an eye on her and instructed her to ignore the Council of State. Two years later, and without consulting the Netherlands nobility, Philip proposed a revolutionary new ecclesiastical organization for the Netherlands: ten new bishoprics, their incumbents to be nominated by the crown and their endowments to come from the huge revenues of the leading abbeys. He also introduced strict new restrictions against heresy.

While Philip's ecclesiastical reform in the Netherlands presumably owed something to a genuine concern for the Dutch church, which he knew to be indolent, corrupt, and tolerant of protestant heresies, these reforms also threatened to overturn the balance of political power within the Netherlands and take the domination of Castile within the empire a step further. Philip would appoint the new bishops, the Netherlands nobility would lose the income of the abbeys, and the bishops would lead a royal party within the Netherlands Estates General. The Netherlands nobles could not possibly assent. Orange, Egmont, and Horn, who held the governorships of the most important provinces and commanded the noble militia or *bandes d'ordonnance*, absented themselves from the Council of State, making the execution of policy impossible. Growing bolder, they demanded the recall of Granvelle, and Philip obliged in 1563. Three years later, bowing to pressure from the lower nobility, Orange and the other magnates demanded religious toleration, and in the spring of 1566 an armed deputation of

---

17. Koenigsberger, "Patronage and Bribery," pp. 166–175, notes in particular that the estates of Holland bribed councillors to maintain economic privileges.

four hundred nobles forced Margaret to suspend the heresy laws.[18]

Like most other sixteenth-century political questions, the issue of proper policy toward the Netherlands immediately became entangled with court politics. The recall of Granvelle resulted largely from an intrigue mounted by Philip II's secretary Francisco de Eraso, an ally of the prince of Eboli, who passed the king reports claiming that Granvelle had not done enough against heresy. Eboli and Eraso opposed Granvelle partly because of their ties to Egmont and Horn, and partly simply because Granvelle had long been an ally of the duke of Alba. The Portuguese Eboli and the Aragonese Antonio Perez may also have opposed Philip's policies in the Netherlands because they regarded them as part of a more general "Castilianization" policy with implications for the Iberian peninsula.[19] Alba in return opposed the recall partly for the sake of his own prestige as a patron and partly because of his firm belief in royal authority. When in 1566 Calvinists in the Netherlands perpetrated the Iconoclastic Fury, smashing ornaments in numerous churches, Alba was vindicated. Philip and the Castilian Council of State decided to impose royal authority in the Netherlands by force. Many argued that Spain's Italian possessions would follow the Netherlands example if nothing was done. The choice of Alba to command the army the king planned to dispatch was logical given his long-standing support of a firm policy, but Alba's numerous following at court unsuccessfully asked him to decline it, fearing for their fate during his long absence.[20]

Philip fought the Netherland rebels for thirty years largely because he refused to moderate his claims to religious and political authority. And although many of the Netherland nobles desperately wanted a compromise settlement of their differences with Philip, they could not agree to surrender their power and patronage or to proceed rigorously against heresy without forfeiting their own position. Between 1567 and 1572 the duke of Alba did manage to execute most of the leaders of the revolt and beat back invasions by William of Orange and Louis of Nassau, but when he attempted to put his rule on a sound footing he could not secure the consent of the Netherlands to new permanent taxes. Instead, in 1572 Wil-

18. Parker, *Dutch Revolt*, pp. 68–84.
19. Elliott, *Revolt of the Catalans*, p. 19.
20. Maltby, *Alba*, pp. 127–136; Parker, *Dutch Revolt*, pp. 87–90.

liam of Orange and the Sea Beggars established themselves in Holland and Zeeland and turned the revolt into a more serious military problem. Alba's terror tactics, including the sack of several towns, convinced many Netherlanders that they had no choice but to side with Orange.

Alba's inability to win a quick victory turned the struggle into a contest of resources. The need to maintain an army in the Netherlands tested the financial resources of the Spanish government, and the need to win a military victory tested the effectiveness of its forces. Both proved inadequate to establish Philip's supreme authority.

The story of Philip's finances reflects the dilemmas of early modern reforming monarchs. Philip did manage to increase his Castilian revenues, although even here inflation ate up much of what he was able to accomplish. Total imperial revenues at Philip's accession seem to have been slightly less than 3 million ducats, and by 1577 he had increased them to about 8.7 million ducats. Subsequent increases to about 11 million at the time of his death were entirely eaten up by inflation.[21] Imports of silver from the new world reached almost 1 million ducats annually by the late 1560s, and rose to 2 million ducats annually late in the reign. Expenditure, however, immediately began to outrun revenue, especially after the beginning of full-scale war in the Netherlands. By the early 1570s the deficit had reached 50 percent.[22]

To finance the war against the Dutch, Philip had to increase borrowing and to return gradually to the *asiento* system within Spain. Under this system, private interests lent money short-term, undertook military operations, or promised to provide supplies in exchange for claims upon future revenues or upon shipments of silver from the Americas. Despite his good intentions, Philip could not resist the temptation to realize the present value of his revenues by pledging them as security for loans. He thereby eliminated any chance of putting his finances on a sound footing. Philip's debts seem to have reached about 20 million ducats in 1560, 50 million in the early 1570s, and perhaps 80 million in the early 1580s.[23]

---

21. Elliott, *Imperial Spain*, pp. 203, 283; Thompson, *War and Government*, pp. 67–72. Philip's principal revenues were the sales tax or *alcabala* and the *servicio, excusado*, and *cruzada*, which came from the church.

22. Elliott, *Imperial Spain*, pp. 67–72, 181.

23. Braudel, *The Mediterranean*, I, 533.

Thus, in 1567, the arrival of a large quantity of silver, together with a lull in the fighting against the Turks, enabled Philip to authorize Alba in 1567 to raise an army of about 30,000 men. Only a minority of them were Spanish regulars, and thousands were raised on credit in Germany, Italy, and Flanders itself, with captains and colonels advancing some or all of the cost of recruiting.[24] Alba well understood that keeping an army in the field was the key to contemporary military success, and in 1568 he successfully avoided battle with William of Orange until much of William's army—also raised in Germany on Orange's own personal credit—had deserted.[25] The nature of the problem changed after 1573, when Orange established a secure military and financial base in Holland and Zeeland. Alba, who had demobilized many of his troops but kept their colonels and captains on retainer to enable him to recall them when the need arose, rapidly increased his strength from 13,000 to 67,000,[26] but he now faced far more serious problems relating to sixteenth-century military technology. To subdue the rebellion, he had to retake a series of strategic towns. The development of new, low brick fortifications—the *trace italienne*—had rendered town walls almost invulnerable to gunfire. No longer was it possible to blast a hole in the walls and pour troops through. Towns could be taken only by blockade and protracted siege, a process which took months. As the Netherlands had hundreds of strategic and increasingly well-fortified towns which had to be taken in a more or less prescribed sequence, the problem of their subjugation became well-nigh insuperable. By the 1570s several Spaniards had commented that it might take many decades to do the job.[27]

A second, equally critical problem also emerged in the early 1570s. The Army of Flanders, like all other contemporary armies, expected to be paid, and when left unpaid, it mutinied. Mutinies had begun by late 1573, when Alba was recalled from the Netherlands. They started among Spanish troops, whose pay had frequently been withheld to satisfy the German mercenaries. Mutinous episodes followed a well-established pattern. Troops whose

24. Maltby, *Alba,* pp. 139–143.
25. Ibid., pp. 161–204.
26. Parker, *Army of Flanders,* p. 27.
27. For the classic statement of these problems, see Parker, *Army of Flanders,* pp. 3–21.

pay had long been in arrears suddenly refused to fight, elected their own representatives to negotiate with their superiors, and frequently began collecting contributions from the surrounding countryside in place of their pay. Army commanders generally had no choice but to settle on the best terms they could make. With characteristic firmness, Alba double-crossed one of his first mutinous units at Haarlem in 1573, executing many of the ringleaders after agreeing to a settlement, but this only made later rebels harder to satisfy.[28] The mutinies continued after Alba's departure. By 1575 the Army of Flanders, now risen to 80,000 men, cost 1.2 million florins a month to maintain—more than the entire income of Castile and the expected treasure from the Indies. Complete catastrophe occurred after September 1575, when Philip, driven to bankruptcy, suspended payment on all his debts. Concluding that they now had no chance of being paid, the troops devoted themselves to plundering the countryside. Both the towns and the Spanish authorities paid them large sums of money to avoid pillage. Spanish authority collapsed completely, and the Spanish-dominated Council of State even allowed the estates of Brabant to raise troops to fight the mutineers. In the midst of the chaos the Spaniards scored a tremendous military success, the capture of Antwerp, but lost any political benefits when the unpaid soldiery sacked the town and left 8,000 dead.[29]

The events of 1575–1577 exemplified the basic dilemma of early modern monarchs. Only by raising armies could they increase their authority, but their revenues rarely sufficed to keep their armies in the field long enough to achieve their objectives. The result was a cycle of levies, bankruptcies, and mutinies—a cycle which tended to continue simply because it reflected contemporary economic, political, and social structures. A temporary recovery began when Philip II made terms with his bankers. Fifteen years had elapsed since his last state bankruptcy of 1560. In that time, despite a substantial increase in Castilian revenues and silver deliveries from the New World, Philip had borrowed until his annual revenues had been completely anticipated, thus making it impossible to pay the interest or principal on his loans. His suspension of payments in 1575 did *not*, however, represent a complete repu-

28. Parker, *Army of Flanders*, pp. 202–203.
29. Parker, *Dutch Revolt*, pp. 169–186.

diation of his debts. Instead, after many months of negotiations, Philip successfully converted many of his short-term cash obligations into long-term annuities, or *juros,* which the bankers sold to pay their own debts. As soon as agreement was reached, the bankers began advancing more more money in exchange for new claims on future revenues.[30] Within a short time Philip's half-brother Don Juan had raised a new army, won a battle over William of Orange, and reestablished the Spanish position in the southern Netherlands.

The Dutch, of course, paid for their long struggle with Spain with the help of Europe's most highly developed financial network, backed by their important position in European trade, especially in the Baltic. They improved their position further beginning in the 1580s by beginning to trade with the Spanish and Portuguese empires in the East and West Indies (Philip II had inherited the crown of Portugal in 1580), the first of a series of threats to the Spanish commercial monopoly. By the late 1590s, the war had become a Spanish attempt to reimpose the official commercial monopoly with the Americas, as well as a struggle for royal authority.[31]

Cycles of boom and bust governed the course of the war in the Netherlands until the truce of 1609. Because Philip periodically reestablished his credit, because shipments of silver from the Indies increased dramatically in the 1580s, and because financial shortages and mutinies also troubled the young Dutch republic, the duke of Parma, Alexander Farnese, scored some major successes in the mid-1580s but without bringing the rebellion in sight of completion. Then in 1597 Philip declared a new bankruptcy, capping a series of new and even larger mutinies in the Army of Flanders. After his death in 1598 his son Philip III supplemented the expense of the war with a lavish court, leading to his first bankruptcy in 1607—the event that finally brought the war to a temporary end.

The international aspects of the revolt of the Netherlands induced Philip to try other strategies for ending it. Like rebellious factions in France during the sixteenth century and Germany in the early seventeenth, Orange and his allies had no trouble enlist-

---

30. Braudel, *The Mediterranean,* I, 501–508.
31. Geyl, *Revolt of the Netherlands,* and Parker, *Dutch Revolt,* give the best short accounts of the developments on the Dutch side. On the Dutch republic itself, see below, pp. 166–168.

ing foreign help. At various times they received assistance from different French factions and from Elizabeth I of England. In return, Philip consistently supported the French Catholic party, supplying armed aid during the civil wars of the 1560s and large sums of money after 1584, when the Protestant Henry of Navarre became heir to the throne of France. The Army of Flanders intervened directly in the French civil wars to save Paris from Henry of Navarre in 1590. But Philip's alliance with the Catholic League masked real differences of interest, and he alienated much of the league after 1589 by putting forth his own daughter as a candidate for the French throne in violation of Salic law.

During most of his reign Philip had avoided an open break with Elizabeth of England, but his attitude changed after 1585. Philip had counted upon Parma's capture of Antwerp in that year to induce the rebels to negotiate, and he blamed their failure to do so on the subsidy treaty they concluded with Elizabeth in 1585.[32] Now his agents also sponsored several plots against Elizabeth and corresponded with Mary, Queen of Scots. In addition, Philip eventually decided to attempt the invasion of England in 1588.

The Armada of 1588, which Philip counted upon to break the rebels' spirit in the Netherlands and win a decisive victory, instead helped demonstrate the limits of what sixteenth-century states could accomplish. Although the mounting of the expedition was an extraordinary achievement, it was doomed almost from the beginning by a faulty strategic conception and a lack of coordination between the fleet itself and Parma's troops in the Netherlands. The plan adopted early in 1587 called for a large amphibious expedition which would rendezvous in the channel with a special force drawn from the Army of Flanders.[33] The cost was estimated at 3.5 million ducats—not an insuperable obstacle, since Philip's silver receipts from the Indies had risen to almost 2 million ducats per year. Parma's troops would either conquer England and enable Philip to place its crown upon his daughter's head, or simply force Elizabeth to make peace, end her support of the rebels, and tolerate Catholicism in England.[34] The duke of Medina Sidonia sailed with 130 ships in May 1588.

The armada sailed, however, without any agreement about

32. Parker, "Spain, Her Enemies," p. 35.
33. Garrett Mattingly, *The Armada* (Boston, 1959), pp. 75–78.
34. Parker, *Philip II*, pp. 152–153.

what it should do. The plan called for the armada to meet the duke of Parma's forces, which would sail into the channel in small boats, and escort them across the channel for the invasion of England. But Philip's orders urged Medina Sidonia to avoid battle with the English fleet until after Parma had landed, evidently counting upon his ships to intimidate the English from interfering with the invasion. Meanwhile, Parma did not believe that he could cross the channel in the small boats of his command, and was counting on a convoy which Medina Sidonia never considered. The gap between their conceptions did not become apparent until the decisive moment of the battle, when Parma seized upon a variety of excuses not to embark his men.

An excellent new study confirms that the armada was a vast organizational enterprise without a definite strategic rationale and, as such, very characteristic of sixteenth-century warfare in general. While its plans reflected Philip's overwhelming need to deal some sort of decisive blow to Elizabeth's power—and thereby to cripple the Dutch revolt, whose success he now ascribed to her support—they never reflected a clear strategy or even a clear military objective. Philip himself definitely specified less-than-maximum objectives for the campaign, including Elizabeth's simple withdrawal of support from the Dutch, respect for Spanish rights at sea, and toleration of the Catholic religion, and he also seems to have hoped at times that a mere naval victory or the occupation of Ireland might manage to achieve these objectives. Many Spaniards, led by Medina Sidonia himself, plainly doubted the success of the enterprise by the time it sailed, and some hints suggest that it sailed largely because of the expense of keeping it in port.[35]

Driven out of its formation by English fireships on August 8, the armada suffered more heavily in a new battle and was almost driven aground on the Dutch coast by wind and tide. During the next few days winds prevented the fleet from sailing back into the channel and eventually left Medina Sidonia with no choice but to sail around the British Isles and home. Slightly more than half of the ships arrived home, and many of their crewmen died of disease during the return voyage. The armada, like the Army of Flan-

---

35. Felipe Fernández-Alvarez, *The Spanish Armada: The Experience of War in 1588* (Oxford, 1988), pp. 72–134.

ders, could not achieve the political purpose for which it had been designed. Its failure, like the mutinies of 1576, illustrates the inability of the Spanish state to achieve the tasks Philip had set for it.

The demands of Philip's wars led to a series of military, financial, and political catastrophes near the end of his reign. During the 1590s silver shipments from the Indies reached a new high of over 2 million ducats per year.[36] Even this boon, however, could not finance the continuing campaign against the Netherlands, new expeditions against the British Isles, and large-scale financial intervention in the French civil wars. The crown's revenue during the 1590s totalled only about 10 million ducats—an increase of only 25 percent since the 1570s, which after adjustment for inflation probably worked out to a decline.[37] Financial pressure finally began to threaten Philip's authority within Spain. In 1590 the Castilian Cortes, which had been notably subservient throughout the reign, had voted a large new tax, the *milliones*, to pay for the armada, but by 1592 it refused to vote more taxes and bluntly requested that the king scale down his foreign commitments. Only a four-year campaign of bribery and intimidation overcame its resistance. In 1591 Philip's attempts to appoint a non-Aragonese viceroy in Aragon led to armed revolt. Philip put the revolt down fairly easily, but widely left Aragonese privileges intact.[38] Then in 1597 a new financial crisis compelled Philip to end his reign in exactly the way he had begun it: with a new state bankruptcy and a peace with France. He died in 1598. The war in the Netherlands dragged on until 1609, when a new state bankruptcy and new mutinies in the Netherlands forced Philip III to conclude a twelve-year truce.

Philip II's reign illustrates how particular political, economic, and social arrangements can result in long and costly wars that states are unable to bring to a successful conclusion. Military and financial considerations made the conquest of the Netherlands impossible, which raises the question—recently posed by a leading authority—of how the Dutch revolt could last so long.[39] Strategically the subjection of the Netherlands seemed hopeless, and the defeat of their English and French patrons more hopeless still. But

36. Elliott, *Imperial Spain*, p. 181.
37. Ibid., pp. 282–283.
38. Parker, *Philip II*, pp. 183–190.
39. Geoffrey Parker, "Why Did the Dutch Revolt Last So Long?" in Parker, *Spain and the Netherlands*, pp. 45–63.

Philip II remained committed to his view of royal authority; silver continued to arrive from the Indies, and his bankers remained willing to supply his armies in return for it; the Army of Flanders continued to fight, although periodic revolts made military success even less likely; and at home, one faction would always support the war, even though others would just as inevitably oppose it. The same factors, combined with new developments, led Spain to renew the war against the Dutch under Philip IV and Olivares and to pursue other bold plans for strengthening the monarchy.

Olivares and the Union of Arms

Spain's struggle with the Netherlands resumed in 1621. Factional struggles set the course of Spanish foreign policy during the reign of Philip III (1598–1622). Philip's favorite, the duke of Lerma, had come into power as the leader of a peace faction, and during the 1610s he generally preferred operations against the Turks in the Mediterranean to land war in Europe. The opposing Zuñiga-Olivares faction began to argue for much more vigorous reassertion of Spanish interests in Italy, the Netherlands, and Germany, where they favored support for the Austrian Hapsburgs against the German Protestants.[40] These men, often acting independently, took many of the decisions that involved Spain in the Thirty Years' War. They negotiated the treaty of 1617, which traded Spanish rights to the imperial succession for Philip III's overlordship of Milan and Sündgau in Alsace, encouraged the emperor Matthias to take drastic action against the Bohemian rebels, and decided to occupy the Valtelline in 1620.[41] How much they did so out of conviction, and how much simply because they opposed Lerma and his peace policies, is not possible at this time to say.

The Spanish government's decision to let the truce with the Netherlands lapse in 1621 reflected a more complex mix of material interests and *reputación*, or prestige. Jonathan Israel's recent work suggests that the renewed Spanish-Dutch war was the first of the

40. See Bohdan Chudoba, *Spain and the Empire, 1519–1643* (Chicago, 1952), pp. 210–211; J. H. Elliott, "A Question of Reputation? Spanish Foreign Policy in the Seventeenth Century," *Journal of Modern History*, 55, no. 3 (September 1983): 479–481.

41. Chudoba, *Spain and the Empire*, pp. 210–249; Peter Brightwell, "The Spanish Origins of the Thirty Years' War," *European Studies Review*, 9, no.4 (September 1979): 409–432.

great mercantilist struggles of the seventeenth and eighteenth centuries. During the truce the Dutch had made serious commercial inroads in the Spanish and Portuguese empires—inroads which translated themselves into a substantial loss of revenue and influence for the king of Spain. Their industries had also developed some markets within Spain itself. Thus, while the Spanish government in Brussels favored renewing the truce, the Council of the Indies and the Council of Portugal both opposed it. The Spanish government insisted upon a Dutch withdrawal from the Indies both in talks on renewing the truce and during intermittent peace negotiations in the years 1621–1640.[42] And from the beginning of the new war, the Spanish government sought new ways to hurt the Dutch by threatening their economic power.

In 1622, when Philip III died, the war against the Dutch became the responsibility of Philip IV's favorite, the count duke of Olivares, who led the Spanish government until 1643. Olivares, like his French rival Richelieu, combined a thoroughly traditional approach to his own career with certain more modern conceptions of domestic and foreign policy. His career shows how impossible it was to impose modern concepts of uniformity and strategy upon the world of the early seventeenth century.

Olivares had achieved power by carefully building up a following at court and cultivating the heir apparent. His faction had consistently advocated the resumption of a more vigorous foreign policy, but in the early stages of his career he had sought above all to attain the status of a grandee and eclipse the rival branch of his family, led by the duke of Medina Sidonia.[43] Throughout his career he concentrated upon finding places for his relatives, and he fell into despair when a series of deaths made it impossible for him to found a dynasty. In power, however, he became a reformer, with grandiose plans for both the internal and foreign policy of the empire.

Not only did Olivares intend to defeat the Dutch by combining military, economic, and diplomatic pressure, in the early stages of his rule, at least, he seems also to have dreamed of imposing a Spanish-led peace over all of Europe, possibly leading to the even-

42. Jonathan Israel, *The Dutch Republic and the Hispanic World* (Oxford, 1982), handles these issues in great detail.

43. Elliott, *Olivares*, pp. 15–45.

tual eclipse of the Protestant religion.[44] Perhaps because of his own lack of real military experience, he had a most unwarranted faith in the political efficacy of military power, as well as a naive belief in the utility of allies such as the Hapsburg emperor. New land campaigns against the Dutch followed a familiar course: a series of sieges, in which apparently brilliant victories such as the Spanish capture of Breda in 1625 temporarily affected morale but never brought either side within sight of a decisive victory. The viceroys in Brussels lost interest in the war long before Olivares did, and in 1628 Spinola, the commander of the Army of Flanders, journeyed to Madrid to try to convince Olivares to make peace.[45] But Olivares continued to believe that the Dutch might be compelled to concede his demands, either through economic pressure, or by enlisting the help of others, or—shades of Philip II—by the defeat of their allies.

Thus, believing that the wealth and power of the Dutch stemmed largely from their control of European trade and their encroachments upon the Indies, Olivares tried to found new trading companies to supplant them. Like Colbert later in the century, however, he found that he could do relatively little to increase the enterprise of his own traders. He especially aimed at reducing Dutch control of trade with the Baltic, and planned in the late 1620s to found a new trading company with the help of the Hapsburg emperor, whose general Wallenstein had established himself on the Baltic. But Wallenstein's failure to take Straslund and the intervention of Sweden in the war put an end to these plans. In addition, whenever the Hapsburg side had gained the ascendancy in the Thirty Years' War in Germany, the count duke expected them loyally to assist their cousin by committing troops against the Dutch, but only once in the late 1630s—and then only briefly—did the Hapsburg emperor actually do so.[46] The Catholic League of German princes, led by Maximilian of Bavaria, also refused to help him.[47] During the 1620s, when England briefly entered the war on the Dutch side, he talked of invading Ireland, and in the late 1630s his hopes for English intervention on his side had to be abandoned

44. For the latter contention, see Eberhard Straub, *Pax et Imperium* (Paderborn, 1980).
45. Elliott, *Olivares*, pp. 334–354.
46. Grete Mecenseffy, *Habsburger im 17. Jahrhundert: Die Beziehungen der Höfe von Wien und Madrid während des dreissigjährigen Krieges* (Vienna, 1955), describes this difficult relationship in considerable detail.
47. Elliott, *Olivares*, pp. 352–353.

owing to the domestic difficulties of Charles I. Nowhere, however, was his policy more ambitious or less successful than with regard to France.

Like Philip II before him, Olivares soon concluded that the foreign assistance that the Dutch enjoyed—specifically from the French—was the key to their resistance, and as early as 1626 he was discussing plans for an invasion of France that he hoped might be decisive.[48] Two years later, during the siege of La Rochelle, he briefly made an alliance with France, but this relationship collapsed when the French king Louis XIII backed the duke of Nevers's claim to the succession of Mantua in 1627–28. Typically, Olivares now decided that a sudden military stroke from Milan against Mantua would restore the Spanish king's reputation, damage that of Richelieu and Louis XIII, and hasten favorable peace with the Dutch. But despite some help from the emperor, Olivares's intervention achieved almost nothing, and he had to acknowledge Nevers's claims in 1631. Spain won a tremendous victory in 1634, when a new army under the command of the king's brother the cardinal-infante marched from Italy into Germany and routed the Swedes at Nördlingen. But largely because of that victory, the French entered the war in the following year, and the quick, decisive victory of which Olivares had talked for about a decade once again proved to be illusory. Following once more in Philip II's footsteps, he also tried from time to time to start a new civil war in France, or at least to support a coup d'état against his great rival Richelieu, but these projects also failed.

In the meantime, Olivares made some determined efforts to reform the structure of the Spanish government and the finances of the Spanish empire. Here he appears as something of a modern reformer, but one whose attempts at reform led to disaster. Recognizing that the system of governing councils tended to paralyze action, he instead created ad hoc juntas to deal with special subjects ranging from the reform of morals and dress to military operations. Although the system scored some successes, he complained increasingly during his tenure of office that his orders were not obeyed. His most important attempted innovations involved Castilian finances and his attempts to draw upon the resources of the rest of the empire.[49]

48. Ibid., pp. 245–252.
49. On Olivares's reforms, see J. H. Elliott, *Richelieu and Olivares* (Cambridge and New York, 1984), pp. 51–59, 67–68.

The financial situation in 1618 had not improved since the days of Philip II. Castilian revenues in 1621 were estimated at only 9.7 million ducats. At the same time, the crown had sold *juros* amounting to more than 100 million ducats, and annual interest payments totalled more than 5 million. Numerous royal revenues, including the sales tax of *alcabala*, had either been alienated in return for cash payments or designated as security for *juros*. The government had no force of officials with which to collect its revenues, and private farmers and local town oligarchies customarily took hefty cuts of their own. The crown continued to conduct foreign operations in Flanders and Italy with the help of the Genoese *asentistas*, who contracted to make payments in silver or bills of exchange in return for claims upon government revenues and licenses to export silver from the Indies.[50]

Olivares's plans to reform the system got almost nowhere. In 1623 he tried to abolish the *milliones*, a consumption tax dating from the 1590s, and to replace most existing taxes with a single levy on towns and villages. He also proposed a system of national banks financed by a one-time levy on property and income. But Castilian towns forced him to summon the Cortes, which rejected these proposals.[51] Interestingly enough, Olivares—unlike Philip II—never seriously pursued the option of entrusting the finances of the kingdom to royal officials. Indeed, in 1625 he wanted to end the role of the Council of Finance and turn the main Castilian taxes over to tax farmers, who he thought would be more efficient, and ten years later he complained that while Castile paid about 9 million escudos in taxes, only 3 million actually reached the crown, the rest going to office holders.[52] By 1627 the strain of war had forced Olivares into a new state bankruptcy, and he seized upon the occasion to break off relations with the Genoese bankers, whom public opinion customarily blamed for the government's poverty, and to substitute Portuguese bankers in their place. The overall financial condition of the crown did not, however, improve as a result.

Between 1627 and his fall in 1643 Olivares imposed a few small new taxes, including special payments from office holders, money

50. See Antonio Dominguez Ortiz, *Politica y hacienda de Felipe IV* (Madrid, 1960), pp. 91–108, 176–181, 193–195, 315–318.
51. Elliot, *Richelieu and Olivares*, pp. 69–71.
52. Elliott, *Olivares*, pp. 232–233, 477.

payments from clerics and nobles in lieu of feudal service, and a stamp tax. On the whole he continued to depend upon *asentistas* to provide money and services in return for future claims. Whenever large new foreign expenditures arose, he confiscated large amounts of private silver at Seville, compensating the owners with copper vellón or with *juros*. He also levied forced loans in silver.[53] Despite bitter protests from the merchants to whom the silver belonged, the government resorted to this stratagem several times: in 1625, when part of the treasure fleet failed to arrive; in 1629–30, to pay for the Mantuan war; in 1635–1637, after the renewal of war with France; and in 1639. Finally, in 1642, the government had to promise not to take this step again. In the meantime, the government periodically juggled the relative values of silver and vellón in order to accumulate more silver at the expense of the citizenry. Chronically short of funds with which to raise troops, the government increasingly had to turn local defense and recruiting over to local magnates such as the duke of Medina Sidonia.[54] All this did not prevent two more state bankruptcies, in 1647 and 1653.

Olivares's proposal for a Union of Arms, which he unveiled in late 1625, was his most important and seemingly most modern innovation. In an effort to distribute the burdens of empire more evenly, it asked each realm to raise and maintain a quota of armed men, ranging from 44,000 each from Castile and the Indies to just 6,000 each from Valencia and Sicily, and totalling 140,000. But most of the quotas were wildly optimistic, reflecting inaccurate estimates of population, and even a journey by Philip IV to Catalonia and Valencia in 1626 failed to secure much effective help. In its first year the scheme furnished only 2,000 men.[55]

Olivares subsequently focused upon Catalonia. From 1627 through 1640 he tried to persuade the Catalonian Cortes to contribute more money. Even after the outbreak of open war with France in 1635 the Catalonians resisted, and in 1637 an attempt to raise troops for an invasion of France failed dismally. Finally in 1640, after the French had invaded Catalonia, Olivares dispatched an army of 10,000 men to defend the kingdom. Lacking funds, he ordered that they be billeted among the population, in defiance of a specific provision of the Catalonian constitution. After numerous

53. Ortiz, *Politica y hacienda*, pp. 227–236, 281–309.
54. Thompson, *War and Government*, pp. 146–159.
55. Elliott, *Olivares*, pp. 245–271.

clashes between the troops and the local population, an armed insurrection broke out in 1640, and rebels murdered the Viceroy and opened relations with the French. Determined to suppress the revolt but desperately short of manpower, Olivares tried to mobilize the Portuguese nobility to do the job. This induced them to join the rest of Portugal in yet another rebellion against the crown, fueled partly by new taxes and Portuguese opposition to the Union of Arms.[56] Olivares quickly concluded that a truce with the Dutch had become essential even if Dutch encroachments upon Brazil were left untouched, but the Dutch made terms with the Portuguese rebels instead and failed to begin serious talks with the Spaniards until 1646.[57]

Discredited by these disasters, Olivares now suffered the collapse of his position within Castile. In 1641 his kinsman Medina Sidonia apparently conspired to lead an Andalusian revolt against him. Other near relatives plotted his disgrace because he had legitimized his bastard son and thereby deprived them of their inheritance. In January 1643 he left office, giving way to his nephew, Don Luis de Haro. Four years later Haro declared a new state bankruptcy, and new revolts broke out in Sicily and Naples. The Spaniards finally made terms with the Dutch in 1648, agreeing even to close the Scheldt and free Amsterdam from the competition with Antwerp. Eleven years later they surrendered important border territories to France in the Peace of the Pyrenees.

The failure of Spanish foreign policy stemmed from a combination of contemporary military realities and the inadequacy of imperial finances. The strength of the defensive, the unreliability of mercenary troops, and the lack of reliable, adequate revenue prevented the Spaniards from winning a decisive victory in the Netherlands or in Italy, and ultimately led to revolts in Catalonia, Portugal, Naples, and Sicily. The surplus required to fight the crown's numerous wars came only from Castile and from the New World. After substantial growth in Castilian revenues under Philip II, however, Castilian revenues stabilized or even fell, and silver shipments also declined after 1600. Attempts to improve the efficiency of the Castilian government failed; indeed, as Thompson has shown, the

56. Ibid., pp. 305–522.
57. Israel, *Dutch Republic and Hispanic World*, pp. 315–336.

crown progressively sold off more and more of its authority in the late sixteenth and early seventeenth centuries in return for short-term financial contributions. Revenues consistently fell far behind expenditures, and the crown declared bankruptcy at fairly regular twenty-year intervals.

The size of the Spanish empire, the crown's concern with its communications such as the "Spanish Road" from Italy to Flanders, the continuing (though usually frustrating) alliance between the Austrian and the Spanish Hapsburgs, and the number and variety of Spain's military undertakings from 1559 through 1659 have led several historians to take a view of Spanish (or Hapsburg) power nearly as exalted as that of Olivares himself, and to see the history of this chaotic century as the story of a Spanish attempt to impose unified control over all Europe, comparable to attempts by Napoleon and Hitler. In so doing, historians seem to have repeated, in a sense, the mistakes of Olivares, who, as J. H. Elliott has recently noted, followed "a global strategy in which it was taken for granted that no problem could be treated in isolation, but was intimately related to what was happening elsewhere," and "carefully [drew] up his plans for the coming year, laying down exact figures for the numbers of men and the sums of money required in each of the theatres of war, only to have his generals report that they lacked the men and resources to comply with their orders."[58] Another modern feature of Spanish political life during this century was the stream of pamphlets and books produced by the *arbitristas,* who so confidently laid down the sweeping, uniform administrative measures that would restore Spain's mythical lost greatness, and from whom Olivares borrowed a good deal. Yet the reality with which the crown had to deal was very different, and his attempts (like Philip II's) to impose his vision upon it cost the monarchy, its citizens, and all of European society very dearly.

Simply put, the Spanish crown could not impose its political or military authority over the Dutch, Catalan, or Portuguese aristocracy, much less win a decisive victory over France or conquer England. Silver from the Indies enabled it to field armies with the help of Genoese and Portuguese *asentistas,* but these armies frequently proved to be unreliable instruments and could not win the decisive victories which the crown demanded of them. This, more than

58. Elliott, *Olivares,* pp. 361, 505.

anything else, made the wars of the period—especially the Spanish-Dutch conflict—last so long. Nor could Philip II or Olivares count reliably upon help from the Austrian Hapsburgs or turn the French Catholic League to their advantage. The interests of European princes diverged too much to allow them to form reliable coalitions.

The question of how the Spanish monarchy actually paid for its wars is critical to an understanding of the social and economic impact of warfare in the years 1559–1659. Some evidence suggests that taxes severely impoverished Castile, leading to a decline in population, an absolute decline in economic welfare, and the depopulation of large rural areas. In addition, Europe as a whole paid much of the costs of Spain's wars. As we have seen, the crown customarily made annual contracts with *asentistas*—German, Italian, or Portuguese bankers, for the most part—who made specie and bills of exchange available at specified times and places in return for claims upon future revenues or upon silver shipments from America. The investigations of Richard Ehrenberg and Fernand Braudel suggest that the *asentistas* did not simply lend their own money, but rather acted as middlemen for thousands of European investors, large and small, who put their money in the bills of exchange of prominent bankers. This, of course, helps explain why the Genoese, in particular, continued to lend to the crown year after year, long after the crown's inability to make good on its debts had become apparent.

During the latter half of the sixteenth century the influx of gold and silver which helped the crown finance its wars was largely, if not exclusively, responsible for European inflation—in effect, a general tax upon the whole economy. In addition, the periodic Spanish state bankruptcies, in which the crown (and subsequently the *asentistas*) paid off their short-term debts in *juros* which generally traded well below their face value and were frequently repudiated altogether, effectively confiscated large portions of the savings of European investors. Although the bankers themselves sometimes suffered, they seem to have managed to pass on their losses. Inflation and repudiation allowed Spain to finance its wars by levying a general tax upon the European economy and by confiscating part of the savings of the European public. The Castilian monarchy and nobility's attempt to maintain and extend their holdings imposed a heavy economic burden not only upon their own subjects, but also upon Europe as a whole. Their efforts reflect the disparity between the aristocracy's pretensions and available resources—a disparity which had equally important effects in other parts of Europe.

French Politics from the Wars of Religion to the Death of Mazarin

Many histories of France identify the years from 1559 to 1661 as a period in which the chaos of the religious wars gave way to the absolute monarchies of Henry IV, Louis XIII, Richelieu, and Mazarin. Richelieu in particular has become known as a founder of bureaucratic absolutism at home and of the balance-of-power foreign policy abroad. In recent years, however, new treatments of the seventeenth century have revised the idea of absolutism as it actually developed in seventeenth-century France, both before and during the reign of Louis XIV.[1] In fact, the history of French politics during the years 1559–1659 testifies more to the persistence of premodern political structures than to the emergence of a prototypical modern state. The factional conflicts which tore France apart during the latter half of the sixteenth century remained extremely important under Richelieu and Mazarin, and the crown never established itself upon a secure political or financial footing. The Fronde of 1648–1652 showed just how much remained to be accomplished. Indeed, France during the years 1559–1659 embodied the ideal type of the early modern society and state more closely than any other European nation. Although the monarchy obviously established its authority more successfully during the first half of the seventeenth century than in the latter half of the sixteenth, the change was quite marginal, and did not reflect a fundamental institutional change.

The Wars of Religion

From 1559 through 1598, French politics revolved around a never-ending, often violent struggle among three factions led by the

1. Sharon Kettering, *Patrons, Brokers, and Clients in Seventeenth-Century France* (New York, 1986); David Parker, *The Making of French Absolutism* (New York, 1983); and William Beik, *Absolutism and Society in Seventeenth-Century France: State Power and Provincial Aristocracy in Languedoc* (New York, 1985).

Guise, the Montmorency, and the Bourbon families. The crown never imposed its authority over the factions, and Henry IV brought the civil wars to an end only by buying them off. Though religion helped hold these parties together, their conflict was primarily political. It was not new. At the time of the accidental death of Henry II in 1559 these three factions had already dominated French political life for some time. Henry II's death undoubtedly gave the factional conflict freer play, but the French civil wars sprang more from the structure of French politics and society than from a dynastic accident. Henry II would undoubtedly have had to deal with many of the same problems as his widow and sons, and might not have been much more successful.[2]

Each of the three leaders of these factions—Francis, Anne of Guise, Montmorency, and Anthony of Bourbon—wielded extraordinary political, economic, and governmental power. The lands of the Guise lay mainly in eastern France, those of the Bourbons in the south and west, and the Montmorency domain largely in the center, but all three had some territory and clients in other parts of the country. Having the ear of the monarch, they disposed of enormous patronage. During the 1550s the French church had effectively passed under the control of the Guises, led by the duke's brother, the cardinal of Lorraine—a fact which undoubtedly helped predispose the Bourbons toward Calvinism. As constable, Montmorency exercised considerable control over military appointments. Lastly, these three men and their clients held most of the most important provincial governorships and thereby commanded the local gendarmerie and made recommendations for local appointments. They could also establish their influence over local fiscal and administrative officials and even usurp the collection of royal taxes—a step they frequently took during the forty years of civil war about to begin. During the civil wars the gendarmerie disintegrated, and provincial governors maintained their power through alliances with associations of Catholic or Huguenot noblemen, clergy, and townspeople. By the 1590s they had developed onerous systems of taxes and forced loans which supported the nobility at the expense of the rest of the population.[3]

2. This is the theme of Lucien Romier's extraordinary history, *Les origines politiques des guerres de religion.*

3. Romier, *Le royaume de Cathérine de Medici,* pp. 211–230; Harding, *Anatomy of a Power Elite,* pp. 21–55, 68–80.

Other aspects of French political, economic, and religious life also contributed to the prevailing instability. The end of the Italian wars left the French lesser nobility in a difficult situation. Although systematic studies have not been undertaken, they seem to have been declining both economically and politically. The custom of partible inheritance had narrowed their landed economic base, and their revenues were not keeping pace with inflation. They also were losing power to the new and growing class of office holders, both because they could not afford venal offices and because they lacked the necessary educational qualifications.[4] The nobility was accustomed to war. Returning home, nobles might expect to serve the local governor in the local gendarmerie and to receive handsome salaries from the crown. Should the royal purse prove inadequate, however, they would become an important source of social unrest. As it was, dueling and vendettas became major social problems almost as soon as the troops returned home in 1559.[5]

The spread of Calvinism also created new local political groupings that played a critical role in the civil wars. John Calvin himself, who orchestrated the spread of his religion through much of France from Geneva, emphasized the importance of noble conversions and achieved considerable success, especially in the south and southwest of France. Although some nobles and their wives undoubtedly converted out of conviction, others coveted church lands and the patronage of church offices. When a leading noble converted, clientage relationships spread the new religion downward, reinforcing existing political and social ties. The leading converts to Calvinism were Louis Bourbon, prince of Condé; Montmorency's nephew, Gaspard de Coligny; and Anthony of Bourbon's son Henry, and the Bourbon party ultimately became the patron of Calvinists around France. In response, the Guises later took advantage of the Catholic reaction against Calvinism.

Although the extraordinarily complex conflicts of the years 1559–1598 have been divided into no less than eight civil wars, they fall into a remarkably consistent pattern. As soon as one fac-

4. We should perhaps repeat that the officer class was not yet independent, and that most officers owed their jobs to the patronage of leading court figures. Still, noble representatives consistently protested the sale of office at meetings of the Estates General; Mousnier, *La venalité des offices*, pp. 63–71.

5. Romier, *Le royaume de Cathérine de Medici*, pp. 161–208; J. H. M. Salmon, *Society in Crisis*, pp. 92–100; Harding, *Anatomy of a Power Elite*, pp. 6–45.

tion seemed to have established its influence over the monarch, at least one of the others would begin a conspiracy against it. After raising an army—often with the help of a foreign subsidy—the rebels generally issued a manifesto claiming to be acting on behalf of the king, whom they proclaimed to be a captive of evil men pursuing goals inimical to the best interests of France. The crown, with the help of one or two of the remaining factions, would attempt to subdue the rebels but could rarely win a decisive victory. Instead, each conflict was settled by a new royal edict which forgave the rebels' usurpations of royal authority, paid off their troops, and redistributed fortunes and favors. Within a few years, the cycle would begin again.[6] While some historians have blamed the breakdown of authority upon the immaturity of Francis II and Charles IX, structural factors seem more to blame. Conflicts began under the regency of Catherine de Medici, who effectively ruled from 1559 through 1568, and continued during the majority of Charles IX and under the rule of Henry III, who came to the throne in 1574. We shall look successively at the activities of the three main factions and at the crown's attempts to cope with them.

The heads of the house of Bourbon during this period were Anthony of Bourbon, king of Navarre, who died of battle wounds in 1562; his brother Louis, prince of Condé, killed in battle in 1569; Anthony's son Henry of Navarre, the future King Henry IV: and Louis's son Henry, who died in 1588. All were Calvinists. From 1562 until 1572 they generally allied themselves with Montmorency's nephew, the Huguenot Gaspard de Coligny. On four occasions—in 1562, 1567–1570, 1574–1576, and 1579–80—they proclaimed that the king had fallen under hostile and dangerous influences and put an army in the field. In each case they sought more favor and offices for their leaders and freer exercise of the Calvinist religion. They sometimes plotted to kidnap the royal family and murder the Guises, and in 1562 the duke of Guise was assassinated by Poltrot de Mere, a Calvinist nobleman whom Coligny had placed in Guise's household as a spy.[7] Twice they were

---

6. The best accounts of the religious wars are J.-H. Mariéjol, *La réforme et la ligue: L'édit de Nantes (1559–1598)* (Paris, 1911); James Westfall Thompson, *The Wars of Religion in France, 1559–1576* (New York, 1909); Harding, *Anatomy of a Power Elite*; and Salmon, *Society in Crisis.*

7. Thompson, *Wars of Religion*, pp. 168–189. The Guises not unnaturally blamed Coligny for the murder. Under torture, Poltrot implicated the admiral in the crime, and

threatened with extinction. After the massacre of St. Bartholomew, when Henry of Navarre and Henry, prince of Condé, had to profess Catholicism and languish under virtual house arrest at court, the Huguenot stronghold of La Rochelle successfully resisted a royal siege. After 1585, when the Guises won complete ascendancy over Henry III and committed him to the extirpation of heresy, Henry of Navarre again led his party into the field in self-defense. He entered into an alliance with the king in 1588 and claimed the French throne when the king was assassinated a year later.

The Bourbon armies came from their clienteles in the southwest and the south, the garrisons they controlled as provincial governors, and hired mercenaries, especially from Germany. They sometimes hired princely German military entrepreneurs such as John Casimir of the Palatinate or the duke of Zweibrücken. Commanders initially raised the money for recruitment by pawning their possessions, securing loans from Huguenot towns, or obtaining foreign subsidies. Elizabeth I, who seems to have feared the ascendancy of the Guises because of Mary of Guise's claim to her throne, may have given some assistance to the Tumult of Amboise, an abortive rising in 1560, and she provided some troops in 1562 and money in 1569. Her allies showed little gratitude, ignoring various promises they had made to her when the time came to make peace. Elizabeth intervened openly on the side of Henry IV after 1588.

The conflict in France also became intertwined with the Dutch revolt. Condé rose in 1567 partly because of the duke of Alba's march from Italy to the Netherlands and the arrest of Egmont and Horn. He claimed that all these moves reflected a general strategy for the extirpation of Protestantism—a strategy which Protestant propaganda claimed falsely that Alba and Catherine de Medici had adopted at their meeting in Bayonne in 1564. Then, in 1568, Coligny concluded a formal treaty with William of Orange, noting that both their sovereigns were misled by evil counsellors who

although Coligny denied complicity in the murder, he admitted some knowledge of Poltrot's intentions and added that the death of Guise "is the greatest good that could happen to this Kingdom and to the church of God, and particularly to me and my family, and also because, if it please Her Majesty the Queen, it will be the means of bringing peace." Henry Dwight Sedgwick, *The House of Guise* (New York, 1938), pp. 171–175.

sought to destroy true religion, the nobility, and all gens de bien.[8] The Edicts of Longjumeau (1568) and St. Germain (1570) specifically guaranteed the French possessions of Orange and his brother, Louis of Nassau. Coligny spent the years 1570–1572 trying to persuade Charles IX to intervene on the side of the Dutch, and the Huguenots mounted an unsuccessful intervention of their own in 1572 before the massacre of St. Bartholomew put an end to these plans. Until 1588 they did not win a single battle, but their capacity to maintain men in the field sufficed to control large parts of France.

The various edicts which put an end to the Bourbon uprisings all began by confirming the rebel leaders in all their governorships and other offices, and forgiving their local usurpations of royal power during the conflict.[9] On several occasions the Bourbons also forced the crown to pay off their foreign troops, who would otherwise have refused to disband. The edicts also defined the rights of Protestant worship in various parts of France. These provisions showed that the nobility retained the leadership of the Huguenot party. While several of them granted full liberty of worship to noblemen within their homes, they sharply restricted the rights of urban bourgeois Calvinists, who sometimes complained bitterly that their leaders did not take them into account. In addition, beginning with the Peace of St. Germain in 1570, the edicts specifically guaranteed the Huguenots the right to maintain fortified towns, including La Rochelle, and provided for *chambres mi-parties*, or mixed judicial bodies, to hear cases between Catholics and Protestants. Because of Catholic resistance this concession was seldom put into effect, but the grant of the right to maintain fortified places confirmed, in effect, that the king of France was not master within his realm.

The Guises were, if anything, more insatiable than the Bourbons. While they enjoyed the predominant influence at court during most of the period 1559–1588, they ultimately sought to bring the whole of France under their political control. The death of Henry II in 1559 left the Guises in virtually unchallenged command of the government thanks both to the offices they held and

8. Salmon, *Society in Crisis*, p. 173.

9. These include the Edict of Amboise (1563); the Edict of Longjumeau (1568); the Edict of St. Germain (1570); the Edict of Boulogne (1573); the Peace of Monsieur (1576); the Edict of Poitiers (1577); and the Treaty of Fleix (1580).

to Francis II's marriage to Mary of Guise. Economical and haughty, they quickly antagonized the Bourbons and alienated the lesser nobility by cutting the generous pensions paid by Henry II. Catherine de Medici also resented their ascendancy and quickly moved to redress the balance in favor of Anthony of Bourbon after the death of Francis II in late 1560. The Guises immediately sought the help of Philip II and toyed with the idea of marrying the widowed Mary to Don Carlos, the ill-fated heir to the Spanish throne.[10] They eventually persuaded Bourbon to join them in exchange for their help in securing Philip's recognition of his status of king of Navarre. Then, in March of 1562, Guise's retinue surprised and attacked a Protestant service in Vassy, in eastern France. Later that year, the Guises triggered Condé's rising by taking the royal family into informal custody. Philip II provided some troops, and the Guises forced Condé to stay in the field through the winter of 1562–63, but they suffered disaster when Duke Francis was assassinated. Although the family emerged as the patron of Catholic religious associations during the mid-1560s, the Guises were not religious fanatics. At one time they actually dangled the hand of Mary of Guise, now Queen of Scots, before Condé, hoping to detach him from Coligny and the Huguenot party.

The surviving Guises became more violent after the assassination of the duke. During the civil wars of 1567–1570 they plotted the arrest of the Huguenot leaders and at one point even offered the crown of France to Philip II should Charles IX and his brothers die without issue.[11] In 1572 the Guises resorted to assassination to eliminate the influence of Coligny, whom they still blamed for the assassination of Duke Francis. Their threats had generally kept Coligny away from court since 1563, and in August 1572, they apparently arranged his assassination in Paris just before the wedding of Henry of Navarre and Margaret of Valois. When the assassination failed, they persuaded Catherine de Medici and Charles IX that only the wholesale massacre of the Huguenot leadership could avoid Huguenot retaliation.[12] The Guises' triumph seemed

10. See the text of their treaty in N. M. Sutherland, *The Massacre of St. Bartholomew and the European Conflict, 1559–1572* (New York, 1973), pp. 347–350.

11. Thompson, *Wars of Religion*, pp. 304, 336.

12. Sutherland, *Massacre of St. Bartholomew*, pp. 312–346, summarizes the still-controversial evidence regarding the responsibility for the massacre, which probably rested with the Guises. Both the reputed marksman, Maurevert, and the house from which he fired seem to have had some connection with the Guises, who had been

complete, but within two years they had lost the support of the Montmorencys. They failed to subdue their opponents in the south and southwest or to prevent the defection of the king's brother, the duke of Anjou. The Peace of Monsieur in 1576 once again restored equilibrium among the three factions.

Within another year, the Guises had formed the Catholic League, a far-reaching network of Catholic nobles and townsmen dedicated to the maintenance of the Catholic religion. Such leagues had been important at least since the first civil war of 1562–63. Although several royal edicts had attempted to ban them, they remained the institution which linked the lower nobility and leading townspeople to the provincial governors in much of France. The Catholic League now formed councils of town notables, clergymen, and gentry who spread propaganda among the people, collected taxes, and tried to maintain order. Although the league had a general council sitting in Paris, it remained highly decentralized.[13] When the new king Henry III called the Estates General in 1576, the league-dominated deputies insisted that he immediately restore religious unity.[14] A year later Henry did begin a new war against the Huguenots and cut back their privileges significantly.

The Guises achieved almost complete ascendancy in French politics after the death of the heir apparent, the duke of Anjou, in the Netherlands in 1584. The Protestant Henry of Navarre was now heir to the throne, and the Guises joined with Philip II and Navarre's uncle the cardinal of Bourbon in a Holy League for "the defense and conservation of the Catholic, apostolic and Roman religion" and for the extirpation of heresy in France. Philip provided a subsidy of one million livres, and the league took over the city of Paris and many other parts of France, usurping government authority and collecting taxes. Henry III capitulated in June 1585, promising to eliminate all Protestant rights at once, disinheriting Henry of Navarre, paying off foreign troops the Guises had hired, showering their followers with pensions, governorships, and

---

scheming to kill Coligny since 1563 and had recently received encouragement from the pope. No hard evidence suggests that Catherine de Medici planned the initial murder of Condé, and early diplomatic reports blamed the Guises for the assassination. See Wallace McCaffrey, *Queen Elizabeth and the Making of Policy, 1572–1588* (Princeton, 1981), pp. 172–173.

13. Harding, *Anatomy of a Power Elite*, pp. 84–98.

14. Mariéjol, *La réforme et la ligue*, pp. 173–188.

other offices, and giving them the control of specified fortresses.
The duke in January 1588 issued a new ultimatum asking for his
appointment as lieutenant general of the army, the murder of
Huguenot prisoners, the sale of Huguenot property to pay the
league's debts, and recognition of the league's right to garrison
towns. Supported by the people of Paris, whom the league had
turned into a political force, the Guises drove the king out of the
city in July 1588 and forced him to call the Estates General. But
when the Estates General met at Blois in December 1588, Henry III
invited the duke of Guise to a private audience, where he was assassinated. His brother the cardinal of Guise was arrested and assassinated as well.[15]

Although the Guise party survived under the leadership of the
late duke's brother, the duke of Mayenne, the structure of the
league began to crack after the assassination of Henry III in 1589.
The league initially supported the succession of the cardinal of
Bourbon, Henry IV's uncle, but upon his death it divided its support among candidates put forward by Philip II, the house of Lorraine, the Guises themselves, and the house of Savoy. An Estates
General called by the league in 1593 could not resolve this problem. In the meantime, a series of violent conflicts arose between
urban democratic factions within the league, such as the Paris Sixteen, and the noble provincial and town governors who up until
now had controlled these factions. In Paris, Mayenne eventually
executed several of the leaders of the Sixteen. Eventually, after
Henry IV's conversion to Catholicism in 1593, Mayenne decided to
come to terms with the king.[16]

In the meantime the powerful Montmorency faction tacked back
and forth between the Bourbons and the Guises while building up
their own position in Languedoc. The aged constable Anne of
Montmorency fought with the Guises in the first and second civil
wars, losing his life on the battlefield during the second. During
the early 1560s a passionate affair between Anne's second son,
Henry of Montmorency-Damville, and Mary of Guise strengthened the alliance. After the constable's death, his sons helped negotiate the compromise Edict of St. Germain. Damville, who had

15. Ibid., pp. 238–262, 325–379; De Lamar Jensen, *Diplomacy and Dogmatism: Berna-
dino de Mendoza and the French Catholic League* (Cambridge, Mass., 1964), pp. 41–72, 130–
152.

16. Salmon, *Society in Crisis*, pp. 247–273; Mariéjol, *La réforme et la ligue*, pp. 389–392.

become governor of Languedoc in 1563, built up an extensive following and generally stayed on reasonable terms with the Huguenot communities in the province.

After the massacre of St. Bartholomew, Damville initially participated in the new campaign against the Huguenots, but in 1575 he switched sides to protect his position against the Guises and the duke of Joyeuse, a favorite of Henry III. The bargain he struck with Henry of Navarre in that year turned Languedoc, the Dauphiné, and Provence into a virtual state within a state, and the Peace of Monsieur confirmed his enormous power. Damville now maintained independent relations with foreign princes and refused even to send delegates to the Estates General. But in 1577 Catherine de Medici successfully reconciled Damville and Montmorency to the crown with new promises of favor and office, and they fought against the Huguenots from 1578 through 1581. While Damville consistently respected the Huguenots' rights of conscience, they frequently resisted his attempts to collect royal taxes.[17]

Damville, who succeeded to the Montmorency title in 1579, came under attack from the Catholic League in 1582 and formed a union of *politiques* and Huguenots in response. "He governeth himself marvellously well," an English envoy wrote, and "is marvellously beloved where he is, and hath a great number of gentlemen that follow and do depend on him."[18] Montmorency remained almost impregnable in Languedoc. In 1590 he joined Henry IV in exchange for a promise of enormous estates. In the end this promise was not kept, but Montmorency's domains provided much of the money with which Henry IV financed his campaigns during the 1590s.

From 1559 through the mid-1590s the French monarchy lacked the material, political, and moral resources necessary to put an end to civil conflicts. Catherine de Medici, the most powerful member of the royal family until the early 1580s, tried to conciliate the various factions but could not always avoid taking sides, while Henry III tried to built up a faction of his own. During the 1560s Catherine seems to have realized that the triumph of any one faction was neither likely nor desirable, and she therefore agreed to

17. Franklin Charles Palm, *Politics and Religion in Sixteenth-Century France: A Study of the Career of Henry of Montmorency-Damville, Uncrowned King of the South* (Gloucester, 1969), gives a fine account of these developments.

18. Ibid., p. 154.

the relatively generous settlements that secured numerous Protestant rights. So unpopular were these measures, however, that she was frequently unable to persuade the parlements to ratify them, and during the 1560s she aroused Protestant suspicions as well. In May 1565, Catherine met with Philip's representative, the duke of Alba, and her daughter, Elizabeth, Queen of Spain, in Bayonne. Catherine planned to discuss new dynastic marriages, but because Philip had insisted that no heretic be present at the meeting, even the prince of Condé, European Protestants suspected a plot. In 1572 Catherine made another attempt to conciliate the factions by marrying her daughter, Elizabeth, to Henry of Navarre, but after the massacre of St. Bartholomew it became an article of faith among Protestants that she and Alba had planned the slaughter of Protestants all over Europe.

From time to time Catherine did make a determined effort to assert royal authority, either alone or together with one of the factions. Thus in early 1566, a series of royal edicts sought to improve administration, suppress unnecessary judicial offices (which Francis I and Henry II had proliferated to raise more money), and strip the uncontrollable royal governors—rapidly emerging as the leaders of Protestant and Catholic leagues—of their power to raise taxes and hold fairs. The renewal of the civil wars in the following year put an end to such plans. Fighting together with the Guises from 1568 through 1570, the monarchy successfully put armies in the field but could not keep them there long enough to subdue the Huguenots. Mutiny was a constant threat, and on several occasions royal forces simply melted away. The crown was even more helpless at sea, where Protestant privateers based in La Rochelle marauded at will and opened relations with the Dutch Sea Beggars. The extraordinary concession of fortified towns in the Edict of St. Germain reflected the balance of forces. Even after the massacre of St. Bartholomew, which left the Huguenot party almost leaderless, the crown and the Guises could not reduce the town of La Rochelle. In the meantime the people of France suffered the ceaseless plundering of all the fighting forces. To most of them, high politics must have seemed a visitation like the plague.[19]

Rivalries *within* the royal family increased political chaos. From 1570 through 1572, as Charles IX fell under Coligny's influence, his

19. This account is based on Thompson, *Wars of Religion*, pp. 326–421; Salmon, *Society in Crisis*, pp. 168–183; Harding, *Anatomy of a Power Elite*, pp. 55–68; and Palm, *Politics and Religion*, pp. 50–79.

brother Henry, duke of Anjou, became patron of the Guises. After Henry succeeded his brother in 1574, his younger brother Francis, duke of Alençon, emerged as an ally of the Bourbons and a political power in his own right. In September 1575 Alençon escaped from court and emerged at the head of an army in alliance with the *politiques*. Soon Henry III's control of France was reduced to the Ile-de-France and the Guise strongholds of Burgundy and Champagne. Bankrupt, he finally made peace in May 1576, confirming the rights of the Huguenots and the independent power of Montmorency and Henry of Navarre, and granting a huge apanage in the Loire valley to Alençon.[20] A few years later, Henry III endorsed his brother's involvement in the Dutch revolt in order to get him out of France.

Materially the crown was growing weaker, not stronger. Adjusting for inflation, the king's revenue in 1574 had fallen about 33 percent since the death of Francis I.[21] In each war the crown had attempted to make do with forced loans from the towns (especially Paris), forced sales of church property, and loans from foreign financiers. Nor did the crown enjoy any reservoir of support in the country at large. The general resentment of court corruption and extravagance which Trevor-Roper discussed in his essay on the 1640s seems to have pervaded France as early as the late sixteenth century. When the Estates General met at Blois in 1576–77 the king reported a debt of 100 million livres, but such was the resentment of the deputies toward the court and the suspicion of "foreign favorites" that no new revenues were granted. Henry III also attempted to bring the Catholic League under royal control, but without success.[22]

Henry's attempts to build up his own party only increased this resentment. He lavishly rewarded his favorites, the *mignons* Joyeuse and Epernon, and the effeminacy of the court became the subject of numerous pamphlets. Court life further degenerated into anarchy when a series of fatal bouts of swordplay broke out among followers of the king, Anjou, and the Guises. Disgust with the king became so general by early 1580 that some Huguenot nobles discussed with the Guises a plan to depose him and confirm the Huguenots' privileges. Religious allegiances remained

20. Thompson, *Wars of Religion*, pp. 454–524.

21. Royal revenue had risen from 9 million livres in 1546 to only 12 million in 1574, while prices had at least doubled. Wolfe, *Fiscal System*, p. 103.

22. Mariéjol, *La réforme et la ligue*, pp. 173–188.

powerful among townspeople but seemed to have become almost irrelevant at the upper reaches of society.[23]

As we have seen, Henry III in 1585 fell entirely under the influence of the league, only to turn the table on the Guises by assassinating them in late 1588. He promptly made an alliance with Henry of Navarre but was himself assassinated by a Catholic friar in August 1589. His heir apparent, Henry IV, never put an end to factional struggles and rebellions, but he did bring the civil wars to an end. Henry IV has been portrayed as an apostle of toleration and a founder of absolutism, but he was neither. Instead, he was perhaps the cleverest politician of sixteenth-century Europe—a crafty, cynical man who understood the nature of contemporary politics.

After several years of struggle—including an unsuccessful siege of Paris, raised by the duke of Parma—Henry in 1593 asked to be received into the Catholic faith. He then embarked upon a long series of complex negotiations with the Catholic magnates. In late 1595 he settled with Mayenne, the leader of the Guise party, in terms reminiscent of the earlier edicts that had ended the various episodes of civil war. Highly detailed articles absolved Mayenne of a multitude of usurpations of both royal and clerical revenue, and even of coining his own money. Henry also assumed Mayenne's debts to the tune of approximately 1 million livres and gave him an indemnity of 2.6 million more. Mayenne received the right to garrison three secure places and became governor of Ile-de-France. Aumale, Joyeuse, the young duke of Guise, and many others seem to have received similar (although probably somewhat less generous) terms, as well as important governorships and other posts. In many cases Henry did try to reduce their power bases by forcing them to assume new positions in other parts of the country, but he did not dispossess them. Henry's adherents, of course, also deserved rewards, and Montmorency-Damville assumed his father's old post as constable. Not one magnate suffered for treason, even those like Joyeuse who had collaborated openly with Philip II. Towns, too, sold their allegiance dearly, with Paris leading the way with the price of almost 1.5 million livres. By 1598 the cost of buying the allegiance of France had reached about 24 million livres—more than 80 percent of the annual revenue.

The willingness of the Catholic chiefs to submit to royal author-

23. Ibid., pp. 188–200; Salmon, *Society in Crisis*, pp. 196–206.

ity probably owed something to the financial distress in which they must have found themselves after more than five years of continuous war—by far the longest continuous conflict of the era. It also owed something to the conflict that had developed within the league between the magnates and the democratic movements that had emerged in Paris and in other cities—movements that threatened the social order. Money, however, played the key role. After one important submission Henry was congratulated for his subjects' decision to render unto Caesar that which was Caesar's. "Don't say that they have rendered [*rendu*] it to me!" replied Henry. "Say rather that they have sold [*vendu*] it!"[24]

In 1595 Henry took another major step toward reconciliation by declaring war on Spain. For the first time since 1559, the whole French nobility could turn its violent impulses outward. Within France, however, the most independent and recalcitrant minority of all, the Huguenots, had not yet come to terms with the crown. Since Henry's abjuration in 1593 their relationship with him had not been easy, and for a time they had planned to secede from the realm. They had extorted large sums from him in return for troops to use against the Spaniards, and in 1596–97, dissatisfied with his failure to guarantee their position, they held a national assembly. Their chance came when the Spaniards captured Amiens, leaving Henry too desperate for their help to put off making terms. The result was the Edict of Nantes, issued in 1598.[25]

Like the earlier edicts issued at the conclusion of the civil wars, the Edict of Nantes represented the maximum which the Protestant party had been able to extort from the crown. Henry IV gave more *not* because of his Huguenot past but because he had no choice. As soon as he became a Catholic king the Huguenots became a major political problem for him, and subsequent evidence shows that he, like his grandson Louis XIV, hoped that French Protestantism would eventually disappear. In 1598, however, he had to meet their demands. The Huguenots secured liberty of conscience and liberty of worship in all places specified in the 1576 Peace of Monsieur and in two towns per *bailliage* or *sénéchausée*. They also secured the right to maintain 51 garrisoned towns and 150 additional places of refuge, the expenses of which would be

24. Wolfe, *Fiscal System*, pp. 214–225 (quotation on p. 218); Mariéjol, *La réforme et la ligue*, pp. 389–392, 403–406; Harding, *Anatomy of a Power Elite*, pp. 105–170.

25. Mousnier, *Assassination of Henry IV*, pp. 138–158.

paid by the crown, and the right to hold political assemblies. Other provisions similar to Henry's treaties with the Catholic magnates forgave them their usurpations of royal revenues, their minting of coins, and their extraordinary levies.[26]

Rather than favor one faction or another, Henry IV pursued a calculated policy of balance—a policy similar to that of Elizabeth I, and the only one which under the circumstances had any chance of success. "The wisest philosophers," wrote Henry's chancellor Bellièvre at the time of the Edict of Nantes, "have for long taught us that it is impossible to avoid sedition in a kingdom, if persons of worth see themselves rejected and lose hope of achieving the dignities they think they have merited by their birth and virtue."[27] It remained impossible for Henry to keep them all satisfied, but he did his best.[28]

During the remainder of Henry's reign he attempted to improve the crown's position, concentrating, with the help of the duke of Sully, on the royal finances. By negotiating better terms with creditors and tax farmers Sully managed drastically to reduce the royal debt, estimated at almost 300 million livres by 1600, and to run a surplus in most years. By 1610 the surplus had reached 15 million livres out of a revenue of 33 million. Nothing like this ever occurred before or after in any early modern country. At the same time, Sully used his position to accumulate a huge private fortune and create a reliable clientele of his own.[29] Henry and Sully also introduced a major institutional innovation, the *paulette*, in an apparent attempt to reduce noble patronage and power. The *paulette* of 1604 imposed an annual payment on holders of venal offices, including the vast majority of financial and judicial officials. In return the officers received the long-sought right to bequeath their office to their heirs. Though justified at the time as a financial measure, some later evidence suggests that the *paulette* aimed at releasing the office holders from the patronage of the magnates and making them a new, independent class.[30] This step may indeed

26. Wolfe, *Fiscal System*, pp. 225–230; Salmon, *Society in Crisis*, pp. 292–313.

27. Salmon, *Society in Crisis*, p. 318.

28. David Buisseret, *Henry IV* (London, 1984), pp. 160–161.

29. On Henry's reign, see Wolfe, *Fiscal System*, pp. 214–239; J. Russell Major, *Representative Government in Early Modern France* (New Haven, 1980), pp. 375–396; and Salmon, *Society in Crisis*, pp. 309–326.

30. See Mousnier, *La venalité des offices*, pp. 557–567. Years later Richelieu claimed that Sully had privately given him this explanation.

have reduced the power of the nobility, but it also created an independent officer class that later seriously contested royal authority.

Despite Henry's political brilliance, his hold over the country remained tenuous. Both the Catholic and Protestant churches regarded him with suspicion, and despite his efforts to reduce fortified places around the country, the position of the nobility remained dangerously strong. Conspiracies and revolts continued.[31] He faced essentially the same problems as the monarchs of the previous half-century, and his greatness lies in his genius at manipulating contemporary politics rather than in the foundation of any new, absolutist institutions. Nor was he guided by any new conception of "reason of state." A man of his time, he had on the eve of his death embarked upon a war with Spain, largely because Archduke Albert of the Spanish Netherlands refused to hand over Charlotte of Montmorency, whose husband, the prince of Condé, had carried her across the border to escape the king's romantic attentions.[32] The history of the next forty years confirmed his failure to make any decisive institutional changes in French politics.

Louis XIII, Richelieu, and Mazarin

Although French governments maintained somewhat more order during the first sixty years of the seventeenth century than they had since the death of Henry II, noble conspiracies and religious rebellions continued to play a vital role in French political life until the beginning of the rule of Louis XIV. The crown remained weak financially and institutionally, while the magnates were as greedy, jealous, and unreliable as ever. Even more serious conspiracies hatched within the royal family, where Louis XIII had to contend with the intrigues of Marie de Medici and his brother Gaston d'Orléans, known as "Monsieur." While the crown occasionally met such revolts with firm measures, it frequently found itself compelled to make generous terms with the rebels to restore order, just as it had during the religious wars. Thus in 1602 Henry IV executed his old friend Marshal Biron, who had led a wide-ranging conspiracy of discontented magnates. The duke of Bouillon,

31. See Mousnier, *Assassination of Henry IV, passim.*

32. This conclusion, however fantastic it may seem, is forcefully and effectively argued in J.-H. Mariéjol, *Henri IV et Louis XIII* (Paris, 1911), pp. 126ff., and confirmed by Buisseret, *Henry IV,* pp. 173–174.

prince of Sedan and son-in-law of William of Orange, fled to Germany after taking part in the same conspiracy and did not submit to Henry until 1608. After the king's death—which may have been the result of a conspiracy that never came to light[33]—the prince of Condé, Bouillon, the duke of Nevers, and Henry IV's bastard son the duke of Vendôme staged a series of risings culminating in Condé's arrest in 1616. In early 1617 Louis XIII arranged the murder of his mother's favorite, Concini, and began to rule himself. Although he bestowed important provincial governorships and large pensions upon his mother, she continued to conspire against him until her exile in 1631. The Protestants, led by the duke of Rohan, also revolted several times during the 1620s.[34]

The advent of Armand-Jean du Plessis, Cardinal Richelieu, as the king's first minister in 1624 has long been regarded as a turning point in the history of France, if not indeed of the modern world. Both in theory and in practice, many have argued, Richelieu put the authority of the French state on a new basis and vastly increased its strength. He has also been credited with the restoration of the European balance of power, and with moving both his country and the European continent a step closer to modernity. "Richelieu's political thought," Friedrich Meinecke wrote sixty years ago, "centered round the proposition, that in all State activity the ruling force was to be, purely and exclusively, *raison d'état*, the 'public interest,' purified of all particular and private motives and of all materially egotistical constituents."[35] A more recent treatment has argued that in internal affairs, "the Cardinal's many undertakings were consistently directed towards one major, comprehensive end: state-building."[36]

In part, this traditional view reflects Richelieu's skill as a memorialist and handler of public opinion. Few statesmen have imposed their view of themselves upon posterity more successfully than he. A series of more recent studies have painted a considerably more mixed and subtle picture of his achievements. Without attempting to deal with his entire career, we may usefully examine some of its

33. This is clearly the view of Mousnier, *Assassination of Henry IV.*

34. The best sources on the political history of the reigns of Henry IV and Louis XIII are Mariéjol, *Henri IV et Louis XIII*, and Victor-L. Tapié, *France in the Age of Louis XIII and Richelieu* (New York, 1974).

35. Friedrich Meinecke, *Machiavellism: The Doctrine of Raison d'Etat and Its Place in Modern History* (New Haven, 1957), p. 167.

36. William F. Church, *Richelieu and Reason of State* (Princeton, 1972), p. 173.

most important aspects: the course of his rise to power, the nature of the state he led, his relationship to the traditional sources of power in French society, the extent of his financial reforms, and the goals and achievements of his foreign policy.

Richelieu secured and held power by entirely traditional methods. A nobleman from a family fallen on relatively hard times, Richelieu entered the church to keep the bishopric of Luçon in his family—a fact which did not prevent him, years later, from piously advising Louis XIII to reserve bishoprics for persons of exemplary merit.[37] At court he rose rapidly under the patronage of the favorite Concini and the Queen Mother, Marie de Medici, whose chaplain he became and who secured him numerous livings. His first brief tour as foreign minister ended in 1617 with Concini's fall, but the Queen Mother subsequently secured his cardinal's hat. "Madam," he wrote on that occasion, "this purple for which I am beholden to your Majesty will ever call to my remembrance the solemn vow that I have made to shed blood in your service." Whether or not he remembered this vow, he subsequently honored it mainly in the breach.[38]

Further intrigues raised Richelieu to the post of first minister in 1625. His subsequent description of the state of France upon his accession would have fit the late sixteenth century perfectly well: "I can truly say," he wrote Louis XIII more than ten years later, "that the Huguenots shared the state with you, that the Greats behaved as if they were not your subjects, and the most powerful governors of provinces as if they were sovereign in their offices."[39] In 1625 he proposed the most sweeping reforms: reorganization of the royal councils, implementation of the Tridentine decrees and other church reforms, abolition of dueling, reduction of the royal household expenses, and abolition of venality of office. But as one of the leading students of the period has noted, few if any of these reforms were ever effected.[40] By the time he wrote the *Testament politique* Richelieu regarded both the venality and the hereditability of office as unfortunate evils that simply could not be suppressed. He never published the Tridentine decrees, whose provisions against pluralism would have been an extreme personal embar-

37. *Testament politique du Cardinal Richelieu*, ed. Louis André (Paris, 1947), pp. 151–152.

38. Tapié, *France*, pp. 127, 130–138.

39. Richelieu, *Testament politique*, p. 93; all translations of this work are my own.

40. Tapié, *France*, pp. 138–153.

rassment, and his vehement complaints against dueling reflect his inability to stop it.[41] Indeed, at the key moment of his ministry, in 1630, Richelieu explicitly chose foreign intervention over the domestic reforms favored by his chief rival, Marillac.[42]

Pamphleteering played a major role in French as well as Spanish politics, and Richelieu retained several skilled writers to defend himself and his policies. Like every contemporary favorite, he was frequently accused of misleading the king and misusing the power of the state for his own purposes. His pamphleteers answered that he consistently put the interests of the state and the true religion above all else, and they have been remarkably successful in imposing this view upon history.[43] It is clear, however, that Richelieu's use of favor and patronage was entirely characteristic of his age. He was every bit as solicitous of the welfare of himself and his family and friends as Antonio Perez, Olivares, Wallenstein, Lord Burghley, or the duke of Buckingham.

Having achieved power through the intercession of the Queen Mother, Richelieu increased it by continually courting Louis XIII and by cleverly manipulating the patronage system. He extended his clientele when possible by arranging advantageous marriages for his nieces, and he found numerous places for his male relatives. At one time he even toyed with the idea of marrying a niece to the king's brother, Gaston d'Orléans. He personally purchased the offices of admiral of the west and admiral of the Levant from the dukes of Montmorency and Guise, partly because of his interest in sea power. Gradually he packed the emerging royal ministry, composed of the chancellor, secretaries of state, and superintendents of finance, with his "creatures," men long linked to him by family and business ties.[44] He certainly did not neglect his own private interests. Although his own finances remain shrouded in obscurity, he clearly amassed a very large fortune.[45]

More significant, Richelieu never really attacked the power of

41. Richard Herr, "Honor vs. Absolutism: Richelieu's Fight against Dueling," *Journal of Modern History*, 27, no. 3 (September 1955): 281–286.

42. Richard Bonney, *Political Change in France under Richelieu and Mazarin* (Oxford, 1978), pp. 29–35.

43. Church, *Richelieu and Reason of State*, is based upon these pamphlets.

44. Orest A. Ranum, *Richelieu and the Councillors of Louis XIII* (Oxford, 1963); Kettering, *Patrons, Brokers, and Clients*, pp. 157–191.

45. Joseph Bergrin, *Cardinal Richelieu: Power and the Pursuit of Wealth* (New Haven, 1985), gives a perceptive account of Richelieu's accumulation of wealth and power but concedes that many of his dealings remain obscure; see esp. pp. 243–256.

the great magnates who had dominated French politics since 1559. The importance of provincial governors had diminished little since the late sixteenth century, and Richelieu tried to secure the most important governorships for himself and his most trusted associates.[46] The Code Michaux of 1629 forbade governors to raise troops and accumulate arms in the provinces, but its enforcement never got off the ground.[47] Richelieu's most important ally among the magnates was the prince of Condé, to whom he gave several important governorships and other favors, and to whom he eventually married a niece. He appointed Condé commander of the army detailed to crush the Huguenots in 1628 in order to prevent an alliance between the Huguenots and discontented magnates. When Richelieu executed Condé's brother-in-law Montmorency in 1632, he arranged for Condé to receive Montmorency's estates.[48] While harsh toward disobedient nobles, Richelieu believed in the prerogatives of the noble order. "Forgetting nothing that will maintain the nobility in the virtues of its ancestors," he wrote, "one should also omit nothing which will allow it to conserve its wealth, and procure the means which will allow it to acquire more."[49]

The destruction of the Huguenots' independent power was Richelieu's most striking concrete political achievement. When in 1627 the English duke of Buckingham allied himself with Soubise, son of the duke de Rohan, and landed near La Rochelle, Richelieu successfully besieged the town, secured its surrender in 1628 in return for a simple guarantee of religious liberty, and razed its fortifications to the ground. In the following year a royal army originally raised for service in Italy crushed Rohan in the Protestant stronghold of Languedoc, and the subsequent Edict of Alais revoked the Protestants' military and political privileges. These measures removed one, though by no means the only, source of armed rebellion against the crown. They also provided effective propaganda against the pro-Spanish *dévot* party, which consistently criticized Richelieu's foreign policy for its partiality toward Dutch and German heretics.[50] Yet Rohan himself submitted only in exchange

46. See Tapié, *France*, pp. 159–174; Bonney, *Richelieu and Mazarin*, pp. 284–318; and Orest Ranum, "Richelieu and the Great Nobility: Some Aspects of Early Modern Political Motives," *French Historical Studies*, 3, no. 2 (Fall 1962): 184–204.

47. Tapié, *France*, pp. 264–267.

48. Henri d'Orleans, duc d'Aumale, *Histoire des princes de condé pendant les XVIe et XVIIe siècles* (Paris, 1863–1896), III, 250–256.

49. Richelieu, *Testament politique*, pp. 220, 224–229.

50. Tapié, *France*, pp. 175–202.

for substantial favors, and he later won fame and honors as a general in the Thirty Years' War.

Despite this success, however, Richelieu did not establish his government's authority on a firm basis of generally recognized authority. Throughout his tenure in power he had to deal with an almost continuous series of conspiracies—episodes which, although he surmounted them successfully, testified to his inability to overcome the structural chaos of French politics. As a parvenu of relatively modest origins, he, like Wallenstein in Germany, inevitably aroused the resentment of many princes and magnates, all the more so because of his successful manipulation of patronage. Their opposition posed unusually serious problems because of the support they received both from the royal family itself and from personal favorites of the emotionally unstable king. Marie de Medici, who had raised Richelieu to power, rapidly came to resent him, and the king's brother, Monsieur—Gaston d'Orléans, heir to the throne until 1638—became another center of intrigue.

The story of Monsieur's relations with Richelieu raises serious questions about the cardinal's methods. Twice, in 1624 and 1626, Richelieu ordered the imprisonment of Gaston's confidant d'Orano simply because he feared d'Orano's influence, and in 1626 he arrested and eventually executed Henri de Talleyrand, count of Chalais, whom an informant had accused of plotting to assassinate the king. Curiously, while V. L. Tapié and William Church both treat this episode as a worthy exercise of state authority, Gaston's biographer argues that Chalais was probably innocent, and that Richelieu simply sought to intimidate his patron.[51] In 1630, suspecting a plot by Gaston and Marie de Medici, Richelieu imprisoned Marie and sent troops after Gaston when he took her side. The heir apparent fled to Lorraine, and Richelieu eventually had to buy him back by rewarding his servants with new offices and paying 200,000 livres' worth of debts. In 1631–32 Gaston fled to Lorraine again and raised another rebellion with the help of Henry, duke of Montmorency. As Richelieu wrote in his *Testament politique*, he insisted upon Montmorency's execution to show other magnates that Monsieur's patronage would give no immunity against punishment.[52] In 1641 the king's favorite St.-Mars met the same fate after he joined Monsieur in another conspiracy against

51. Georges Dethan, *Gaston d'Orléans, conspirateur et prince charmant* (Paris, 1959), pp. 41–67.

52. Richelieu, *Testament politique*, p. 124.

Richelieu. Like other Protestant and Catholic nobles who rebelled against the cardinal, Monsieur frequently accepted help from foreign princes. Loyalty toward the crown or the state, in short, hardly seemed more secure than it had been under the Valois, and Richelieu maintained his position through good intelligence and judicial terror.

A contemporary classic, Corneille's *Le Cid*, tells of two leading nobles who eventually bow to their King's injunction to put their personal quarrel aside and fight for the glory of the monarchy. Richelieu's foreign policy may well have reflected the same fundamental idea, one which had already been articulated by French political theorist Jean Bodin.

Like Olivares, Richelieu had a well-developed theory of his government's international interests. The welfare of the French crown, he seems to have believed, depended on the maintenance of reliable clients on France's borders, as well as at home, and upon the maintenance of royal prestige on a level at least equal to that of the Spanish throne. His sensitivity to his monarch's prestige and reputation has been likened to that of Olivares.[53] The most active phase of his foreign policy began in 1628, immediately after the suppression of the La Rochelle revolt, when he supported the claims of Charles, duke of Nevers, to the succession of Mantua and Montferrat against the Spanish and Austrians. The defense of Nevers would inevitably involve France in a long war and, as Chancellor Marillac pointed out, would doom any major domestic reforms. An Italian campaign would also mean the absence of Louis XIII from France, an especially dangerous contingency since Monsieur had taken refuge in Lorraine, and Marie de Medici opposed the war. Richelieu argued, however, that a rapid campaign would make Louis XIII "the most important monarch in the world, and the most esteemed." He carried the day, conveniently dispatching the duke of Rohan, whose revolt had just been completed, to begin the Italian campaign in late 1629 and following with his own army in March 1630. The seizure of the important fort of Pinerolo made the campaign a success, though far from a definitive one. The conflict did not come to an end; indeed, it was the beginning of a struggle that lasted for thirty years, until the Peace of the Pyrenees. Nor did the domestic struggle cease: in exile

53. Elliott, *Richelieu and Olivares*, p. 41.

in 1631 Monsieur issued a manifesto attacking Richelieu's virtual monopoly of patronage, complaining that taxation had already become oppressive, and arguing that Richelieu had pushed for the Italian war "for his vanity, his ambition and his interest, and to the disadvantage of France."[54] But Richelieu had won a victory, and he now became definitively associated with an anti-Hapsburg foreign policy, just as the Olivares-Zuñiga connection had come to personify Spanish intervention in Italy, Germany, and the Netherlands.

Still, Richelieu proceeded with great caution. On the whole his statements and his policies suggest that he sought simply to build up and maintain a network of reliable clients among France's immediate neighbors. He felt that the minor potentates of western Germany and northern Italy should look to Paris rather than to Brussels, Vienna, or Madrid for protection and patronage; otherwise they might serve the interest of the king's foreign and domestic enemies.[55] And while he sometimes spoke of a European-wide struggle between France and Spain, he preferred insofar as possible to let others bear the burden of resisting Madrid. "A singular prudence," he wrote the king in the *Testament politique*, had allowed him "to occupy the forces of the enemies of your state by those of your allies, putting your hand to your purse rather than your arms, and entering into open warfare only when your allies could no longer subsist alone."[56]

The notable prudence with which Richelieu steered clear of war until 1635 reflects his senses of the weakness of the French state. Because his opposition to the Hapsburgs placed him in alliance with the Dutch and with German and Swedish Protestants, the *dévot* party, which in 1630 came to include Monsieur and Marie de Medici, argued that he was betraying the true religion and keeping the war in Italy going to increase his own power. French finances remained very fragile, having been heavily strained by the brief Italian campaign. So it was that French opposition to Hapsburg pretensions in Germany confined itself to subsidies to the Dutch

54. Richard Bonney, *The King's Debts: Finance and Politics in France, 1589–1661* (Oxford, 1981), p. 156; my translation.

55. The danger was exemplified by the behavior of Charles, duke of Lorraine, a military entrepreneur who had fought on the side of Emperor Ferdinand II at the Battle of the White Mountain, and who began sheltering Gaston d'Orléans in 1629. See Wilhelm Mommsen, *Kardinal Richelieu: Seine Politik im Elsass und im Lothringen* (Berlin, 1922), pp. 50–69.

56. Richelieu, *Testament politique*, p. 134.

and to Gustav Adolf of Sweden—subsidies equal only to about three million livres annually.[57]

Such a policy may have been realistic, but it was not particularly successful. Like Olivares, Richelieu found it almost impossible to manipulate the parties to the German war to his advantage. Richelieu watched anxiously as Wallenstein, Tilly, and the Spaniards occupied Germany, and his attempts to set up a third party failed. In the *Testament politique* he bragged of having secured Wallenstein's dismissal at Regensburg in 1630 and boasted of having won the allegiance of the elector of Bavaria, "until then inseparably attached to the House of Austria," but in fact Wallenstein had opposed Spanish influence within the empire, and after his dismissal Maximilian of Bavaria refused to accept a French alliance. Nor was Richelieu successful in the following year in arranging an effective treaty of neutrality between Gustav Adolf of Sweden and the Catholic League. After Gustav Adolf's victory at Breitenfeld Richelieu proclaimed the need to "put an end to the over-mighty power of the house of Austria *and the king of Sweden.*"[58] He began occupying strongpoints in Alsace and Lorraine in self-defense. Schemes to induce the Swedish army to enter the Hapsburg hereditary lands, and later to help make Wallenstein king of Bohemia, met with no success.[59]

After the Spaniards and imperial forces defeated the Swedish army at Nördlingen on September 6, 1634, war could no longer be avoided. With full knowledge of both the military and financial dangers involved, Richelieu embarked upon war after a further delay of six months.[60] To secure help he made far-reaching concessions both to the Dutch and to the Swedes, involving the possible partition of the Spanish Netherlands and the recognition of Sweden's claim to the archbishopric of Mainz.[61] He also failed to prevent the almost immediate conclusion of peace between the emperor and the electors of Saxony and Brandenburg.

Richelieu avoided war as long as possible partly because of France's military weakness. He undertook no major military re-

57. Ibid., p. 163.

58. Georges Pagès, *The Thirty Years War, 1618–1648* (New York, 1970), pp. 116–130; Richelieu, *Testament politique,* pp. 116–117, emphasis added.

59. Tapié, *France,* pp. 296–324.

60. See Pagès, *Thirty Years War,* p. 174. The Spanish seizure of the elector of Trier, a French client, was the pretext for his intervention.

61. Ibid., pp. 182–183.

forms. The army was a tangle of offices and commands, shot through with rivalries and crippled by vague lines of authority. Officers accumulated as many commands as they could, viewing each as an addition to their fame and fortune. France had virtually no standing army. The only battleworthy troops available belonged to the Protestant military entrepreneur Bernhard of Saxe-Weimar, whom Richelieu enticed into French service in exchange for a large annual subsidy and a promise of the territory of Alsace.[62] French arms, indeed, fared very poorly for the first few years of war, during which the Spaniards invaded France and threatened Paris more than once. Richelieu originally gave many important commands to his relatives, clients, and friendly churchmen, whose military credentials were less than distinguished.[63]

The war also exposed the weakness of the French financial system, whose performance had never been particularly impressive. During the last years of Henry IV's reign the crown's revenue had reached about thirty million livres annually—less, as we have seen, than the revenue of Francis I, once inflation is taken into account. Furthermore, only about one-third of these revenues came from sources directly under control of the crown—the taille levied by royal officials in the *pays d'élections*, and the *parties casuelles*, including the annual payments of office holders under the *paulette*. Over half the revenue came from farmed indirect taxes—a highly unreliable source, since farmers customarily renegotiated their leases whenever proceeds did not come up to expectations—and from *deniers extraordinaires*, including loans, sales of rentes on existing taxes, and contracts allowing financiers the right to collect existing taxes. More than half of the crown's revenue, in short, was collected by private parties who generally managed to protect their own interests at the expense of the crown and the public. The civil wars and the Italian wars had largely been financed by the creation of new offices. Income from the *parties casuelles* almost doubled during the late 1620s and early 1630s, while receipts from the taille actually fell.[64] Even before 1635, Richelieu's superintendant of fi-

---

62. Louis André, *Michel Le Tellier et l'organization de l'armée monarchique* (Paris, 1906), pp. 23–24. There is no work on the army under Richelieu.

63. D'Aumale, *Histoire des princes*, III, 262–268; see also Geoffrey Parker, *The Thirty Years' War* (London, 1984), pp. 149–153.

64. The figures come from Bonney's superb work, *The King's Debts*, pp. 310–313. The taille began to rise again in the early 1630s.

nance, Boutiller, had no choice but to let tax contracts to financiers at exhorbitant rates. Richelieu began the the war without the slightest delusion that current revenue would suffice to finance it. One *partial* expedient emerged at a royal council in April 1635: "By increasing his majesty's forces, which are already very large, it will become difficult for him to pay them all on time," but "they can be maintained without giving them a lot of money if instead we give than more freedom than they have had hitherto to live off the country, although not so much that they become completely undisciplined and disobedient."[65] This the French soldiers did, like their Swedish, imperial, and Spanish counterparts, but to an extent that depopulated large parts of Germany and could not therefore continue indefinitely. This tactic could not in any event suffice, and Richelieu and Boutiller ultimately relied on two other expedients.

One expedient was institutional, and although much misunderstood and somewhat overrated, it carried with it the germ of a new form of government. The dispatch of royal intendants with particular commissions to carry on important tasks, both with armies and in the provinces, was not a new feature of French government, but Richelieu vastly expanded it to help pay for the war. Beginning in 1638 he dispatched intendants to nineteen provinces, including two *pays d'états*, to collect the taille and a new sales tax,and they stayed for ten years. Mostly drawn from the Paris *maîtres de requêtes*, the crown's senior fiscal officers, they replaced inefficient and corrupt *élus* and increased the taille receipts from about 36.3 million livres in 1635 to 72.6 million in 1643. Special brigades of troops assisted them, as did some financiers, who soon farmed much of the taille in exchange for immediate advances. The intendants did not yet threaten the power of the provincial governors; on the contrary, they cooperated with them and assisted them.[66] But even discounting for a moment the political problems these measures involved, they hardly sufficed to finance the conflict. While the taille doubled, loans and tax contracts tripled. Richelieu also created numerous new offices and increased the *droit annuel*.

65. Pagès, *Thirty Years War*, p. 190.
66. See Bonney, *Richelieu and Mazarin*, pp. 29–56, 163–190, 214–232; see also Harding, *Anatomy of a Power Elite*, pp. 204–212. Thus when the intendants were recalled in 1648 the three most powerful governors kept theirs.

In an important article, Orest Ranum has shown that Richelieu and Louis XIII tried very hard to increase the authority of the intendants. The authority the intendants claimed, however, was anything but impersonal and bureaucratic. It was entirely personal, based upon their presumed status as embodiments of the king himself, and they tried to impose it through courtesy—that is, by insisting that local elites treat them with the respect due the monarch. Both Richelieu and Louis XIII, indeed, obsessively used courtesy and ritual to increase the king's authority, and Louis XIII was far less accessible to Frenchmen of all types than previous kings. To restrict access to the monarch, and to insist that subjects speak to him and his creatures with proper respect, are undoubtedly ways of strengthening royal authority, but they seem considerably less modern than Philip II's insistence upon doing business on paper.[67]

Richelieu's control over both foreign and domestic events seems to have weakened in the last years before his death. Abroad France's fortunes improved after Bernhard of Saxe-Weimar captured the key strategic position of Breisach in 1639, and Bernhard's subsequent death released Richelieu of his obligation to make him territorial prince of Alsace. With France and Spain both nearing exhaustion, peace feelers began, but Richelieu insisted on keeping Pinerolo, Alsace, and the duchy of Lorraine. In 1640 revolts in Catalonia and Portugal further inspired Richelieu to dream of a complete victory, but no end to the war was in sight when he died.

In the meantime, Richelieu's policies had alienated enormous sections of the French body politic. The war benefited a few great magnates like Condé, his son Enghien, and Turenne, who won fame if not fortune fighting the Spaniards, It also helped the increasingly important financiers, who profited from most of the government's financial transactions but whose patience by 1642 was also becoming exhausted. But the conflict embittered many: the sovereign courts, who resented the creations of new offices, the increases in the *droit annuel*, and the growing power of the intendants; the people in town and countryside, who called for immediate remission of taxes and confiscation of the wealth of the financiers; and various princes of the blood and members of the royal family who resented Richelieu's influence.

67. Orest Ranum, "Courtesy, Absolutism, and the Rise of the French State, 1630–1660," *Journal of Modern History*, 52 (September, 1980): 426–451.

Tax revolts in towns and in the countryside became endemic during the late 1630s, all the more so because of poor economic conditions. In each case the common people who actually paid the taxes secured the support of local elites: the urban oligarchies, who seem to have supported the artisans in fear of their lives and property, and the lower rural nobility, who feared that the exactions of the central government would leave them with nothing for themselves. Towns resisted a forced loan which Richelieu attempted to levy in 1636 for three years, and ultimately forced the government to withdraw the sales tax he had introduced in 1640. In the countryside widespread peasant revolts, aided by local gentry, plagued the southwest from 1635 through 1637 and struck Normandy in 1639.[68] The alienation of the country from the court, which Trevor-Roper postulated as the source of the crisis of the 1640s, undoubtedly existed in much of France. From the 1560s through 1614, the infrequent meetings of the Estates General had consistently criticized the extravagance of the court, the burden of taxation, and the role of financiers. Now, confronted by intendants who used troops to repay financiers' advances, the gentry, peasantry, and urban artisans revolted.

Had these revolts been accompanied by an uprising among the magnates Richelieu's position would have become far more critical, but this he managed to prevent. Further conspiracies took place, but with the help of numerous royal troops and his impressive sources of intelligence, he was able to put them down. In 1641 the duke of Bouillon, the count of Soissons, and the duke of Guise staged an insurrection, which collapsed when Soissons, a popular figure in Paris, fell in battle, possibly the victim of a spy of Richelieu's. Even then Richelieu was not too proud to pardon Bouillon, who submitted when the revolt collapsed. We have seen that in the following year he also uncovered the Cinq-Mars conspiracy, which Olivares had subsidized, and executed Cinq-Mars. On the whole Richelieu remained on good terms with the provincial governors, who do not seem to have felt threatened by the intendants and whom he seems to have regarded as the single most important group of officials in the realm.[69]

Richelieu died in 1642. In the context of his time he may well

68. Bonney, *Richelieu and Mazarin*, pp. 318–344; Roland Mousnier, *Peasant Uprisings in Seventeenth-Century France, Russia, and China* (New York, 1970), pp. 32–149.

69. Tapié, *France*, pp. 412–424; Richelieu, *Testament politique*, pp. 256–261.

have been a great statesman, but not because of any fundamental innovations in domestic or international affairs. "One is often inclined to believe that the course of events was under Richelieu's control to a greater extent than was the case," writes V.-L. Tapié.

> Moreover, for us to acknowledge as we look back centuries later that the cardinal was far from able to put his programme into full effect, that he continually had to make do with compromise arrangements and that the evil which he succeeded in arresting at one point often reappeared at another, involves no depreciation of his qualities; if anything the reverse is nearer the truth. This superlative architect of French unity and absolute monarchy failed to do everything that he wanted and often did things which he had not reckoned on doing. In the event the structure which he left, although undoubtedly imposing, was in many respects incomplete and fragile.[70]

Richelieu created no new basis of loyalty to the French crown. He achieved and extended his power by the clever manipulation of patronage, and he triumphed over numerous conspiracies only through a mixture of good intelligence, ruthless punishments, and bribery. In foreign policy the Battle of Rocroi a few months after his death and the concurrent political collapse of the Spanish empire left France in a strong position, but even here his lasting achievements have been exaggerated. And while by means of various expedients he managed roughly to double the revenue of the crown by the time of his death, his methods moved the crown rapidly toward bankruptcy, alienated large portions of the body politic, and inevitably led within a few more years to a new collapse of royal authority. Though Richelieu remains perhaps the most successful of early seventeenth-century political figures, he failed significantly to alter the rules of seventeenth-century politics.

Much the same can be said of his successor. Like Richelieu, Mazarin, an Italian prelate who had played a leading diplomatic role in the Italian wars, quickly rose to power by establishing his personal ascendancy over the Queen Mother—now Anne of Austria, widow of Louis XIII (who died within months of Richelieu), and mother of the child Louis XIV. He too carefully deployed his power in the service of his family, arranging good marriages for his nieces and spending millions to secure a cardinal's hat for his brother. He also amassed an enormous fortune, which saved his government

70. Tapié, *France*, p. 336.

during the Fronde and still totalled 37 million livres when he died in 1661. (By comparison, total French government expenditures in 1663 were 42 million livres.)[71]

Mazarin managed to continue the struggle against Spain and the empire for five more years, with mixed results. Ironically, despite the general war-weariness which had inclined Richelieu toward peace for the last few years of his life, the decisive victory of Rocroi in 1643 made an immediate treaty with Spain impossible, especially since Anne of Austria and the Italian Mazarin were vulnerable to accusations of betraying French interests.[72] Although mutinies sometimes disturbed the progress of French troops, a series of campaigns in Bavaria led by Turenne eventually led to peace with the empire on terms favorable to France's clients in 1648. Mazarin strengthened France's position in Alsace both legally, by assuming the imperial rights over the territory, and effectively, by securing the occupation of the fortress of Breisach and cutting the "Spanish Road" from Italy to Flanders. Before a peace treaty could be signed with Spain, however, France collapsed internally.

In retrospect, indeed, it seems extraordinary that the crash did not come much sooner. Financially and politically the condition of the French monarchy in 1648 was far inferior to that of 1789. From 1643 through 1648 the new superintendant of finance, d'Hemery, had borrowed the staggering total of 381 million livres—substantially more than the total loans of the monarchy during the preceding thirty years. By 1648 the taille had been anticipated for the next four years. In the meantime, d'Hemery revoked many payments to local officials which had come out of direct taxes, while bowing to pressure and reducing those taxes overall. The Parlement of Paris resisted new fiscal edicts and called for stricter limitations upon the profits of the financiers. Finally, in late 1647, the crown took two more drastic measures: it essentially confiscated the revenues of French towns and announced that the office holders' *droit annuel* would be renewed only in return for a heavy forced loan.[73] In the spring of 1648 Mazarin asked parlementaires to renounce their salaries for four years in return for the renewal of the *paulette*. The financial condition of the French crown was worse, if anything, than that of the Spanish.

71. Bonney, *Richelieu and Mazarin*, pp. 419–439.
72. Bonney, *King's Debts*, p. 143.
73. Ibid., pp. 197–201.

Mazarin could continue his policies only as long as royal officials, including both the traditional financial and judicial officers and the new intendants, could provide enough revenue to persuade the financiers to make additional loans. The officers, however, now refused to do this, all the more since the separate Dutch peace with Spain boded ill for the future course of the war. Thus in response to Mazarin's attack on their prerogatives, the sovereign courts of Paris, meeting together in the Chambre St.-Louis, asked for the recall of the intendants and a full legal inquiry into the financiers. Mazarin apparently saw no choice but to give in. He recalled the intendants—save for a few attached to the most powerful provincial governors—and he tried to use the attack on the financiers for his own benefit by cutting interest payments from 15 to 6 percent. He could not, however, accept additional demands calling for wide-ranging control of finances by the Parlement, and in January 1649 he led the court out of Paris to prepare to crush the capital by force.[74]

Mazarin might now have prevailed over the office holders had he retained the support of the magnates, but this he failed to do. Like Richelieu, he had monopolized patronage for five years and had acquired plenty of powerful enemies. Although initially both Monsieur and Condé remained faithful to the crown, the Parlement secured the support of Condé's brother Conti and his brother-in-law Longueville, the duke of Bouillon, and, worst of all, Bouillon's brother Turenne, who tried unsuccessfully to bring his army in Germany into France on the side of the Parlement. By February 1649, faced with the threat of Spanish intervention, Mazarin gave in to the Parlement's demands to restrict borrowing and bought off the rebellious princes with pensions and governorships. At the same time, just as the Paris Parlement had defied the government, various local parlements defied their governors, and anarchy threatened much of France.[75]

Since he had not yet reestablished the royal finances, Mazarin, like a Valois king, had no choice but to try to build up a suitable coalition of magnates. During 1649 he attempted by means of marriages to do so, but Condé put obstacles in his way, and Mazarin ultimately decided upon the prince's arrest in January 1650.

74. For details of the Fronde, I am relying mainly on Ernst H. Kossmann, *La Fronde* (Leiden, 1954); see esp. pp. 36–78.
75. Ibid., pp. 79–143.

Twenty-one months of anarchy followed. Condé's party formed an army in southwest France and brought about his release, Turenne led a Spanish army into France, Monsieur entered into a loose alliance with Condé, and Mazarin in February 1651 had to flee the country. By late 1651 Condé had accepted Spanish help and established a virtually independent regime in southwest France, collecting royal revenues like his sixteenth-century ancestors. In the midst of the turmoil the lesser nobility forced Anne of Austria to call a meeting of the Estates General for 1651, but both the royal party and the princes opposed this step, and the Estates never met. In the fall of 1651 Louis XIV attained his majority and Mazarin returned to France at the head of an army raised with his own funds.[76] Public finance had almost entirely ceased to function, and the army supported itself partly from the cardinal's private fortune and partly from levies off of the land. Turenne had also been bought back onto the side of the king, and Mazarin bought the loyalty of other commanders.[77] Royal forces won a series of important victories against Condé, Nemours, and Beaufort. Peace was restored by 1653. Monsieur eventually won his way back into royal favor by denouncing the counselors who had supposedly led him astray, but Condé had to flee to Spain.[78]

"We must stop," wrote the great French historian Ernest Lavisse during a succinct narrative of these events, "and consider all these facts, these levies of arms and negotiations with the enemy, which today would be crimes but which at that time astonished almost no one. The explanation lies in the incompleteness of the state."[79] Indeed, the crisis illustrates the failure of new institutions or new patterns of loyalty to emerge by the time of the Thirty Years' War. The edifice of war finance, based upon a steady flow of loans from the financiers secured by the exactions of the intendants, had alienated the office holders, the provincial gentry, and the urban and rural poor. Simultaneously, customary jealousies among the magnates had persisted, increasingly focusing upon the all-

---

76. The money for the army actually came from the new superintendant of finance, La Vieuville, whom Louis XIV had appointed at Mazarin's behest, and who had advanced it as a kind of down payment on existing royal debts to the cardinal. Bonney, *King's Debts*, pp. 229–233.

77. André, *Michel Le Tellier*, pp. 122–123.

78. Ibid., pp. 187–259.

79. Ernest Lavisse, *Louis XIV, de 1643 à 1685* (Paris, 1908), p. 50; my translation.

powerful figure of Mazarin. The confrontation with the Parlement of Paris had led to a complete collapse of his authority. Payment of taxes ceased throughout France, and Condé called out not only his own regiments fighting in Picardy but also his clienteles in several different parts of France and the officers of fortified places within the provinces he governed. Without any firm institutional base, Mazarin tacked broadly for two years between various parties of princes and frondeurs in maneuvers of astonishing complexity, yet found himself forced to leave the country. He ultimately saved himself only by making new alliances and pledging his private fortune. In the meantime, he forfeited most of the major foreign gains of the last twenty-five years. By 1652 France had lost Tuscany, the fortress of Casale, most of the gains in Flanders, and Catalonia. France's attempts to benefit from the Spanish imperial crises of the early 1640s had ended in a disastrous failure. For the moment, at least, Richelieu's grandiose schemes had gone the way of those of Olivares. A balance of power reasserted itself—a balancing reflecting the exaggerated aims of both the Spanish and French crowns.

Mazarin managed after the Fronde to return to the system of the 1640s. Determined to continue the war, he worked hard with the help of the new financial officials Servien and Fouquet to establish a renewed, dependable relationship with the financiers. To do so he had to restore the intendants and reimpose heavy direct taxation, steps which by 1655 led to renewed trouble in the countryside. By 1658 the crown was hopelessly overextended once more, and bankruptcy threatened again. The Peace of the Pyrenees in 1659 represented a compromise. France yielded some conquests in Franche-Comté and in parts of Flanders in return for gains in Artois and Roussillon and Spanish withdrawals from Germany, where Mazarin had amassed a considerable clientele of minor princes. The treaty also provided for Louis XIV's marriage to Philip IV's daughter, and left Louis with a possible claim to the entire Spanish inheritance if her dowry was not paid. Still, the war had been a near thing, and many had feared another general rising on the eve of the decisive Battle of the Dunes.[80] The Peace of the Pyrenees also allowed for the return of Condé, to whom Louis XIV promised the governorship of Burgundy.

80. Bonney, *King's Debts*, pp. 242–264; Lavisse, *Louis XIV, de 1643 à 1661*, pp. 66–77.

Generations of historians have identified the rule of Richelieu and Mazarin as a key episode in the development of absolutism and the era of the modern state. The two cardinals undoubtedly mobilized more resources than any French monarch had previously commanded, overcame the threats to their authority posed by the nobility, office holders, and members of the royal family, and won some important victories in war. Yet they failed significantly to alter the basis of political loyalty within France, to establish a new institutional structure of monarchical authority, or to expand crown revenues on a lasting basis. Indeed, it is far from clear that they intended such changes.

Sixty years ago Friedrich Meinecke wondered how a figure like the duke of Rohan could combine in one lifetime a long series of rebellions and conspiracies against royal authority—often assisted by foreign money—with subsequent devotion to Richelieu and the principle of "reason of state," which in Meinecke's view the cardinal embodied.[81] The contradiction was more apparent than real. Although the idea of reason of state had begun to circulate in political pamphlets, leading political figures still acted primarily on the basis of a careful calculation of their personal interests. Both Richelieu and Mazarin exploited their own positions shamelessly. In the nine years after the Fronde Mazarin amassed one of the greatest fortunes in the history of the old regime, comprising abbeys, properties, duchies, lands in Alsace granted by the king, diamonds, claims on the throne, and cash—including large deposits near the borders of France in case he should ever have to flee again. He had also safeguarded his position among the magnates by marrying his nieces into important families.[82] On his deathbed he worried about the future of his family, not about the strength of the French state. The conspiracies of Gaston d'Orléans, the fortunes of Richelieu and Mazarin, the erratic performance of French armies in the Thirty Years' War, and the anarchy of the Fronde all reflected the political development of early seventeenth-century France—a state which in many ways had not changed since the era of the wars of religion, and which cannot be judged to form a part of the modern era.

81. Meinecke, *Machiavellism*, pp. 183–188.
82. Bonney, *King's Debts*, pp. 260–261.

The Thirty Years' War

Like Philip II and Charles I of England, the Holy Roman Emperor Ferdinand II, beginning in 1618, tried to increase his political and religious authority—first within the kingdom of Bohemia, where Protestant noblemen had revolted against his rule, and subsequently within the rest of the empire. Encouraged by the Jesuits, he dreamed at one point of rolling back the advances made by Protestantism since 1555, and in the late 1620s his army seemed to have given him real authority over all Germany. His efforts also brought about the intervention of Spain, Sweden, and France, and an armed struggle that lasted for thirty years, ending with a peace that left the position of the emperor within the empire essentially unchanged. The Thirty Years' War, however, was not merely another case of a European monarch trying and failing to increase his authority. No conflict shows more clearly the continuing power of the European aristocracy and, above all, the ways in which early modern armies served themselves, rather than their legal sovereigns.

To understand the conflict, we must look first at Germany in the late sixteenth century. Historians have often tended to regard the Holy Roman Empire of the German Nation as a medieval anachronism, left far behind during the early modern period by its religious disunity and political fragmentation. Such a picture can hardly be disputed with respect to the late seventeenth and eighteenth centuries, but the generally placid decades between 1555 and 1618 suggest a very different view. The organization of the Holy Roman Empire, one might easily argue, more closely reflected the actual balance of political power in the late sixteenth century than that of the French monarchy or the Spanish empire. The Holy Roman Emperor made no pretense of exerting effective control over the empire and wasted little money or lives in attempting to secure it. The leading German families' status as territorial princes gave their aspirations more legitimacy than those of the magnates of France or the Netherlands, while focusing their attention upon their own lands rather than upon the imperial court. The limited extent of their territory may in some respects have been a blessing, since their credit was rarely good enough to put armies in the field. And the imperial diet and imperial courts provided peaceful means for the ajudication of disputes which at the very least could immobilize the participants for years at a time. The empire, in short, had discovered relatively effective ways and means of gratifying its leading subjects, who posed correspondingly less of a problem for their sovereign ruler.

A variety of other factors also helped give Germany such unusual political stability during the second half of the sixteenth century. Charles V's religious settlement, the Peace of Augsburg, established both Catholicism and Lutheranism as legal religions in 1555, although its provisions left plenty of room for future controversies. Moreover, Charles's immediate successors, Ferdinand I (1556–1564) and Maximilian II (1564–1576), both supported toleration while hoping for an eventual Christian reunion. Meanwhile the German princely houses struggled for power within the numerous ecclesiastical principalities scattered throughout Germany, whose bishops were elected by cathedral chapters before being confirmed by the pope. Although the Peace of Augsburg had required any ecclesiastical prince who converted to Protestantism to resign, many Protestants successfully secured election and even managed to receive papal confirmation. Ecclesiastical livings provided a peaceful battleground for German princely houses. The houses of Wettin and Hohenzollern, sovereign in Saxony and Brandenburg, contested the bishoprics of east central and northern Germany together with the ducal houses of Mecklenburg and Pomerania; local dynasties generally ruled the chapters of central Germany, including Magdeburg, Bremen, Osnabrück, and Lübeck; while the Austrian Hapsburgs and the Bavarian Wittelsbachs divided the Catholic livings of the south and west.

Developments outside Germany also helped keep the peace. Germans who became military enterprisers and soldiers found employment elsewhere. German military enterprisers played a critical role in both the Dutch and Spanish armies in the Netherlands and frequently joined in the French civil wars. In addition, in the southeast the Hapsburgs waged campaigns against the Turks from 1593 through 1606. The end of the civil wars in France, the truce between Spain and the Dutch in 1609, and the truce between the emperor and the sultan unhappily coincided with an increase of political tension within Germany.[1]

---

1. Redlich, *German Military Enterpriser*, I, 157–162, points out that virtually all the important commanders of the Thirty Years' War had received their training in these campaigns.

Beginning with the accession of Rudolf II in 1576, religious conflict became somewhat sharper, and armed conflicts began again. Some Protestant princes and cities refused strictly to observe the terms of the Peace of Augsburg, and some Catholics sought military aid in response. Thus, when in 1582 the elector of Cologne tried to convert his territory to Protestantism, his chapter revolted, elected a Wittelsbach prince as elector, and defeated the Protestants with the help of Duke William V of Bavaria and Spanish troops from the Netherlands. During the 1590s a long struggle between Protestant and Catholic canons in Strasbourg, who supported rival candidates from the houses of Brandenburg and Lorraine, led to an eventual Catholic victory in 1604.[2] When in 1605 Catholics secured a judgment in the Reichshofrath—an imperial court—against the town of Donauwörth, which had refused to tolerate Catholicism within its walls, the Protestants argued that the court had exceeded its authority. Three years later the Catholic duke Maximilian of Bavaria took matters into his own hands and crushed the town. The Regensburg Reichstag of 1608 broke up as a result of this episode, and rival parties formed the Protestant Union and the Catholic League to protect their interests.[3]

Such religious conflicts undoubtedly helped lead to the eruption of the Thirty Years' War in 1618, but the outbreak of the war also reflected the same political trends responsible for so much conflict in France, the Netherlands, and England. Thus, the war began when several German princes—the emperors Matthias and Ferdinand II, Duke Maximilian of Bavaria, and Elector Frederick of the Palatinate—decided to increase their own authority, promote their chosen religion, and acquire new lands and honors by force. In addition, various foreign princes—the king of Spain, the king of Denmark, the Dutch States General, the king of Sweden, and the king of France—tried to take advantage of the situation to attract more foreign clients and provided some of the wherewithal to fight the war. Finally, an entire generation of military enterprisers on all sides attempted to use the conflict to make their fortunes, either by raising troops, levying contributions, or earning favors up to and including territorial sovereignty from the princes who

2. See Moritz Ritter, "Die Ursprung des Restitutionsedikts," *Historische Zeitschrift*, 76 (1896): 62–102.

3. Bruno Gebhardt, *Handbuch der deutschen Geschichte*, 3 vols. (Stuttgart, 1970), II, 154–156.

employed them. Most famous among these entrepreneurs were Ernst von Mansfeld, Christian of Halberstadt, Tserclaes of Tilly, Bernhard of Saxe-Weimar, and, of course, Albrecht von Wallenstein, perhaps the single most characteristic figure of the whole era. And in this war, as elsewhere, the leaders of the two coalitions experienced the same difficulties in winning decisive victories, maintaining the loyalty of their allies, and keeping their armies in being.

Religion played at least as complex a role in this conflict as in the French civil war. Only very briefly did the Thirty Years' War seem likely to impose religious unity upon the Holy Roman Empire. While in the late 1620s elements within the Catholic party dreamed of rolling back all Protestant gains since 1555, and possibly even of eliminating Protestantism from Germany altogether, these plans never became practical and had quickly to be abandoned after the intervention of Sweden in 1631. In addition, religion never overcame a host of political conflicts *within* the Catholic and Protestant parties, of which the long and extraordinarily complex struggles among the emperor Ferdinand, Maximilian of Bavaria, the Spaniards, and Wallenstein are only the most notable. The war was a war of ambition, an anarchic free-for-all of violently changing fortunes and power relations in which the main actors rarely if ever thought of anything but themselves. To see how its origins and course reflected the nature of European politics in the early seventeenth century, I shall begin with the Catholic side, focusing on the Hapsburgs, Maximilian of Bavaria, Wallenstein, and the Spaniards, and then examine the motives of the German Protestants, the Swedes, the French, and the neutral party within Germany.[4]

The Catholic Party

The Austrian Hapsburgs began the war in 1618 to increase their authority within their own hereditary domains. During the 1600s

---

4. A good short narrative by E. A. Beller can be found in *The New Cambridge Modern History*, 14 vols. (Cambridge, 1957–1979), IV, 306–358. Parker, *Thirty Years' War*, is somewhat more comprehensive than Pagès, *Thirty Years War*, which overemphasizes the role of France. Polisensky (with the collaboration of Frederick Snider), *War and Society in Europe*, provides an exhaustive bibliography, and T. K. Rabb, *The Thirty Years' War: Problems of Motive, Extent, and Effect* (Boston, 1964), excerpts much fine literature and provides a stimulating introduction. By far the most detailed work is Moritz Ritter, *Deutsche Geschichte im Zeitalter der Gegenreformation und des dreissigjährigen Krieges* (Stuttgart, 1889–1908).

the emperor Rudolf II had tried to rebuild a Catholic party in Bohemia, Moravia, Hungary, and the various duchies of present-day
Austria. In response, in 1609 the Bohemian estates had forced Rudolf to grant them the Letter of Majesty, extending liberty of conscience and a modified liberty of worship, as well as political guarantees to the Protestant nobility similar to the concessions enjoyed
by the Huguenots in France. Conflicts became more serious after
the succession of Ferdinand of Styria as king of Bohemia in 1618.
An energetic Counter-Reformation prince, Ferdinand had already
strengthened his position throughout his domains with the help
of the Jesuit order. Ferdinand was not a religious fanatic. Like
Philip II, he regarded religion primarily as a bulwark of the state,
and heretics primarily as disloyal subjects. Both in Styria and Bohemia, he used religious differences as a pretext for attempts to
strengthen princely authority at the expense of his estates.[5] He
was supported by the Spanish ambassador, Oñate, who had by
now established a strong pro-Spanish party in Vienna.[6]

The conflict escalated in the spring of 1618, when the Bohemian
Protestants revolted, raised an army, annulled Ferdinand's election
as king, and chose Frederick V, the Calvinist elector of the Palatinate, as their new king, while sharply reducing royal power. The
estates of other Hapsburg domains rapidly followed suit, and by
1620 those of Moravia, Silesia, Upper and Lower Austria, and
Hungary had joined the Bohemian estates in a confederation denying Ferdinand's authority. The confrontation between the estates and the Hapsburgs resembled the struggle between the
Netherlands and Philip II, and one Czech historian has argued
that Dutch and Spanish models respectively inspired the Estates
and the imperial court.[7]

Encouraged by Ambassador Oñate, the imperial court decided
in early 1619 to try to subdue Bohemia by force. But Ferdinand,
who succeeded to the imperial throne in March 1619, disposed
only of the most limited revenues, and like most German princes,
he lacked any access to commercial credit.[8] The troops with which

5. For an excellent portrait, see Leopold von Ranke, *Geschichte Wallensteins*, ed. Helmut Diwald (Düsseldorf, 1967), pp. 133–148; see also Hans Sturmberger, *Kaiser Ferdinand II und das Problem des Absolutismus* (Munich, 1957), and Parker, *Thirty Years' War*,
pp. 6–11, 83–87.

6. Gebhardt, *Handbuch*, pp. 153–159.

7. V. L. Tapié. "The Hapsburg Lands, 1618–57," in *New Cambridge Modern History*, IV,
503–530; Polisensky, *War and Society in Europe*, pp. 1–13.

8. Redlich, *German Military Enterpriser*, I, 238.

he successfully subdued the rebels by 1621 came from three sources: the Spaniards, the wealthy Counter-Reformation militant duke Maximilian of Bavaria, and military entrepreneurs drawn from among the Catholic party within the empire. Like the factions of the French or Spanish nobility, these claimants would never be able to agree on a common program, or even recognize the primacy of any one of their claims for compensation. Both the Catholic and Protestant coalitions were in a sense syndicates, the claims of whose members exceeded the possible profits available. The wars lasted so long largely because of the disproportion between princely and aristocratic ambition on the one hand and the resources of Germany on the other.

Thus, the Spaniards provided several thousand troops from Italy and the Netherlands to crush the Bohemian rebels at the Battle of the White Mountain in late 1620 in order to maintain the Hapsburgs on the imperial throne. Their troops occupied the Lower Palatinate in 1620. They asked in return for a say in the disposition of the Palatinate and help in their renewed war against the Dutch. Duke Maximilian of Bavaria, leader of the Catholic League and the richest prince in the empire, raised an army of perhaps 10,000 men to seize the electoral dignity from his Wittelsbach cousin, Frederick V of the Palatinate—a tactic pioneered in the sixteenth century by Maurice of Saxony, who had managed a similar coup. In 1619 Ferdinand verbally promised Maximilian the electorate, pledged him full indemnity for his assistance, and allowed Maximilian to occupy his own Hapsburg hereditary lands as security.[9] Ferdinand's work within the hereditary lands was far from over. The reestablishment of Catholicism turned out to be extremely difficult, leading at one point to a serious peasant revolt in Upper Austria.[10] But the difficulty of satisfying the various Catholic claimants, combined with the presence of at least a few Protestant leaders still willing to fight, spread the war further into Germany.

While Catholic armies moved into new territories—either to subdue resistance or to find new sources of support—members of the Catholic coalition came forward with new claims. This in turn brought additional Protestant princes into the war. In 1622, Tilly led the unpaid armies of the Catholic League into northern Ger-

9. Dieter Albrecht, *Die Auswärtige Politik Maximilians von Bayern, 1618–35* (Göttingen, 1962), pp. 3–5, 44–49.
10. Parker, *Thirty Years' War*, pp. 91–92.

many in pursuit of the Protestant general Christian of Brunswick and began levying contributions. His presence enabled a Catholic candidate to win election as bishop of Osnabrück, a diocese previously in Protestant hands. The emperor also laid claim to Christian's previously Protestant diocese of Halberstadt, which King Christian IV of Denmark also coveted. In 1625 the Danish king, whose family held numerous ecclesiastical livings in northern Germany, intervened on the Protestant side with the help of English money.[11] Fortune continued to favor the Catholics, and after the defeat of the Danes, the Peace of Lübeck left them in full control of Germany.

Both the emperor and the league now wanted to reorganize the empire and restore Catholicism to at least the position of 1555. As we have seen, ever since the 1560s Catholic complaints against Protestant usurpations of the Peace of Augsburg had begun accumulating. As soon as the imperial and league armies began to win victories in the Palatinate, bishops and religious orders had begun proceedings to regain their lands. Buoyed by further military successes, the ecclesiastical rulers of Mainz, Trier, and Cologne began to call for the complete restitution of church property seized since 1555 and the elimination of Calvinism.[12] The papal curia, which owed large unpaid subsidies to the Catholic League, encouraged restitution as an alternative to payment, and Maximilian of Bavaria endorsed the idea in 1627, partly because he had so far failed to secure some of the livings which he coveted for his family.[13] Most leading politicians in Vienna had initially opposed such drastic measures for fear of breaking up the unity of the empire, but in 1628 the emperor's Jesuit confessor, Lamormaini, climbed on the bandwagon, hoping to use the income of restored church lands to endow Jesuit schools and colleges. He apparently persuaded Ferdinand, who had already made a liberal provision of restored church lands for his second son, that to fail to take full advantage of the Catholic victories would amount to a refusal of God's grace.[14] Ferdinand therefore issued the Edict of Restitution in 1629. The

11. Parker, *Thirty Years' War*, pp. 72–81, points out that Christian also wanted to avoid the intervention of his rival, Gustav Adolf of Sweden.

12. Ritter, "Die Ursprung des Restitutionsedikts."

13. Albrecht, *Die auswärtige Politik Maximilians von Bayern*, pp. 197–203.

14. See the highly original study by Robert Bireley, *Religion and Politics in the Age of the Counterreformation* (Chapel Hill, 1981), pp. 36–43, 52–61, 130–150.

edict called for the return of all secularized bishoprics, abbeys, and endowments, and reaffirmed the illegality of Calvinism.

Ferdinand II appeared briefly to have established unprecedented political and religious authority over the Holy Roman Empire, but his triumph was quite illusory. To begin with, the edict very quickly brought about the defection of the Protestant electors of Brandenburg and Saxony and the intervention of the king of Sweden. In addition, as we have seen the Catholic League was bound to raise claims that conflicted with the plans of Ferdinand and the Jesuits. Most important of all, however, the emperor's military victories and his new army rested neither upon the imperial revenue nor upon the allegiance of the troops to himself. The man who had put Ferdinand II in control of Germany, the imperial general Albrecht von Wallenstein, was the outstanding aristocrat of his age, loyal only to himself, possessed of his own ideas for the proper future of Germany, and detested by the league. The story of Wallenstein's career—so exemplary of early modern politics—shows how impossible any ideas of Catholic, imperial absolutism within Germany really were.

No early modern figure has aroused more historical controversy than Wallenstein, and he deserves the attention he has received.[15] No politician of the early seventeenth century, including Olivares and Richelieu, seems better to have understood the nature of the world he lived in, the opportunities for advancement it offered, and the nature of contemporary power.

Born in 1583 to an undistinguished Bohemian Protestant noble family, Wallenstein entered imperial service as an ensign in the army in 1603. By 1606 he had converted to Catholicism, a decision reflecting the increasing Catholic militancy at the court of Rudolf II. A relation helped get him a position within the household of the archduke Matthias, and in 1608 he married a wealthy heiress and took possession of large Moravian estates. In 1610, during the political controversy in Moravia that led to the deposition of Rudolf II as Margrave, he commanded troops raised by the Moravian estates, and in 1617 he raised troops to help Ferdinand of Styria fight the Venetians. In early 1618, after the beginning of the Bohe-

---

15. An excellent introduction to the literature can be found in Rabb, *Thirty Years' War.* I have relied most heavily upon Golo Mann, *Wallenstein: His Life Narrated* (London, 1976), and Leopold von Ranke, *Geschichte Wallensteins,* which remains extraordinarily informative and provocative.

mian revolt, he raised troops on behalf of the Moravian estates again. In 1619, however, he betrayed his employers, murdered his second-in-command, looted the Moravian treasury, and led his troops across the Moravian border into imperial service. Outlawed by the Moravian estates, he had his revenge after the Battle of the White Mountain in late 1620.

Although Wallenstein did not participate in that battle himself, no one benefited more from its results. Like any early modern faction, those in the Catholic party that had supported the emperor wanted rewards for their help, and they persuaded the emperor to confiscate the estates of the Bohemian rebels. By lending money to the emperor, Wallenstein secured liens upon the huge properties of his rebel cousins, the Smirickys, and he purchased many large confiscated estates in central Bohemia with the assistance of a distant relative, Adam von Waldstein, president of the newly convened Court of Confiscations. He also joined a syndicate of financiers and traders in precious metals which secured the right to coin debased currency and used it to buy more land. When in 1625 the imperial exchequer protested the accumulation of properties at lower than market prices, Wallenstein mollified the emperor by giving him a large loan.[16] Wallenstein's first wife had died in 1614, and he now married the daughter of a leading Austrian official family with close connections to Prince Eggenberg, the president of the Imperial Privy Council. He also achieved the dignities of Count Palatine and prince of the empire.[17]

Having used the traditional tools of favor and influence to become a territorial magnate, Wallenstein used military entrepreneurship to make himself perhaps the most powerful man in the empire. In 1625, when Christian of Denmark intervened in the war on the Protestant side, he raised an army of 20,000 men for the imperial service, beginning his spectacular career as the greatest military enterpriser of them all. In 1627 his enormous Bohemian properties were consolidated as the duchy of Friedland. His household swelled to almost 1,000 persons, and he handed out numerous fiefs, often to colonels and captains in his armies. Within Friedland he monopolized the administration of justice and the production and sale of beer and coined money bearing his

16. The debasement of the currency had been disastrous for the Bohemian economy: see Parker, *Thirty Years' War*, pp. 88–90.

17. Mann, *Wallenstein*, pp. 1–191.

own likeness. He imported artisans and built an iron factory to manufacture cannon. He built castles and townhouses. Then, in late 1627, after he and Tilly had virtually cleared Germany of the Danes and other Protestant forces, Wallenstein persuaded Ferdinand to dispossess the reigning dukes of Mecklenburg, who had sided with the Danes, and hand their duchies over to him. He became general of the Oceanic and Baltic seas, and began building an imperial Baltic fleet.[18]

Wallenstein exploited the financial weakness of his ruler more cleverly than any other early modern nobleman. In raising his armies he relied upon his own credit, borrowing money from his own colonels and accumulating large claims upon the emperor which ultimately could be satisfied only with new grants of territory. His credit, which rested largely upon the wealth of the duchy of Friedland, became the foundation of the imperial army.[19] Once raised, the army supported itself out of contributions, preferably from enemy territory but sometimes from allied territory as well. Wallenstein often authorized his colonels to collect his debts to them in the form of contributions, while collecting the emperor's debts to himself in the form of territorial grants. Wallenstein tried to keep contributions within reasonable bounds in order to enable occupied territory to continue to pay them, and like his rival, King Gustav Adolf of Sweden, he seems to have done what he could to prevent undisciplined pillaging. By the end of his life, however, he had apparently raised armies of a size which German territories simply could not support out of current income. Significantly, he secured and carefully maintained an exemption from the burden of quartering troops for the duchy of Friedland, leaving his credit intact.[20]

Ferdinand II owed his new position of eminence not to the princes of the league or the Jesuits but to this master of early modern politics. And remarkably enough, Wallenstein, unlike Maximilian or Lamormaini, evidently understood that the emperor could not retain his new position if he attempted to enforce religious absolutism and undo the religious changes of the previous seventy years. Lacking any strong personal commitment to Catholicism, Wallenstein employed many Protestant officers in his

18. Ibid., pp. 211–252.
19. Redlich, *German Military Enterpriser*, I, 238–245.
20. Mann, *Wallenstein*, pp. 276–277, 308–316.

army, tolerated Protestants within Friedland, and did nothing at all to disturb the Lutheran religion in Mecklenburg. He opposed any attempts drastically to roll back Protestantism within the empire, both because of their effects upon his army and because he knew that they would make it extremely difficult to maintain the loyalty of the electors of Brandenburg and Saxony, who had played a crucial role in the emperor's success. He also seems to have understood that Germany could not indefinitely support armies on the scale of his own. By 1629 he favored an immediate peace within the empire on the basis of religious parity—a peace which would enable the costly armies to be disbanded and which would isolate Germany from the Dutch-Spanish war. He bitterly opposed the Edict of Restitution and even informed John George of Saxony that he would not help enforce it.

The opposition to Wallenstein emerged at the imperial diet of Regensburg in 1630. Ferdinand originally called the electors together to elect his son as king of the Romans—thereby making him his designated successor—but their deliberations focused instead upon his alliance policies and upon Wallenstein's future. Ferdinand had recently sent troops to Italy to help the Spaniards against the French, and the electors, led by Maximilian of Bavaria, wanted to recall them to protect the empire from foreign intervention. Moreover, the electors wanted Ferdinand to dismiss Wallenstein and disband the imperial army, which they regarded as a new and dangerous institution. Wallenstein insisted upon levying contributions at his own discretion, and territorial princes had been dispossessed for his benefit. The league had already asked for the dismissal of all Protestant officers within the imperial army, and at Regensburg its representatives asked for the formation of a new *Kriegsdirektorium* that would regulate the levying of contributions and for the dismissal of Wallenstein.[21] Not only the electors, but also Lamormaini—who resented Wallenstein's opposition to the Edict of Restitution—now demanded the general's recall, and Ferdinand II agreed to it in 1630. Part of the imperial army was paid off and the rest put under Tilly's command after Ferdinand refused to accept Maximilian as its commander, and the electors vetoed the choice of Ferdinand's son. As if to emphasize their power, the elec-

---

21. See Albrecht, *Die auswartige Politik*, pp. 263–302, and especially Ranke, *Geshichte Wallensteins*, pp. 149–165.

tors refused to elect a king of the Romans, partly because Maximilian seems to have believed that he might secure French or papal support for the imperial succession.[22]

Maximilian and the other Catholic electors had won a stunning victory, but their policy, premised upon the full enforcement of the Edict of Restitution, was doomed. John George of Saxony rightly believed that many of the Catholics meant to go even further, especially after the emperor refused to postpone restitution for fifty years. Meanwhile, the Swedish king Gustav Adolf had decided to make the edict his pretext for intervention in the German war.[23] Although the protestant electors initially shied away from Gustav Adolf, they eventually concluded that they had to make terms with him. Maximilian and the league actually welcomed his intervention, hoping to profit from new confiscations at the expense of the north German princes who joined him. Even John George of Saxony, who hoped until the last minute to preserve his neutrality, went over to Gustav Adolf in September 1631 after Tilly's sack of Magdeburg.

The political situation changed completely a few weeks later, when the combined Swedish and Saxon armies annihilated Tilly's forces at the Battle of Breitenfeld. Once again, the emperor turned to Wallenstein, and once again he found that he could reestablish his authority within Germany only by creating a new and independent power more than equal to his own. This time, Wallenstein, exploiting to the full the position of an early modern magnate, essentially discounted imperial authority altogether and tried to establish himself as a fully independent power in international politics. The last phase of his career provides the best example of both the opportunities and the dangers of early modern politics.

After Breitenfeld, Ferdinand II had no choice but to authorize Wallenstein to reconstitute his army virtually on his own terms. With the German Protestants firmly in Gustav Adolf's camp and the league increasingly solicitous of the patronage of Richelieu, he had to restore his independent military power as soon as possible. Ferdinand apparently promised Wallenstein to revoke the Edict of Restitution, reconfirmed his debts to the general, gave him the Silesian duchy of Glogau to compensate him for the loss of Meck-

22. Ranke, *Geschichte Wallensteins*, pp. 149–165; see also Mann, *Wallenstein*, pp. 496–533.

23. See below, pp. 103–104.

lenburg to the Swedes, and even gave him the right to distribute confiscated properties to his own commanders. Wallenstein immediately attempted to detach Saxony from Gustav Adolf by promising to rescind the edict, but the Swedish king had definitely established his authority over the German Protestants. The problem of peace had been further complicated by Gustav Adolf's own territorial demands, including Pomerania. In November 1632, after a year of marches and countermarches, Wallenstein fought Gustav Adolf at Lützen. The Swedes and their allies forced the imperial army to withdraw from the field, but Gustav Adolf was killed.

Wallenstein now tried and failed to arrange peace terms based upon a reversion to the religious situation of 1618 within most of the empire and 1622 in Bohemia. The Catholic League refused to accept these conditions, or to allow the Palatinate and the electoral title to revert to the heirs of Frederick V after Maximilian's death. Denied peace and desperate to assure his son's position before his death, Ferdinand II called upon the Spaniards to intervene again. This enraged Wallenstein, who wanted to keep Spanish armies out of Germany at all costs.

One phase of the war was already over: the imperial court, bowing to reality, had abandoned its extreme religious aims. Shortly after Lützen, Cardinal Pazmany, a leading imperial figure, affirmed the need for a compromise peace. "If there were hope either of completely subduing the Empire or radically extirpating heresy, it would be impious and execrable to raise the question of a settlement," he wrote. "But given the present state of affairs and considering the situation in France, Belgium, Italy and the Indies as well as the exhaustion of the princes and provinces, it seems morally impossible (divine miracles, reserved to the supreme heavenly council, do not enter into the deliberation), whereby [sic] the resources of the empire could be totally destroyed."[24] Ferdinand II was above all anxious to secure the succession to the empire for his son and to make the Catholic religion secure within the Hapsburg hereditary domains, once again threatened by the presence of important Bohemian emigres within the Swedish army. He was not, however, willing to accept the terms Wallenstein discussed with Saxon representatives, which would have accepted 1618 as the base year in settling religious and territorial questions

24. Bireley, *Religion and Politics*, pp. 189–190.

in the rest of the empire, because he was determined to keep Magdeburg, Bremen, and Halberstadt for his second son. He also refused to renounce the Edict of Restitution without the consent of Bavaria and Mainz, which was not yet forthcoming.[25]

Wallenstein now prepared to arrange peace himself. He had entered into secret relations with foreign princes even before his recall. Although these negotiations have been labeled as treasonous by several distinguished German and Czech historians, we know very well that they were not in the least unusual. During this period such connections had been opened by diverse figures including Condé, the dukes of Guise, Marie de Medici, and Gaston of Orleans in France; William of Orange, Horn, and Egmont in the Netherlands; the duke of Norfolk in England; and various other German military entrepreneurs such as Christian of Brunswick and Ernst von Mansfeld, to name only a few of the most distinguished cases. Those who entered into these negotiations ran the risk of execution or assassination for treason, but many ran that risk. One must nonetheless pay tribute to the breathtaking scale of the plans Wallenstein discussed with the Swedes and the French. Thus during 1631, before his recall, Wallenstein asked a Czech intermediary negotiating on behalf of Gustav Adolf for 12,000 troops. This force, he said, would enable him to win over much of the imperial army, which he would indemnify at the expense of the Jesuits prior to taking revenge upon his other enemies, such as Maximilian of Bavaria. Gustav Adolf apparently found the proposal too risky.[26]

After Gustav Adolf's death at Lützen, Wallenstein tried to take advantage of the extraordinary powers Ferdinand had given him at the time of his recall to make himself the arbiter of Germany's destiny. In peace talks with the Saxons he discussed the revocation of the Edict of Restitution, which neither the Jesuits nor the princes of the league were willing to contemplate, and the eventual restoration of part of the Palatinate or the electoral title to the Protestant Elector, which Maximilian refused to discuss. Simultaneously, Wallenstein's authority suffered a major blow when Ferdinand II acceded to a Spanish request to raise an army of 24,000 men in Milan and march it through Germany to safeguard Spanish com-

25. Ibid., pp. 190–209.
26. Ranke, *Geschichte Wallensteins*, pp. 178–180; Mann, *Wallenstein*, pp. 559–569.

munications with the Netherlands. Wallenstein was unable to prevent the army's entry into Germany, although its commander, Cardinal Infante Don Ferdinand, remained theoretically subordinate to him. He was still determined to try to avoid involving the empire in Spain's quarrels with the Dutch and the French, and the Spaniards at the imperial court, who had favored his recall in 1631, now joined his enemies.

Richelieu's envoy Feuquières, who had established contact with leading Bohemian exiles, now opened talks with Wallenstein as well. Feuquières apparently offered him the kingdom of Bohemia to get him to break openly with Ferdinand, but Wallenstein declined, perhaps fearing for his estates in Friedland. In talks with the Saxons in the summer of 1633, however, he was willing to offer freedom of conscience within the Hapsburg hereditary lands—a demand to which Ferdinand would never have agreed—and to promise Saxony the bishoprics of Magdeburg and Halberstadt, which Ferdinand had reserved for his son Leopold William. All the parties to the talks apparently assumed that Wallenstein himself would also have to receive a large new domain to compensate him for the loss of Mecklenburg—possibly one carved from Baden and Württemberg—and perhaps an electoral hat as well. (The general, it may be noted, had previously dreamed of becoming king of Denmark, sacking Rome, or leading a crusade against Constantinople.) But the Swedish chancellor Oexenstiema refused to work for these terms unless Wallenstein would break openly with the emperor, and this he would not do. In the fall the talks broke down—partly because of the imperial court's failure to meet the Protestant conditions—leaving Wallenstein in a rage.[27]

Wallenstein, then, had discussed rebellion against the emperor but had not committed it, and when imperial agents searched his papers after his death, they found no evidence that he had intended to do so. He did take an oath to his colonels in January 1634 to remain in command in exchange for their promise to remain faithful to him, but Ranke interprets this as an attempt to reassure them that he would ultimately make good on his promises of money and land, rather than as preparation for rebellion.[28] In the meantime, the Catholic electors resented the concessions he

27. Ranke, *Geschichte Wallensteins*, pp. 224–253.
28. Ibid., pp. 280–294.

threatened to make for the sake of peace, the Jesuits still hoped to maintain the Edict of Restitution, and Oñate, the Spanish ambassador in Vienna, was reporting on Wallenstein's intrigues and claiming that he intended to usurp either the Bohemian or the imperial crown. Ferdinand II still needed the support of the Catholic electors to secure his son's succession, and Spanish money to carry on the war. After the Spaniards offered subsidies to buy off some of Wallenstein's leading subordinates and ensure the loyalty of his army, the temptation to eliminate the general proved too great. In February 1634 the emperor announced that Wallenstein had entered into a conspiracy to deprive his rightful overlord of his lands and honors, and asked the imperial army forthwith to disregard his commands. Betrayed by his generals, who acted out of mercenary motives, Wallenstein fled to Eger, where he was assassinated by English officers recruited by his subordinate Piccolomini.

"He always lived in the midst of his grand designs," wrote Ranke more than a century ago, "in which nevertheless the public interest was mixed up with his private aims, though, if we do not misunderstand him, the former predominated. And it was all clothed in a self-confidence that blinded even Wallenstein himself."[29] While one may doubt that "the former predominated," Wallenstein undoubtedly believed that he could realize his own ambitions most easily within the framework of a compromise peace. Meanwhile, he never seems to have realized how many problems Ferdinand II might solve by eliminating him. After having encouraged his assassination, Ferdinand could restore the duchy of Mecklenburg without having to carve out a new domain for Wallenstein along the Rhine. He handsomely rewarded the generals who betrayed Wallenstein with portions of the duchy of Friedland, thereby creating the Bohemian dynasties that dominated Bohemian politics until the Second World War. Ferdinand's large cash debts to Wallenstein were also wiped out. Wallenstein's concern for the welfare of his domains and of all Germany, which so entranced Ranke, carried little weight in the context of early modern politics. Having abandoned dreams of ruling Germany, the emperor found it easier to abandon him as well.

Ferdinand II subsequently won some new military victories, but he and his son never reasserted their more extreme war aims. The future Ferdinand III joined the new Spanish army recruited in Italy

29. The translation is Rabb's: see Rabb, *Thirty Years' War*, p. 66.

by the cardinal-infante and annihilated a weakened Swedish army at Nördlingen in September 1634. The remaining Swedish contingents retreated to the north and west, leaving the Hapsburgs and Maximilian fully in control of southern Germany once again. Rather than press his advantage, however, Ferdinand was more than willing to make peace. The Peace of Prague in 1635 made major concessions to the most powerful electors, both Catholic and Protestant. Thus Magdeburg, which Ferdinand II had coveted for his son Leopold William, was given to the son of John George of Saxony for life, and John George himself retained the two Lusatias, which he had originally acquired in exchange for his help in suppressing the Bohemian revolt, as an imperial fief. In general the year 1627 became the base year for determining the fate of church lands, leaving the Catholics with considerable gains in southwest and central Germany and protecting the Counter-Reformation within the Hapsburg lands, but not disturbing the situation in the north and east. The emperor granted an amnesty to most of the Protestant estates who had taken up arms against him after the intervention of Gustav Adolf, but not to Frederick of the Palatinate or to the Bohemian rebels. Maximilian of Bavaria, who had recently married Ferdinand's daughter, received the electoral title and the Lower Palatinate in perpetuity. For the sake of peace, both the Jesuits and the Wittelsbach princes of the league had to abandon the grandiose schemes they had hoped to implement under the Edict of Restitution. And although the Jesuits and the elector of Cologne argued that the revocation of the Edict of Restitution violated a sacred trust, both Ferdinand and Maximilian concluded on the basis of the exhaustion of their treasuries and of Germany as a whole that the continuation of the war was out of the question. A critical paper by the imperial privy council argued that the conquest of Germany was impossible, and that Ferdinand must concentrate on assuring the imperial succession for his son—an increasingly critical problem owing to the emperor's declining health—and maintaining the Catholic religion within his hereditary domains. The Spaniards also advocated peace within Germany, hoping to enlist Austrian help in their impending war against France. Ferdinand ultimately accepted these recommendations, recognizing the impossibility of transforming the political or religious structure of the empire.[30]

---

30. Bireley, *Religion and Politics*, pp. 209–230.

The Austrian Hapsburgs had given up any intention of increasing their imperial authority while retaining their gains within their own domains. Thus, although the Peace of Prague called for the formation of a single imperial army, the implementation of this provision left the army divided into four independent contingents commanded respectively by Ferdinand's son the king of Hungary, Maximilian of Bavaria, John George of Saxony, and George William of Brandenburg. Recent studies have concluded that neither Ferdinand II nor Ferdinand III had any intention of eliminating electoral authority or using the Peace of Prague as a basis for imperial absolutism.[31] At the Regensburg Electoral Convention of 1636–37, Ferdinand II, with the help of Spanish subsidies, finally arranged his son's election as king of the Romans only months before his death. Henceforth the war in Germany continued mainly because of the intervention of France and the obstinacy of the Swedish army. Conflicts within the Catholic coalition continued, and the estates of the empire asserted new rights during peace talks. At a new Reichstag in Regensburg in 1640–41 the Protestants established the principle that the organization of the empire would be a subject of peace negotiations,[32] and when peace talks finally opened, the German estates won the right to take part in the talks.[33] The unity of the coalition collapsed again in 1647. After the Swedes and the French had occupied Bavaria, Maximilian independently secured a cease-fire and agreed to work for peace.[34]

At the Peace of Westphalia in 1648, the Austrian Hapsburgs essentially secured the implementation of their original program of 1618. They made no religious concessions whatever regarding the hereditary lands and provided no compensation for the Bohemian émigrés. Other clauses of the treaty, however, effectively renounced any increase in the Hapsburgs' power within the empire. The emperor finally revoked the Edict of Restitution, which the Peace of Prague had simply suspended for forty years. The peace

31. This is the view both of Bireley, *Religion and Politics*, and Heiner Haan, "Kaiser Ferdinand II und das Problem des Reichasabsolutismus: Die Praager Heeresreform von 1635," in Hans Ulrich Rudolf, ed., *Der Dreissigjährige Krieg: Perspectiven und Strukturen* (Darmstadt, 1977), pp. 261–264.

32. Kathrin Bierther, *Der Regensburger Reichstag von 1640-41* (Kallmunz, 1971), pp. 314–327.

33. Parker, *Thirty Years' War*, pp. 173–174.

34. Hermann Freiherrn von Egloffstein, *Baierns Friedenspolitik von 1645 bis 1647* (Leipzig, 1898), pp. 150–158.

reinstated the ecclesiastical reservation forbidding new secularizations of bishoprics, abbeys, and monasteries, but it established 1624 as the standard year for the restoration of religious rights, before the imperial and league armies had begun undoing secularizations in central and northern Germany. Although Ferdinand III deeply regretted the loss of Alsace to France and the need to abandon the Spaniards, the weariness of the other Catholic states, combined with the Swedish occupation of much of the Hapsburg hereditary lands, forced him to make peace. The most obvious winners on the Catholic side were Maximilian of Bavaria, who became an elector, and Wallenstein's colonels and generals, whose betrayal of him earned them the domains of the duchy of Friedland. The political structure of the empire had not changed significantly as a result of the war.

The Protestant Coalition and the Role of the Swedish Army

The problems of the Protestant coalition closely resembled those of the Catholic side. The Protestant cause initially combined the Bohemian Protestant nobility, attempting to defend their considerable power and privileges; a reckless and ambitious prince, the Calvinist Frederick V of the Palatinate, who played roughly the role of his cousin Maximilian of Bavaria, albeit without the same success; and two ambitious military entrepreneurs, Ernst von Mansfeld and Christian of Brunswick. Subsequently, after the defeat of this original coalition and the apparent Catholic victory of 1629, Gustav Adolf of Sweden descended upon Germany, crushed a Catholic army, and seemed during 1632 to dispose of opportunities comparable to those enjoyed by Ferdinand II three years earlier. After Gustav Adolf's death, however, the power of the Swedes in Germany proved to be almost as ephemeral as Ferdinand's. And just as Ferdinand won his successes only by acquiring enormous debts to Wallenstein, the Protestants restored equilibrium in Germany only by incurring huge debts to the Swedish army. The extraordinary tenacity of that army prolonged the war for years and eventually secured for its officers the permanent endowment which Wallenstein had tried and failed to win for himself.

The Protestant militants who began the war never succeeded in mobilizing a united Protestant party behind them. The estates of the Hapsburg hereditary domains, led by Bohemia, revolted in

1618 from a mixture of political and religious motives, recognizing that Ferdinand II intended to use the Counter-Reformation to strengthen himself in Bohemia as he had done in Styria. But when Frederick V of the Palatinate, a Calvinist and the leader of the Protestant Union, accepted the crown of Bohemia from the Bohemian estates in 1619, his fellow Protestant princes refused to take up arms on behalf of his claim. Instead, they signed a neutrality treaty with the Catholic League at Ulm in July 1620. The Lutheran John George of Saxony even allied himself with the emperor in exchange for the two duchies of Lusatia rather than support the pretensions of his Calvinist cousin. Frederick V also failed to get any substantial help from his father-in-law, James I of England, who disapproved of his conduct and hoped to marry his son Charles to the daughter of the king of Spain. Since Frederick and the Bohemian estates failed to find any real counterweight to the intervention of Maximilian and the Spaniards, their defeat was a foregone conclusion.

Even the dispossession of Frederick V did not move the majority of the Protestant princes to action, and for several years the emperor's only opponents were Frederick, the margrave of Baden, and two military entrepreneurs, Mansfeld and Christian of Brunswick, the Protestant administrator of Halberstadt. By 1622 Mansfeld, one of the most active of all military entrepreneurs, had abandoned Frederick V and led his troops into Alsace, where they lived off the land. He successively negotiated with Louis XIII and the duke of Bouillon in France—then engaged in a brief civil war—with the Spanish, and with the Dutch, with whom he ultimately managed to make terms.[35]

Like the Spaniards, however, foreign Protestant monarchs now tried to exploit the conflict in Germany for their own ends. In 1625 King Christian IV of Denmark intervened on the Protestant side, hoping to secure several rich north German bishoprics for his son. He raised an army with the help of subsidies from Charles I of England, whose support for the Protestant cause pleased the militant Protestant party in Parliament, and from the Dutch, who sought to protect their eastern frontier against the Hapsburgs. The threatened princes of the lower Saxon circle also joined him, as did Mansfeld and Christian of Brunswick. But in 1626–27 Tilly and

---

35. Redlich, *German Military Enterpriser*, I, 211–220.

Wallenstein drove him from the mainland, leading to the Peace of Lübeck and the Edict of Restitution.

In the wake of the Protestant catastrophe, Gustav Adolf decided in 1630 to intervene in the conflict. Like Ferdinand II in 1629, Gustav seemed by 1632 to have virtually all of Germany at his feet, but after his death the Swedes, like the Hapsburgs, rapidly had to abandon any dreams of revolutionizing Germany or radically upsetting the prewar religious settlement.

Since the mid-sixteenth century, the Swedish monarchy had been fighting almost continuous wars against the Danes, the Russians, and the Poles. The most distinguished historian of modern Sweden has tentatively concluded that the Swedish monarchy's wars reflected a sincere concern for the defense of the monarchy's holdings against dangerous neighbors, a generally warlike ethos which pervaded much, though not all of the nobility, and—though this in his opinion was less important—a desire to control Baltic commerce, partly as a means of financing war.[36] In the case of the German war, Roberts argues that Gustav Adolf feared the power of the Hapsburgs along the Baltic coast, especially after Wallenstein began the construction of an imperial fleet. He also sought to make Protestantism secure in northern Germany to provide a buffer against the empire.[37]

At the same time, it seems clear that war had become a virtual economic necessity for Gustav Adolf, and that his wars reflect dilemmas of early modern politics with which we have become so familiar. Although the small kingdom enjoyed by contemporary standards an effective administration and valuable copper and iron mines, annual income was only about 1.5 million talers, a fraction of French or Castilian revenues in this period. The Swedes, indeed, were successful militarily not because of their domestic revenues, but because they recognized well before 1630 that "war must nourish war," and that Sweden itself could not be relied upon to finance new acquisitions. After 1632, in fact, Sweden provided practically nothing for the army in Germany. Their army lived off of tolls collected in occupied Baltic ports, intermittent French and Dutch subsidies, and above all, contributions within Germany it-

36. Michael Roberts, *The Swedish Imperial Experience, 1560–1718* (Cambridge, 1979), pp. 1–42.

37. Michael Roberts, "The Political Objectives of Gustav Adolf in Germany, 1630–32," in Roberts, *Essays in Swedish History* (London, 1967), pp. 82–110.

self. The huge army that Gustav Adolf raised could be supported only through levies upon the population, and indeed, it soon became clear that it was too large to live off the current income of occupied Germany. Well before his death, the king had begun complaining about the exhaustion of the country.[38]

In addition, like the original imperial attack upon Bohemia and Tilly and Wallenstein's march into northern Germany, Gustav Adolf's intervention was a massive exercise in land speculation on behalf of the colonels and captains who raised the bulk of his troops. Gustav Adolf landed in 1630 with about 40,000 men, of whom less than half were Swedes. He immediately raised an almost equal number, drawing upon German military entrepreneurs whose claims would eventually have to be satisfied. Among these were many Bohemian émigrés, who would never regain their lands without a total victory over the Hapsburgs, and numerous German Protestant princes, including Bernhard of Saxe-Weimar, who soon commanded a corps in the Swedish army. During 1631 the treaties which Gustav Adolf concluded with various German Protestant allies showed a large and increasing concern for a Swedish say in the disposition of all territory conquered from the enemy.[39] This concern undoubtedly reflected the need eventually to satisfy his army.

After Gustav crushed the Catholic League's Army in September 1631, the problem of satisfying various Protestant claimants emerged almost at once. Rather than pursue the remnants of Tilly's army or march upon Vienna, Gustav Adolf decided to move down the Main valley to the Rhine. He collected huge new contributions and made numerous donations to his colonels and captains and to various minor German princes. As his chancellor Oexenstierna pointed out after the king's death, much of the conquered territory had already passed out of his hands to make good arrears of pay, although Gustav always reserved the right to call upon the recipients for help and to levy contributions within their domains.[40]

---

38. See Roberts, *Swedish Imperial Experience*, pp. 43–55; Sven Lundkvist, "Schwedische Kriegsfinanzierung 1630–35," in Rudolf, ed., *Der Dreissigjährige Krieg*, pp. 298–303; and Theodor Lorentzen, *Die Schwedische Armee im Dreissigjährigen Kriege und ihre Abdankung* (Leipzig, 1894), pp. 1–5. Lundkvist argues that the Swedes specifically copied Wallenstein's careful levies of contributions.

39. Roberts, "Gustav Adolf in Germany," pp. 87–93.

40. Michael Roberts, *Gustavus Adolphus: A History of Sweden, 1611–1632*, vol. 2 (London, 1958), pp. 538–551, 622–626.

The needs of Gustav Adolf's army, which reached 100,000 men, influenced the politics of the Protestant side of the war much in the way that Wallenstein's army transformed the balance of power on the Catholic side. To assure their interests and the cohesion of their armies, both men insisted upon far-reaching concessions in their dealings with their allies. In negotiations with Pomerania, Hesse, the dukes of Mecklenburg, Frederick of the Palatinate, and the elector of Brandenburg, Gustav Adolf attempted to secure pledges of vassalage and insisted upon the right to dispose of conquered territory and fortified places. Although some of his partners had no option but to accede to his demands, his imperious attitude worried many of his allies from the beginning, and the electors of Saxony and Brandenburg in particular clearly feared his leadership and his long-term designs.

The king's ultimate aims remain controversial. Many Catholic contemporaries accused him of wanting the imperial title for himself, and despite the lack of any firm evidence for this, some subsequent historians endorsed this verdict. In fact, he probably did not have such sweeping designs, but he did intend to make substantial territorial acquisitions along the German Baltic coast, retain a strong say in the affairs of northern and central Germany, and keep large territorial acquisitions to reward his army. He also wanted a well-organized Protestant League, probably with himself at its head, to maintain an army and defend the peace. Such aims could not possibly be reconciled with the independent interests of his Protestant allies. As on the Catholic side, the spoils of war, however impressive, could not satisfy all the combatants.[41]

The problem of achieving a victory which would enable the spoils to be divided became far more serious in 1632, after Wallenstein managed to raise a huge army of his own. Despite the conquest of Bavaria, Gustav Adolf had to move once again into central Germany to defend Saxony against Wallenstein in the summer. As Roberts has pointed out, it was increasingly clear that he could prevail only by the conquest and administration of virtually all of Germany, which would make it impossible for the emperor to maintain an army. At the same time, however, the exhaustion of Germany was making it impossible to support forces of his own that could accomplish this task.[42] The size of both the Protestant

41. Ibid., pp. 619–673.
42. Ibid., pp. 761–762.

and imperial armies peaked in 1632. And at Lützen, near Leipzig, Gustav Adolf not only failed to win a complete victory over Wallenstein but also lost his life.

The subsequent history of Sweden's involvement in the Thirty Years' War is perhaps the most revealing episode of the conflict. Despite the loss of the king, the exhaustion of their forces, the desertion of most of their allies, and the increasingly limited nature of their territorial goals, the Swedes under Oexenstierna continued the war from 1633 through 1648 in order to satisfy their army and maintain their credit as military entrepreneurs. In the end, they prevailed.

Although Oexenstierna had originally viewed his king's German adventure unenthusiastically, he decided after Lützen that Sweden could not withdraw without an indemnity, some safeguards for its allies, and territorial concessions along the Baltic coast. Although Oexenstierna is generally seen as a highly capable bureaucrat, he had territorial ambitions and seriously dreamed of becoming the elector of Mainz. In April of 1633 he organized the Protestant estates within the Heilbronn League and extorted a renewal of French subsidies from Richelieu, who had to depend upon Sweden to protect French interests. But John George of Saxony deserted the Swedes, contributions fell short of projected levels, and the army, seeking recognition of its claims, threatened mutiny during the spring and summer. Oexenstierna eventually signed away most of Sweden's conquests to his colonels and generals, saving only Mainz and Worms for himself and Osnabrück for Gustav Adolf's illegitimate son. Nonetheless, during the next year much of the army deserted, and August 27, 1634, the combined imperial, Bavarian, and Spanish forces annihilated the remainder of the Swedish army—reduced now to about 36,000 men—at Nördlingen. Retreating northward, the army lost all its conquests in central and southern Germany.[43] The Protestant commander Bernhard of Saxe-Weimar defected and went into French service, and almost all of Sweden's Protestant allies acceded to the Peace of Prague in 1635.

Despite the demands of the Swedish Reichsrat and peasant revolts in Sweden, Oexenstierna in 1635 refused to make peace with-

---

43. Lorentzen, *Die Schwedische Armee*, pp. 33–70; Sigmund Goetze, *Die Politik des schwedischen Reichskanzlers Axel Oxenstierna gegenüber Kaiser und Reich* (Kiel, 1971), pp. 90–128; Parker, *Thirty Years' War*, pp. 156–161.

out an indemnity for his German and Swedish officers, without which the Swedish crown would have great difficulty ever raising an army in the future. And from 1635 through 1649, the Swedish army, showing extraordinary determination, remained in the field until the Swedish government had secured both the territorial concessions and the cash indemnity that it demanded. Oexenstierna initially had to make a treaty with his leading officers, promising that six of them would take part in any future peace talks. On several occasions unpaid officers threatened to mutiny, but the strong personalities of the leading Swedish commanders—Baner, Torstennsohn, and Wrangel—and emergency payments always kept the situation in hand. Sweden itself was destitute, but since the Swedes had almost no German allies left the army could draw freely upon Germany for contributions.

During the lengthy peace talks during the early 1640s, the emperor and the German estates flatly rejected demands for an indemnity. By late 1647 however the Swedes and the French had conquered Bavaria and much of Bohemia, leaving the emperor with no choice. Even after the Swedes had secured a territorial indemnity including western Pomerania, Bremen, Verden, and Wismar, both sides knew that the Swedish army would simply live off the land if funds were not found to pay it off. In the following year the imperial estates agreed in principle to an indemnity of five million talers, but the army, now entrenched in the Hapsburg domains after an impressive series of victories, refused to disperse for more than another year, until the Germans provided more adequate guarantees of payment. When the money was paid, Oexenstierna, King Charles Gustav, and Sweden's leading generals used the large sums they received to pay off their debts to their subordinates. The Swedish government also distributed much of the territory it acquired in northern Germany to the soldiers. The army was now composed almost entirely of Germans, and most of the indemnity therefore stayed in Germany. The few remaining Swedes who had accumulated debts received places within Sweden.[44]

The Protestant estates of Germany regained most of their original position under the peace, which also established Calvinism as a legal religion within the empire. The emperor restored almost all

44. Lorentzen, *Die Schwedische Armee*, pp. 74–213.

of the Protestant princes who had fought against him, including those like the duke of Württemberg and the landgrave of Hesse-Cassel who had refused to accept the Peace of Prague. Even the new heir to the Palatinate, Charles Louis, regained the Lower Palatinate and a seat in the electoral college, although the Bavarians retained their new electorate and the Upper Palatinate as well—a partial payment for the services they had initially provided the emperor in 1618. The princes also explicitly received the right to make alliances with foreign princes—a right they had exercised for centuries, and of which the emperor had briefly and ineffectively attempted to deprive them in 1635. The new ecclesiastical settlement inevitably opened the way for numerous new quarrels over the fate of secularized bishoprics and also called into question the status of numerous towns. These quarrels continued for decades, but without provoking general war. The situation returned in this respect to the era of 1559–1618.

The Thirty Years' War had its most important political and religious effects within the Hapsburg hereditary domains, where the Protestant religion never recovered. But the failure of the war to achieve very many dramatic political or religious changes in the rest of the empire reflects the disproportion between the ends of men like Ferdinand II and Gustav Adolf and the means they had to achieve them.[45] Ultimately, the wars stemmed from the ambition of the whole German ruling elite. The initial conflict over Bohemia and the subsequent military campaigns unleashed the ambition of German princes great and small, from the emperor and the duke of Bavaria to the minor princes who raised regiments and companies for service in the various armies. The persistence of these ambitions gave the war its particularly destructive character. As long as foreign princes could provide initial advances with which to recruit troops and as long as German territory could provide contributions to keep them alive, the war went on. Only a few of the princes and commanders emerged wealthier than they started, and many did not even survive, but virtually all of them fought as long as they could.

45. It is true, as Geoffrey Parker has recently argued, that after the settlement of 1648 neither religion nor Hapsburg imperialism ever again led to a general war in Germany (*Thirty Years' War*, p. 217), but one must also note that the balance of power within the empire was roughly the same in 1648 as in 1618, and that the primarily German phases of the war, which ended with the Peace of Prague in 1635, largely revolved around unsuccessful attempts to overturn that balance.

In the meantime, Germany suffered enormous losses in both wealth and population. Like Philip II's wars against the Netherlands, these were wars which the European economy could not finance, but no stream of American silver enabled the princes to finance this war through inflation. Instead the armies kept themselves alive through the most ruthless exploitation of Germany, with devastating economic and demographic consequences. The German princes—who by 1635 at the latest had generally realized the extent of their disastrous folly—found themselves completely unable to control the forces they had unleashed. The war levied a continuous tax on the German economy, which probably reduced Germany's population by between 30 and 50 percent. The enormous destruction of the war, which a few historians have rather quixotically disputed, has now been confirmed beyond any doubt. The discovery of a few areas that suffered very little does not alter the general picture.[46] Unable to remake Germany—owing to the political, economic, and military realities of the time—princes and soldiers literally levied a tax in blood for three decades. The war ultimately represented a kind of *reductio ad absurdum* that highlighted the illogic of seventeenth-century politics. Not for almost two centuries—and then for entirely different reasons—would such a destructive war take place again.

The English Civil War in European Perspective

At least two schools of English historians have ascribed to the years 1642–1660 a pivotal role in the political development of Great Britain. The Whigs, perhaps inspired by the great narrative work of S. R. Gardiner but led ideologically by G. M. Trevelyan, first argued that the victory of the Parliamentary party had secured the survival of English liberty. Later, Marxists led by R. H. Tawney and Christopher Hill suggested that the war grew out of the rise of the middle class, embodied in the gentry and urban merchants to

46. On this point, see T. K. Rabb, "The Effects of the Thirty Years' War on the German Economy," *Journal of Modern History*, 34, no. 1 (March 1962): 40–51, and Henry Kamen, "The Economic Effects of the Thirty Years' War," *Past and Present*, 39 (April 1968): pp. 44–61, both of which survey the literature. The most authoritative single survey of this problem is Günther Franz, *Der Dreissigjährige Krieg und das deutsche Volk* (Stuttgart, 1961), which gives the figure of 30 to 50 percent. Parker, *Thirty Years' War*, pp. 210–211, plumps for a more conservative figure of 15 to 20 percent.

whom they assigned crucial roles in the conflict. Criticism of the Marxist view resulted in the gentry controversy of the early 1950s, in which Tawney, Hugh Trevor-Roper, Lawrence Stone, and J. H. Hexter exchanged polemics of unusual ferocity. In 1977, a special issue of the *Journal of Modern History* devoted to new interpretations of the conflict, followed by lengthy rejoinders from Hexter and others, showed that the old controversies had lost little of their fervor.

The vast historiography of the English civil war, however, has seldom tried to place it in a comparative European perspective.[1] And thus, however well-trodden and strewn with illustrious dead and wounded the battleground may be, an attempt to reinterpret the civil war in light of contemporary Continental events may produce interesting results. Indeed, not only have the various controversies of the last few decades failed to produce a consensus, but the opposing parties have fought each other virtually to a standstill. The major theoretical interpretations have been severely questioned by detailed empirical studies, and little new has emerged to take their place. And it is clear, based upon the foregoing analysis of Continental European politics from 1559 to 1659, that many similarities between British and Continental politics have been largely overlooked by historians.

In fact, when one looks at the politics of the British Isles from a Continental perspective—and more specifically at the civil war of the 1640s—one finds the same underlying political structures that led to so much contemporary conflict in Europe. Like Continental politics, the politics of the kingdoms of England, Ireland, and Scotland during the late sixteenth and early seventeenth centuries are characterized by the leading role of the aristocracy, the importance of patronage and faction, the frequent incidence of violence (most notably, but not always, in Ireland and Scotland), the divisive influence of religion, and the material weakness of the crown. Whereas the traditional tendency to focus solely on England has encouraged an emphasis on distinctive aspects of English politics, a broader view including Ireland and Scotland suggests that the United Kingdom (including Scotland after 1603) was every bit as much an aristocratic empire as its Continental contemporaries. Moreover, the English civil war, like the Thirty Years' War and the

1. One exception is Perez Zagorin, *Rebels and Rulers, 1500–1660* (Cambridge, 1982).

Catalonian rebellion, grew out of a monarch's attempts to increase his religious, political, and economic power in various different parts of his domains.

In addition, as in the revolt of the Netherlands and the Thirty Years' War, the behavior of armies determined much of the course of the conflict. Like monarchs on the Continent, Charles I and the Parliamentarians generally lacked the money to pay their armies and had to take far-reaching measures as a result. Charles I had to call Parliament in the first place because of the disintegration of his own army and the invasion of the Scots, who demanded arrears of pay before they would withdraw. A few years later Parliament decided upon the abolition of episcopacy and the sale of bishops' lands to raise money to pay off its forces. Beginning in 1646, the Parliamentary New Model Army mutinied to secure arrears of pay and subsequently purged Parliament to stop a settlement with Charles I. Under Cromwell the Commonwealth sold off crown lands and confiscated vast Irish lands to satisfy its soldiery, but the revolutionary regime never found a settlement which would satisfy both the army and the nation, and it collapsed when the unpaid army finally mutinied again.

The English civil war did present some novel features. The rebels against Charles I included elements both similar and dissimilar to Continental rebels. The men who in 1640–41 initially seized the Parliamentary initiative and subsequently raised the standard of Parliamentary rebellion against the king represented a classic aristocratic faction, albeit one in which non-noble landowners played very significant roles. They originally sought not sweeping constitutional change, but power. Within the Long Parliament, however, another faction of far more radical gentlemen who did *not* enjoy aristocratic patronage played an increasingly important role as time wore on, largely because of Charles's failure to come to terms with the more traditional opposition. But while the rebels included truly revolutionary elements, the results of the conflict from 1640 through 1660 were dubiously revolutionary at most and do not support the idea that England had experienced a decisive class struggle. On the whole, then, and despite some significant differences, English politics during the 1640s resembled Continental politics a great deal, and the course of the civil war reflected contemporary European-wide power structures as much as they did any particular English tradition of liberty.

Before examining the civil war in more detail, we must review the somewhat calmer period of the late sixteenth and early seventeenth centuries. After the accession of Elizabeth I in 1559, purely *English* politics were relatively tranquil. England underwent only two armed rebellions under Elizabeth and James I: the northern rising in 1569–70 and the Essex Rebellion of 1602. Both resembled contemporary Continental rebellions. The duke of Norfolk in 1569 had been indirectly in contact with Philip II and rebelled partly in sympathy with the Catholic party, while Essex's followers staged their almost comical rising to protest their exclusion from office. But the rarity and insignificance of these episodes clearly distinguishes England from the rest of Europe. Much of the credit goes to the leading politicians during this period. The crown possessed a most impressive amount of patronage, and until the 1630s it seems to have distributed it fairly equally. Elizabeth's skill at balancing the Burghley and Leicester factions is famous, although the balancing act broke down in 1602 after Essex, who had inherited Leicester's patronage, lost the queen's favor. Burghley's son Robert Cecil shared the royal patronage with the Howards in the early years of the reign of James I, and when Buckingham became the king's favorite, he sold office impartially to the highest bidder and thus probably retarded the growth of an organized, hostile faction.[2]

Meanwhile, the British crown in the late sixteenth and early seventeenth centuries usually avoided becoming involved in the wars on the Continent. This also increased stability at home, not least because it limited the demands the crown had to make upon the people. Factions frequently did attempt to make capital out of foreign policy issues, but Elizabeth I, James I, and Charles I usually resisted their warlike impulses. In 1560 William Cecil, the future Lord Burghley, won credit with Elizabeth by mounting an invasion of Scotland (then prey to French influence), but only because the invasion was a quick success. By the 1580s the earl of Leicester had become the patron of the Puritans and the prime advocate of intervention in the Netherlands to support the Protestant cause. Elizabeth, who had for financial and other reasons consistently inclined against intervention in that conflict, eventually agreed to an expe-

2. Conrad Russell, *The Crisis of Parliaments: English History, 1509–1660* (Oxford, 1971), pp. 285–288; on Elizabethan politics, see Wallace MacCaffrey, *The Shaping of the Elizabethan Regime* (Princeton, 1968), and *Queen Elizabeth and the Making of Policy.*

dition but forced the earl to spend a large portion of his own fortune upon it.[3] The resulting war with Spain and Essex's expedition to Ireland wrecked Elizabeth's finances. During the next reign, James I's favorites, the Howards, developed a notorious connection with the crown of Spain, which together with James's natural pusillanimity kept England out of the early stages of the Thirty Years' War. Under both James I and Charles I the Parliamentary opposition continually pressed the crown to support the Protestant cause in the Thirty Years' War, and Buckingham, in search of personal glory, succeeded in 1624–1626 in involving England in simultaneous war with both France and Spain. With the exception of Elizabeth's war with Spain, all these conflicts remained brief.

The English crown in the late sixteenth and early seventeenth centuries avoided financial catastrophe with a combination of penury at home and caution abroad. Elizabeth's annual revenue, like that of the French crown, failed to keep pace with the inflation of the sixteenth century, but she made do by cutting expenditures, keeping salaries low (and thereby increasing official corruption), leasing monopolies, and selling crown lands. When during the 1590s she had to make much higher demands on Parliament to pay for the indecisive war with Spain, the House of Commons agreed only with considerable misgivings, and the counties put up some resistance.[4] James I made peace with Spain. He increased pensions and other expenditures, but his revenues also increased, and during his reign the royal debt grew from £400,000 pounds to just £900,000. Both James and Charles I contented themselves with the money they could collect with or without the consent of Parliament, rather than satisfying the opposition by giving it a larger share of power over revenue and expenditure or by adopting its foreign policy and making a real commitment to the Protestant side in the Thirty Years' War. Their revenue was, by Continental standards, very low. Castilian revenues in 1621 reached almost 10 million ducats; Charles I's revenue peaked in 1640 at £858,000, about a third of the same total.[5]

3. Charles Wilson, *Queen Elizabeth and the Revolt of the Netherlands* (Berkeley, 1970), pp. 96–104. The intervention suffered from the customary contemporary problems of mutiny and treachery.

4. R. B. Wernham, *After the Armada: Elizabethan England and the Struggle for Western Europe 1588–1595* (Oxford, 1984), pp. 559–568.

5. Frederick C. Dietz, *English Public Finance, 1558–1641*, vol. 2 (2d ed., New York, 1964), p. 285. I am using an exchange rate of 4 ducats to the pound, which I believe to

Another source of English political stability has been noted by Stone and Hexter: the decline of large aristocratic armed bands in the countryside, owing at least partly to royal attempts to restrict them. The English upper classes continued to breed their share of soldiers. During much of the reign of Elizabeth Ireland provided ample opportunities for military adventure, and in the early seventeenth century some English gentlemen became military entrepreneurs in Germany, even participating in the assassination of Wallenstein. Within England, however, large-scale armed conflict ceased to be a common form of political struggle. The aristocracy could no longer count upon the local gentry to rise to defend its interests—a fact undeniably connected to a more general erosion of the links between noblemen and gentlemen.[6]

In addition, despite intense anti-Catholic feeling and the growing Puritan critique of some established church institutions and practices, England undoubtedly benefited under Elizabeth and James I from a relatively latitudinarian attitude toward religious practice. As Nicholas Tyacke has recently pointed out, Puritanism managed to exist within the church of England until Archbishop William Laud and others introduced Arminianism in the 1620s. As long as the church hierarchy remained weak—and it was notoriously weak under Elizabeth—and as long as local lords and gentlemen controlled most parish appointments, religion was unlikely to lead to serious political conflicts.[7]

Finally, Parliament, and especially the House of Commons, had already provided a forum for the realization of ambition and the resolution of certain kinds of conflicts which on the Continent often ended in violence. Parliament was, to begin with—in a much-quoted phrase of G. R. Elton's—"a point of contact between the rulers and the ruled," and, as such, it could mediate conflicts,

---

have been roughly valid throughout the century. Conrad Russell has argued that the debates on foreign policy in 1624, when Buckingham wanted large subsidies for a foreign war, showed that the Commons simply had no conception of the financial requirements of European war. Russell, "Parliament and the King's Finances," in Russell, ed., *The Origins of the English Civil War* (New York, 1973), pp. 91–116.

6. Significantly, William Wentworth advised his infant son, Thomas—the future earl of Strafford—not to seek a firm connection with noblemen but simply to avoid their enmity. *Wentworth Papers, 1597–1628*, ed. J. P. Cooper, Camden Fourth Series, vol. 12 (London, 1973), no. 1. See also Stone, *The Crisis of the Aristocracy*, pp. 201–214.

7. Nicholas Tyacke, "Puritanism, Arminianism, and Counter-Revolution," in Russell, ed., *Origins of the English Civil War*," pp. 120–143.

including conflicts over taxes, which on the Continent led to revolt. Whether or not members actually represented their voting and nonvoting constituents, and however they were actually chosen, they did show real independence in their dealings with the crown. Less than half of early Stuart members of the Commons owed their seats to the patronage of the crown or the peerage, and they responded skeptically to the crown's financial demands.[8] Meetings of the French Estates General during the late sixteenth century had expressed similar feelings, but after 1614 the Estates General did not meet. The clashes between Parliament and king during the 1620s, in which Parliament frequently refused to meet the king's demands in full, were a more peaceful counterpart of the numerous tax revolts against Richelieu. Parliament and Parliamentary consent were not yet essential to effective royal rule, however. Several authors have recently noted that Charles's non-Parliamentary government from 1628 through 1640 was more successful than it has often been given credit for. Ship money, a tax the king imposed without consent, was collected without great difficulty during the late 1630s, and the opposition leader John Hampden lost his famous court case against it. By avoiding any intervention in Continental affairs Charles kept himself on a sufficiently secure financial footing.[9]

The House of Commons fulfilled other stabilizing functions. Opposing country gentry factions could fight for status in elections, instead of in armed combat, and it is clear that many did so. A seat in the House of Commons could also be a stepping stone to influence in London and at court. Thus Thomas Wentworth of Yorkshire entered Parliament after a series of electoral battles with his local rivals, the Saviles; emerged in 1628 as a leader of the anti-court faction; and then, suddenly and without warning, became Viscount Wentworth and entered the king's service.[10] While Parliament was in session, royal ministers and opposition leaders alike

8. See Derek Hirst, *The Representative of the People? Voters and Voting in England under the Early Stuarts* (Cambridge, 1975), pp. 132–153, and John K. Gruenfelder, *Influence in Early Stuart Elections, 1604–1640* (Columbus, 1981), pp. 213–223. Mark Kishlansky, *Parliamentary Selection: Social and Political Choice in Early Modern England* (New York, 1986), argues that both national and local authorities tried to avoid truly contested elections before the civil war, thus weakening Hirst's conception of the representativeness of the institution.

9. See especially J. S. Morrill, *The Revolt of the Provinces* (London, 1976), pp. 13–31.

10. C. V. Wedgewood, *Thomas Wentworth, First Earl of Strafford: A Revaluation* (London, 1961), pp. 28–73.

could fight their battles in the Parliamentary arena. Beginning in the 1620s the procedure of impeachment and trial by the House of Lords became a means of disgracing an opponent—a substitute, one might suggest, for the kind of blackmail so common in the court of Philip II or the assassination conspiracies against Richelieu. Since the king retained the power of pardoning convicted offenders, the two Houses could not strike down a favorite without his assent, but the procedure allowed him to sacrifice servants who had become too unpopular. Buckingham apparently arranged the impeachment of the Lord Treasurer Cranfield in 1624, and the earls of Pembroke and Arundel, working with the queen, managed the impeachment of Buckingham in 1626, which Charles I eventually stopped. In this as in other cases, Conrad Russell has remarked, "the concerns of court and country found a point of contact."[11]

Relatively quiet England, however, occupied the same position within the domains of the crown of England as Castile did within the Spanish empire. Ireland in particular had become an outlet for the violent ambitions of the English nobility, which tried intermittently to exploit it in the same way that the Castilian nobility drew upon Italy and other parts of the Iberian peninsula. Elizabeth's regime controlled Ireland militarily with the help of numerous local garrisons and encouraged Englishmen from all classes to settle there. After numerous rebellions, which frequently sought and at one point obtained some Spanish assistance, the English established their authority firmly by the end of Elizabeth's reign.[12] James I continued attempts to increase the Protestant party and establish its political supremacy within new Irish political institutions. Various legal tricks enabled "new English"—that is, Protestant—settlers to claim title to land under regrants from the crown, and thereby to enrich themselves, often without actually settling on the property.[13]

The kingdom of Scotland was fully sovereign and separate from England, and was ruled by different monarchs until the death of

11. Conrad Russell, *Parliaments and English Politics, 1621–1629* (Oxford, 1979), pp. 15–17, 198–202, 266–322.

12. Steven G. Ellis, *Tudor Ireland: Crown, Community, and the Conflict of Cultures, 1470–1603* (London, 1985), pp. 228–320.

13. Aidan Clarke, with R. Dudley Edwards, "Pacification, Plantation, and the Catholic Question, 1603–23," in T. W. Moody et al., eds., *A New History of Ireland*, vol. 3 (Oxford, 1976), pp. 187–232.

Elizabeth I and the accession of James VI of Scotland as James I of England in 1603. It experienced political conflicts during the second half of the sixteenth century very similar to contemporary conflicts in France or to the Bohemian civil war of the 1610s, and these conflicts frequently involved England as well. From 1561 until 1568 Mary, Queen of Scots, a Catholic, granddaughter of the duke of Guise, widow of the French king Francis II, and Catholic claimant to the English throne as well, tried to rule over a confused political and religious situation in which Calvinist reformers had won over most of the country from the still-established Roman Catholic church. The struggle between the factions was unusually bloody and devious even by contemporary standards, featuring armed risings, intervention from both France and England, and the murder of Mary's Catholic husband, Darnley, and her hasty remarriage to a Protestant, Bothwell, who was suspected of Darnley's murder. Mary was deposed in 1567 and fled to England, where Elizabeth I imprisoned her, and a further civil war was settled in 1573 by Elizabeth's intervention.

After plotting Elizabeth's assassination with Spanish encouragement, Mary was executed in 1587. Her son James I, who had begun to rule in 1581, accepted the supremacy of reformed doctrine, but waged a long battle with the Presbyterian Kirk for the right to appoint bishops and control church lands. Foreign plots, intrigues, and murders continued to play a major role in Scottish politics until James's accession to the English throne in 1603. During the rest of his reign, he made some further progress in reestablishing bishops, whom he could use to strengthen his own party and his authority in Scotland as well as England.[14]

The events that preceded the English civil war in 1640–1642 resemble developments in other parts of Europe quite closely if one looks at them from the standpoint not merely of England, but of the British Isles as a whole. The religious and financial innovations and the favoritism of Charles I in England, Scotland, and Ireland closely resembled the policies of Philip II in the Netherlands. They provoked a rebellion in Scotland similar to the Bohemian revolt against Ferdinand II, a rising in Ireland, and widespread discontent within England itself.

14. William Croft Dickinson and George S. Pryde, *A New History of Scotland*, 2 vols. (Edinburgh, 1961–1965), I, 322–369, II, 1–7.

Of all Charles's policies, his religious innovations seem to have provoked the greatest unrest.[15] The more controversial religious changes of the first half of the sixteenth century came not from the Puritans but from the Arminians, led by Archbishop Laud. The most important Arminian challenge to the prevailing orthodoxy lay not in the emphasis on ritual and ornamentation, but in the challenge to the Calvinist doctrine of predestination, which had been accepted as Church of England orthodoxy by 1600. The Arminian belief in sacraments as a key to grace outraged Puritans who identified this doctrine with Catholicism—and Charles's grants of office to prominent Catholics in the 1630s, as well as his wife's Catholicism, heightened their suspicions. Under Laud, Arminianism became orthodoxy.[16] Arminianism also aroused bitter opposition in Scotland, leading to rebellion in 1637. In both England and Scotland, Charles and Laud were trying to increase their ecclesiastical patronage and alter religious practice—steps similar to those taken by Philip II in the Netherlands and Ferdinand II in Bohemia.

Other events which led to war in Scotland and rebellion in Ireland had Continental parallels. Like Ferdinand II in Bohemia and Olivares in Catalonia, Charles had undertaken important reforms which would substantially have increased his power. Only a few months after becoming king, in October 1625, he had declared a sweeping revocation of royal grants and gifts, designed to reassert royal control over vast former church lands held by the nobility and to increase payments from office holders. And when in 1637 Charles and Laud insisted upon the introduction of the English Prayer Book in Scotland, the Scots made the National Covenant, pledging to maintain their existing religion.[17] Meanwhile, in Ireland Thomas Wentworth used various means to increase the revenue of the crown and force both Catholic Old English and Protestant New English settlers to pay more to the crown for clear title to their land, while preparing new plantations that would dispossess

15. This contradicts a famous statement by Cromwell, but the Short and Long Parliaments in their early stages put more emphasis upon religious problems than upon anything else, including ship money. See Samuel R. Gardiner, *History of England from the Accession of James I to the Outbreak of the Civil War, 1603–42*, 10 vols. (London, 1883–84), IX, 98–118, 218–293.

16. Tyacke, "Puritanism, Arminianism, and Counter-Revolution", pp. 120–143.

17. David Stevenson, *The Scottish Revolution, 1637–1644: The Triumph of the Covenanters* (London, 1973), esp. pp. 15–87.

the Irish Catholics. His uniformly heavy hand managed by 1641 to alienate all the major Irish factions and to make them more than willing to cooperate with Charles's enemies in Scotland and England.[18]

Like Philip II and Ferdinand II, Charles, Laud, and Wentworth (later earl of Strafford) were determined reformers rather than corrupt skeptics. It was their relatively modern tendency toward uniformity and their insistence on principle, as well as their monopoly of patronage, that proved their undoing. Wentworth, both as president of the Council of the North and lord deputy in Ireland, antagonized one and all by his dislike of corruption and his all too impartial exercise of royal authority. "Ruinous though his success may have been," Gardiner commented upon Strafford's career, "in his devotion to the rule of intelligence he stands strangely near to one side of the modern spirit. Alone amongst his generation his voice was always raised for practical reforms . . . Strafford regarded [existing] society as full of abuses, and sought in the organization which was ready to his hand, the lever by which those abuses might be removed."[19]

In 1638, the Scots raised an army led by Alexander Leslie, who had led troops against the Hapsburgs in the Thirty Years' War. The opening campaigns ended inconclusively and left Charles bankrupt. He recalled Wentworth from Ireland and created him earl of Strafford, and Wentworth persuaded him to call Parliament in 1640. When the Short Parliament made inconvenient demands, Charles quickly dismissed it. New Scottish victories and the Scottish occupation of the north of England forced Charles to call Parliament again, and the Long Parliament—one of the most carefully studied assemblies in history—was called in the fall of 1640. Then in 1641 the Catholics rose in Ireland to undo some of Wentworth's plantations.

In calling Parliament, Charles I was appealing to the country, and a recent work by John Gruenfelder suggests that the early Stuart kings did not dispose of a reliable clientele in the counties. From 1614 through 1624 only 8 to 10 percent of the seats in the House were secured by the court's clients. This figure fell below 5

18. Aidan Clarke, "The Government of Wentworth, 1632–40," in Moody, ed., *New History of Ireland*, III, pp. 243–269; see also p. 289.

19. Gardiner, *History of England*, IX, 370; see also Wedgewood, *Thomas Wentworth*, p. 231, on Wentworth's distinctive outlook.

percent during the 1620s, rose to 6.2 percent in the spring elections of 1640, and fell to 4.6 percent in the fall, despite an all-out effort on Charles I's behalf.[20] In the meantime, the peerage generally managed to elect about a quarter of the seats in the House, peaking at 30.5 percent in 1625 and falling to a low of 22.1 percent in the elections to the Long Parliament.[21]

Interpretations of the civil war depend largely on particular views of the class basis and aims of the opposition in the Long Parliament. Whereas Whig historians, led by G. M. Trevelyan, have argued that the Parliamentary leaders were simply fighting for "English liberty and religion" rather than for the interests of a particular class,[22] Tawney, Trevor-Roper, and Stone have all argued that the House of Commons represented the interests of a distinct class, the gentry, although they differ on the source of the gentry's concerns. More recently, Paul Christianson and Clayton Roberts have suggested that the Lords, rather than the Commons, dominated the early sessions of the Long Parliament, only to be subjected to severe criticism by T. K. Rabb and especially by J. H. Hexter, who in early 1978 reiterated his Whig view that the Commons fought principally to secure freedom and liberty.[23]

From a Continental perspective, these questions have additional interest. If the House of Commons was fighting primarily either for liberty or for the interests of a distinct gentry class in opposition to the aristocracy, then the civil war differed fundamentally from noble revolts in the Netherlands, France, Catalonia, and elsewhere, and the war deserves to be called the English Revolution. Recent research, however, suggests that in its early stages the con-

---

20. Gruenfelder defines court patronage quite narrowly, to include nominees by the lord wardens, the duchies of Lancaster and Cornwall, the Prince's Council, the councils of the North and Wales, and the Privy Council; see *Influence in Early Stuart Elections*, pp. 59–109. In cases like the duke of Buckingham he apparently distinguishes patronage distributed in an official capacity (specifically as Lord Warden) and in a purely personal capacity.

21. Gruenfelder, *Influence in Early Stuart Elections*, p. 222. Gruenfelder's figures are tentative, but he believes that the figures for aristocratic patronage are probably conservative; see p. 169.

22. G. M. Trevelyan, *England under the Stuarts* (New York, 1960), p. 188.

23. See the articles by Christianson and Roberts in the December 1977 issue of the *Journal of Modern History*, and J. H. Hexter, "Power Struggle, Parliament, and Liberty in Early Stuart England," in ibid., 50, no. 1 (March 1978): 1–50; also Derek Hirst, "Unanimity in the Commons, Aristocratic Intrigues, and the Origins of the English Civil War," in ibid., pp. 51–71.

flict was another faction fight, in which the opposition in the Lords and Commons sought simply to replace Strafford, Laud, and their creatures as the ministers of Charles I. Recent treatments have agreed that great lords led the Parliamentary opposition of 1641–42. Hexter, the self-identified Whig and biographer of John Pym, agreed in 1978 that Pym and Hampden—opposition leaders in the Commons—belonged to a well-established faction led by the earls of Bedford, Warwick, and Essex and Viscount Saye and Seale. Gruenfelder's election data confirms the importance of the Bedford-Pym faction, which threw its weight behind 35 candidates in the spring of 1640 and 37 in the autumn, and elected 32 and 35 of them, respectively. Most of these candidates became firm Parliament men during the civil war.[24] But Hexter reiterates, following his earlier "Storm over the Gentry," that throughout the early Stuart period, "the central and recurrent conflict was over liberty and the rule of law"—and more specifically over the rights and privileges of Parliament. The Triennial Act of March 1641, in his view, tried to settle the conflict by giving Parliament an independent existence, thereby balancing the king.[25]

Yet Essex, Pym, and the rest of their faction clearly had a good deal more on their minds than the establishment of the independent power of Parliament and the rights of Englishmen. It even seems possible to argue, though much more difficult to know for sure, that they regarded these blessings as means rather than as ends in themselves. Not satisfied with the Triennial Act and the subsequent abolition of the prerogative courts, Bedford, Essex, Pym, and the rest sought to replace the king's ministers with themselves. Specifically, Bedford planned to become lord treasurer with Pym as chancellor of the exchequer. Essex deeply resented the honors which Charles had given to Strafford instead of himself, despite Essex's numerous services in the campaign against the Scots. The Triennial Act, as Hexter notes, was the first piece of *legislation* passed by the Long Parliament, but before passing it the House of Commons had dealt with other nonlegislative business

24. Gruenfelder, *Influence in Early Stuart Elections*, pp. 183–202. Other peers did much less well, confirming Lawrence Stone's argument that the opposition peers had maintained their influence among the lower orders more successfully than peers associated with the court; see Stone, *The Causes of the English Revolution* (New York, 1972), p. 136.

25. Hexter, "Power Struggle," pp. 46–47; see also J. H. Hexter, "Storm over the Gentry," reprinted in Hexler, *Reappraisals in History* (Aberdeen, 1961), pp. 117–162.

apparently regarded as more pressing—the impeachment of Strafford and Laud.[26] Nor was the opposition committed to a reduction in the king's power. Had they indeed persuaded Charles to take them into office, Bedford and Pym planned to solve the king's long-standing financial problems by introducing a series of new taxes—including many of the same taxes that Pym later imposed on behalf of Parliament.[27] In *The Causes of the English Revolution* Lawrence Stone maintains that the conflict was "more than a mere rebellion against a particular King,"[28] but in its first stage the conflict seems to have been *less* than a rebellion against a particular king. From the standpoint of Bedford, Pym, and the rest, it seems to have been a movement against a particular faction and its policies, similar to innumerable French and Spanish conspiracies, in which Parliament was a key weapon. Meanwhile they did not scruple to use other far more questionable weapons, including an invitation to the Scots to continue their war against Charles in order to bring him to heel.

At the same time, Gruenfelder's work confirms that the House of Commons was not simply a tool of aristocratic faction. It contained large numbers of independent gentry—including a number who played a prominent and truly revolutionary role in later stages of the civil war. In fact, the number of independent members elected in 1640 increased relative to earlier Stuart Parliaments. Court and aristocratic patronage, Gruenfelder estimates, secured 145 places in the Parliament of 1604, 174 in 1624, 140 in 1628, and 132 in the Long Parliament—meaning that patronage failed to secure 326 places in 1604, 311 in 1624, 350 in 1628, and 361 in the fall of 1640. Throughout the early Stuart period, in short, the House of Commons was made up mainly of independent gentry and town oligarchs whose strongest ties bound them to their local community. Indeed, both Gruenfelder and Derek Hirst have found that borough and county constituencies showed an increasing reluctance to elect outsiders, who had presumably been put forward by

26. Gardiner, *History of England*, IX, 218–293.

27. On these points, see Brian Manning, "The Aristocracy and the Downfall of Charles I," in Manning, ed., *Politics, Religion, and the English Civil War* (London, 1973), pp. 37–82; Clayton Roberts, "The Earl of Bedford and the Coming of the English Revolution," *Journal of Modern History*, 49, no. 4 (December 1977): 600–616; Russell, "Parliament and the King's Finances"; and Vernon F. Snow, *Essex the Rebel* (Lincoln, 1970), pp. 237–264.

28. Stone, *The Causes of the English Revolution*, p. 48.

powerful patrons, during Charles I's reign. The number of outsiders elected peaked at 129 in 1625 and fell to 79—about one-sixth—in the Long Parliament.[29] The role of these independent members in the civil war emerges from several monographs, including Hexter's *Reign of King Pym* and David Underdown's *Pride's Purge*, which focus upon the divisions within the Parliamentary side of the civil war and help explain how the war eventually did become more revolutionary.

The independent or "country" members did almost unanimously oppose Laud's religious innovations and Charles's financial innovations, and these members supported the impeachment of Strafford, the Triennial Act, and the abolition of the prerogative courts. Many of them, however, began to waver in late 1641 when Pym tried to use Parliament to force Charles to give power to the opposition. Approximately half of them apparently refused in December 1641 to support the Grand Remonstrance, in which Parliament claimed both the right to choose the king's ministers and the right to control the armed forces. Thus Perez Zagorin has argued that with the Grand Remonstrance the opposition leaders lost the support of the country. We shall see that it would be more accurate to say that they lost the support of a large part of the country, and that while some country members showed more caution than the opposition leaders, others showed more zeal.[30]

Three reasons explain why the war now became a revolution in which the king was executed, episcopacy and the House of Lords abolished, Parliament purged, and a great deal of land confiscated and resold, both in England and Ireland. First, Charles I, ignoring the precedents of numerous rebellions against French Valois and Bourbon kings and the more recent example of Ferdinand II, chose the role of Philip II in the Netherlands and absolutely refused to make terms with his enemies. Second, Charles's obstinacy progressively discredited the original opposition leadership, who wanted an eventual agreement with him, and brought to the fore a new, far more radical group of opposition leaders drawn from among the independent members of Parliament. Third, and from a European-wide perspective most interesting, Parliament, having raised armies of its own and called upon a Scottish one as well,

29. Gruenfelder, *Influence in Early Stuart Elections*, p. 225.
30. See Perez Zagorin, *The Court and the Country: The Beginning of the English Revolution* (New York, 1970), pp. 251–294.

increasingly found its policies determined by the need to satisfy these armies. This problem was all the more difficult because Parliament, like the sovereigns of Europe, simply could not pay the army out of current revenue. The New Model Army, in particular, emerged as a political force in 1646, and for fourteen years it proved every bit as determined, and at least as influential politically, as the Swedish army in the Thirty Years' War.

Hexter has shown how the House of Commons divided after the civil war began. Among the perhaps two hundred members of Parliament who did remain sitting after the war began, three rather vague and shifting groups emerged: a peace party, led by Denzil Holles; the middle group, led first by Pym and later by Oliver St. John, which cooperated closely with the remaining opposition peers like Essex; and an extreme war party led by Sir Arthur Haselrig, Henry Martin, and Sir Henry Vane, Jr. These three groups included about half of the remaining members, and the rest belonged to no party at all.[31] The peace party, like much of the country at large, obviously regretted the outbreak of civil war and wanted a settlement with Charles I on almost any terms. Only Charles's utter obstinacy allowed Pym to persuade Parliament to undertake harsh wartime measures in 1642–43. The nucleus of the middle group was the thirty or so members, Pym included, who had been elected in 1642 with the patronage of the aristocratic opposition. They wanted a settlement with Charles, but only on favorable terms. The war party, composed of independent gentry, had far more radical aims. Its members wanted the unconditional surrender of Charles; they showed a great hostility toward both the king and the Lords from the beginning; they wanted the abolition of episcopacy; and a few declared themselves republicans very early in the war. Religious differences, it has clearly been shown, did not determine these parties. The terms "Presbyterian" and "Independent" had no precise meaning in these times, and very few members of Parliament seem to have had definite ideas regarding the organization of a new English church. But of the existence of a politically radical war party from an early stage there can be no doubt—and this party took the lead in the conflict after the traditional elites failed to compromise.[32]

31. Hexter, *The Reign of King Pym* (Cambridge, Mass., 1941), pp. 31–62, 67.
32. On these points, see especially David Underdown, *Pride's Purge: Politics in the Puritan Revolution* (Oxford, 1971), pp. 45–65.

The civil war, then, grew out of a relatively traditional aristocratic factional struggle, but the House of Commons, upon which the opposition faction relied for support, included large numbers of relatively independent members drawn from other segments of English society. Had the opposition come to terms with Charles I in the early stages of the war, English politics would not have undergone fundamental changes. The opposition leaders began with limited aims: once Charles sacrificed Strafford, Laud, and a few other lesser figures and took them into office, they would have no further quarrel with him. They apparently planned to undo Laud's religious innovations and reassert lay control over the church, although only a minority of the Commons as yet had any thought of abolishing episcopacy. They did secure the abolition of the prerogative courts and the Councils of the North and Wales, which by increasing local at the expense of central power undoubtedly pleased the country members a great deal, while protecting the opposition leaders against arbitrary arrest. On the other hand, they intended to increase the royal revenue with the consent of Parliament—a step which would probably have been unpopular with many independent members and with the country at large. Even the condemned Strafford himself, remarkably enough, seems to have believed that the conflict was best settled by giving power to the opposition. In his last letter to Charles, urging him to bow to the Act of Attainder which Pym had forced through after impeachment had failed, Strafford hoped that his own death would bring about "that blessed agreement which God, I trust, shall ever establish between you and your subjects."[33]

During 1641 Charles seemed ready on several occasions to yield to the opposition, and only the untimely death of the duke of Bedford may have prevented a compromise. But Charles continually antagonized the opposition by negotiating in bad faith, attempting to build up his own faction at court, intriguing with foreign powers, trying to reach a settlement with the Scots, and finally trying to arrest opposition leaders.[34] This, more than anything else, brought about the war and the subsequent attempted revolution.

The civil war was not settled on relatively traditional terms because Charles never abandoned hopes of total victory. Thus in

33. Quoted in Gardiner, *History of England*, IX, 362.
34. See Manning, "The Aristocracy and the Downfall of Charles I," and Gardiner, *History of England*, vols. 9 and 10.

early 1643 he refused an offer of mutual demobilization before talks began, a piece of obstinacy which helped Pym mightily in his efforts to stiffen the House of Commons against the royalist cause. During the early and militarily inconclusive stages of the war, the Parliamentary leaders, like French Catholic and Protestant rebels in the sixteenth century, carefully maintained the fiction that they were fighting the king's evil councillors rather than the king himself, and in the winter of 1644–45 they offered a settlement based on the abolition of episcopacy and the exclusion of prominent royalists from a general pardon. Charles, who now believed that God had been punishing him for the sacrifice of Strafford, utterly refused.

The continuation of the war further divided the Parliamentary side. In 1644 a coalition of the middle group and the war party agreed to entice the Scots into the war by signing the Solemn League and Covenant, in which the Scots tried to commit the English to setting up a thoroughly Presbyterian church. But during the next two years, various divergences both of ends and means became apparent. The war party, in which Oliver Cromwell had emerged as a prominent member, now began to argue that peers like Essex and Manchester, whose armies had performed erratically, did not really want to win the war. In response, the old peace party—which had been joined by some of the now-dead Pym's adherents in the middle group—struck up an alliance with the Scots designed to settle the war on the basis of a Presbyterian church and a restored monarchy. The Self-Denying Ordinance of 1645, which sought to remove all sitting members of Parliament from military office, deprived Essex and Manchester of their commands and amalgamated their men—not without difficulty—into the New Model Army. But the peace leaders, including Denzil Holles and Philip Stapleton, dominated the Committee of Both Kingdoms, which directed the war, and after the New Model Army soundly defeated Charles in 1646 they began seriously negotiating for a settlement again.[35]

By now most of England was heartily sick of the war, and especially of the Parliamentary armies and the unprecedented taxes needed to maintain them. The Newcastle Propositions of July 1646

---

35. On these points, see Underdown, *Pride's Purge*, pp. 45–65, and Mark A. Kishlansky, *The Rise of the New Model Army* (Cambridge, 1979), pp. 26–51. Cromwell, of course, was exempted from the provisions of the Self-Denying Ordinance.

asked Charles to accept the Solemn League and Covenant, harsh measures against Catholic recusants, Parliamentary control of the fleet and militia for twenty years, and an end to the truce which Charles had arranged with the Irish rebels. The Parliamentary leaders had now managed to get the Scots to withdraw from the war in exchange for a money payment raised by the sales of bishops' lands. They now intended to disband the New Model Army as well and send a new army to Ireland to crush the rebellion there. This led to a further crisis.

Part of the issue between the Parliamentary leaders (and their allies in the City of London) and the New Model Army was ideological. The army included many republican elements, some Levellers, and a good many supporters of an independent church settlement. The two most recent students of the 1646–47 crisis, however, have argued that the army's most pressing concerns, like those of the Spanish army in the Netherlands and the various armies of the Thirty Years' War, were financial. The soldiers of the New Model Army wanted their arrears of pay and an indemnity for their acts while under arms. In March an army petition refused to sign up for Irish service until these demands were satisfied. But when Charles in May 1647 offered to accept most of the Newcastle Propositions, including a three years' trial of Presbyterianism and Parliamentary control of the militia, the Parliamentary leaders tried to disband the army again.[36] Refusing to disband, officers and men, led by Colonel Thomas Fairfax, marched on London and secured the withdrawal from Parliament of eleven members (including Denzil Holles) whom they rightly suspected of trying to make a deal with the king that would betray their interests.[37]

This scenario repeated itself almost exactly in the second half of 1648, after Charles, with the help of the Scots and the discontented counties, had unleashed the second civil war. After Charles's defeat and his surrender, the survivors of the Parliamentary middle group, undeterred by his repeated betrayals in the past, reopened

36. See Valerie Pearl, "London's Counter-Revolution," in G. E. Aylmer, ed., *The Interregnum: The Quest for a Settlement, 1646–1660* (London, 1972), pp. 29–56.

37. Both Ian Gentles, "Arrears of Pay and Ideology in the Army Revolt of 1647," in Brian Bond and Ian Roy, eds., *War and Society* (New York, 1975), pp. 45–66, and Kishlansky, *Rise of the New Model Army*, pp. 179–222, agree that the army acted mainly out of concern for its arrears of pay. Kishlansky, p. 206, notes that some soldiers, deserted by their officers, elected their own commissioners, just like soldiers in the Army of Flanders described by Geoffrey Parker.

negotiations at Newport. Charles eventually agreed to Parliamentary control of the militia for twenty years and even to the temporary abolition of episcopacy, but the war party rightly suspected him of stalling while he sought to escape or secure foreign help. In December he apparently yielded on almost all points, and despite everything, a majority of the House of Commons was still willing to reach agreement. The army, however, was not. Led by Colonel Thomas Pride, the army on December 6 purged Parliament, eventually imprisoning or secluding about 230 members. During the next two months the remaining members repudiated the negotiations with Charles, tried and executed him, abolished the House of Lords, and established the Commonwealth.[38]

Thanks to David Underdown, we know a great deal about the political purposes of the New Model Army officers who carried out the purge—including Cromwell's son-in-law, Henry Ireton—and a great deal about the revolutionary members of Parliament who cooperated in it and staged the trial of the king. The officers were not Levellers—the Leveller movement had always been a minority within the army, and its influence had peaked in 1647—but they now believed that Charles simply could not be trusted, and that his reinstatement would lead rapidly to an almost complete restoration of the old order, at considerable cost to themselves. They buttressed their argument with appeals to the verdict of Divine Providence: Charles's repeated defeats, they believed, testified to the Lord's judgment upon him. Even before the purge they had asked Parliament for a fundamental reform of the government which, while leaving Parliamentary suffrage essentially unchanged, would have firmly enshrined the supremacy of Parliament and the electorate. The remonstrance also asked for judicial proceedings against Charles, if only to prove that the king could not be above the law.[39]

Underdown's most interesting conclusions relate to the 71 revolutionary members—only 15 percent of the whole House[40]—who cooperated in Pride's Purge and staged the trial of the king. Only 28 of these 71 were original members of the Long Parliament; 53 had been chosen in recruitment elections, which some suspected of having been managed by county committees to secure radical

38. Underdown, *Pride's Purge,* pp. 106–207.
39. Ibid., pp. 123–126.
40. The House had replaced royalist members with recruiting elections after 1645.

members. Significantly, of the 28 original members, 15 have been firmly identified as members of the war party in the early stages of the conflict—that is, they were among those who had shown very early hostility to the king and the House of Lords.[41] They were, by and large, men who had been elected without court or aristocratic patronage. Dividing gentry members into the greater gentry (closely allied to the peerage), county gentry (knights and their sons, who held high county offices), and lesser gentry, Underdown found higher percentages of the victims of the purge among the two more distinguished groups, and higher percentages of the purgers who were lesser gentry or merchants. The victims tended to come from older and more established families than the purgers; the purgers' median income seems to have been much lower; and they held much greater claims against the revolutionary government. Religiously, they included higher proportions of sectaries and independents, at least according to Underdown's rather tentative definitions.[42]

Underdown's minute scrutiny of this group is justified by their unusual historical significance. One must remember that they were a small minority—less than 20 percent of the Parliamentary members then sitting—and that they held extreme views. They did, however, seize political power in December 1648 and carry out a political revolution, and no other similar group ever achieved anything comparable in sixteenth- or seventeenth-century Europe. Having said that, one must note at once that they never had much chance of building a national consensus around their vision of the future of England—as many other leading political figures recognized. Both Cromwell and Thomas Fairfax, the two most important military commanders, had favored a settlement with Charles I and opposed the purge, and Cromwell subsequently opposed the abolition of the House of Lords.[43] The purgers, in short, would never have achieved political prominence, much less power, but for the split in the ruling elite that dated back to 1640, and they proved unable to keep power after 1649. Their revolution

41. Underdown, *Pride's Purge*, p. 403. Twelve more former war party members subsequently returned to Parliament in February, after the king was dead—that is, they were "conformists," to use Underdown's term.

42. Ibid., pp. 230–256, 404–407. Hexter earlier argued quite effectively that these religious terms are virtually meaningless.

43. The peerage itself was not abolished, and peers subsequently sat with the Commons.

was a product of extreme circumstances, destined to collapse within a relatively short time.

This episode does move closer to the mainstream of European politics when the revolution is analyzed from another angle. It was the leaders of the New Model Army, not the Parliamentary revolutionaries, who planned and carried out the purge that led to the trial of the king. And the steadily increasing role of the army within the Parliamentary side parallels contemporary Continental events. Much of the course of the English revolution reflected the problems of raising, maintaining, and paying off sixteenth- and seventeenth-century armies.

Like every contemporary European monarch who embarked upon a war, Parliament had from the beginning found itself short of funds. Pym's excise and income from sequestrated estates enabled Parliament to keep armies in the field from 1642 through 1646, but Parliament had to borrow about £1 million a year.[44] To secure loans, Parliament—like both sides in the Thirty Years' War—offered land as security, and many of Parliament's revolutionary *political* measures secured the land they needed. Parliament began pledging land in late 1641, when Pym used the excuse of a Catholic rebellion in Ireland to raise a Parliamentary army. Wildly exaggerating the extent of the rebellion—and therefore, the extent of the rebels' lands—Parliament tried to borrow £1 million for the new Irish Adventurers Company with Irish land as security. They eventually raised £300,000, but failed to suppress the rebellion until after Charles I's execution.[45] Still, Parliament had committed itself to a major redistribution of Irish land.

Parliament faced a new financial crisis in 1646. With popular discontent over the cost of the war on the rise, the Parliamentary leaders decided to buy the Scots' army out of the conflict. To do so they needed a cash payment of £200,000. They solved their problem by abolishing episcopacy—a step which had long been debated, but not yet taken—and by asking their creditors to double their loans and accept bishops' lands as security. Sales of bishops' lands even-

---

44. One scholar estimates Parliament's revenues during the war at about £2 million annually, with expenditures of £3 million—compared to royal revenue of 1640 of £860,000. H. J. Habbakuk, "Public Finance and the Sale of Confiscated Property during the Interregnum," *Economic History Review*, 2d ser., 15, no. 1 (1962): 70–88. See Dietz, *English Public Finance*, p. 285.

45. Karl S. Bottigheimer, *English Money and Irish Land: The Adventurers and the Cromwellian Settlement of Ireland* (Oxford, 1971), pp. 30–113.

tually retired £660,000 in debt but raised virtually no new cash.[46] Later that year, as we have seen, Parliament tried to disband the New Model Army, to which it owed substantial arrears, and send a new army to Ireland finally to suppress the revolt and redeem its promises to the adventurers. This led to the army revolt, the exclusion of the eleven members, and partial payment of arrears.

Both Mark Kishlansky and Ian Gentles have concluded that financial rather than ideological considerations governed the army's behavior in 1646–47, but no one seems to have asked the same question about the army's behavior in the fall of 1648. Its opposition to the Treaty of Newport, culminating in Pride's Purge, undoubtedly owed something to suspicions that Charles's restoration would vastly reduce its chances of collecting its arrears.[47] In any case, once the king had been tried and executed, the Rump Parliament confiscated the crown lands and put them up for sale, giving tenants and soldiers first priority of purchase. Soldiers were given the option of exchanging their arrears for debentures which could be used either to buy crown land or sold on the open market. These sales retired about £1.5 million of additional debt, but, like the sales of bishops' lands, they raised almost no new cash. Most of the purchasers were gentry or officers, some of whom had bought up their soldiers' debentures.[48] In the same year Parliament put dean and chapter lands up for sale, but these sales have not been systematically studied.

Parliament's needs, however, remained unfulfilled. Cromwell finally embarked for Ireland in 1649, brutally conquered it, and ultimately redistributed more than a third of the land in Ireland.[49] Parliament also put English royalist land up for sale in 1651, although

46. Ian Gentles, "The Sale of Bishops' Lands in the English Revolution, 1646–1660," *English Historical Review*, 95, no. 376 (July 1980): 573–596.

47. Underdown, *Pride's Purge*, p. 122, notes that the House of Commons on November 15, 1648, voted to grant the king's request to return to London and reclaim his lands and legal revenues, and that this step helped put Ireland and the army on the road to revolution. Not to make too much of what is now only a single piece of evidence, it seems quite possible that the army leaders realized that Charles's gain would be their loss.

48. Ian Gentles, "The Sales of Crown Lands during the English Revolution," *Economic History Review*, 2d ser., 26, no. 4 (November 1973): 614–635.

49. Bottigheimer, *English Money and Irish Land*, pp. 3, 115–142. Although we know little about who actually got the land, Bottigheimer states that whereas English and Scottish Protestants held 41 percent of the land in Ireland in 1640, they owned 78 percent in 1688.

the royalists themselves repurchased the vast majority of it, thereby turning the measure into a disguised fine.[50]

Although no one has systematically analyzed the political role of the army during the interregnum, it seems clear that its role was if anything even greater than in 1646–1649. Despite all the financial expedients noted above, arrears of pay remained a key issue. Interestingly enough, the extreme political ideas which had gained a foothold in the army made little headway after the execution of the king. The Parliamentary Rump moved quickly back toward the center, rejecting the army's Agreement of the People, standing by plans for a disciplined national church, and crushing the Leveller mutinies of 1649.[51] These measures antagonized remaining radicals in the army, led by Major General Thomas Harrison. In early 1652 the Rump declared war upon the Dutch to enforce the Navigation Act, and in the fall it had to confiscate the estates of six hundred additional royalists to help pay for it. The army apparently cherished the hope that new elections would return a more friendly assembly, and in early 1653 they persuaded Cromwell to dissolve the Rump.[52]

Cromwell was now head of government in fact, six months before he became lord protector in December 1653. We need not discuss the complex series of assemblies and constitutional devices which he adopted in his search for a lasting settlement. Recent historians, on the whole, have given Cromwell considerable credit for a conciliatory temper. As already noted, he had favored a settlement with the king at the time of the Treaty of Newport. He also tried to secure better treatment for royalists after the dissolution of the Rump. Yet neither he nor anyone else could solve the two problems that faced the Commonwealth regime: the financial problem, and, in G. E. Aylmer's words, the difficulty of reconciling constitutional government with minority rule.[53] The army's views on religion represented a very small minority of the popula-

50. Joan Thirsk, "The Sales of Royalist Land during the Interregnum," *Economic History Review,* 2d ser., 5, no. 2 (1952): 188–205.

51. Underdown, *Pride's Purge,* pp. 258–296.

52. This admittedly vast oversimplification of a long series of complex events is based upon Blair Worden, *The Rump Parliament, 1648–1653* (Cambridge, 1974); see also Austin Woolrych, "Oliver Cromwell and the Rule of the Saints," in Ivan Roots, ed., *Cromwell: A Profile* (New York, 1973), pp. 50–71.

53. G. E. Aylmer, "The Quest for a Settlement, 1646–1660," in Aylmer, ed., *The Interregnum: The Quest for a Settlement, 1646–1660* (London, 1972), pp. 3–28.

tion, and the country, as the elections to Barebone's Parliament in 1653 showed, still deferred to its traditional leaders, who far outnumbered the radicals in the new assembly.[54]

The Commonwealth's credit collapsed in 1654, and the rule of the major generals, instituted in the following year after a royalist rising, was the next financial expedient. Cromwell empowered the major generals to collect new fines from several broadly defined categories of royalists, but this was not enough. "The only way the state could have paid its way in the long run," H. J. Habbakuk has written, "was by drastically reducing its military and naval commitments and releasing an income to service a debt. But how could it reduce the army substantially? It was the foundation of the regime, and its support against a royalist revival; and in any case they could not easily disband troops without paying their arrears, and this they were not in a position to do."[55] Cromwell secured some more cash by making an anti-Spanish alliance with Mazarin, but by 1659—a year after Cromwell's death—the Commonwealth's credit collapsed once and for all. Much of the army mutinied and disintegrated, and General Monk marched his troops in from Scotland and invited Charles II to return to England.

The failure of Charles I to reach agreement with the opposition in 1640–1642, as the rules of early modern politics required him to do, had led to the civil war. The civil war created the New Model Army, which rapidly built up claims upon Parliament that were difficult, if not impossible, to satisfy. Acting together with a small group of allies within Parliament, the New Model Army in 1648–49 supplanted England's traditional political leadership. During the next ten years, with Cromwell at its head, it tried to impose its rule. As an extreme regime, however, it could not command a consensus; and like the duke of Alba in Holland, it lacked the financial and administrative resources necessary to maintain its rule indefinitely. The crisis in English politics, which so much of the country seems to have regretted for so long, came to an end when the army finally collapsed.

The revolutionary phase of the civil wars, moreover, left virtually no legacy behind it. As Hexter and Zagorin have both pointed out, Charles II returned essentially under the terms of the legisla-

54. Woolrych, "Oliver Cromwell and the Rule of the Saints."
55. Habbakuk, "Public Finance and the Sale of Confiscated Property," p. 85.

tion of 1641—with the significant exception of the Triennial Act. Wardship and the prerogative courts remained abolished, stripping the king of important weapons against his political opponents. But Charles II's relations with his Parliaments were quite similar to those of James I. As before, Parliament argued with the monarch over money and foreign policy; as before, it impeached ministers who had become too powerful; as before, the king managed without Parliament for long periods of time.[56] Significantly, both crown and church lands returned to their original owners— and royalists, it is now quite clear, had generally succeeded in retaining their lands during the interregnum.[57] Only in Ireland did wholesale land transfers last. Thus landed wealth, still generally the basis of political power, remained in essentially the same hands. Most striking of all, considering the fervor of the revolution, is the lack of lasting religious change. Arminianism and Laud's ceremonial innovations disappeared, but episcopacy was immediately reestablished, confirming that the Puritans on the Parliamentary side had never really agreed upon the shape of a new national church. Indeed, recent research has found that some bishops had continued to ordain priests during the 1640s, and that many churches seem to have observed old rituals during the 1650s.[58] A recent study argues effectively that most politically active gentry saw the critical religious problems facing England in the years 1660–1688 in the same way as their forefathers had seen the issues of 1621–1641. The critical issue, in both cases, was resistance to Catholicism and popish innovations.[59]

England in 1660 still found itself in a transitional period—a transition between the age of feudal retainers, which had gradually receded under the Tudors, and a new age in which elections to the House of Commons would become the decisive battlefield in aristocratic factional conflict. In the meantime, both Charles I and the New Model Army, like various Continental sovereigns, had made

56. See below, pp. 157–159.

57. Joan Thirsk, "The Restoration Land Settlement," *Journal of Modern History*, 26, no. 4 (December 1954): 315–328; I. M. Green, *The Re-Establishment of the Church of England, 1660–63* (Oxford, 1978); and C. D. Chandaman, *The English Public Revenue, 1660–1688* (Oxford, 1965), pp. 110–111.

58. J. S. Morrill, "The Church in England, 1642–49," in Morrill, ed., *Reactions to the English Civil War*, pp. 90–114.

59. Michael Finlayson, *Historians, Puritanism, and the English Revolution: The Religious Factor in English Politics before and after the Interregnum* (Toronto, 1983).

their own bids for political supremacy and religious change, and both had failed. England during the century 1559–1659 enjoyed more peace and prosperity than the nations of Europe, but its politics showed many of the same features, especially after 1640, when Charles I, emulating Philip II, Richelieu, Olivares, and Ferdinand II, tried to increase his authority beyond his means.

The Failure of the State

The history of major conflicts from 1559 through 1659 shows clearly that while Charles Tilly's definition of the post-1500 European state—distinguished by its control of "a well-defined, contiguous territory," its "tendency to acquire a monopoly over the concentrated means of political coercion within its territory," and its differentiation from other organizations—may reflect the pretensions of a few European governments, it does not reflect political reality.[1] The factions that supported monarchs and favorites were not differentiated from other factions, monarchs possessed very little centralized authority, and both monarchs and aristocrats ignored the theoretical territorial limits of princely authority. Above all, monarchs generally lacked the element of political power which Max Weber also defined as the essence of statehood: a monopoly of legitimate force. Tilly's argument reflects one of the most common tendencies of modern historians, the tendency to exaggerate the pace of political change, particularly with respect to the growth of central authority.[2] In reality, those European monarchs and favorites such as Philip II, Charles II, Ferdinand II, Richelieu, and Mazarin who tried to claim exclusive political authority simply showed how inadequate the political, financial, and military foundations of their authority were. Because contemporary monarchies lacked the essential features of statehood, even the fundamental distinction between internal and international conflict only occasionally applies to the wars of the late sixteenth and early seventeenth centuries.

The chaos of the years 1559–1659 grew out of the ethos of the European nobility. The nobility may have fought so fiercely for land, honors, money, and prestige partly out of economic need,

1. Tilly, "Reflections on the History of European State-Making," p. 27.
2. An even more striking example of this tendency is Joseph R. Strayer, *On the Medieval Origins of the Modern State* (Princeton, 1970).

and the history of the Thirty Years' War, in particular, suggests that the aristocracy was growing too quickly for the economy to support all its members in the style to which they were accustomed. But since many of the struggles involved parties who were all enormously rich, and since so many quarrels grew out of noneconomic issues, and often out of purely personal ones, one must conclude that conflict owed more to the prevailing aristocratic temperament, a social and psychological phenomenon which needs more systematic analysis. At the same time, European monarchs—themselves very much imbued with the aristocratic ethos—made claims upon their subjects' loyalties and resources which they could not consistently enforce. The wars which resulted served the interests of nobles and other soldiers who wanted to fight, and of bankers and provisioners who made them possible. Yet they achieved very little and imposed a huge cost upon the population of Europe.

The political conflicts of the period 1559–1659 had severe economic and demographic consequences. In the years 1567–1609 the primary conflict in Europe—and the primary place of employment for military entrepreneurs—was the Spanish-Dutch war in the Netherlands. The Dutch managed to finance much of their half of the war out of loans from Amsterdam merchants, and thanks to the prosperity of Dutch trade, they managed to repay them. The Spaniards, however, financed the war mainly with gold and silver imported from the New World—the sixteenth-century equivalent of printing money. In addition, as we have seen, Philip II periodically repudiated his short-term obligations in ways which also had the effect of increasing the amount of negotiable currency in circulation. These measures contributed mightily to the European inflation of the second half of the sixteenth century—an inflation which acted as a disguised tax upon European society.[3] Evidence also suggests that France suffered economic and demographic decline during the period of the civil wars, as well.[4]

Beginning in 1618, the soldiery of Europe found employment in Germany. During the next fifteen years the size of armies swelled

3. Redlich, *German Military Enterpriser,* I, 157–162, points out that the Austro-Ottoman war in Hungary also provided employment for late sixteenth- and early seventeenth-century soldiers.

4. Buisseret, *Henry IV,* pp. 178–180, also concludes that France was probably at a Malthusian peak around 1550.

rapidly, until by 1632 both the imperial and Swedish armies numbered about 100,000 men. Very little Spanish silver found its way into Germany, however, and the inability of the European economy to finance war on such a scale became immediately apparent. First, in subsequent years these armies melted away, falling to about one-quarter of their peak size before the end of the war. Second, the remaining soldiers—left without adequate payments from their home governments—began the ruthless exploitation of the battle areas which eventually depopulated large parts of Germany. Confiscations financed the Thirty Years' War, with devastating demographic effects. It is almost certainly not a coincidence that the population of Europe as a whole, which grew during the sixteenth century, declined significantly in the first half of the seventeenth.[5]

Statesmen like Elizabeth I, Henry IV, and even Richelieu recognized the limitations of their authority and the destructiveness of war and often sought to avoid it. Their temperaments did not however prevail within the European ruling class of the late sixteenth and early seventeenth centuries. For the most part, Europe in the years 1559–1659 was the scene of an endless struggle for wealth, power, and influence—a struggle which endured despite the inability of European society to finance it or even to reward the victors. The only real result of the conflict was the impoverishment and depopulation of much of Europe—and, perhaps, a revulsion against anarchy which helped European princes establish more stable authority in the second half of the seventeenth century.[6]

5. On the economic effects of the Thirty Years' War, see above, p. 109. On European population, see Roger Mols S.J., "Population in Europe, 1500–1700," in Carlo M. Cipolla, ed., *The Fontana History of Europe: The Sixteenth and Seventeenth Centuries* (Glasgow, 1974), pp. 38–44.

6. This is suggested by Rabb, *Struggle for Stability*, pp. 100–145.

2   The Age of Louis XIV

The entire art of politics consists in playing upon circumstances.

—Louis XIV, king of France and of Navarre

The Coming of a New Era

European domestic and international politics changed dramatically after 1661. In the previous century, monarchs' attempts to assert their authority had produced chaos. Now, by increasing their resources and carefully moderating their goals, European princes placed their authority upon a sure footing. Many things, to be sure, remained the same. The aristocratic ethos still ruled the upper reaches of society and politics, and the atmosphere of politics still reeked of suspicion, treachery, and hatred. War, moreover, remained a normal feature of European life, occupying well over half the time between 1659 and 1713, and the populations of Europe still suffered from the burden of paying for the ruling class's favorite pursuit. But during this period, and for the first time, the control of international politics passed definitely into the hands of the European monarchies. The general strengthening of European states which had failed to occur in the late sixteenth and early seventeenth centuries took place in the era of Louis XIV. Political institutions changed only marginally, but Louis XIV and his fellow monarchs nonetheless solved the key problems of allegiance and revenue far more successfully than their fathers and grandfathers. Their conduct of international politics played a key role in their success.

European monarchs in the late seventeenth century acquired new political and economic resources and vigorously asserted new rights, both domestically and internationally. The most obvious symbols of new monarchical authority were the standing army, which enabled princes to co-opt the inherent violence of the aristocracy and to deal much more harshly with independent political or religious entities, and the lavish court, which kept the great men of the realm around the prince. Both of these required increased revenue, which came from an increase in commerce, from the authority exercised by the army, and in many cases—crucially, from our perspective—from participation in international politics. Specifically, whereas in the sixteenth century monarchs frequently fought one another by subsidizing factions within foreign countries, in the late seventeenth century they preferred to subsidize foreign princes. The large, intricate, and rapidly shifting coalitions that fought the wars of the late seventeenth century strengthened princes throughout Europe, since the richer members of a coalition generally paid the poorer to raise and maintain troops, and these troops frequently served a domestic purpose. Meanwhile, the instruments of war passed firmly into the control of European states, where they have remained except in times of the most extreme crisis ever since.

Wars now revolved mainly around two types of issues: the dynastic rights of princes, who sought to extend their rights and increase their inheritance abroad as well as at home (the Spanish succession, of course, was the single most important dynastic question of the period); and the trading rights of their peoples, who fought for larger shares of Europe's growing wealth and trade. The English and French became leading players in the mercantilist struggle for trade and profit, which in the previous century had concerned mainly the Spanish, the Portuguese, and the Dutch. In peacetime states fought over trade with the help of navigation acts, tariffs, and other restrictions, while in wartime they turned to naval warfare and overseas expeditions. Economic growth and economic warfare did not upset the prevailing political and social structure. Trade, like the right to raise an army or administer a vacant estate, was a privilege granted by the monarch, and monarchs and their ministers used these privileges to strengthen their own parties within their domains. But the growing emphasis upon trade as a source of conflict shifted warfare slightly from the land to the sea, where it was generally much less destructive.

During this period European monarchs also developed new techniques to keep wars within well-defined territorial and temporal limits. They generally fought slow-moving, careful, almost ritualistic campaigns based upon siege warfare; they carried on active diplomacy even in the midst of conflicts; they were generally willing to moderate their territorial claims; and they negotiated frequent, relatively even-handed peace treaties. Although war was only slightly less frequent in the era of Louis XIV than in the preceding century, peace treaties were much more so, with no less than three general European settlements between 1661 and 1715. Monarchs generally fought wars for limited aims. Publicists frequently accused rival monarchs of seeking total victory over their enemies, and one or two of them briefly dreamed of it, but opportunities for complete victory repeatedly proved illusory, and the peace treaties arrived at reflected an explicit conception of a balance of power.

To understand the sources and consequences of European international conflict in the era of Louis XIV, we must look first at the policies of the major European monarchies. Their attempts to strengthen themselves not only led to war, but also to political change within smaller states. From 1661 through 1688 the French monarchy led the way, but after 1688 the British monarchy and the Dutch republic increasingly copied Louis XIV's foreign policy. An examination of political developments within individual states will enable us also to understand the nature of international conflict itself, the ways in which the European powers controlled it, and its overall impact upon Europe in the late sixteenth and early seventeenth centuries.

The France of Louis XIV

Just as both the domestic and international politics of the years 1559–1659 reflect the weakness of contemporary European monarchs, the politics of the years 1661–1715 reflect their growing strength. But domestically and internationally, European monarchs increased their resources, built stronger instruments of power, and, for the most part, combined their growing strength with a careful assertion of their legal rights to improve their position. They also showed considerable tactical flexibility and frequently resorted to negotiation when force failed to achieve their ends. Louis XIV was the first monarch not only to undertake these changes but also to spread them through the rest of Europe by means of his foreign policy.

Many nineteenth- and twentieth-century historians have exaggerated the nature of Louis XIV's domestic achievements. He did not break the power of the nobility, or build his regime upon a new, more bureaucratic form of legitimacy, or command the absolute obedience of his subjects.[1] Instead, he took advantage of the ethos of the ruling class in ways begun by Richelieu and Mazarin. One of the most eminent French authorities on the early modern period has suggested that Louis XIV, far from intending to substitute more modern concepts of authority for the ties between *maîtres* and *fidèles* that held together the networks of the upper reaches of society, tried instead to become the sole *maître* to whom all *fidèles* would pledge their lives and fortunes.[2] Another very recent study argues that Louis actually restored some of the precedence and prestige of the nobility of the sword, and showed by his distribution of new honors that he had no intention of raising any other class to challenge them. His power, in short, depended upon the manipulation, rather than the elimination, or aristocratic values.[3]

Louis seems to have managed the nobility in two main ways. By forcing the leading nobles to wait upon him at court, he forced them to compete for his personal favor and for many seemingly trivial marks of distinction, kept an eye on their intrigues, and made it impossible for them to maintain the large retinues which had made their forefathers laws unto themselves in the countryside.[4] The court also remained the source of substantial favors, ranging from outright gifts and pensions—which Louis seems to have dispensed quite liberally—to commercial and industrial concessions and advantageous marriages.[5] Monarchs all over Europe zealously copied Louis's lavish court, sometimes with the help of subsidies from Louis himself.

Louis's power—like that of Richelieu and Mazarin before him—rested on his own intricate system of patronage, and his most important clients behaved in highly traditional ways. The members

1. See Roger Mettam, *Power and Faction in Louis XIV's France* (New York, 1988), pp. 13–44.

2. Mousnier, *Les institutions de la France*, vol. I, *Société et état*, pp. 85–93.

3. Mettam, *Power and Faction*, pp. 200–202.

4. Kettering, *Patrons, Brokers, and Clients*, pp. 220–222; Mettam, *Power and Faction*, pp. 45–57.

5. David Parker, *The Making of French Absolutism* (New York, 1983), pp. 141–142. No systematic study of Louis's use of pensions seems to exist. Recent studies tend to confirm the argument of Perry Anderson, *Lineages of the Absolutist State* (London, 1974), that noblemen of the late sixteenth century began to rely on the crown for the distribution of the national economic surplus, rather than directly collecting it themselves.

of Louis's inner council all came from three families—the Colbert, Le Tellier, and Phélypeux clans. Although not among the oldest noble families in France, these clans had already achieved distinction through service to the crown and amassed large fortunes, and during Louis's reign they intermarried both with each other and with families from the older nobility.[6] And while keeping many of the leading nobles at court, Louis also built an elaborate network of friendly nobles throughout the country—a network without which, in the view of the most recent student of the subject, he would have found it impossible to govern France.[7]

Jean-Baptiste Colbert—whom so many historians have cited as the purveyor of a new, more bourgeois style of government—emerges from recent treatments as a generally traditional figure, far more similar to Wallenstein than to Gladstone. Like Richelieu and Mazarin, Colbert built an elaborate network of provincial clienteles which drew local officials into the royal orbit. Colbert had emerged from the legal bureaucracy, but he, like Antonio Perez and William Cecil a century earlier, used his power to acquire offices, castles, and seigneuries for himself and his large family.[8] And although Colbert championed the government, headquartered in Paris, against the claims of the court in Versailles, he specifically acknowledged the primacy of traditional warlike values over all others. "Apart from glorious actions of war," he wrote in 1665, "nothing celebrates so advantageously the greatness and genius of princes than buildings."[9]

Financially, Roger Mettam has recently argued, Louis and Colbert depended far more upon negotiation and the cooperation of local officials and less upon the authority of the new intendants than many historians of "absolutism" have suggested. The provincial estates, in particular, frequently insisted upon reconfirmation of local privileges before meeting the crown's demands and often failed to pay promised revenues.[10] Like Philip II a century earlier,

6. François Bluc, "The Social Origins of the Secretaries of State under Louis XIV, 1661–1715," in Ragnhild Hatton, ed., Louis XIV and Absolutism (Columbus, 1976), pp. 85–87.

7. Mettam, Power and Faction, pp. 44–47, 53–54.

8. See Daniel Dessert and Jean-Louis Journel, "Le lobby Colbert, royaume, ou une affaire de famille?" Annales, ESC, 30, no. 6 (1975): 1303–36.

9. Quoted in Gilette Ziegler, At the Court of Versailles: Eye-Witness Reports from the Reign of Louis XIV (New York, 1966), p. 26.

10. Mettam, Power and Faction, pp. 268–277.

Colbert initially managed to substitute his own officials for bankers in the collection of the revenue. He reduced annual debt service from 30 million French livres to 8 million and increased revenue from about 37 million livres in 1661 to 65 million in 1671.[11] But his reforms, like Philip's, did not survive Louis's first major war. During the conflict with the Dutch in 1672–1678 all the old practices of anticipating revenues, relying upon financiers, and debasing the coinage resumed as before.[12]

Colbert's attitude toward economic life was highly traditional. While he sought to encourage French industry, he held the already outmoded view that the sum of the world's commerce was fixed, and he therefore simply sought to divert it to his own creatures at the expense of enemies both foreign and domestic.[13] His own economic program focused almost exclusively upon projects of military, colonial, and naval interest, rather than upon the general economic health of the country. Furthermore, he generally failed either to interest many Frenchmen in his companies and reforms or to turn much of a profit. He did manage to attract some foreign artisans into France—concentrating, like Wallenstein, upon specialists in armaments—but in general his attempts to restructure the French economy so as to increase the power of the state met with little success.[14]

"The royal bureaucracy," concludes a recent study, "certainly never detached itself from the complex maze of lineages, clienteles and patrimonial interests from which it had emerged . . . Absolutism did not involve any dramatic break with the past."[15] Struggles over policy, as Louis himself fully recognized, generally turned on struggles for power at court, within which policy simply became a pretext. "I had no doubt," Louis wrote to the dauphin describing the presumed state of opinion regarding the continuation of war in 1668, "that those who were employed in the war would unconsciously favor its continuation, and moreover, it was easy to see

---

11. Goubert, *Louis XIV*, pp. 119–123.

12. Inès Murat, *Colbert* (Charlottesville, 1984), is a fine short treatment.

13. See C. W. Cole, *Colbert and a Century of French Militarism*, 2 vols. (New York, 1939); Lionel Rothkrug, *Opposition to Louis XIV: The Political and Social Origins of the French Enlightenment* (Princeton, 1965), pp. 179–211; and Edmond Silberner, *La guerre dans la pensée économique du XVIème au XVIIIème siècle* (Paris 1939), pp. 7–11, 33–38.

14. Mettam, *Power and Faction*, pp. 189–192, 288–306.

15. Parker, *French Absolutism*, p. 159.

that the people whom I employed in my other councils, finding it inconvenient to follow me to the armies and being jealous of those who did, would naturally all be for peace." [16] And all the while, the government's role in society reflected the values of the greatest aristocrat, Louis himself, greedy for glory and eager for war. Power, glory, and war were the business of the monarchy, and the French state in the second half of the seventeenth century was *more* oriented toward war than in the second half of the sixteenth. Louis, however, carried on war in such as way as to strengthen the monarchy rather than weaken it.

Louis did create one vital new instrument of his authority, the standing army. He used the army to co-opt the violence endemic to European society in the seventeenth century and to assert his claims both against his own subjects and against foreign states. "We find ourselves obliged," Louis wrote Marshal Turenne in 1659, before he had assumed real power, "for the conservation of our state as much as for its glory and our reputation, to maintain . . . in peace as well as in war, a great number of troops, both infantry and cavalry, which will always be ready and in good condition to act to keep our people in the obedience and the respect that they owe us, to insure the peace and the tranquility that they have won . . . and to aid our allies." [17] After Louis began to rule in 1661, the army grew from a few thousand men in 1661 to 72,000 in 1667 and 120,000 in 1672, and reached more than 150,000 even in the peacetime years of the early 1680s. [18] Louis and his secretaries of state for war, Michel Le Tellier and his son Louvois, worked hard to bring the army under firmer royal control. Louis refused to replace the colonel-general of France when he died early in the reign because, as he wrote in his memoirs, "the appointment of subordinate officers which had been attached to [the office] gave [the colonel-general] the means of placing his followers everywhere and gave him more control than the king himself over the principal forces of the state." [19] Regiments were no longer named for their officers, the

---

16. Louis XIV, King of France, *Memoires for the Instruction of the Dauphin*, ed. Paul Sonnino (New York, 1970), p. 258.

17. John B. Wolf, *Louis XIV* (New York, 1968), p. 148.

18. Camille Rousset, *Histoire de Louvois et de son administration politique et militaire*, 4 vols. (Paris, 1862–63), IV, 80–102; also Lavisse, *Louis XIV, de 1643 à 1685*, p. 238.

19. Sonnino, ed., *Memoires*, p. 44.

state tried to pay regular salaries, and Louis and his ministers attempted to introduce promotion by merit as an alternative to venality as a means of filling vacancies. They also tried to set up more magazines and supply depots around the country and to regularize the collection of contributions, so that troops need not be left to live off the population unless Louis, for political reasons, wanted them to do so.[20] Both Louis and his fellow European monarchs also seem to have been able to raise larger armies simply because the average soldier's wages were declining in the latter half of the seventeenth century.[21] The organization of the army, however, retained many traditional aspects. Colonels still bought their regiments and even retained the right to sell their subordinate commissions. The problem of phantom soldiers—for whom colonels happily collected pay—continued to plague the military administration throughout the reign.

The army became a highly effective instrument for the enforcement of royal authority, and Louis used it both to put down peasant insurrections and to strip rival power sources of their authority. The quartering of troops upon rebellious areas—the so-called *dragonnades*—could both crush and deter local revolts like those of the first half of the century. Louis used the army to put down rebellions like those in Brittany in 1675, to intimidate provincial estates, and to reduce the power of towns—most notably in Marseilles, where he undertook in 1661 the first important initiative of his reign.[22] And the army played the crucial role in bringing about the almost complete elimination of Protestantism in France, beginning with the dragonnades against unconverted Huguenots undertaken by the intendant Marillac in Poitou in 1681.[23] Troops remained capable of the most frightful cruelties, so that the mere threat of a dragonnade often ended a local disturbance. International conflict provided another means of supporting the army: "My various ideas always obliging me to maintain a great number of troops, it would be more convenient for me to thrust them upon

20. Rousset, *Histoire de Louvois*, III, 315–322; A. Corvisier, *La France de Louis XIV, 1643–1715: Ordre intérieur et place en Europe* (2d ed., Paris, 1979), pp. 176–197. Mettam, *Power and Faction*, pp. 220–223, also notes that attempts to replace billeting of troops with contributions did not get very far.

21. Redlich, *German Military Enterpriser*, II, 51–53.

22. Parker, *French Absolutism*, pp. 122–125.

23. Elisabeth Labrousse, *"Une foi, une loi, un roi"? La révocation de l'Edit de Nantes* (Paris, 1985), pp. 167–196.

the domains of the King of Spain than to feed them constantly at the expense of my subjects," Louis wrote bluntly in 1666.[24]

Louis's policy toward the nobility also helped ensure that rival sources of military power would not arise, as they had during the previous century. A recent work confirms the traditional view of the importance of the Versailles court, where the nobility became Louis's retinue, and where it was impossible for them to maintain large households of their own.[25] The court intrigues absorbed energies that might earlier have been spent in the organization of local revolts, and provided opportunities for profit to replace those that had come earlier from the forcible appropriation of royal revenues.[26] Louis's control of violence was not absolute, and like Richelieu, he never managed to stamp out dueling, but by bringing the aristocracy within his orbit, he drastically reduced the incidence of local rebellions. When serious rebellions did occur, he combined force with compromise[27]—just as he did in foreign policy.

Louis's policy toward the Huguenots gives an excellent example of his political technique and parallels many of his foreign policy initiatives. He began by bribing the relatively few remaining Huguenot nobles to convert to Catholicism while undertaking a series of measures to restrict Huguenot rights to the letter of the Edict of Nantes. Thus in 1665 he eliminated the Protestant commissioners who had shared responsibility for enforcing the terms of the edict, and he subsequently began restricting public Protestant worship and limiting the participation of Protestants in certain occupations. Ironically, the final drive against the Huguenots began in 1681, after an edict exempted newly converted Huguenots from the quartering of troops. Marillac, the intendant of Poitou, began quartering troops only among unconverted Huguenots, and this technique proved so successful that it was extended to other districts as well. The final revocation of the Edict of Nantes in 1685 was undertaken only after these measures had reduced the

24. Sonnino, ed., *Memoires*, p. 123. Mettam, *Power and Faction*, pp. 239–240, argues that the army played a relatively minor role in governing the kingdom in normal times but confirms its role in religious policy and in dealing with some peasant revolts.

25. Kettering, *Patrons, Brokers, and Clients*, pp. 230–232.

26. An excellent brief description is J. Levron, "Louis XIV's Courtiers," in Hatton, ed., *Louis XIV and Absolutism*, pp. 130–153.

27. Mettam, *Power and Faction*, pp. 310–319.

Huguenot presence substantially.[28] And since no great magnates still professed Protestantism, these steps would not lead to a new aristocratic rising.

The diplomacy and military strategy of Louis XIV, which established the pattern of international relations during the period of his reign, followed a similar pattern. The king continuously asserted his rights, including the right to be regarded as Europe's leading sovereign, his dynastic rights of inheritance, commercial rights, and claims to compensation for the gains of other powers. His claims, while often supported by extreme and specious propaganda, usually had some legal foundation. Louis was willing to pursue his claims diplomatically, and he used bribery—in the form of subsidies—to secure support for himself among other European princes. He undertook war only after much diplomatic preparation, and then watched for opportunities to conclude an advantageous peace. He generally took care not to risk his armies unnecessarily or to embark upon overly ambitious operations. His wars sometimes began with grandiose claims, but he frequently modified his aims for the sake of peace, worked hard to divide hostile coalitions, and usually took a reasonable attitude toward the demands of others. Louis loved war for its own sake, but he carefully moderated his passion so as to prevent it from threatening the foundations of his authority. Although France suffered heavily from the effects of his wars, Louis maintained the confidence of the ruling elites and never allowed those sufferings to grow to the point where another revolt like the Fronde might take place.

"Glory," Louis wrote early in his reign, "is not a mistress who can be neglected, nor is one ever worthy of her first favors if he is not always working for new ones."[29] Louis sought from the beginning the stature of the leading monarch in Europe. His insistence upon his own precedence led during the 1660s to violent clashes in London, where his ambassador disputed the honors given to his Spanish colleague, and in Rome, where Louis felt that the pope had not shown him adequate respect.[30] Similarly, he found it natural that he, or another member of his house, should occupy the elective office of Holy Roman Emperor, and sought the votes of the electors in many complicated negotiations. By the early 1680s, in-

28. Labrousse, *La révocation de l'Edit de Nantes,* pp. 113–196.
29. Sonnino, ed., *Memoires,* p. 37.
30. Louis André, *Louis XIV et l'Europe* (Paris, 1950), pp. 55, 59–61.

deed, he had secured promises from a majority of the imperial electors to vote for him or his son should an election either of a new Holy Roman Emperor or a new king of the Romans be held, but the emperor Leopold eventually outmaneuvered him and secured the election of his son Charles as king of the Romans in 1689, while Louis was at war with most of Europe.[31] He also tried more than once to secure the election of a French candidate to the elective throne of Poland, but he never succeeded.[32]

Louis asserted all possible dynastic rights of inheritance, although with respect to the most important dynastic question of his reign, the Spanish succession, he generally showed a willingness to compromise. It is often forgotten that while Louis claimed the succession for his house, he never intended that either he or his son or grandson should rule both France and Spain. He also generally recognized that any Bourbon candidate for the Spanish throne would have to share the empire with rival claimants. Louis's initial claims arose because although his first wife Maria Theresa, the daughter of Philip IV, had given up any rights to the succession at the time of her marriage, Louis claimed that the Spaniards' failure to pay her dowry had invalidated her renunciation. Thus in 1665, when Philip IV of Spain died, Louis's lawyers apparently discovered provisions of the law of the Spanish Netherlands which entitled Maria Theresa—child of an earlier marriage of Philip IV than the new king, Carlos II[33]—to an immediate share of Philip's inheritance. He went to war in 1667 to make good his claims, but in the next year he made a treaty with the other leading claimant, the Holy Roman Emperor Leopold, in which he ceded his rights to the Spanish crown itself in exchange for gains in the Low Countries, Italy, and the Pacific.

Louis varied the breadth of his claims to the Spanish inheritance in response to changes in the balance of power. At the height of his power in the mid-1680s, when the emperor found himself fully

31. H. Vast, "Les tentatives de Louis XIV pour arriver a l'empire," *Revue Historique*, 65, pp. 1–45, discusses Louis's efforts to secure imperial election. By 1682 the electors of Brandenburg, Saxony, and Bavaria were under treaty obligation to support Louis or his son should an election be held, and the elector of Cologne had given a verbal promise to cast the fourth vote in his favor.

32. André, *Louis XIV et l'Europe*, pp. 141–143, 261–269.

33. I shall refer to Charles II of Spain as Carlos II, to distinguish him from his contemporary Charles II of Great Britain. As is well known, he was sickly and not expected to live long or have children. He did remain childless, but he lived until 1700.

occupied with the Turks, and both the English and Dutch were paralyzed by domestic problems, he reverted to attempts to secure the whole succession for his grandson.[34] But after the Nine Years' War (1688–1697), in which he failed to prevail against virtually the whole of Europe, he once again took up partition schemes, arguing indeed that *he* now needed compensation for changes in the balance of power. "I know," he wrote, "how much Europe would be alarmed to see my power raise itself above that of the house of Austria . . . But the power of the Emperor is much enlarged by the submission of the German princes and by the advantageous peace that he has just made with the Porte . . . It is to the general interest that if his becomes great, mine should always be in condition to counterbalance him."[35] In new partition treaties with William III of Great Britain and Holland, he again waived his family's claims to the Spanish throne in exchange for Lorraine and Savoy, whose princes would in turn be compensated with Spanish possession in Italy. He failed to observe the treaties, as we shall see, because of the terms of Carlos II's new will, which gave the whole empire to Louis's grandson or, should he refuse it, to the son of the emperor.

Louis also used legal claims to extend his territory into Germany during the early 1680s. In addition to waging a slow but inexorable campaign to extend the sovereign rights granted the French crown in Alsace by the Peace of Westphalia, he created special courts, the Chambre de Réunions, to argue that additional German territories had once been dependencies of territories which now belonged to himself. Characteristically, he undertook this campaign when the Turkish threat to the Holy Roman Emperor was most serious. The invasions of Flanders and Luxemburg, like the simultaneous dragonnades against the Huguenots, allowed Louis to keep virtually his whole army together even after the Treaty of Nijmegen in 1678, and to support it with massive contributions from foreign soil.[36] In 1684, after a short war with Spain, he made a twenty-year truce with the emperor, leaving the ultimate fate of these gains in doubt. He secured other important territories, including the port of Dunkirk and the Italian fortress of Casale, by purchase, and simply

---

34. André, *Louis XIV et l'Europe*, pp. 235–238.

35. Wolf, *Louis XIV*, p. 499; Wolf does not give the date of this letter, but it seems to come from the 1697–1700 period.

36. Adolphe Leave, *Essai historique sur les négociations de la trève de vingt ans conclue à Ratisbonne en 1681* (Brussels, 1881), *passim*.

took Strasbourg by force at a moment when no one could resist this coup. The king, in short, worked constantly to increase his authority, his territory, and his reputation.

Like Philip II, Louis also enjoyed posing as the defender of the Catholic religion. While struggling with successive popes for authority over the French church, he promoted the exercise of Catholicism both in Britain, where he encouraged Charles II to avow Catholicism, and in Holland, where he included plans to make Catholicism a state-supported religion in his war aims of 1672. Indeed, the Dutch war had both religious aims and dynastic-political ones. As Simon Schama has recently pointed out, both Louis and Charles II of Britain undertook the war partly to crush the Republican pretensions of the Dutch, and ironically intended to establish William of Orange as sovereign prince over a much-reduced United Provinces should they prove victorious.[37]

Louis—no less than Colbert—also keenly felt the right and the duty to promote French commerce at the expense of other nations, to found trading companies, and to encourage the growth of colonies overseas. Both of them, indeed, pursued these aims in order to strengthen French military and naval power, as much or more than for the sake of the general health of the economy. Colbert in the 1660s encouraged the formation of a West India trading company to take the trade of the French West Indies away from the Dutch and instituted a tariff war against Dutch goods.[38] Louis invaded the United Provinces in 1672 with the intention of conquering them and taking over a large portion of Dutch trade. Colbert also began a trade war with Britain in 1674, after the British made peace with the Dutch, and this conflict continued until the accession of James II in 1685.[39] The French carried out privateering wars against the British and the Dutch after 1688, and Louis ordered attacks from Canada against British colonies in New England and New York during the Nine Years' War and the War of the Spanish Succession.[40] In addition, Louis fought to maintain the illegal

37. Simon Schama, *The Embarrassment of Riches: An Interpretation of Dutch Culture in the Golden Age* (New York, 1987), pp. 272–275.

38. Nellis M. Crouse, *The French Struggle for the West Indies, 1665–1713* (New York, 1943), pp. 3–6.

39. G. N. Clark, *The Dutch Alliance and the War against French Trade, 1688–1697* (London, 1923), pp. 63–72.

40. One remarkable royal order, dispatched in 1689, instructed the governor of Canada, after conquering New York, to drive virtually the entire English and Dutch popu-

French trading position at Cadiz, where French merchants bribed Spanish officials for the right to trade with the Indies. Louis occasionally threatened force to secure the return of fines.[41] Finally, Louis after 1700 hoped to secure advantageous trade privileges in the Spanish empire from his grandson Philip V, including the *asiento* to supply slaves and rights to sell French exports. Indeed, Louis apparently valued these prizes more highly than the maintenance of the Bourbon dynasty in Spain. "The principal object of the present war," he wrote in 1709, "is the commerce of the Indies and the riches they produce."[42]

What most distinguishes Louis's foreign policy from the monarchs of the previous century, however, is his careful regulation of the use of force. While embarking upon war far more frequently, Louis almost always combined war with skillful diplomacy and a willingness to make necessary compromises. Thus, while France was at war for approximately thirty of the fifty-four years of his rule, no single war lasted even half as long as Richelieu and Mazarin's struggle with Spain. As a result, his wars—unlike those of Philip II, Olivares, Richelieu, Mazarin, and Ferdinand II—rarely threatened his domestic political power.[43]

Louis began wars three times: in 1667, against Spain; in 1672, against the Dutch; and in 1688, when he occupied Cologne and the Palatinate, attacked the United Provinces, and helped the deposed James II of Britain mount an expedition to Ireland. He was attacked twice: in 1683, when the Spaniards decided to contest the reunions in the Rhineland, and in 1701, when the Anglo-Dutch-Hapsburg coalition decided to fight for the Spanish succession. His first two campaigns began only after the most careful diplomatic preparation. Before attacking Spain in 1667, he made sure of the neutrality of the United Provinces and England, the alliance of Portugal, and the cooperation of Neuburg, Mainz, Cologne, and Münster, who agreed to bar any attempt by the emperor Leopold, with whom Louis's negotiations had failed, to intervene. (As already noted,

---

lation out of the colony. See Francis Parkman, *Count Frontenac and the New France under Louis XIV* (Boston, 1894), p. 189.

41. Albert Girard, *Le commerce français à Séville et Cadix au temps des Habsbourg* (Paris, 1932), pp. 268–334.

42. Quoted in Ragnhild Hatton, *Europe in the Age of Louis XIV* (New York, 1969), p. 215.

43. André, *Louis XIV et l'Europe*, gives the best survey of Louis's foreign policy.

Leopold did agree to a treaty partitioning for the Spanish empire in the following year.) By 1672, he had secured the alliance of Great Britain, Sweden, and several minor German states with subsidy treaties, and the neutrality of the emperor. We shall see that these subsidies, which were subsequently copied by William III and Marlborough, had a critical effect upon their recipients as well and became a key element in their domestic politics. Louis undertook the Nine Years' War without comparable diplomatic preparation, but he was reacting in 1688 to the shock of William III's descent upon England, an event which he knew was likely to upset the whole balance of power.

The issue of war and peace, it is clear, weighed most heavily upon Louis when King Carlos II died in 1700 and offered Louis's grandson Philip the whole Spanish inheritance in his will. He evidently thought long and hard before accepting the will, but concluded that if he failed to do so, the emperor Leopold's son would become the heir to the whole empire, and Louis would have to declare war to secure the Italian territories that the last partition treaty had promised to the French crown.[44] Characteristically, however, Louis could not resist taking maximum advantage of the will, even after the British and the Dutch had recognized Philip as Philip V of Spain. French troops ejected Dutch soldiers from barrier fortresses in the Spanish Netherlands that they had occupied since 1697, and Philip granted the French new trading privileges in the Spanish empire overseas. The English and Dutch, together with the emperor—who claimed the whole inheritance for his son—declared the last great war of the era.

Once in a war, Louis waged it with great care. Although we lack any really systematic studies of his armies, they seem to have been somewhat better organized and better provisioned than those of the Thirty Years' War. They also seem to have moved more slowly and to have relied somewhat less upon exactions from the general population. Louis himself preferred siege warfare to mobile warfare and disliked costly attacks. Some of his campaigns, such as the invasion of Flanders in 1667, resembled a court review, complete with the queen and the current royal mistress. Again and again, as John Wolf has shown, he complained of excessive losses

44. Wolf, *Louis XIV,* pp. 505–507; Mark A. Thomson, "Louis XIV and the Origins of the War of the Spanish Succession," in Ragnild Hatton and J. S. Bromley, eds., *William III and Louis XIV* (Liverpool, 1968), pp. 213–236.

among his troops, especially among the officers. He was determined to keep war off of French soil and succeeded in doing so until the latter stages of the War of the Spanish Succession.[45] Certainly his troops sometimes did leave their fortresses and began living off enemy territory as in the Thirty Years' War, and they began the Nine Years' War in 1688 by laying waste to the Palatinate. Only once, however—in the Blenheim campaign of 1704—did his armies attempt a long-range march into enemy territory.

In sharp contrast to the monarchs of the previous century, Louis immediately began serious peace negotiations when wars went badly or domestic unrest threatened at home, and he showed an impressive willingness to make concessions to bring conflicts to a conclusion. Thus, when in 1668 the Dutch, English, and Swedish governments joined together to resist further French advances against the Spanish Netherlands, he rapidly made peace, even though several of his leading councillors wanted to continue the war. He began the Dutch war in 1672 with ambitious aims, but the next year, when the Dutch saved their northern provinces by flooding, Louis's response could not have been more different from that of Philip II. Rather than beat his head against this new barrier, he turned once again against Spain. By 1675 the war had strained French finances badly, leading to domestic unrest, and Marshal Vauban, one of Louis's military leaders, was already warning that troops stationed at home might be inadequate to cope with a revolt.[46] The eventual peace of 1678 returned all Louis's Dutch conquests in exchange for Franche-Comté and new territorial gains in Flanders at Spain's expense.

When Louis occupied the Palatinate and the electorate of Cologne in late 1688, he offered to withdraw at once if the empire would agree to a few further territorial concessions and confirm his candidate as elector of Cologne.[47] But his enemies, now led by William III of the United Provinces and England, preferred to fight, largely because of their growing strength and the revocation of the Edict of Nantes, which had bolstered their war parties. After some victories on land and defeats at sea, Louis was more than ready for peace by 1693, but the opposition continued to fight. A catastrophic economic crisis in France—partly an effect of Anglo-

45. Cf. Wolf, *Louis XIV*, pp. 213–246, 465–469.
46. André, *Louis XIV et l'Europe*, pp. 171–173.
47. Wolf, *Louis XIV*, p. 444.

Dutch economic warfare—cut revenue from 92 million livres in 1688 to just 60 million in 1697, despite a number of new taxes, and entailed a famine in which at least a tenth of the population seems to have died.[48] With growing opposition to the war developing, rebellion threatened again, and Louis managed by careful diplomacy to detach first Savoy, and then William III himself, from the coalition, and to retain some, though not all, of the territories he had added to his domain since 1678. Knowing his peoples' desire for peace, he wrote privately, he sacrificed his army's gains to the needs of public tranquility.[49]

The War of the Spanish Succession, which Louis had clearly hoped to avoid, grew much larger than any of his earlier wars, and at times the balance of military forces seemed to have turned decisively against him. In addition, the Huguenot Camisard revolt of 1702–1704 took two years and 20,000 men to suppress, although this revolt, unlike those of the previous reigns, was not led by powerful nobles. Thus, as early as 1705, after his troops had stabilized the situation, Louis was willing to negotiate again and to give up both the Spanish Netherlands and the Hapsburgs' Italian possessions in exchange for leaving Spain in the hands of his grandson. What kept the war going were the demands of the opposing coalition, led by the duke of Marlborough, who refused these terms and preferred to seek total victory. By 1709 France was once again on the verge of collapse. Louis was willing to surrender many of his territorial gains on the northeast frontier to get peace, but not to join his enemies to remove Philip V from the throne of Spain, as the opposing negotiators demanded. His generals managed amidst more famine and great difficulty to keep an army in being, and they won a narrow victory over the allies at Malplaquet. In the end, after long negotiations, Louis agreed to give up the Netherlands, Milan, and the two Sicilies on behalf of his grandson. He also gave up important overseas possessions, but he saved the French frontiers of 1697 and left Philip V on the throne of Spain.

Both at home and abroad, Louis XIV had vastly increased royal authority within a generally traditional framework. The Versailles palace, his elaborate court, and Louis's wars diverted the resources of French society to enterprises planned, supervised, and con-

48. Goubert, *Louis XIV*, pp. 215–222.
49. Wolf, *Louis XIV*, p. 487.

cluded by the monarch himself. His social, architectural, and military achievements clearly reflected the values of the aristocracy—values which he enthusiastically shared. Because he so consistently favored the same families, excluded the princes of the blood from policy, and imposed severe hardships upon the population—especially in the last few years of his reign—he inevitably encountered some important opposition. Influential men and their pamphleteers protested Colbert's high-tariff policy from the start, and beginning in the 1690s, when France experienced a very severe economic and demographic crisis, various voices argued that the wars cost too much and imposed excessive sufferings upon the nation.[50] But the intendants, the standing army, and the court had apparently eliminated the possibility of revolts like the Fronde or the risings of the late sixteenth century. The opposition had to pin its hopes upon the succession of the dauphin, around whom it grouped itself during the War of the Spanish Succession. Politics now centered on intrigue rather than rebellion, and the financial and military resources of the state, carefully managed by the monarch, made effective rebellion impossible. This was the real achievement of Louis XIV, and his conduct of war and diplomacy was an essential part of it.

The Maritime Powers and the Hapsburg States

To understand the role of Britain and the United Provinces in the wars of the late seventeenth century, we must begin by shedding the stereotype, so dear to Whig historians, of two fundamentally commercial, middle-class powers, increasingly dedicated to representative institutions, religious toleration, and bourgeois values, whose nature impelled them to oppose the Catholic, monarchical absolutism of Louis XIV. In fact, despite the importance of their representative institutions, the politics of Britain and the United Provinces had a highly baroque atmosphere and revolved around huge pensions, bribery, suspicions of fantastic plots, accusations of spurious children, and assassination.[1] The reigning princes behaved similarly to their great French contemporary. Charles II, James II, and William III used the resources of their states to ad-

---

50. See especially Rothkrug, *Opposition to Louis XIV.*
1. Cf. John Kenyon, *The Popish Plot* (New York, 1972), and Herbert H. Rowen, *John De Witt, Grand Pensionary of Holland, 1625–1672* (Princeton, 1979), esp. pp. 840–893.

vance their own dynastic ambitions, build clienteles, and advance their preferred religion in ways very similar to Louis XIV.[2] Eventually they also copied him diplomatically, using pensions and subsidies to solidify coalitions of minor powers after 1688 in the same way that Louis had done during the first three decades of his reign.

Furthermore, while representative institutions certainly played a much larger political role in the maritime powers than elsewhere, the membership of the English (and, after 1707, the British) Parliament and the Netherland provincial estates and States General did not consistently defend the European balance of power. Both the Whigs in England and the leaders of the Estates of Holland occasionally accepted subsidies from Louis XIV. The ruling classes of both England and the United Provinces in the late seventeenth century may have been somewhat less militarily inclined than the French or perhaps the German, and the peace parties in these countries were often stronger than in France. But these two powers showed themselves at least as willing as the French to resort to war on behalf of their commercial interests. Here, as in France, the sovereign prince (or later, in the United Provinces, Grand Pensionary Heinsius) used war to realize his own dynastic ambitions and strengthen his own party, and fought until the exhaustion of his domains forced him to make peace.

Thus, during the first twenty-five years of Louis XIV's reign, Charles II of Great Britain not only tried to strengthen his position in ways similar to Louis XIV, but did so with Louis's help. After his restoration, Charles managed with the help of Parliament to pay off the army, reestablish the Anglican church, and restore his prerogatives virtually to the level of his father's at the outset of the English revolution. Like Louis, he maintained a fairly lavish court and paid large pensions, and his normal revenue therefore generally proved inadequate to meet his needs.[3] Charles also seems to have decided never entirely to cast his lot with one favorite or faction, instead periodically dismissing and disgracing men who had become unpopular.[4]

Dynastic rights dominated the domestic politics of Charles's

2. William III, of course, was never a reigning prince in the United Provinces, merely stadholder from 1672 until his death in 1702.

3. Chandaman, English Public Revenue, esp. pp. 199–202, 261–275.

4. J. R. Jones, Charles II, Royal Politician (London, 1987), pp. 6–8.

reign. Having no legitimate heir, Charles had to contend after 1669 with increasing pressure for the exclusion of his brother James, duke of York—an avowed Roman Catholic—from the throne. By the mid-1670s, this controversy had made it almost impossible for him to secure additional revenue from Parliament without agreeing to exclusion.[5] In foreign policy, Charles faced pressure from a growing mercantilist lobby. English traders with the East and West Indies and with West Africa came frequently into conflict with the Dutch, and city merchants could count upon the support of a very powerful naval party, led by Charles's brother James. They led England into the second Dutch war in 1664, from which England emerged three exhausting years later with the Dutch colonies in North America.[6]

For most of Charles's reign, Louis helped Charles assert his dynastic rights, encourage particular religious parties—in his case, after 1670, Catholics and Protestant Dissenters—and reduce the power of competing political institutions, including Parliament and the City of London. He did so by paying secret subsidies in return for a variety of foreign policy concessions. Thus in 1670, when the exclusion issue had just arisen and Charles faced a financial crisis, Charles agreed in the Secret Treaty of Dover to declare his own adherence to Catholicism, make it the English state religion, and field fifty ships in a new Dutch war in exchange for an immediate payment of £150,000 (2 million livres) and a wartime subsidy of £225,000 annually.[7] Like many promises in contemporary treaties, Charles's religious promises do not seem to have been serious, but he did in 1672 issue a Declaration of Indulgence legalizing Catholic worship. War aims drawn up for the new war included the annexation of Dutch coastal ports and the installation of Charles's nephew William of Orange as permanent sovereign of the United Provinces.[8] When money ran out in early 1673 Charles had to call Parliament, which forced him to revoke the Declaration of Indulgence and threatened to change the succession. A year later, similar demands led to him to prorogue Parliament and make peace with the Dutch.[9]

5. Ibid., pp. 162–186.

6. Charles Wilson, *Profit and Power: A Study of England and the Dutch Wars* (New York, 1957), pp. 90–142.

7. Keith Feiling, *British Foreign Policy, 1660–1672* (London, 1968), pp. 267–308.

8. J. R. Jones, *Britain and the World, 1649–1815* (Brighton, 1980), pp. 104–105.

9. David Ogg, *England in the Reign of Charles II* (Oxford, 1936), pp. 365–386.

Louis paid Charles further subsidies to remain neutral in 1675–1677, and in 1681–1684, after Charles had definitely decided to do without Parliament for good, Louis made this easier by paying an additional £120,000 annually for three years.[10] Charles also took advantage of his position to revoke the privileges of the City of London. In the early 1680s, as Louis moved unchallenged into Germany and the Low Countries, anti-French feeling increased in England. The Whigs hoped that the international crisis might force Charles to call Parliament, but he managed to avoid doing so. In November 1681 he even warned Louis that the siege of Luxemburg was making his position very difficult, and Louis lifted the siege.[11]

Carefully limiting his involvement in Continental wars and using the help of Louis XIV to maintain his authority, Charles II, like many German princes, took advantage of contemporary international politics to strengthen his position at home. A recent study of his reign concludes that by the early 1680s he had achieved supremacy over his subjects at home in exchange for surrendering his freedom of action abroad, and states that his whole foreign policy, both in war and peace, aimed simply at increasing his authority—a remark that would apply equally well to Louis. Certainly he does not seem to have resented his dependence upon his fellow monarch, whom he had always admired.[12] Because of his conflict with Parliament over religion and the succession, he never disposed of the resources which England's very rapid economic growth was potentially making available.[13] His next three successors embarked upon very different sorts of policies.

The short reign of James II showed that the power of late seventeenth-century monarchs still depended upon the careful management of the aristocracy. James apparently ascended the throne with the intention of copying Louis XIV's army and authority.[14] Although Parliament granted him generous annual revenues when he succeeded in 1685, his attempts to build up a nationwide, largely Catholic party drove the English aristocracy to open resist-

10. Chandaman, *English Public Revenue*, pp. 29–36.

11. For Anglo-French relations generally, see Leopold von Ranke, *A History of England Principally in the Seventeenth Century*, vol. 4 (New York, 1966), pp. 58–195.

12. Jones, *Charles II, Royal Politician*, pp. 187–188.

13. Thus Feiling, *British Foreign Policy*, pp. 1–28, notes that foreign trade increased more than 50 percent between 1662 and 1688, and that the capital of English trading countries was doubling every ten years.

14. J. R. Western, *Monarchy and Revolution: The English State in the 1680s* (Totowa, N.J., 1972), pp. 82–92.

ance by 1688. He also appointed a Catholic, Lord Tyrconnell, as lord deputy in Ireland and began to favor the Catholics there, even moving to return some of the land they had lost under Cromwell. One crisis arose in England early in 1688, when Anglican bishops refused to order the reading of James's latest Declaration of Indulgence and were acquitted at the trial which James himself ordered. Then the birth of James's Catholic son in June 1688, which deprived his Protestant daughter, Mary, of the succession, frightened Protestants throughout the British Isles, and decided Mary's husband, William of Orange, to sail to England to protect his wife's rights. Virtually all of England welcomed William, and a new phase of English history began. While the English aristocracy used the crisis to establish new political rights in relation to the crown, the new king expanded England's role on the Continent.

Beginning in 1688, the role of England and English (and then, after 1707, British) politics in European international relations began to rival that of Louis XIV. The English involvement in the Nine Years' War began as a domestic one, after Louis XIV in early 1689 decided to land James II in Ireland to attempt to begin the reconquest of his throne. Neither William nor the Protestant English aristocracy could possibly ignore this, and an Irish campaign took up much of the next two years. James was defeated and the Protestant ascendancy reestablished in 1691. Subsequently, the English fought the remainder of the Nine Years' War and the War of the Spanish Succession for reasons reminiscent of Louis's own: to secure dynastic rights, to acquire territory, and to expand English trade in the new world. Using its growing economic resources, the government put large armies in the field and financed intricate coalitions of smaller and larger European states.[15] William III and Marlborough, the favorite of Queen Anne, emerged as Louis's virtual equals and rivals on the European stage. In England, as in the rest of Europe, the monarchy undertook these wars together with the ruling aristocracy. But while the goals of the English government did not differ essentially from those of Louis, new institutions emerged to regulate aristocratic factional conflict and to make fundamental decisions of war and peace. Parliament and parlia-

15. The growth in British state machinery, taxes, and military and naval effort is carefully traced by John Brewer, *The Sinews of Power: War, Money, and the English State, 1688–1783* (New York, 1989).

mentary elections became a critical part of the framework within which the crown and the aristocracy carried out foreign policy.

William III certainly did not intend to weaken the English monarchy. This ambitious prince, who had expected since childhood to succeed to the English throne,[16] firmly believed in royal prerogatives and jealously fought for them both in the United Provinces and in Britain. He apparently undertook his expedition to England in 1688 believing that James II had deceived the world and stolen his wife's rights by foisting a supposititious child upon the public.[17] After Louis XIV sheltered James II and landed him in Ireland, Parliament immediately endorsed a campaign against James. After securing Ireland, William III won the support of the Whig party for the war in exchange for a mixture of constitutional concessions and pecuniary inducements. While Parliament approved unprecedented grants of supply and increases in taxation, William reluctantly assented to curbs upon the prerogative, eventually including not only a bill of rights, but also triennial parliaments, an end to censorship, and a parliamentary right to charter trading companies. The Mutiny Act, by making the enforcement of military discipline subject to an annual act of Parliament, removed the danger of a standing army responsible only to the prince. At the same time, William appointed many supporters to lucrative offices, and repeatedly vetoed bills barring placemen from Parliament. Two distinct, though heterogeneous parties, the Tories and Whigs, emerged in both the House of Commons and the House of Lords, but neither party ever monopolized office. William, like Anne after him, quickly learned to rely upon friendly elements of both groups, as well as upon dependents of the court without ties to either party.

As long as France threatened the British Isles with invasion, Parliament supported and financed the war. Expenditure during the war averaged £5 million per year—about one-third of it borrowed—compared with about £2 million annually under James II. But opposition to William's large Continental commitment developed after the threat of a French invasion faded and British foreign trade suffered severely because of the war. The opposition Tories

16. Stephen B. Baxter, *William III and the Defense of European Liberty, 1650–1702* (New York, 1966), pp. 223–224.

17. This at any rate was clearly Mary's belief: ibid., pp. 226–227.

increasingly attacked the combination of city finance, represented by the new Bank of England, and Whig politicians who alone seemed to them to benefit from the war. The opposition won an impressive victory in Parliamentary elections in 1695. By 1697 Britain needed peace almost as badly as France and settled essentially for Louis's recognition of William as lawful king and the loss of some recent French gains in the Treaty of Ryswick.[18]

Like Louis, William wanted to avoid a new war over the Spanish succession, and he immediately began secret negotiations to partition the empire. Both Whigs and Tories now knew how to use foreign policy for their own purposes, and when the English public eventually learned that the second partition treaty had given Spain's Italian lands to the French crown, the Tories violently attacked it for betraying England's trading interest in the Mediterranean. Then, after the death of Carlos II and the accession of Philip V, French claims of privileges in the Spanish empire helped build support for a new war against France. In addition, Louis's recognition of James III as king of England upon the death of his father in September 1701 turned the impending conflict into the War of the English Succession as well, undoubtedly helping to unify the political nation behind it.

Under Queen Anne, who succeeded William in 1702, policy passed under the control of a faction led by one of the most powerful of early modern aristocrats, the duke of Marlborough. The war party also included Godolphin, the first lord of the treasury, and the Whig mercantile and financial interests, among them the Bank of England and the new East India Company. Marlborough—a one-time client of James II who had survived an accusation of treason and become a lieutenant of William's—depended for his favor partly upon his wife's friendship with Anne. Extraordinarily ambitious, he became in 1701 England's chief diplomat and military leader on the Continent. He negotiated the Grand Alliance with the United Provinces and the emperor, promising the Dutch a barrier of fortresses in the Spanish Netherlands; the emperor, the Italian territories of the Spanish inheritance; and the English and Dutch, commercial concessions in the Spanish em-

---

18. Henry Horwitz, *Parliament, Policy, and Politics in the Reign of William III* (Newark, 1977), pp. 311–324; J. R. Jones, *Country and Court: England, 1658–1714* (Cambridge, Mass., 1978), pp. 256–301; P. G. M. Dickson, *The Financial Revolution in England: A Study in the Development of Public Credit, 1688–1756* (London, 1967), p. 10.

pire. When war began Marlborough initially fielded an army of 40,000 men, about half of them British subjects, and British forces eventually exceeded 100,000.[19] As captain-general, subordinate only to Anne (and, until his death, her husband Prince George of Denmark), his authority compared favorably with Wallenstein's at the height of his power, and he used it with equal effect. Although he did not raise troops upon his own account and risk, he disposed very freely of the increasing resources of the British government.

Subsidies paid from these resources enabled Marlborough to assemble a far-reaching coalition against Louis XIV, including Portugal, Denmark, Savoy, Prussia, Saxony, Mainz, Trier, the Palatinate, Hanover, many smaller German princes, and the army of the Hapsburg claimant Charles in Spain itself. Total subsidies paid by the British and the Dutch from 1701 through 1711 seem to have reached about £8 million, of which the British paid about two-thirds—a sum equal to about 64 million French livres, or one year's entire French revenue early in the reign of Louis XIV.[20] Marlborough generally directed allied military operations, and even decided when enemy territory should be laid waste. With the support of his queen and his faction, Marlborough had become the intermediary through which the English revenue and English finance supported the princes and armies of a very large part of Europe.

Like Wallenstein, Marlborough played an independent diplomatic role of enormous importance, apparently combined private and public moneys in highly advantageous fashion, and developed territorial ambitions of his own. At one time he hoped to become governor-general of the Spanish Netherlands, which he reconquered on behalf of the Austrian emperor, and in 1706, after his victory at Blenheim, the emperor actually created him territorial prince of Mindelheim, a principality confiscated from Max Emmanuel of Bavaria. And in 1708, at the height of his power, he bluntly offered the French peace terms in exchange for a bribe of 2

19. Ivor F. Burton, *The Captain-General: The Career of John Churchill, Duke of Marlborough, from 1702 to 1711* (London, 1968), p. 21, is an excellent short study of Marlborough's career.

20. Max Braubach, *Die Bedeutung der Subsidien für die Politik im spanischen Erbfolgekriege* (Bonn, 1923), esp. p. 17; P. G. M. Dickson and John Sperling, "War Finance, 1689–1714," in *New Cambridge Modern History*, VI, 284–285.

million livres—although in fairness, he seems to have refused bribes at other times. This proposal, wrote Marlborough's biographer and descendant, "served interests national, European, and personal at once and equally," echoing Ranke's remarks about Wallenstein's combination of private and public aims.[21] The splendor of Blenheim Palace testifies to the brilliance of his career. He also maintained a long and secret correspondence with James II and his son, presumably as insurance in case the Protestant succession should for some reason fail.

But whereas Wallenstein recognized the advantages of peaceful compromise, Marlborough fought determinedly and ultimately unsuccessfully for complete victory in the manner of Olivares. His military campaigns showed an unusual willingness to force decisive battles. He won several spectacular victories, but the military realities of his time made total victory over Louis XIV impossible. Thus Marlborough agreed in 1707 to fight until the Hapsburg claimant Charles had secured the Spanish throne, from which he would grant the English special privileges in the Spanish empire. But Charles was defeated within Spain, and despite the exhaustion of France, the English and their allies could not force Louis XIV to depose his grandson. Marlborough nonetheless preferred to fight on the French frontiers, perhaps for the sake of maintaining the coalition and his European role, and perhaps because of the benefits which continued to accrue to him and his clientele.[22] Given Marlborough's war aims, the traditional Whig historian's view of the war—that the British fought to maintain a European balance of power—seems quite untenable. After 1709, when the bloody Battle of Malplaquet failed to drive Louis from the field, Marlborough failed to win the support of the Dutch and Austrians for new, ambitious operations.

Marlborough's fall shows that European politics were changing. After the failure of his sweeping plans for total victory, he fell from power not as a result of intrigue or assassination, but rather through the workings of the emerging British constitution. Until 1710, Marlborough and Godolphin had managed with the help of their enormous resources to keep shifting parliamentary majori-

21. Winston S. Churchill, *Marlborough: His Life and Times*, 2 vols. (London, 1947), book 2, pp. 48–50, 499–500. Max Emmanuel regained the territory at the Peace of Utrecht, after Marlborough's disgrace.

22. Burton, *Captain-General*, pp. 193–197.

ties behind them. The government's growing economic strength enabled it to offer places and pensions to many members of the Commons and (to a greater extent) the Lords. The *availability* of these rewards undoubtedly encouraged members of both the Whig and Tory parties to give the war at least their qualified support, and therefore to become eligible for the benefits of office.[23] By 1710, however, the opposition to Marlborough and Godolphin—led by Robert Harley—had devised its own military and naval strategy as a means to rally support. Jealous of Marlborough, the Tories argued that Britain should abandon the Continental campaign and the goals of the Dutch and the Hapsburgs, and concentrate on the Mediterranean and colonial gains. The election of 1710 returned them to power. Eventually they decided to form the South Sea Company to trade with the Spanish empire and to provide a Tory counterweight to the Bank of England.

After taking power in 1710, Harley immediately began working for a compromise peace, which the electorate clearly endorsed in a new election. After preliminary terms had been agreed with the French in 1711, the Whigs—supported by Anne's heir, the elector of Hanover—continued to argue, with Marlborough's support, that the Bourbons should not be left on the throne of Spain, but the Tory ministry carried the day. Shortly thereafter, in early 1712, Marlborough was dismissed. He was accused of appropriating public funds for his own benefit, but, in a reflection of a new, less violent age, he lived out his days in honorable and wealthy retirement.[24] As the fruits of the war the Tories could claim Gibraltar and Minorca, which the navy had seized during the war; Acadia, Newfoundland, and Hudson's Bay, won largely by American colonists without any real help from England itself; Louis's recognition of the Protestant succession; and the *asiento*, or contract to supply the Spanish empire with slaves, together with permission to send an annual ship of goods to sell in the Indies. The last of these gains proved a disappointment, as British traders had trouble realizing them. The South Sea Company—the Tory allies to whom the *asiento* was actually given—experienced enormous difficulties securing and marketing its slaves and probably never made much of

23. Geoffrey Holmes, *British Politics in the Age of Anne* (New York, 1967), esp. pp. 345–420.

24. Burton, *Captain-General*, pp. 185–189.

a profit on this much-prized concession.[25] The trade with the Indies remained quite unregulated after the war, and any British gains probably owed more to the wealth and enterprise of British traders than to Marlborough's victories and Harley's diplomacy.

Nothing, in short, was unique either about the war aims of the British or the men who directed the war. Nor did the British dispose of overwhelmingly superior financial resources. A recent study of war finance and the British economy makes it very clear that the Nine Years' War strained British resources to the absolute limit, and that William's Flanders armies stayed in the field thanks only to large loans from the Dutch States General.[26] Although the credit system of the maritime powers was more modern, a survey of the wars of 1688–1713 shows that Louis XIV borrowed and spent about as much on the wars as his opponents.[27]

Yet in the realm of politics, the British had found new ways of institutionalizing factional conflict, regulating the rise and fall of ministries, reaching decisions on war and peace, and even allowing the people a very limited role in national political life. In France, Louis XIV relied consistently upon the same clienteles to do his business, the French people relied entirely upon his wisdom to decide questions of war and peace, and the aristocratic opposition had to put its hopes in the succession of his son, who eventually predeceased him. In Great Britain, by contrast, monarchs now presided over a regular alternation of factions in power; elections, however undemocratic and corrupt, enabled some of the public to participate in this process; and peaceful changes in the personnel of government had become the main means of changing government policy, especially in questions of war and peace. None of this guaranteed more effective or rational policies, but the development of a system of peaceful political competition represented a major advance for European politics.

The politics of the Dutch republic showed more unique features during the late seventeenth century, precisely because much of the ruling class still did not accept the need for a sovereign prince and

25. John Carswell, *The South Sea Bubble* (Stanford, 1960), pp. 64–68.

26. D. W. Jones, *War and Economy in the Age of William III and Marlborough* (New York, 1988), stresses the role of luck during the War of the Spanish Succession.

27. Dickson and Sperling, "War Finance."

rejected a foreign policy based upon dynastic interests. Indeed, the chronic Dutch suspicion even of their stadholder—an institution which the United Provinces did without for much of the era of Louis XIV—made it somewhat more difficult for them to play the international political game in the late seventeenth and early eighteenth centuries.[28] The issue of princely authority had become critical in the late 1640s, when the stadholder William II of Orange had tried to impose much stronger authority by corrupting the provincial estates and States General. By this time Dutch politics revolved around two factions, known as the States party—led by John De Witt—and the Orangist party. After William II's sudden death in 1650, De Witt had persuaded the States General to abolish the office of stadholder, arguing that the republic would be happier without a prince.[29] An extremely intricate series of provincial and national constitutional arrangements protected the interests of the nobility, the gentry, and the growing urban patriciate—which frequently pursued a very lavish lifestyle itself.[30]

By the mid-sixteenth century, the Dutch had developed a healthy respect for the human and material costs of war, and a theory of lawful and unlawful war which specifically excluded war in pursuit of dynastic ambition.[31] In the early years of Louis XIV's reign, John De Witt hoped to rely upon diplomacy, a militia, and perhaps a Protestant coalition to protect the security of the United Provinces, but the combined Anglo-French assault in 1672 doomed both De Witt, who was brutally lynched, and his policies. Significantly, the powerful Estates of Holland voted in July to make William III of Orange stadholder rather than accept Louis XIV's humiliating peace terms, implicitly recognizing that one prince was necessary to resist another.[32] The subsequent wars against Louis

28. Older and newer surveys of the Dutch republic, its leadership class, its politics, and its culture include: Pieter Geyl, *The Netherlands in the Seventeenth Century*, pts. 1 and 2 (New York, 1961); Rowen, *John De Witt*; Israel, *Dutch Republic and Hispanic World*; Sherrin Marshall, *The Dutch Gentry, 1500–1650* (New York, 1987); and Schama, *Embarrassment of Riches*. I thank Simon Schama for his most helpful comments on Chapters 2 and 3 of this book.

29. Rowen, *John De Witt*, pp. 25–30, 191–238, 380.

30. Rowen, *John De Witt*, pp. 231–241, discusses the constitutional structure; Schama, *Embarrassment of Riches*, focuses on the lives of the ruling elite.

31. The theory is stated in Pieter de la Court, *The True Interest and Political Maxims of the Republic of Holland* (London, 1746). (This edition, like many others, mistakenly attributes the authorship of the work to John De Witt himself.)

32. Baxter, *William III*, pp. 77–78.

XIV, as Simon Schama has recently suggested, turned the United Provinces into a more normal European power both institutionally and philosophically, but they did not lead to anything like a full-scale dynastic policy or to absolutism. After his return as stadholder and head of a large army, William III did not disturb the constitution, but he began packing provincial governments with his own followers wherever possible in a manner perfectly similar to Richelieu, Mazarin, Colbert, or James II. Young and eager, William shared many of the values of his fellow princes, and after 1674, when the territory of the United Provinces was safe once again, he enthusiastically carried on the war for four more years, largely, his biographer affirms, because war was his true profession, and he loved it.[33] The war became increasingly unpopular at home, however, and Holland, the source of more than half the revenue, eventually refused to subsidize the allies. In 1678 the Peace of Nijmegen left Louis XIV, as we have seen, with major gains in the Spanish Netherlands and Franche-Comté.[34]

Indeed, during both the war of 1672–1678 and the Nine Years' War, the States party consistently favored the conclusion of peace as soon as possible, and only in times of grave danger did the whole aristocracy unite behind war. The massive importance of Dutch foreign trade—the key to the wealth of Holland and the United Provinces as a whole—inclined important interests toward peace, since wartime trade suffered from privateering. The Dutch also rejected territorial acquisitions. At times during the Eighty Years' War the Dutch had dreamed of acquiring the Southern Netherlands, but now such acquisitions would lead at once to the opening of the Scheldt, the revival of Antwerp, and a corresponding decline in Amsterdam's trade.[35]

Dutch politics restricted the international role of the United Provinces severely in the 1678–1688 period. The States party's distrust of William increased as a result of his marriage to Mary of York, heir presumptive to the British throne, and their opposition to him was encouraged by bribes paid by the French ambassador, d'Avaux. In 1682 Louis calculatedly insulted William by occupying the principality of Orange, but Amsterdam refused to increase the Dutch army, much less to fight on the side of Spain. States party

33. Ibid., pp. 135–136.
34. Ibid., pp. 127–159.
35. Schama, *Embarrassment of Riches*, pp. 221–257.

propaganda also began to argue, with relatively little justification, that William's court was too rich.[36] The revocation of the Edict of Nantes, however, changed Dutch opinion considerably, and the States General in 1688 agreed to William's expedition to England, which he justified as a means of protecting the Protestant religion. Having agreed, the United Provinces found themselves once again in a defensive war against Louis XIV, who responded to William's success in England with a new attack upon their territory.

Under the leadership of William III and Grand Pensionary of Holland Heinsius, the United Provinces made an enormous financial and military effort during the Nine Years' War and the War of the Spanish Succession. They tried in the meantime, over the objections of the English, to continue their trade with France and the Spanish Netherlands. Their financial contributions to the two wars totaled about £60 million, or roughly half of British expenditure, of which the greatest part was raised by taxes and loans within Holland, where the interest rate remained at an astonishingly low 4 percent throughout the period.[37] They also contributed roughly one-third of the subsidies paid by the maritime powers during the War of the Spanish Succession.

Following the pattern of the 1670s, strong peace parties emerged in both wars as soon as the territory of the United Provinces was no longer threatened. In the Nine Years' War, the Dutch fought, in theory, to secure William of Orange's rights in England and to roll back some of Louis XIV's gains; in the War of the Spanish Succession, they fought to maintain a fortified barrier in the Spanish Netherlands and for a share of Spanish trade. Lacking an ambitious dynasty or a great general like Marlborough after William's death in 1702, the Dutch had only moderate war aims in the war. They hesitated to commit themselves to the Hapsburg claimant to the Spanish throne, and ultimately did so only because the British insisted upon it. The Dutch allowed their navy to fall well behind the British and had therefore to depend upon the British alliance, which Heinsius carefully nurtured, to secure any commercial or colonial gains. In the end, thanks to cynical British diplomacy, they did not receive them. The Barrier Treaty of 1709 promised the Dutch a huge chain of fortresses and some small territorial conces-

---

36. Geyl, *Netherlands in the Seventeenth Century*, II, 162–170.
37. Dickson and Sperling, "War Finance," pp. 294–298.

sions in the Spanish Netherlands and an equal share of any British commercial or territorial gains at Spain's expense, in exchange for support of the Hapsburg Charles III's claim to the Spanish empire. But at Utrecht the British Tory government negotiated for itself only, and the Dutch got nothing but a much-reduced barrier in exchange for the British acquisition of Minorca, Majorca, and the *asiento*.[38] The Dutch did not even receive the full restoration of the liberal French tariff of 1664, and the British, who had resisted a compromise over Spain from 1703 through 1710, received more advantages than the Dutch when they finally did compromise.

The wars of the era of Louis XIV were fought by and for monarchs, and most of their gains and losses could be measured in monarchical prestige. The Dutch, who lacked a monarch for much of the period, had to fight for tangible gain, and few tangible gains were available. Diplomatically this was also an age of treachery, and the Dutch suffered considerably for their loyalty to the British alliance, which the British did not repay.[39] Dependent upon trade and lacking dynastic ambition, the Dutch sought war less frequently than any other major power in the late seventeenth century. In the War of the Spanish Succession they received less return on their investment than any of the other major combatants.

The power of the Hapsburg emperors increased substantially during the era of Louis XIV. Although their sovereignty over Germany remained almost entirely theoretical, and the nobility within their hereditary domains remained extremely independent, they made very large territorial gains from the wars of the period, both against the Turks and in the aftermath of the War of the Spanish Succession.

Two recent analyses have argued that the Hapsburg emperor Leopold I, who reigned from 1657 to 1703, made only very small progress toward the creation of a more centralized state within his hereditary domains, and that the landed aristocracy of Austria, Bohemia, and Hungary retained much more power and wealth

---

38. H. G. Pitt, "The Pacification of Utrecht," in *New Cambridge Modern History*, VI, 462–465; see also Geyl, *Netherlands in the Seventeenth Century*, II, 254–324.

39. See especially J. G. Stork-Penning, "The Ordeal of the States—Some Remarks on Dutch Politics during the War of the Spanish Succession," in *Acta Historiae Neerlandica*, vol. 2 (Leiden, 1967) pp. 107–141.

than their French counterparts.[40] The great magnates acquired properties in different parts of the empire and generally controlled local government, the small central bureaucracy, and the church. The magnates also maintained enormous city and country establishments, quarreled constantly over precedence, and maintained armed retainers who continually fought like their French and English counterparts a century earlier.[41] While troops supported a vigorous Catholic Counter-Reformation—sometimes using tactics similar to Louis XIV's dragonnades—they did not help collect revenue, and the estates of the various provinces remained extremely powerful and independent. Foreign observers specifically contrasted the Hapsburg domains with France, where the crown had clearly managed to mobilize a much larger share of the agricultural surplus, and where local resistance to taxation could be punished by the quartering of troops.[42] Indeed, the distribution of political power within the Austrian domains seems similar to that in France in the late sixteenth century. This emerged most dramatically in 1703 when Hungarian and Transylvanian aristocrats, led by Prince Rákóczi, led a general rebellion against the Hapsburgs. Louis XIV subsidized the rebels handsomely, much as Philip II of Spain had done during the French civil wars of the late 1500s, while Emperor Leopold's British and Dutch allies urged him to negotiate a settlement. Both he and his son Joseph failed to crush the rebellion militarily, and Joseph eventually had to confirm a number of important Hungarian privileges in 1711 to bring the insurrection to a close.[43]

At the same time, however, Leopold and his sons, Joseph I (reigned 1703–1711) and Charles VI, provided their aristocrats with numerous opportunities for conquest, glory, and new estates. The Hapsburgs eventually made far larger territorial gains during the wars of Louis XIV than any other dynasty. These gains included Hungary, reconquered during the 1680s and 1690s, and

40. Jean Bérenger, *Finances et absolutisme autrichien dans la seconde moitié du XVIIème siècle* (Paris, 1975); R. J. W. Evans, *The Making of the Hapsburg Monarchy, 1550–1700: An Interpretation* (Oxford, 1979).

41. Derek McKay, *Prince Eugene of Savoy* (London, 1977), pp. 48–50.

42. Bérenger, *Finances et absolutisme autrichien*, pp. 393–403.

43. Linda Frey and Marsha Frey, "The Rákóczi Insurrection and the Disruption of the Grand Alliance," *Canadian-American Review of Hungarian Studies*, 5, no. 2 (Fall 1978): 17–29.

the Italian territories of Milan, Naples, and Sicily, which Charles VI eventually secured as his share of the Spanish inheritance. Leopold, who won the great victories against the Turks and defeated Louis XIV's attempt to secure the imperial succession in 1690, achieved all this partly by increasing his own revenues and partly with the help of foreign subsidies. His own revenues rose from 4.3 million florins in 1661 (about 19 million livres) to almost 6.4 million in 1683 (about 29 million livres) and 11.8 million florins (about 53 million livres) in 1693. The greatest part of the increase came from new extraordinary taxes and revenues from reconquered Hungary.[44] In the same period, ordinary French revenues increased from 32 million livres in 1661 to 62 million livres in 1683 and 108 million in 1693, consistently totaling about twice as much.[45] In the first two decades of his reign, Leopold I fought only when other powers would provide subsidies. He initially tolerated French expansion, signing a treaty partitioning the Spanish empire with Louis XIV in 1666, and a neutrality treaty in 1671, on the eve of the Dutch war. He joined the Dutch war against Louis in 1673 in exchange for promises of substantial subsidies (between 13 and 20 percent of his total revenue) from the Spanish and Dutch.[46] Threatened by the Turks in 1663–64 and 1682–83, he secured help from the Holy Roman Empire and from Louis XIV in the first case, and massive help from the empire, Poland, and the Vatican in the second.

By the mid-1680s Leopold's revenues had grown, and he could pursue a more aggressive strategy. Financially he occupied a middle position among the powers, sometimes paying subsidies to other powers like the elector of Bavaria, and sometimes receiving them. The war against the Turks threatened Leopold with disaster in 1683, when the grand vizier Kara Mustafa encircled Vienna, and after the siege was lifted with the help of the king of Poland, John Sobieski, Leopold was encouraged to pursue the Turks into Hungary. This task occupied most of his efforts during

44. Bérenger, *Finances et absolutisme autrichien*, p. 349.

45. Venon de Forbonnais, *Récherches et considérations sur les finances de France depuis l'année 1595 jusqu'à l'année 1721*, 2 vols. (Basel, 1758), I, 290, 555, II, 74; A. M. de Boislisle, *Correspondance des contrôleurs généraux des finances avec les intendants de province*, vol. 1, *1683-1699* (Paris, 1874), pp. 583, 593, uses a slightly different accounting for ordinary and extraordinary revenues.

46. Bérenger, *Finances et absolutisme autrichien*, pp. 406–410.

the remainder of the 1680s.[47] Although the Papacy continued to subsidize his wars against the Turks handsomely with the help of Italian and Spanish revenues, he does not seem to have received subsidies from the English or Dutch to fight against Louis during the Nine Years' War. But Leopold did take advantage of Louis's war against the whole empire to secure his son Joseph's election as king of the Romans in early 1690.[48] Like his fellow monarchs, he carefully combined diplomacy and war to increase his power.

Having secured Hungary in the 1690s, Leopold's thoughts turned to the Spanish inheritance. He did not blindly insist upon keeping the Spanish throne within the Hapsburg family but sought to use the succession question to increase his own territorial power. Before the death of Carlos II, Leopold considered renouncing his claims to Spain and the Indies in return for Milan, Naples, Sicily, and Sardinia, and his policy during the war reflects these goals. He began the War of the Spanish Succession by sending Prince Eugene into Italy, and after Eugene's great victory at Turin in 1706, he tried to reassert imperial rights over the whole peninsula. At one point he had seemed willing once again to concede Spain and the Indies to the Bourbons in exchange for Italian territory. It seems quite clear, too, that had Joseph I lived and his brother, Charles, ascended the Spanish throne, a new struggle for Italy between the Hapsburg princes would have begun. The maritime powers, not the emperor, paid for Charles's attempts to establish himself in Spain, and these countries stood to gain far more through commercial concessions than the Austrian Hapsburgs should Charles succeed.[49] After Joseph's death in 1711, Charles gave up the Spanish throne in favor of the empire.

The early years of the War of the Spanish Succession, in which the Austrian government had to cope with a hostile army in Bavaria, rebellion in Hungary, and some disastrous Italian campaigns, suggested that Austria was not equal to the task it had set itself, and in 1704 Vienna seemed to be threatened by a Franco-Bavarian force on one side and the Hungarians on the other. But

47. John Stoye, *The Siege of Vienna* (New York, 1965); see pp. 265–299.

48. Oswald Redlich, *Weltmacht des Barock: Österreich in der Zeit Kaiser Leopolds I* (4th ed., Vienna, 1961), pp. 336–338.

49. Leopold Auer, "Zur rolle italiens in der Öesterreichischen Politik um das spanisch Erbe," *Mitteilungen des österreichischen Staatsarchiv*, 31 (1978): 52–72.

Marlborough's march to the Danube and the Battle of Blenheim removed the threat, and new men in Vienna, led by Prince Eugene of Savoy, enabled the Austrians to play an important role for the rest of the war.[50] They did so, however, only with critical financial help. The British and the Dutch did not directly subsidize the Austrian army during the war, but the Hapsburgs borrowed about 9.4 million guilders from the maritime powers during the war—a sum equal to perhaps a tenth of the emperor's revenue during that period. The maritime powers also assigned many of the German troops they hired to imperial command on the Italian and Netherlands fronts, such as the 8,000 Prussians whom Marlborough hired personally on a visit to Berlin in 1704.[51]

The emperor Charles VI initially rejected the Peace of Utrecht and tried to hold the old alliance of German princes together.[52] He lacked the money, however, and after a year of desultory campaigning, the emperor in early 1714 received Sardinia—previously allocated to Max Emmanuel of Bavaria—and reserved his additional Italian claims at Rastatt. He eventually obtained Naples, Milan, Mantua, and some smaller territories and subsequently exchanged Sardinia for Sicily. Taking advantage of contemporary diplomacy, the Hapsburg emperors had increased their domains enormously without making many institutional changes at home.

Like Hapsburg Austria, Hapsburg Spain changed relatively little in the seventeenth century. The political system remained overwhelmingly decentralized and aristocratic. Both the countryside and the towns increasingly fell under the control of the grandees, and the church, which still controlled vast revenues and handed some of them to the pope, remained an independent power. The crown—especially during the reign of Carlos II—granted large numbers of new titles, diminishing its tax base still further, and often exempted nobles from taxes upon the *juros* from which they now drew large parts of their revenues. The administration of non-Castilian territories continued to eat up all their revenue, and in general, the financial position of the crown did not improve. Although the leading authority on the period has argued effectively that the agrarian economy revived somewhat in the latter part of

50. McKay, *Prince Eugene*, pp. 77–88.
51. Ibid., pp. 90–91, 128–129.
52. Ibid., p. 145.

the seventeenth century, Spain still depended upon foreign manufactures.[53]

Financial and political weakness severely limited Spain's role in international politics. While the flow of silver from the Indies continued and may even have grown, much less of it found its way into the coffers of the crown. Since Spain had almost nothing to sell to the Indies, Spanish America exchanged its silver illegally for goods from England, Holland, France, and Italy. The vast majority of American bullion either went directly from the Indies to other parts of Europe or was transferred to foreign ships without being unloaded at Cadiz. As a result, the Spanish throne only rarely financed European warfare. Spain occasionally paid subsidies to minor powers—most notably during the Dutch war—and in 1682 the Spaniards declared war on Louis XIV despite the unwillingness of any other power to resist Louis's reunions, but such measures reflected only temporary financial surpluses. Unlike Hapsburg Austria, furthermore, the Spaniards never raised large armies at the expense of their allies. Although at home duels and vendettas remained a normal part of political life, the nobility had lost its taste for war, partly because of its expense. Even in the war against neighboring Portugal, the Spaniards in 1666 fielded only 20,000 men.[54]

Thus, until the death of Carlos II in 1700, the general strengthening of the crown so characteristic of the rest of late seventeenth-century Europe had not taken place in Spain. The personality of the monarch, who lacked even the courage to choose his own ministers, contributed to the problem, but the realm's political, economic, and financial problems would surely have hampered a far more energetic prince. The weakness of the crown, as well as the impending demise of the dynasty, undoubtedly encouraged the French, the Austrian Hapsburgs, the Dutch, and the English to believe that they might secure a much larger share of the resources of the empire by placing their own client on the throne when Carlos II finally died. Ironically, despite the enormous resources expended by all the powers in the War of the Spanish Succession, none of them really achieved this goal. Instead, the war strengthened the new Bourbon monarch, Philip V, to the point where he

53. Henry Kamen, *Spain in the Later Seventeenth Century, 1665–1700* (New York, 1980), pp. 16–20, 226–236, 357–372.

54. Ibid., pp. 133–147, 247–248, 350–352.

could more effectively defend Spanish privileges and play a greater independent role in international politics. The gains which all the powers hoped to secure from the war proved largely ephemeral.

Although many of the institutional changes made by Philip V and his French councillors aimed mainly at increasing French influence, these changes eventually made the monarchy much more independent. The Spanish grandees, whose shameless exploitation of the state machinery for their own benefit had become legendary, soon found themselves excluded from influence over the crown. Succeeding where Olivares had failed, Philip V abolished the system of councils that had ruled Spain for more than a century and a half, replacing it with a small *despacho* similar to the French royal council. One council, the Council of Castile, survived, but as in France, secretaries of state within the *despacho* carried out the real business of the state. Late in the war the government also introduced the system of intendants. Partly because of these measures, a number of grandees defected to the Hapsburg claimant Charles after the war began, which in turn reduced their power after his defeat.[55]

The government doubled its revenue during the war despite its failure to introduce many new taxes. Revenue eventually reached about 15 million pesos annually, which equaled more than 50 million French livres, or about half the revenue of the French crown. King Philip confiscated an unprecedented sum of silver—about 7 million pesos, or 21 million French livres, from the 1702 treasure fleet, and he received about 1 million pesos from fleets in 1707, 1709, and 1711.[56] Relying on extraordinary gifts from the church and other sources, the crown managed this without significantly increasing its liability in *juros*. And during the war, revolts in Valencia and Aragon—which were aided, of course, by the Hapsburg claimant and the maritime powers—gave Philip V the excuse to do away with the privileges of the realms of the crown of Aragon and lay the basis for the financial and administrative unity of Spain. Although during this period these kingdoms brought relatively little revenue to Madrid, they supported troops out of extraordinary contributions, and they became more important sources of

55. Henry Kamen, *The War of Succession in Spain, 1700–15* (Bloomington, 1969), pp. 83–117.

56. Ibid., pp. 179–180, 186–192. France took about one-third of the 1702 shipment.

income after the war.[57] Furthermore—despite Louis XIV's patronage of Philip V and his attempts to control him through French advisers and assistance—by the end of the war the Spanish crown had also developed more political independence. This trend may have been inevitable from the beginning, but it accelerated after 1709, when a desperate Louis XIV had to withdraw his troops from Spain and almost abandoned his grandson to make peace. By the end of the war the new assertiveness of the monarchy had made it impossible for any of the warring powers to achieve the commercial gains they had sought at Spain's expense.

When Philip V acceded to the throne in 1701, Louis XIV immediately secured the right of French vessels to enter Spanish American ports—a right which made it impossible to prevent French-American trade. The French sent numerous trading fleets to the Caribbean and above all to the Pacific during the War of the Spanish Succession, making a considerable profit until an enormous glut of goods from all over Europe brought the Indies trade almost to a halt. In response to British privateering, they persuaded the Spaniards to divert treasure fleets to France in 1707 and 1709, and secured several trading privileges within Spain itself.[58] The Spaniards, however, feared direct French encroachments upon the traditional monopoly of trade with the Indies, and thus stalled negotiations which would have given the French regular new rights to export goods across the Atlantic.[59]

Similarly, the British and the Dutch, after committing themselves in 1704 to the Hapsburg claimant to the Spanish empire, received substantial promises of commercial concessions in the Indies, including a 1707 promise to the British to allow a number of British ships to trade directly with Spanish America.[60] British and Dutch smugglers also made expeditions to the Atlantic, Pacific, and Caribbean coasts of the empire during the war, contributing to a massive glut of European products. But the persistence of these depredations, as well as those of the French, persuaded King Philip V's advisers to insist, at the Peace of Utrecht, upon the al-

57. Ibid., pp. 199–241, 309–360.

58. Ibid., pp. 140–196.

59. Geoffrey J. Walker, *Spanish Politics and Imperial Trade, 1700–1789* (Bloomington, 1979), pp. 19–33, 50–66.

60. G. N. Clark, "War Trade and Trade War, 1701–1713," *Economic History Review*, 1st ser., 1, no. 2 (January 1928): 277–278; Walker, *Spanish Politics and Imperial Trade*, p. 72.

most complete reaffirmation of the prohibition against foreign trade with the Spanish empire. The French, desperate for peace, had agreed in the preliminaries to exempt British goods from duties paid at Seville, but the Spaniards refused to honor this concession. The British simply received the *asiento* to supply the Indies with African slaves—a privilege which previously had been in both French and Dutch hands—and the right to dispatch one ship for trading purposes with the annual slave contract. The eventual treaties of peace confirmed the validity of the rules of the reign of Carlos II.[61]

In theory, the Spanish crown emerged from the war with its control over the Indies trade intact; in practice, the trade emerged less subject to anyone's control. Unregulated trade had flourished during the war, and the Spanish colonists in both New Spain (Mexico) and Peru resisted the resumption of regular annual fleets from Cadiz after its conclusion. The British did take advantage of their right to send an "annual ship" to make additional inroads into the trade with New Spain after 1716, but in general the trade became increasingly unregulated, or regulated informally by the American authorities themselves.[62] The relative advantages which various powers might draw from the trade would depend henceforth upon the enterprise of their merchants, rather than upon the strength of the European armies.

The new Bourbon monarchy in Spain emerged from the war shorn of many of its Italian possessions but stronger within Spain itself than ever before. Throughout the Hapsburg domains, the era of Louis XIV had strengthened central authority, though not perhaps as much as in France or Britain. Meanwhile, similar developments were occurring in the smaller states of Europe—especially in Germany, the scene of a remarkably intricate, almost continuous diplomatic struggle which local princes quickly learned to turn to their advantage.

Smaller States during the Reign of Louis XIV

One of the most remarkable features of the era of Louis XIV is the way in which international conflict spread political changes from

---

61. E. W. Dahlgren, *Les relations commerciales entre la France et les côtes de l'océan pacifique (commencement du XVIIIeme siècle)* (Paris, 1909), I, 704–729.

62. Walker, *Spanish Politics and Imperial Trade*, pp. 67–92. The authorities initially made enormous difficulties with the annual ship.

larger, stronger states to smaller and weaker ones. As we have seen, the increased wealth and political cohesion of France, Britain, and the United Provinces enabled these states to field much larger armies and carry on wars without provoking domestic rebellions. The armies also increased their power at home, especially in the French case. At the same time, their foreign policy spread these developments to smaller states. Anxious to copy their betters, the minor princes of Europe—especially in Germany—sought standing armies and glittering courts to increase their power and prestige. The richer states cooperated by financing their military establishments in exchange for diplomatic cooperation. As a result, the authority of smaller princes grew along with that of larger ones, contributing to the general growth of European state power.

A brief survey of the policies of the minor German princes will show how international politics reshaped domestic politics in smaller as well as larger European jurisdictions in the era of Louis XIV. Since most minor princes could not afford to maintain standing armies themselves, they had to find patrons who would finance them in return for military assistance.[1] Subsidies from minor powers enabled minor princes to do without credit from their regimental colonels, who had raised so many regiments on their own account during the Thirty Years' War.[2] Many princes promptly used their armies to increase their authority at home.

A key example is Frederick William of Brandenburg, the Great Elector. Impressed by the exactions of foreign armies within Germany during the Thirty Years' War, he had begun to copy them during the First Northern War against Poland and Sweden, which had won him the duchy of Prussia. After the Peace of Oliva in 1659, however, the estates of his territories, weary of the expense of war, forced him to reduce his army from 22,000 men to 7,000. For the remainder of his reign he took advantage of Louis XIV's wars to keep an army in being, frequently changing sides to get the best possible bargain. During the Anglo-Dutch war of 1665–66 he initially planned to attack the Dutch but reversed course and attacked his neighbor, Christopher Bernard von Galen, the bishop of Münster, when a Dutch subsidy enabled him to raise and maintain 12,000 men. Shortly thereafter, in a highly significant coup, he

1. John Childs, *Armies and Warfare in Europe, 1648–1789* (New York, 1982), pp. 31–37.
2. Redlich, *German Military Enterpriser*, II, 105–106.

made peace with Münster and used his troops to subdue the town of Magdeburg, which had claimed the status of an imperial free city since he had acquired it in 1648. Forced to abandon this claim, Magdeburg subsequently provided him with important revenues.

Frederick William's diplomatic footwork became even more rapid during the Dutch war. Although he had signed a subsidy treaty with Louis XIV in 1669, he refused to join the war against the Dutch, with whom he had both religious and dynastic ties, and supplied 12,000 men—half of them paid for by the Dutch—for the campaign of 1672 against Louis. In 1673 he allowed Louis to buy him out of the coalition with another subsidy treaty, but in 1674 he reentered the coalition against Louis. He won some territory from Louis's Swedish allies but had to return it when his allies deserted him. Now determined to rely exclusively on France, he signed a number of subsidy treaties between 1679 and 1685, supporting Louis's advances into Germany and promising to support him or the dauphin in an election for emperor or king of the Romans. While he made no new territorial gains, he managed to keep 25,000 men under arms after the Dutch war, and eventually to overcome the opposition of the estates of both Prussia and Brandenburg and set up a *Generalkriegskommissariat* to billet troops and levy contributions.[3]

The Great Elector's pro-French policies had become increasingly unpopular by 1685 as a result of Louis's encroachments upon the empire, and the revocation of the Edict of Nantes forced him to recall his minister to the imperial diet, the pro-French Jena, in disgrace. Within a year he had concluded new alliances with the Dutch and the emperor Leopold, who matched Louis's previous subsidies. After he died in 1688, his son Frederick entered the war on the allied side in exchange for further generous subsidies. He also leased his troops to the emperor, now engaged in campaigns against the Turks.[4] During the interval of peace before the War of the Spanish Succession, Frederick marshaled diplomatic support for his own recognition as king of Prussia, which would enable him to maintain a much more lavish court. He secured the vital support of the emperor in 1700 in exchange for promising to sup-

3. See F. L. Carsten, *The Origins of Prussia* (Oxford, 1954), esp. pp. 183–186, 199–201, 218–228, 265–267, and Georges Pagès, *Le grand électeur et Louis XIV* (Paris, 1905), *passim*.

4. Pagès, *Le grand électeur*, pp. 536–544, 556–562; Albert Waddington, *Histoire de Prusse*, vol. II, *Les deux premiers rois (1688–1740)* (Paris, 1922), pp. 14–80.

port his claims to the Spanish succession and to supply 8,000 men in a new war. When the war came he hired out as many troops as he could, and his court became entirely dependent upon the money supplied by the British and Dutch. By 1710 he had 44,000 men under arms—a remarkable total for a power of this size—but fully three-quarters of them were fighting in Flanders or in Italy. Frederick thereby lost the chance to profit from the Great Northern War, either as an ally or an enemy of Charles XII of Sweden. His policies earned from his grandson Frederick the Great the title of *roi mercenaire*.[5]

Two Bavarian electors, Ferdinand Maria (reigned 1651–1679) and Max Emmanuel (reigned 1679–1726), also worked cleverly and without scruple to exploit international politics to increase their own power, privileges, rank, and domains. Their approaches differed. Whereas Ferdinand Maria concentrated upon strengthening his position while avoiding war, Max Emmanuel generally sold himself to the prince who would give him the largest military command. Ruling over domains devastated by the Thirty Years' War, Ferdinand Maria worked carefully to increase his income during his reign, but he never balanced his budget.[6] He initially established a relationship with the French court in the early 1660s, when both Bavarian and French help enabled the emperor Leopold to defend his lands from the Turks. In 1667–68 Bavarian delegates at the Reichstag supported imperial neutrality in the War of Devolutions. In 1670 Ferdinand Maria signed a subsidy treaty with Louis XIV in which the two princes promised each other support in case of the death of either Carlos II of Spain or Leopold, neither of whom, at that time, had an heir. While Louis claimed the Spanish succession and the empire, Ferdinand Maria laid claim to parts of the hereditary Hapsburg lands and the title of king of the Romans. The treaty provided him with a small annual subsidy and promised money to raise 9,000 men should war with the emperor break out. The Bavarian estates, which had met in 1669, never had a full meeting again.[7] During the Dutch war, Ferdinand Maria re-

---

5. Waddington, *Histoire de Prusse*, II, 81–230; Redlich, *German Military Enterpriser*, II, 96–97; Max Braubach, *Die Bedeutung der Subsidien für die Politik im spanischen Erbfolgekrieg* (Bonn, 1923), pp. 104–126.

6. M. Doeberl, *Entwicklungsgeschichte Bayerns*, vol. 2 (Munich, 1928), pp. 81–85.

7. Dieter Albrecht, "Staat und Gesellschaft, 1500–1745," in Max Spindler, ed., *Handbuch der bayerischen Geschichte*, vol. 2 (Munich, 1969), pp. 580–581.

sisted the pressure of imperial and domestic opinion and remained steadfastly neutral in exchange for more French subsidies,
which allowed him to raise a small army.[8]

Max Emmanuel, who succeeded Ferdinand Maria in 1679,
dreamed of military glory, not peace, and used diplomacy to
achieve it. In 1682, influenced by Louis's seizure of Strasbourg,
some uncharacteristically inept French diplomacy, and the new
Turkish danger, he signed a far-reaching subsidy treaty with the
emperor. Leopold promised him far more money (250,000 florins
annually in peacetime) than his father had ever received from
Louis XIV, and pledged Hapsburg lands as security. For the next
five years Max Emmanuel fought with distinction against the
Turks, helping in the relief of Vienna and the reconquest of Hungary. In 1685 he married the emperor's daughter Maria Antonia,
who brought as part of her dowry a promise of the Spanish Netherlands, but Spain refused to agree to this provision. Max Emmanuel returned home in 1687 without profit or territorial gains.
Courting him aggressively, the French suggested that he, following the example of the electors of Mainz and Brandenburg, annex
the imperial cities of Regensburg, Augsburg, and Nuremberg, and
promised him part of Carlos II's Italian inheritance. Instead, however, he renewed the alliance with the emperor in 1688, receiving
the overall command of the campaign against the Turks.

From 1688 through 1714, Max Emmanuel tacked back and forth
among the richer powers. Resentful of the new crown of Prussia
and the newly created electorate of Hanover, he sought a royal
crown and territory in either the Spanish Netherlands or Italy to
constitute a kingdom. In the late 1690s, when his infant son was
briefly recognized as heir to Carlos II, he set his sights on the
whole Spanish empire. While he actually fought with the empire
and the maritime powers during the Nine Years' War and with
Louis XIV during the War of the Spanish Succession, he continually flirted with both sides. Generally disappointed in his rewards, he actually secured the stadholdership of the Spanish
Netherlands with William III's help in 1692, but complained that it
cost him more than it brought, and eventually claimed large debts
from the Spaniards in 1700. Changing course, he allowed Louis

---

8. Doeberl, *Entwicklungsgeschichte Bayerns*, II, 42–70; Andreas Kraus, "Bayem im Zeitalter des Absolutismus (1651–1745)," in Spindler, ed., *Handbuch der bayerischen Geschichte*, II, 410–457.

XIV's troops into the Spanish Netherlands in early 1701 and pledged to lead a neutral party within the empire in exchange for French promises of Hapsburg lands and election as king of the Romans or emperor. During the next year he shamelessly courted both sides, eventually opting to fight with Louis when the emperor refused to promise him either a European kingdom or reliable subsidies. Princely self-interest seems entirely to have motivated this decision, which the Bavarian army generally opposed. He successfully linked up with Villars's French army in 1703 but suffered a catastrophe in 1704, when Marlborough and Prince Eugene defeated his army at Blenheim, drove him out of his territories, and laid them to waste. In a brazen instance of early modern diplomatic practice, he inquired, immediately after Blenheim, whether he might now accept the emperor's last offer of an alliance. Marlborough and Eugene withdrew it. The empire subsequently declared him an outlaw and deprived him of his lands and dignities.

While remaining an ally of Louis XIV, who gave him several commands in the Netherlands from 1705 until 1709, Max Emmanuel reopened talks with the allies, promising to betray Louis in exchange for a kingdom in the Netherlands or Italy. The Hapsburgs, however, refused to make any concessions to him. In the Peace of Utrecht he seemed to have secured either the Spanish Netherlands or Sardinia and his coveted royal crown, but at Rastatt the Hapsburgs forced him to content himself with the status quo ante. Like so many other German princes, the electors of Bavaria earned subsidies, troops, and occasional military glory from the wars of the late seventeenth century, but no territorial gains.[9]

Among the most enthusiastic recipients of subsidy payments during the late seventeenth century were the ecclesiastical rulers of northern and western Germany, including the electors of Mainz, Trier, and Cologne, and the bishop of Münster. The supreme political body within each of these principalities was the cathedral chapter, composed of approximately thirty members, which elected the archbishop-elector or prince-bishop for life. In foreign affairs the bishop or archbishop exercised the prerogatives of a secular prince. The bishops, archbishops, and other members of the

9. Doeberl, *Entwicklungsgeschichte Bayerns*, II, 122–168; see also Max Braubach, "Die Politik des Kurfürsten Max Emanuel von Bayern im Jahre 1702," in Braubach, *Diplomatie und Geistiges Leben im 17. und 18. Jahrhundert* (Bonn, 1969), pp. 148–184.

cathedral chapters sometimes came from German ruling houses like the Wittelsbachs but more frequently stemmed from a number of wealthy Rhineland families such as the Leyen, Schönborn, Fürstenberg, and Metternich houses. Many of them obtained office as a political favor and lacked any real religious vocation.[10] Their domestic and foreign policies closely resembled those of their lay counterparts, and they frequently raised and rented troops to the leading powers in exchange for subsidies, and used both the troops and the money to increase their power and prestige at home.

One such prince was the Wittelsbach Max Henry, elector of Cologne from 1650 through 1688, and bishop of Liège for much of the same period. Throughout his tenure he waged a continual battle with his estates, which resented his attempts to increase his civil and military establishment.[11] For most of his reign, Max Henry, who cared more for alchemy than for politics, relied upon two French clients, the brothers William and Egon von Fürstenberg, to conduct his affairs.[12] Recruited by Mazarin, who helped both of them obtain lucrative sees, the Fürstenbergs emerged as Louis XIV's principal negotiators in Germany during the preparation for the War of Devolutions. During 1666 and 1667, Max Henry of Cologne, Philip William, duke of Jülich and Berg, and John Philip of Schönborn, elector of Mainz, all signed subsidy treaties which enabled them to raise several thousand soldiers in exchange for remaining neutral in the coming war. A further subsidy treaty in late 1669 enabled Max Henry to raise another 8,000 troops with which he hoped to subjugate the city of Cologne, which had fought for its independence from the elector for centuries. The Dutch in their turn sent troops to defend Cologne, and Max Henry's troops eventually participated in the early stages of the Dutch war.[13] The

10. For a close look at one chapter, see Max Braubach, "Das Kölner Domkapitel und die Wahl von 1688," *Annalen des historischen Vereins für den Niederrhein*, 122 (1933): 51–117.

11. L. Ennen, *Frankreich und der Niederrhein, oder Geschichte von Stadt und Kurstaat Köln seit dem 30jährigen Kriege bis zur französischen Occupation, meist aus archivalischen Dokumenten* (Cologne and Neuss, 1855), pp. 174–176. The estates included the cathedral chapter, counts, knights, and towns.

12. See Max Braubach, *Wilhelm von Fürstenberg (1629–1704) und die französische Politik im Zeitalter Ludwigs XIV* (Bonn, 1972).

13. Braubach, *Wilhelm von Fürstenberg*, pp. 166–274; Karl Junkers, *Der Streit zwischen Kurstaat und Stadt Köln am Vorabend des Hollandischen Krieges (1667–1672)* (Düsseldorf, 1935), pp. 52–56.

Dutch eventually occupied the electorate in 1673, forcing Max Henry into a monastic retreat, and in the next year imperial troops kidnapped William von Fürstenberg, who had become one of the most hated figures in Germany.

At the close of the war the era of French influence seemed to be at an end, but Max Henry found himself in a new struggle in his other domain, the bishopric of Liège. The city of Liège, a hotbed of popular urban politics, had been occupied by the French during 1675–76, and the French troops, obliging the popular party, had destroyed the town's fortifications before they left, leaving the popular party firmly in control of the city.[14] William von Fürstenberg decided to regain favor by securing Louis XIV's help against the town, and after several years of negotiations he reached an agreement in 1682. Louis promised French forces to subdue the city of Liège and money to rebuilt its citadel, and paid the elector a new annual pension. In exchange, Max Henry agreed to favor peace within the empire—that is, to allow Louis's reunions of imperial territory to continue—and to allow the French to retain garrisons in other parts of Liège. In 1682 Louis provided him with money to raise about 2,000 troops to settle another quarrel with the city of Cologne; in 1683, he may have provided the money that enabled Max Henry to buy his election as bishop of Münster; and later that year, a new subsidy treaty enabled Max Henry to raise a new army. After the signature of the Truce of Ratisbon in August 1684, Max Henry used the troops to occupy Liège, execute the leaders of the opposition, and rewrite the constitution so as to end popular elections of the town government. Loath to disband his troops despite pressure from his estates, Max Henry hired out 6,000 of them to the emperor to fight the Turks.[15]

The electorate of Cologne became a key European diplomatic battleground in 1688, when the cathedral chapter, under pressure from Louis XIV, held an election to select a coadjutor (and almost certain successor) for the aged Max Henry. Helped by a large subsidy from Louis, William von Fürstenberg was elected over the Wittelsbach Joseph Clement, but Pope Innocent XI refused to confirm the election, leading eventually to Louis's occupation of Co-

14. Henry Lonchay, "La principauté de Liège, la France et les Pays-Bas au XVII et au XVIII siècle: Etude d'histoire diplomatique," *Mémoires couronnés et autres mémoires publiés par l'Académie royale des sciences, des lettres et des beaux-arts de Belgique*, 44 (1899): 84–114.

15. Braubach, *Wilhelm von Fürstenberg*, pp. 349–398; Lonchay, "La principauté de Liège," pp. 84–114.

logne in late 1688. Only six years later, however—while the Nine Years' War was still raging—Louis actually *supported* the election of Joseph Clement as prince-bishop of Liège, which territory was taking part in the war against him. In 1697 Joseph Clement lost a bitter battle with the estates of Liège, who forced him to demobilize all his forces and began moving closer to France.[16] Between 1697 and 1701, Joseph Clement became embroiled in new quarrels with his estates, and the emperor Leopold backed the estates' assertions of their rights. In 1701, on the eve of the War of the Spanish Succession, Joseph Clement signed a neutrality treaty with Louis, under which the French government provided him with money to raise more troops and a pension for himself. He hoped to stay out of the war, but when Mainz and Trier signed subsidy treaties with the English and Dutch, he had to invite French troops in to protect himself. His estates, backed by the emperor, had refused to support his attempts to keep an army in being.[17] Again and again, electors of Cologne had accepted French subsidies so as to raise armies and strengthen their domestic authority.

A similar pattern characterized French relations with the electorate of Mainz. The policies of Elector John Philip von Schönborn, who held the post from 1647 until his death in 1673, show a strange mixture of patriotism and self-interest. They included both attempts to develop a more effective common defense of the Holy Roman Empire and mutually advantageous subsidy agreements with Louis XIV. During the 1600s and early 1670s John Philip used his position as archchancellor of the empire, which he held *ex officio* as elector of Mainz, to encourage schemes of imperial defense.[18] But poverty, domestic difficulties, and his desire for a major inter-

---

16. Paul Harsin, *Les relations extérieures de la principauté de Liège sous Jean Louis d'Elderen et Joseph Clément de Bavière (1688–1718)* (Liège and Paris, 1927), pp. 97–149.

17. Günther Tücking, *Der Streit Zwischen den Kurfürsten Joseph Klemens von Köln und seinen Landständen in den Jahren, 1688–1701* (Würzburg, 1934); Max Braubach, *Die Politik des Kurfürsten Joseph Clemens von Köln bei Ausbruch des Spanischen Erbfolgekrieges und die Vertreibung der Franzosen vom Niederrhein* (Bonn, 1925). Braubach argues that Joseph Clement's relationship to his pro-French cousin, Max Emmanuel of Bavaria, determined his decision.

18. The archchancellor was one of the most important members of the Reichstag. As head of the imperial directory, only he could initiate discussions within the Reichstag as a whole, a deputation of it, or the college of electors, and no decision of any of these bodies could become law without passing through his hands. See Josef Wysocki, *Kurmainz und die Reunionen: Die Beziehungen zwischen Frankreich und Kurmainz von 1679 bis 1688* (Mainz, 1961), pp. 161–167, on the functions of the archchancellor.

national role still drove him into Louis's arms on several occasions.[19] Although John Philip also held the bishopric of Würzburg, his domains could never support his adventurous policies. His efforts to keep at least 1,000–2,000 men under arms left his successor with an increased debt and mortgaged revenues.[20] Beginning in 1657 John Philip was a leader in Mazarin's League of the Rhine, helping to keep the empire neutral in the continuing Franco-Spanish war, and using the alliance to strengthen his position at home. When in 1663 the town of Erfurt, which had claimed the status of an imperial free city ever since the Peace of Westphalia, explicitly denied his authority, John Philip called upon his fellow members of the League of the Rhine and marched upon the town in 1664 with 15,000 troops, including 6,000 Frenchmen. Unable to resist and deserted by the protestant elector of Saxony, the town gave in and lost all its political privileges. The use of French troops was extremely unpopular in Germany, but this was far from the last time that French help enabled a German prince to subdue his subjects.[21]

During the mid-1660s John Philip supported various schemes for the defense of the empire, but he maintained his alliance with France in early 1667 and refused to allow Spanish troops recruited in Bohemia to pass through his territories on the way to the Spanish Netherlands.[22] In 1670 he asked the Mainz chapter to elect a coadjutor. He hoped to secure the election of his own nephew, but the French had already promised their support to Lothar Frederick von Metternich, the bishop of neighboring Speyer. Lothar Frederick easily won election with the help of 70,000 Reichstaler supplied

19. See Georg Mentz, *Johann Philipp von Schönborn, Kurfürst von Mainz, Bischof von Würzburg und Worms, 1605–1673: Ein Beitrag zur Geschichte des siebzehnten Jahrhunderts* (Jena, 1896); Claude Badalo-Dulong, *Trente ans de diplomatie française en Allemagne: Louis XIV et l'electeur de Mayence, 1648–1678* (Paris, 1956); and Hans Goldschmidt, *Zentralbehörden und Beamtentum im Kurfürstentum Mainz vom 16. bis zum 18. Jahrhundert* (Berlin and Leipzig, 1908).

20. Goldschmidt, *Zentralbehörden in Mainz*, pp. 107–124. Mentz, *Johann Philipp von Schönborn*, pp. 106–119, paints a slightly brighter picture of the financial situation and estimates annual income very tentatively at 100,000 Reichstaler. Louis XIV sometimes provided as much as one-third of that figure.

21. Mentz, *Johann Philipp von Schönborn*, pp. 70–91; Bertrand Auerbach, *La France et le saint empire romain germanique depuis la paix de Westphalie jusqu'à la révolution française* (Paris, 1912), pp. 106–121.

22. Badalo-Dulong, *Diplomatie française*, pp. 114–115; Braubach, *Wilhelm von Fürstenberg*, pp. 115–131.

by the French.[23] With the Dutch war looming in 1671–72, John Philip tried to organize an anti-French coalition and even allied himself with the emperor, Trier, and Saxony in January 1672. He reverted to neutrality, however, when the Dutch war actually began. Although John Philip was planning to go over to the anti-French side at the time of his death early in 1673, his successor, the French client Lothar Frederick von Metternich, refused to do so. Even after the empire declared war on France in 1674, he remained in contact with France and allowed the coalition only the most limited use of his territory. Subsidies might have converted him to a more active policy, but the emperor Leopold would not pay them. Lothar Frederick died the next year.[24]

In 1679, after two very brief reigns, the Austrian-supported candidate Anselm Francis von Ingelheim won over the French-backed Christopher Rudolf von Stadion.[25] But whatever Anselm Francis's original allegiance, circumstances rapidly converted him to a pro-French policy. Despite—or perhaps because of—Louis's reunions, which steadily advanced French troops toward his territory, he consistently supported Louis's efforts to make a new peace or truce which would leave the French king in possession of most or all of his new acquisitions. At the Frankfurt peace conference of 1681–82 and at discussions in the Reichstag during the next two years, he used his powers as archchancellor to thwart Vienna's attempts to get the empire to take a strong anti-French stand, and thereby helped conclude the twenty year Truce of Ratisbon. Louis XIV rewarded him with 20,000 Reichstaler in 1682, 10,000 in 1683, and 30,000 in 1684. Anselm Francis may have felt that he had no choice but to take any steps that would lessen the risk of war. During the

23. See Max Braubach, "Politische Hintergrunde der Mainzer Koadjutorwahl von 1670," in Braubach, *Diplomatie und geistiges Leben in 17. und 18. Jahrhundert: Gesammelte Abhandlungen* (Bonn, 1969), pp. 54–74. Curiously, despite the French government's aggressive financial intervention in this and several other canonical elections, Louis XIV in the early 1680s seems to have developed scruples forbidding such simoniacal practices, and he actually forbade them in elections to the bishoprics of Bamberg and Würzburg in 1683. See Wysocki, *Kurmainz und die Reunionen*, p. 114.

24. Although even relatively recent studies such as Badalo-Dulong, *Diplomatie française*, have stated that Mainz joined the anti-French coalition, Klaus Mueller, "Wien und Kurmainz, 1673–1680: Ein Beitrag der kaiserlichen Diplomatie im Reich," *Rheinischer Vierteljahresblatter*, 32 (1968): 332–360, shows that this was not the case.

25. Mueller, "Wien und Kurmainz," pp. 360–401. Anti-French feeling was so strong in 1679 that Stadion asked William von Fürstenberg, who went to Mainz to help influence the election, not to support him openly.

Dutch war Mainz had suffered heavily from the exactions of both sides, and in a new war French troops would surely occupy the electorate before help could arrive. Anselm Francis held fast to this reasoning, and when war broke out in 1688 he peacefully handed over his fortifications on the left bank of the Rhine rather than resist the French. Perhaps Mainz in the early 1680s would not have resisted French power in any case, but the French government sensibly encouraged its electors to pursue unpopular pro-French policies by easing their financial burdens.[26]

Another German ecclesiastical prince who took advantage of contemporary international politics was Christopher Bernard von Galen, the bishop of Münster from 1650 to 1678. Indeed, in the opinion of Fritz Redlich, Galen was the first German prince to use subsidies to become a military enterpriser, in search of the power and profit which troops could bring him.[27] Münster had powerful estates, including the cathedral chapter, the knights, and the towns. Upon the death of Ferdinand of Bavaria, who had held both the see of Münster and the electorate of Cologne, the Münster chapter, angered at the financial contributions it had had to pay Ferdinand during the Thirty Years' War, elected Galen, a local magnate, rather than another Wittelsbach. In a highly significant letter to the pope written shortly after his election, Galen noted that much of the Catholic nobility of Münster, lacking opportunities for service to their own state, had converted to Protestantism in order to take positions in the army or government of neighboring Sweden, Holland, Brunswick, or Hesse. The bishop's subsequent policies suggest that he planned to give them ample opportunities for service closer to home.[28] During the 1650s Galen picked a quarrel with the city of Münster. Like the struggle between Erfurt and John Philip von Schönborn, the dispute turned both on religion—Protestantism maintained a foothold in Münster—and political privileges. The United Provinces adopted the role of the protector of Münster, and the Holy Roman Emperor refused to help Christopher Bernard impose his will on the city. In the late 1650s Christopher Bernard formed a league with Max Henry of Cologne and

26. See Wysocki, *Kurmainz und die Reunionen*, *passim*, on Anselm Francis's policy; figures for subsidies are on pp. 167–168.

27. Redlich, *German Military Enterpriser*, II, 8–12.

28. Wilhelm Kohl, *Christoph Bernhard von Galen: Politische Geschichte des Fürstbistums Münster, 1650–1678* (Münster, 1964), pp. 26–33.

John Philip of Mainz to secure more power at home and abroad, but the Münster estates refused to provide troops to make it effective. In 1658 he contemplated joining the Franco-Spanish war to replenish his treasury with Spanish subsidies, but his plans had not matured when the war came to an end.[29]

Christopher Bernard's chance to build up his army and treasury finally came in 1666, when the British promised him 500,000 Reichstaler to put an army in the field against Holland during the second Anglo-Dutch war. This escapade ended in disaster. Beaten by the dukes of Brunswick and the elector of Brandenburg, Christopher Bernard had to return to his estates bankrupt, and only a reconfirmation of their privileges in both war and peace secured needed funds. Down but not out, the bellicose bishop searched for a way to avoid disbanding all his troops. In a startling reversal, he initially proposed a subsidy treaty to the Dutch, and when they failed him, he turned to Louis XIV. A subsidy treaty with Louis signed in May 1667 gave him 36,000 Reichstaler annually to maintain about 3,000 men and enabled him to escape the disarmament mandated by his recent peace treaty with Holland.[30]

Christopher Bernard reentered the lists in 1672, when Louis's subsidies enabled him to put at least 10,000 men into the field as an ally against the Dutch. Although his troops, fighting alongside those of the elector of Cologne, won some initial successes on the Ijssel riverfront in 1672, the intervention of Brandenburg and the empire the next year left him in a disastrous position. Like the elector of Cologne, he made peace with the Dutch in May of 1674, but unlike Max Henry, he did not sit out the rest of the war. Anxious as always to keep men under arms, he changed sides and took part in the successful north German campaigns against France's ally, Sweden.[31] As Redlich has pointed out, Christopher Bernard's campaigns concentrated on the reduction and ransoming of fortified towns and on the conquest of winter quarters for his troops. While he claimed both to be fighting for the Catholic religion and for territorial aggrandizement, the only profit which he ever actually drew from his campaigns was financial—suggesting that this was his real goal.[32]

29. Ibid., pp. 131–151.
30. Ibid., pp. 242–256.
31. Ibid., pp. 335–417.
32. Redlich, *German Military Enterpriser*, II, 11–12.

After his death in 1673, Christopher Bernard was succeeded by a member of the Fürstenberg family and then, in 1683, by Max Henry of Cologne. Under him, conflicts with the Münster estates continued, and although Max Henry levied some troops in Münster, he had to turn successively to Louis and the empire to maintain them. Max Henry's successor, Frederick Christian von Plettenberg, became a Dutch client and raised troops in exchange for Dutch subsidies during the War of the Spanish Succession. In 1706 Frederick Christian died, and the Dutch eventually secured the election of their candidate Francis Arnold von Metternich.[33]

The electorate of Trier became another diplomatic and military battleground in the late seventeenth century, although we know much less about its domestic politics. During the Thirty Years' War, Richelieu and Mazarin had supported the elector Philip Christopher von Sötern against his cathedral chapter and estates in return for the right to occupy Trier's strategic fortresses. His successor, Charles Gaspar von der Leyen, elected in 1652, quickly became a Hapsburg client and sold his vote to Emperor Leopold in 1658. He changed course and joined the League of the Rhine in 1660 after Leopold had failed to pay promised subsidies, securing an annual French payment of 15,000 Reichstaler. Trier was both small and impoverished by the Thirty Years' War, and the League of the Rhine committed him to put only 500 troops in the field. In the Dutch war Charles Gaspar initially declared neutrality and allowed French troops to pass through his territory, but he joined the anti-French coalition in late 1672.[34]

Charles Gaspar and his nephew John Hugo von Orsbeck, who succeeded him in 1676, were promised Spanish subsidies, paid through the governor-general of the Spanish Netherlands, but they rarely arrived, and after the Dutch war John Hugo decided to cooperate with France.[35] The reunions took substantial portions of electoral territory, but John Hugo was powerless to act. In April

33. Max Braubach, "Holland und die geistlichen Staaten im Nordwesten des Reichs während des spanischen Erbfolgekrieges," in Braubach, Diplomatie und geistiges Leben, pp. 185–230.

34. See two articles by Rene Pillorget, "La France et l'électorat de Trèves au temps de Charles-Gaspard de la Leyen," Revue d'Histoire Diplomatique, 78 (1964): 7–34, 118–147, and "Jean-Hugues d'Orsbeck, Electeur de Trèves, et la politique des réunions (1678–1688)," ibid., 79 (1965): 315–337.

35. Alfred Sprunk, "Die Trierer Kurfürsten Karl Kaspard von der Leyen und Johann Hugo von Orsbeck und die Statthalter der Spanischen Niederlanden von 1675 bis 1700," Rheinische Vierteljahrsblätter, 32 (1968): 318–331.

1684 he joined with Cologne, Brandenburg, and Denmark in a new pro-French alliance, thus helping Louis to conclude the Truce of Ratisbon. Even then he had to allow Louis to destroy fortifications within his territory, and he seems to have been simply trying to make whatever terms he could.[36] After the outbreak of war in 1688, however, Trier rejoined the anti-French coalition in return for new promises of Spanish subsidies, and after 1693, when William of Orange arranged the appointment of Max Emmanuel of Bavaria as captain-general of the Netherlands, William tried to cultivate a new relationship with John Hugo.[37] The Dutch also persuaded John Hugo, who reigned until 1711, to join the imperial coalition in the War of the Spanish Succession in 1702, and they subsidized his troops.[38] Here again, the maritime powers continued the pattern established by Louis XIV in the years 1661–1688.

Several other German princes behaved in a similar manner. The elector John George of Saxony sought French subsidies to raise troops and crush his enemies in a coup d'état during the 1660s, and became a French client. But the poor Saxon domains could not support much of an army, and the elector played a very minor diplomatic role in the 1660s and 1670s.[39] Subsequently Saxon contingents fought briefly on the side of the empire during the Nine Years' War. The elector Frederick Augustus, however, won election as king of Poland in 1697. In December 1700, after the death of Carlos II, Frederick Augustus concluded a far-reaching subsidy treaty with Louis XIV and planned to fall upon the Hapsburg hereditary domains. But by the time war broke out he had changed sides, and in 1703 war between Poland and Sweden forced him to drop out of the war against Louis. Four years later Frederick Augustus withdrew from the war with Sweden and turned to the allies for the money he needed for his army and court. He eventually put 10,000 men in the field, financed by the British.[40]

The three duchies of the house of Brunswick—Lüneburg, with its capital of Celle, Kalenburg, with its capital of Hanover, and Wolfenbüttel—all hired out troops during the wars of Louis XIV. Duke John Frederick of Hanover cleverly kept a large army in

36. Pillorget, "Jean-Hugues d'Orsbeck."

37. Sprunk, "Die Trierer Kürfursten," pp. 325–328.

38. Max Braubach, "Kurtrier und die Seemächte während des spanischen Erfolgekrieges," in Braubach, *Diplomatie und geistiges Leben*, pp. 197–220.

39. Bertrand Auerbach, *La diplomatie française et la cour de Saxe, 1648–1680* (Paris, 1887), pp. 132–199, 488–490.

40. Braubach, *Die Bedeutung der Subsidien*, pp. 65–68, 126–132.

being with the help of French subsidies during the Dutch war without ever having to take an active part in the war.[41] His successor Ernest August, like so many other contemporary princes, concentrated upon securing new dignities for himself, specifically, the hat of a ninth elector of the Holy Roman Empire. He took advantage of Emperor Leopold's simultaneous wars with Turkey and France to secure the position in 1692, in exchange for a large money payment and a promise of 6,000 men to fight against the Turks.[42] His successor, the elector George Louis, was also recognized as heir to the British crown in 1701 and willingly provided troops to the British and Dutch, who paid for them, during the War of the Spanish Succession.[43] The ninth electorate in turn angered some neighboring, related princes, and one of them, the duke of Brunswick-Wolfenbüttel, raised 12,000 men for Louis XIV, in exchange for subsidies, during the same war.[44]

A recent study of the duchy of Württemberg describes the attempts of members of the ducal house to turn themselves into miniature monarchs, complete with court and standing army, in unusual detail. The estates of Württemberg enjoyed impressive power, and during the early decades of Louis XIV's reign they managed to prevent the prince regent, Frederick Charles, from realizing his ambition to lead an army in the field on one side or the other. In 1688, however, French armies came to Württemberg, and Frederick Charles got his wish. After he officially created a standing army and imposed new taxes, the estates argued that his measures "mocked the very premises of a legitimate, Christian, German-oriented, non-Machiavellian polity." Frederick Charles was eventually overthrown, but his nephew Duke Eberhard Louis won a confrontation with the estates over the question of a small standing army after the end of the Nine Years' War. Eberhard Louis took advantage of the War of the Spanish Succession to field a much larger army—paid for by imperial and Dutch subsidies—and he managed after the end of the war to maintain that army in peacetime.[45]

The experience of the minor German states during the era of

41. Georg Schanth, *Geschichte Hannovers im Zeitalter der neunten Kur und der englischen Sukzession, 1674–1714*, vol. 1 (Hildesheim, 1938), pp. 41–49, 116–142.

42. Redlich, *Weltmacht des Barock*, pp. 345–347.

43. Braubach, *Die Bedeutung der Subsidien*, pp. 133–136.

44. Ibid., pp. 57–63.

45. James Allen Vann, *The Making of a State: Württemberg, 1593–1793* (Ithaca, 1984), pp. 133–184.

Louis XIV suggests some general observations. To begin with, in the first three decades of his reign, Louis XIV won the alliance of many German princes even though ties with France were both unpopular with the public and unlikely to yield many gains in foreign policy. A very strong anti-French feeling in German public opinion that began with the War of Devolutions made alliances with France extremely unpopular, and a huge pamphlet literature castigated German princes who received French subsidies throughout Louis's reign.[46] In addition, the German princes almost never received territorial gains as a result of their participation in these wars. Yet both greater and lesser German princes accepted these subsidies either because of the lack of other revenues, or because of quarrels with their estates and towns. The German princes wanted to increase their resources and free themselves from the control of any domestic institutions, and subsidies enabled them to do this.[47]

Second, Louis XIV, for reasons not altogether clear, often spent a few tens of thousands of livres (out of a budget of more than 50 million) to secure the allegiance of minor German princes who clearly lacked the strength to oppose him in any case. Many of his alliances with German princes had a marginal military value at best, all the more so since some of them, as Redlich argues, undoubtedly pocketed their money rather than raise all of the troops they had promised, or pay the troops in full. Louvois, indeed, seems to have argued during the preparations for the Dutch war that France should simply occupy German territories and levy contributions from them, instead of paying their princes to raise armies—but except with respect to the Palatinate, with which Louis declined to sign a subsidy treaty, Louvois lost this argument.[48]

46. See Hubert Gillot, *La règne de Louis XIV et l'opinion publique en Allemagne* (Paris, 1914), esp. pp. 105–112. The unpopularity of Louis and of the German princes who cooperated with him is also a major theme of Auerbach's classic, *La France et le saint empire*; see for example pp. 126–135. Auerbach notes that pro-French delegates to the Reichstag were often subject to physical attacks.

47. On the problem of estates generally, see F. L. Carsten, *Princes and Parliaments in Germany from the Fifteenth to the Eighteenth Century* (Oxford, 1959). Carsten's argument that German estates were attempting to uphold the liberty of all citizens against their princes has come under attack from several German historians; see Guenter Birtsch, "Die landständische Verfassung als Gegenstand der Forschung," in Dietrich Gerhard, ed., *Ständische Vertretungen in Europa im 17. und 18. Jahrhundert* (Göttingen, 1969), pp. 32–55. Birtsch's argument that the estates merely sought to uphold particular privileges which they regarded as fundamental laws of their territory is convincing, but in either case, the fundamental struggle for political power between princes and estates is clear.

48. Volker Sellin, *Die Finanzpolitik Karl Ludwigs von der Pfalz: Staatswirtschaft im Wiederaufbau nach dem dreissigjährigen Krieg* (Stuttgart, 1978), pp. 61–72.

Even at the very height of his power in the early 1680s, Louis carried on long and complicated talks with the minor German princes whose territory he had taken in the reunions so as to arrange the truce of 1684, rather than simply take what he wanted and dare his enemies to take it back.[49] Whatever his motives, his strategy surely increased princely authority.

Finally, in currying favor with the German princes, Louis—and, later, the Dutch and the British—benefited from the structure of the Holy Roman Empire. Imperial political institutions were extremely active during Louis's reign. The Peace of Westphalia in 1648 had given the Reichstag the task of rewriting the imperial constitution, and its three colleges of electors, princes, and imperial free cities sat in almost continuous session after 1662. Many of the discussions dealt with schemes for the common defense of the empire, but these plans never got anywhere owing to the princes' reluctance to surrender any real authority over their troops or finances.[50] More important, the actual functions of the institutions of the empire tended to perpetuate the division of the German states rather than unite them and often exacerbated conflicts which foreign princes could exploit. The Reichstag and the other imperial institutions tended to confirm privileges held under the empire. In practice, then, the Reichstag and the imperial courts usually sided with the lesser estates—the minor princes, towns, and local estates—in their quarrels with the electors and other stronger princes, who constantly sought to expand their authority at their subjects' and their weaker neighbors' expense. Even the emperor, to whom some quarrels were appealed, frequently took the risk of offending a powerful prince rather than give a judgment that might undermine the complex structure of privileges upon which the empire was based.[51]

The institutions of the Holy Roman Empire, then, stood directly in the way of princes seeking to establish their authority and increase their independence. Foreign help provided a counterweight. The bishop of Münster and the elector of Mainz got no support from Emperor Leopold I in their respective quarrels with the towns of Münster and Erfurt, but Louis XIV willingly helped

49. These talks are covered in great detail by Wysocki, *Kurmainz und die Reunionen.*

50. Auerbach, *La France et le saint empire*, pp. 2–4 and *passim.*

51. Carol M. Rose, "Empire and Territories at the End of the Old Reich," James A. Vann and Steven W. Rowan, eds., *The Old Reich: Essays on German Political Institutions, 1495–1806* (Brussels, 1974).

them in return for appropriate concessions in the diplomatic sphere. More generally, on two occasions—in 1654 and in 1670—the full Reichstag recognized princes' rights to call upon their subjects for the resources necessary to maintain armies, either for self-defense or to make legal alliances, but the emperor refused to support these resolutions.[52] Louis XIV did assist the princes in the task he had attempted to complete in France: the strengthening of princely authority. More than one hundred years later, the French revolutionary governments and Napoleon helped the minor German lay princes complete the task of dismantling the empire.

The Political Achievement of the Late Seventeenth Century

In the late sixteenth and early seventeenth centuries, the violent ethos of the European aristocracy and the pretensions of European monarchs wreaked havoc over much of the Continent. The wars of the late seventeenth and early eighteenth centuries differed fundamentally from the conflicts of the previous century not because of any basic changes in military strategy or tactics, but because they occurred within a different political context and followed different political principles. Louis XIV and his fellow monarchs fought partly in the pursuit of wealth—though they drew no more monetary profit from their wars than their immediate ancestors—but more for their glory. Louis, Charles I, William of Orange, the Great Elector of Brandenburg, Max Emmanuel of Bavaria, and all the rest fought to enhance their power and prestige, and to a remarkable extent they succeeded. As a result, war, which in the previous century had weakened the authority of European states, now strengthened it.

The princes of the late seventeenth century accomplished this feat in several ways. To begin with, their financial resources grew. The critical increases in revenue in France, Great Britain, and the United Provinces—which paid for so many of the wars of the age—stemmed from a mixture of higher taxes on the countryside and a growth in international commerce. In addition, improved credit mechanisms in England, helped by the founding of the Bank of England, enabled the English monarchy to raise more money in

52. Doeberl, *Entwicklungsgeschichte Bayerns*, II, 59.

loans, although not more than Louis XIV.[1] Still, one should not exaggerate the increased efficiency of government finance in the late seventeenth century, much less suggest that war now showed a profit. During the War of the Spanish Succession Louis XIV had to resort to all the desperate financial expedients so familiar to Philip II, Richelieu, Mazarin, and Olivares. More significant, both the French and the British governments managed after the Peace of Utrecht to repudiate a larger portion of their accumulated debt by means of Mississippi and South Sea Bubbles. Their repudiation was more complete, in practice, than anything Philip II had ever achieved. In Britain, the South Sea Bubble reduced government debt service by more than £1 million per year, perhaps a quarter of the total.[2]

The great new achievements of European monarchs were more political than financial. They began with a series of compromises with their aristocracies over the issues which had led to so much conflict during the preceding century. Louis XIV carefully balanced several factions in his distribution of favors and patronage, rather than allowing a single favorite like Richelieu or Mazarin to monopolize them, and thereby helped avoid a new Fronde; English monarchs respected the claims of different factions and allowed them to make themselves felt in Parliament and in elections; and Emperor Leopold and his sons, respecting the power of their aristocracy, did not challenge their power but provided them with ample military employment against the Turks, in Italy, and in Germany. Monarchs also handled religious issues in a variety of new ways. Louis XIV outlawed Protestantism only after most of the leading Protestant nobles had converted to Catholicism, while English kings allowed a measure of religious toleration but generally restricted political power to aristocrats of the established faith. Monarchs also provided one another with the means to raise ar-

1. See Dickson and Sperling, "War Finance."

2. This figure is from Brewer, *Sinews of Power,* pp. 125–126, and is compared to his figure 2.1, p. 39. More research is needed here. The best short treatment of these episodes, Carswell, *South Sea Bubble,* does not try to estimate the actual financial significance of these operations. In each case, holders of government debt were given the option to exchange their holdings for shares in the new Mississippi and South Sea companies, designed respectively to exploit French possessions in Louisiana and the new *asiento.* After a boom in the shares of these companies which induced many government creditors to exercise their option, they both collapsed, giving a very big shock to European credit and wiping out the government debts that had been exchanged for their shares.

mies, largely putting an end to aristocratic military entrepreneurship and finally bringing the instruments of violence under their control for the first time. These armies enabled several princes to increase religious uniformity and reduce the privileges of towns.

Equally important, Louis XIV and his fellow monarchs changed the nature of war by redefining the stakes of conflicts. Louis himself, who undoubtedly set much of the tone of the era beginning in 1667, took care not to define them rigidly, or to commit himself to specific projects, territorial gains, or increases in wealth. He fought for his own glory, evaluating every step as it bore upon "the good of my service"—and this, more than anything else, gave him the flexibility necessary to control the scope and length of his wars. To Louis his glory never required either the complete obedience of his subjects or the utter defeat of his enemies. Certainly he tried to increase his dynasty's territory in every war, and except in the Nine Years' War he achieved this goal, but he concentrated above all upon seeming to control events. While at times his glory demanded that he begin war, at other times it required him to make peace as well. He repeatedly showed a willingness to respect the claims of other powers in order to secure some of his own, and his rivals joined in establishing the principle of the balance of power in European diplomacy. Only twice in this era did a power or coalition seek a total victory. In 1673, after the brilliant success of his initial campaigns against the Dutch, Louis dreamed of completely subjugating them, and in 1709 Marlborough actually hoped to force Louis to throw his own grandson off the throne of Spain. These bids for total victory were the exception rather than the rule, however, and both of them soon turned out to be illusory. The treaties of Nijmegen, Ryswick, Utrecht, and Rastatt were compromises.

Freedom of action characterized the diplomacy of the European powers and often culminated in diplomatic treachery. Major and minor princes took sides in the wars of this period without regard to tradition, religion, or loyalty. With the exception of the United Provinces, every European state fought both with and against the French during the reign of Louis XIV. Quite a few of their rulers, moreover—including the king of England, the elector of Brandenburg, and the duke of Savoy—changed sides in the middle of the same war, and several, such as Max Emmanuel of Bavaria, shamelessly took bids from both sides throughout entire conflicts. Here, as with respect to the control of military force, monarchs had taken over the role of the great aristocrats of the late sixteenth and early seventeenth centuries. Whereas in the earlier period magnates like the Guises, Condé, and Wallenstein had turned to foreign sovereigns when they felt slighted by their own, now European princes abandoned one rich patron for another as soon as it suited them to do so. No sanctions hampered this practice. Even the most treacherous princes, such as Max Emmanuel, generally emerged from conflicts with their domains restored.

The idea of the balance of power, which as we have seen both William III and Louis XIV invoked when it suited them to do so, reflected the limitations that all the powers imposed upon their war aims. The balance was also maintained as a result of the generally cautious military tactics of the period, which tended to rule out a complete victory, and by the flexible diplomacy of the princes, which encouraged them to change sides whenever they could gain by doing so. But no power, certainly not England, showed any special devotion to the balance. Charles II initially cooperated in Louis's attempts to destroy the Dutch, and thirty years later Marlborough sought a complete victory for his own side. He, not Louis XIV, bore the responsibility for the prolongation of the War of the Spanish Succession, which might easily have ended on roughly the same terms around 1707, had it not been for the allied attempt to produce a total victory.

It is not only inaccurate, as Roger Mettam has shown so clearly, but also ironic that Louis XIV has come down through history as the personification of an absolute monarch who eliminated rivals to his authority and thereby enjoyed the unquestioning obedience of France. Louis himself, as his memoirs show beyond doubt, held almost exactly the opposite view: that no prince could count implicitly upon his subjects' obedience and therefore must secure and maintain that obedience by a ceaseless vigilance and a knowledge of the dangers to his authority. Wise decisions, he wrote, could only be reached after the most careful study; rebellions like the Fronde were natural phenomena, encouraged by ineffective government; and the Huguenots could only be won back to the fold by patient efforts. In foreign affairs, he noted, one could not expect other powers to observe treaties, or the king of Spain to consent to anything that would raise the prestige of France. Above all, he constantly weighed the desirable against the possible.[3] Far from commanding unquestioning obedience, the monarch constantly had to steer a careful course between the rocks and shoals both at home and abroad, and had to deal from time to time with inevitable collisions and the leaks they brought about. The entire art of politics, he wrote, consists of playing upon circumstances, and his career thoroughly reflects that view. The rest of Europe followed his lead.

The new pattern of international conflict which emerged in western Europe in the latter half of the seventeenth century—a pattern based on frequent wars, generally cautious military tactics, rapid diplomatic changes of front, subsidies from richer to poorer powers, almost continual peace negotiations, and a general willingness to compromise issues—did not extend to northern and eastern Europe. The Great Northern War, in which Sweden first seemed to have defeated but subsequently succumbed to an alliance of Denmark, Poland, Russia, and some minor German powers, took place over an enormous territory, and Charles XII in particular sought complete victories over his opponents by occupying their capitals. Like the Austro-Turkish wars, the Great Northern War led to much more far-reaching territorial changes, suggesting a considerably different pattern of warfare in the east of Europe than in the west.[4] This indicates once again that political changes, rather than economic or technological changes, were responsible for the limitations which the central and western European powers observed in international conflict.

In western and central Europe, the new pattern of international relations lasted well into the eighteenth century. A new diplomatic reversal occurred immediately after the treaties of Utrecht and Rastatt. War continued between Philip V of Spain and Emperor Charles VI over the disposition of Spain's old Italian possessions, which Louis XIV—but not Philip V of Spain—had conceded to the emperor and the duke of Savoy. In 1718, three years after Louis XIV's death, the French regency and the British crown joined together with Emperor Charles VI to drive the Spaniards out of Si-

3. Sonnino, ed., *Memoires, passim.*
4. See Ragnhild Hatton, "Charles XII and the Great Northern War," in *New Cambridge Modern History*, VI, 648–680.

cily, and in 1720 Philip V finally made peace on terms laid down by the new Quadruple Alliance of Britain, France, the United Provinces, and the Holy Roman Empire—an alliance of the four main opponents in the War of the Spanish Succession.

During most of the rest of the eighteenth century wars remained entirely a prerogative of European monarchs. They still revolved mainly around dynastic questions such as the Polish and Austrian succession, and around mercantilist conflicts among Britain, Spain, and France. Rapid changes of diplomatic front, betrayal of allies, and compromise peaces—often encouraged by economic exhaustion—characterized the wars of 1733–1735, 1740–1748, and 1756–1763. Highly disciplined armies now moved and fought according to rigidly laid down patterns and campaigned only a few months of the year. In sharp contrast both to the eras that preceded and followed, eighteenth-century armies almost never lived off the land. And they were no more successful in inflicting decisive defeats upon one another than the armies of the era of Louis XIV.[5] The scale of conflicts grew, reflecting the economic and demographic growth of Europe as a whole, and the maritime balance of power changed somewhat in favor of the British, who made important gains in North America and India during the Seven Years' War.[6] While war remained quite frequent during the eighteenth century, it also remained very limited in scope, duration, and effect. Frederick the Great of Prussia specifically argued that the civilian population should not even be aware that wars were taking place,[7] and certainly he and his fellow monarchs came nearer to that ideal than their predecessors or successors. To a remarkable extent, war had become simply the business of those engaged in it, and the rest of society supported the aristocracy's proclivity for periodic conflicts without much damage to itself. War never threatened the domestic political structure of any European nation dur-

5. See especially Walter L. Dorn, *Competition for Empire, 1740–1763* (New York, 1940), pp. 80–121, 325–342. Dorn, whose contribution to the *Rise of Modern Europe* series has most unfortunately been taken out of print, shows very clearly how even the campaigns of Frederick the Great inevitably ended indecisively because of the limitations of contemporary armies.

6. Brewer, *Sinews of Power*, traces the expansion of the British war machine during the eighteenth century. The British, of course, suffered an important setback in the War of American Independence.

7. Ibid., pp. 82–83.

ing most of the eighteenth century, and the economic, intellectual, and cultural life of Europe experienced a unique era of growth and achievement.

Although war remained a wasteful and cruel burden upon European peoples, and the gains of the various European crowns remained fairly small in comparison to the resources expended, the monarchs of the era of Louis XIV had scored a great triumph by dedicating war to objectives which, if not generally beneficial, were at least achievable. The new pattern of international relations which emerged in the late seventeenth century enabled domestic and international politics to assume a much more stable shape, and allowed for tremendous advances in other areas of European civilization.

3 The Revolutionary and Napoleonic Era

> Reason of state being the rule of policy, aggrandizement was its aim. "He who gains nothing, loses," wrote Catherine II. The idea of the greatness of the state was intimately linked to that of the extent of the state.
>
> —Albert Sorel

> Radical though it may have been, the Revolution made far fewer changes than is generally supposed, as I shall point out later. What in point of fact it destroyed . . . may be summed up as everything in the old order that stemmed from aristocratic and feudal institutions, was in any way connected with them, or even bore, however faintly, their imprint.
>
> —Alexis de Tocqueville

The Enlightenment and European International Politics

In the late eighteenth century a profound intellectual change, pregnant with consequences for domestic and international politics, came over Europe. On the surface politics had changed relatively little since the era of Louis XIV. Monarchies and aristocracies still dominated politics and economic life, and faction still played a key role in political conflict.[1] We have seen that international politics did not change fundamentally in the first half of the century, and that states resorted to war from familiar dynastic and mercantile motives.[2] The two major mid-century conflicts, the War of the Austrian Succession and the Seven Years' War, both revolved around the same two major issues: the struggle between the Aus-

---

1. Faction has of course been thoroughly studied in the case of Great Britain thanks to Sir Lewis Namier and his students. Historians of Continental Europe in this period have generally focused upon individual monarchs and ministers.
2. Here see also Geoffrey Best, *War and Society in Revolutionary Europe, 1770–1870* (New York, 1982), pp. 15–17.

trian emperor and the Prussian monarch for Silesia, and the struggle between Britain and France for colonial possessions. Diplomacy also remained a treacherous game of sudden changes like the diplomatic revolution of 1756, in which Louis XV of France made an alliance with Austria, and Britain's abandonment of Prussia in 1761. Since the European economy was growing—albeit largely within its traditional agricultural and commercial framework—and European populations were increasing, governments fielded somewhat larger armies as the century wore on.[3] Wars also imposed larger financial burdens upon states, but until the American War of Independence the British and the French governments—the two most heavily affected—managed to meet their burdens with loans.[4] The late eighteenth century, however—the age of the Enlightenment and of enlightened despotism—witnessed some critical intellectual and political changes which prepared the way for a new and distinct era of general war in Europe, from 1792 through 1815. Writers spread new attitudes toward the purpose of government and the role of reason in public life, and European governments promptly adapted these attitudes to their own purposes. A new view of the nature and purpose of international conflict became a critical factor in European international politics beginning with the first partition of Poland in 1772.

The essence of the Enlightenment, perhaps, was its belief in happiness as the goal of human existence and reason as the source of human happiness.[5] Here we are concerned above all with its influence upon domestic and international politics, as reflected in the behavior of the so-called enlightened despots such as Frederick the Great and the emperor Joseph II; the French revolutionary governments; and Napoleon. The influence was in many ways indirect, largely because the great Enlightenment thinkers understood

3. Only in Prussia, however, did the state mobilize a definitely higher *proportion* of the adult male population as the century wore on. André Corvisier, *Armies and Society in Europe, 1494–1789* (Bloomington, 1979), p. 113.

4. Michel Morineau, "Budgets de l'état et gestion des finances royales en France au dix-huitième siècle," *Revue Historique*, 264, no. 2 (October–December 1980): 289–336. Reversing a traditional view, Morineau argues that French government finances did not become significantly weaker than British until after the American war.

5. In this section I am relying mainly upon Ernst Cassirer, *The Philosophy of the Enlightenment* (Princeton, 1951); Paul Hazard, *European Thought in the Eighteenth Century: From Montesquieu to Lessing* (New Haven, 1954); and Alfred Cobban, *In Search of Humanity: The Role of the Enlightenment in Modern History* (New York, 1960). Cobban points out (pp. 135–138) that David Hume specifically challenged the independence of reason in the midst of the Enlightenment.

some of the critical problems of translating theory into practice. Men like Voltaire, Montesquieu, Hume, and Rousseau combined, in varying measures, a belief in a universally valid reason with a healthy respect for things as they were.[6] On the one hand, they dreamed of more just societies founded upon reason; on the other, they saw greed, ambition, and folly behind the behavior of many princes. In this respect they were wrestling with perhaps the most critical problem of modern civilization, the reconciliation of man's moral imagination with reality, and they were far too sophisticated to content themselves with any simple answers.

European princes, however, found it quite easy to adapt Enlightenment ideas to their own needs. They used reason as their sixteenth- and seventeenth-century forefathers had used religion: as a weapon in their continuing battle to extend their authority, in relation to both traditional domestic institutions and other monarchs. "The enlightened despotism of the physiocrats and philosophes," as Georges Lefèbvre wrote, "offered sovereigns suggestions they could reconcile with their traditional policy insofar as they found them capable of favoring the enrichment of their states and the growth of their power."[7] This was especially easy in the domestic sphere. Enlightenment thinkers asked the state to weaken or suppress traditional irrational institutions such as the church, economic monopolies, and archaic local institutions. The state, the prevailing wisdom held, could promote the welfare of the whole society by promulgating uniform laws, removing barriers to economic activity, and reducing the role of superstition in intellectual life.

Such ideas could help governments increase their revenues, and especially after the end of the Seven Years' War in 1763, which left all the major European countries with large new debts, European monarchs undertook a wide-ranging series of economic, fiscal, political, and even social reforms. All these reforms reflected the new intellectual climate, with which many princes were intimately familiar.[8] Economically the reforms tried to improve agriculture, to

6. This is a major theme of another important work, Friedrich Meinecke, *Historism: The Rise of a New Historical Outlook* (New York, 1972), which treats the main Enlightenment thinkers.

7. Georges Lefèbvre, "Le despotisme éclairé," *Annales Historiques de la Révolution Française*, 21 (1949): 101.

8. A fine short summary of these developments is John G. Gagliardo, *Enlightened Despotism* (London, 1967), esp. pp. 21–59.

make the collection of taxes more efficient, and to encourage freer trade within their realms. Other changes reduced or even eliminated the privileges of religion and religious orders (the Jesuits, of course, were expelled from both France and Austria in the late eighteenth century), tried to set up a new and independent judiciary, and sought to substitute salaried officials for venal or hereditary office holders. Monarchs also tried to make primary education compulsory and improve the status of peasants. All these measures were designed to increase the general welfare and the power of the state, reflecting a new, revolutionary conception of the proper role of government. The new rationalism did not necessarily call for more representative institutions, but it promised to reorder political, economic, and social life. Both monarchs and revolutionaries could hold the new beliefs, since they focused upon the results of government action, rather than its nature. Tocqueville noted long ago that many Enlightenment writers seemed to care more about the implementation of their favorite reforms than about the means by which they might be promulgated, and Elizabeth Fox-Genovese has recently confirmed that the French physiocrats put their faith in authoritarian government to implement the reforms in which they believed.[9] Reason was a new weapon against traditional privilege, which still stood in the way of centralizing monarchs.

The influence of Enlightenment thought upon international affairs was far more subtle. The major Enlightenment thinkers themselves had relatively little to say about international politics. None of the great Enlightenment thinkers was primarily concerned with issues of power politics, and several of them viewed the subject with distaste.[10] Nevertheless, contemporary statesmen quickly adapted Enlightenment thought in ways that not only sanctioned their traditional aspiration toward territorial expansion but actually encouraged it. In the hands of men like Frederick the Great, Joseph II, William Pitt the Elder, the leaders of the French Revolu-

9. Alexis de Tocqueville, *The Old Regime and the French Revolution* (Garden City, 1955), pp. 157–169; Elizabeth Fox-Genovese, *The Origins of Physiocracy: Economic Revolution and Social Order in Eighteenth-Century France* (Ithaca, 1976), pp. 304–305.

10. This emerges very clearly from Meinecke, *Historism*, pp. 54–198, which deals with Voltaire, Montesquieu, Hume, Gibbon, and Robertson. Rousseau was perhaps the most skeptical with respect to international politics. See Stanley Hoffmann, "Rousseau on War and Peace," in Hoffman, *The State of War: Essays on the Theory and Practice of International Politics* (New York, 1965), pp. 54–87.

tion, and Napoleon, reason became a new excuse for territorial expansion, as well as for the growth of the power of the state within their own societies.

Thus, the Enlightenment's rejection of traditional authority and privilege tended to encourage territorial expansion in parts of Europe where the church and other theoretically anachronistic institutions still enjoyed territorial sovereignty. Well before 1789, princes and pamphleteers had begun to regard noble privileges, church lands, and ecclesiastical territories as ripe for reform. After the first partition of Poland, Frederick the Great secularized large church lands and predicted that the French government would eventually take the same step to pay off its debts. Joseph II closed convents and confiscated monastic lands within his domains, and he attempted to remove most noble privileges to create a more unitary state. Lesser German princes already cast covetous eyes upon imperial free cities and ecclesiastical territories, arguing that they had survived beyond their time.[11] Similar views may have encouraged Joseph II's numerous projects of expansion into the Ottoman empire as well. The contemporary climate encouraged supposedly young and vigorous monarchies to expand at the expense of supposedly corrupt, worn-out anachronisms, and such expansion, as we shall see, played a critical role in the wars of the French Revolution and Napoleon.

Reason and enlightenment, however, did not provide any sanction for the expansion of one enlightened despot at the expense of another. As Meinecke noted, this kind of expansion could not be justified based upon the welfare of the inhabitants of the territory that changed hands, if both their old and new rulers administered them according to the same enlightened principles.[12] The solution to this problem lay in another aspect of Enlightenment thought. Led by Frederick the Great, Enlightenment rulers simply postulated a tendency to expand not as a consequence of reason but rather as an observed, inescapable historical fact. "Of all states, from the smallest to the biggest," Frederick wrote in 1743, "one can safely say that the fundamental rule of government is the principle of extending their territories. This passion is as deeply rooted in every ministry as universal despotism is in the Vatican." "Keep it

11. Klaus Epstein, *The Genesis of German Conservatism* (Princeton, 1966), pp. 276–288.

12. Meinecke, *Machiavellism*, pp. 306–307, shows that Frederick the Great discussed this contradiction before his accession to the throne.

firmly fixed in your mind," he wrote in 1768, "that there is no great ruler who does not cherish the idea of extending his dominion."[13] Such maxims turned international conflict into a natural law like those which in the view of the philosophes governed other aspects of economic and political life. They also turned the pursuit of expansion into a necessity, since any prince who departed from the theoretically prevailing pattern must eventually find himself in an inferior position.

Frederick, indeed, built a broader philosophy of kingship upon the necessity of expansion. Regarding himself simply as the "first servant of the state"—a phrase he actually borrowed from his father[14]—he renounced any right to indulge merely personal whims, and relentlessly set about the fulfillment of his duties. His compulsive bourgeois work habits and personal asceticism reflected these beliefs. Historians like Meinecke have generally lauded these aspects of his character, but they had serious consequences. Combined with Frederick's belief in the natural tendency toward territorial expansion, they turned aggrandizement into a duty which the monarch must pursue. Frederick recognized that his policies also reflected his own yearnings for glory but justified even these as necessary for the greater good. Princely ambition, he argued, was needed to give states a unifying purpose. It distinguished Prussia from states like the Netherlands and Sweden, whose parliamentary institutions had led them into impotence and sloth. The prestige of the state required expansion.[15] Frederick also expressed concern for the welfare of his people and did his best to promote economic growth, although it is not altogether clear whether he regarded such measures as ends in themselves or as means to the greater glory and power of the state.

Joseph II of Austria, an equally dedicated and ascetic ruler, used the principles enunciated by Frederick to embark upon a frenzy of activity. More deeply influenced by Enlightenment philosophers, he called as early as 1760 for a larger army, a smaller bureaucracy, a broader tax base, and the encouragement of industry and agricul-

13. Ibid., pp. 301–302. On Frederick's thought, see also Arnold Berney, *Friedrich der Grosse: Entwicklungsgeschichte eines Staatsmannes* (Tübingen, 1934), and Theodor Schieder, "Friedrich der Grosse und Machiavelli—das Dilemma von Machtpolitik," *Historische Zeitschrift*, 234, no. 2 (April 1982): 265–294.

14. Robert Ergang, *The Potsdam Führer: Frederick William I, Father of Prussian Militarism* (New York, 1941), p. 45.

15. See Berney, *Friedrich der Grosse*, pp. 260–273, and Meinecke, *Machiavellism*, p. 302.

ture. He believed that all citizens should work for the good of the nation, and he worked for his subjects' happiness whether they wanted it or not.[16] Once in power he pursued all these reforms, while also undertaking numerous schemes for territorial expansion. These included the exchange of Belgium for Bavaria, a partition of the Ottoman empire, and additional imperial acquisitions in Italy.[17] Joseph's unwillingness to risk decisive battles on behalf of his aims, however, and the poor performance of his troops against the Turks after 1787, left him without significant accomplishments.

The growing belief that states had not only a right but a duty to expand at their neighbors' expense also influenced politicians as diverse as Catherine the Great of Russia and the elder William Pitt. Even those who disliked the new principles on moral grounds, such as Maria Theresa of Austria, or who did not believe that acquisitions would benefit their countries, like the count of Vergennes, French foreign minister from 1774 to 1787, found themselves forced to observe these rules. The obsession with aggrandizement could only encourage aspiring diplomats to develop new and ambitious projects.[18]

The new ideas triumphed dramatically in 1772, in the first partition of Poland. This step had no legal justification whatever. Catherine the Great, Frederick the Great, and Maria Theresa each took a portion of the kingdom simply because they found it useful to do so, and Voltaire, scornful of the existing Polish constitution, lauded them for having performed a service to humanity. The partition of Poland, as Albert Sorel noted, helped institutionalize the principle of compensation in European international politics, thereby sanctioning the parallel expansion of the stronger European states at the expense of the weaker and foreshadowing the diplomacy of the revolutionary and Napoleonic periods.[19] In subsequent years Joseph II, in particular, proposed several new terri-

---

16. See Henri Pirenne, *Histoire de la Belgique*, 7 vols. (Brussels, 1900–1932), V, 397–398.

17. See Paul von Mitrofanov, *Joseph II: Seine politische und kulturelle Tätigkeit* (Vienna and Leipzig, 1910), pp. 113–234.

18. See Orville T. Murphy, *Charles de Gravier, Comte de Vergennes: French Diplomacy in the Age of Revolution, 1719–1787* (Albany, N.Y., 1982), pp. 211–221.

19. Albert Sorel, *L'Europe et la révolution française* (Paris, 1885–1904), esp. vol. I, *passim*. A remarkable critique of Sorel's work can be found in Pieter Geyl, *Napoleon, For and Against* (New Haven, 1949), pp. 254–307.

torial rearrangements, such as the partition of the Ottoman empire in Europe, which lacked any historic or dynastic justification. Intellectually the way had been cleared for a sweeping reorganization of Europe.

Still, before 1789, the idea of reason—like that of princely glory under Louis XIV—was essentially an intellectual gloss upon the practice of dynastic politics. In the long run, of course, it threatened entirely to undermine dynastic authority and to destroy the legitimacy of existing European political institutions. Despite Frederick the Great's attempts to justify princely ambition as useful to the state as a whole, reason did not necessarily favor the maintenance of monarchy. Equally significant, the substitution of reason for historical tradition or dynastic right as the organizing principle of the European community could threaten the legitimacy not only on the frontiers of the kingdom of Poland but of almost any frontiers within Europe. Reason provided no obvious rules for redrawing frontiers, and it therefore might allow for almost any changes imaginable—all the more so since nationalism, which became the new organizing principle of the international community one hundred years later, had not yet developed any influence. In theory anyone might acquire and rule any territory in Europe, as long as their rule seemed designed to liberate their subjects from privilege, encourage happiness, and follow the dictates of natural law.

In practice, the enlightened despots, whose resources were far from unlimited, applied the new ideas of international politics very selectively, balancing their expansionism with a high degree of caution.[20] Frederick the Great turned Prussia into an important European power by acquiring Silesia and West Prussia, but although he also wanted to annex the electorate of Saxony, he became much more careful after the Seven Years' War and did nothing to disturb the peace of Europe during the last twenty years of his reign. The instruments of warfare still restrained ambitious princes. European armies of the eighteenth century remained cumbersome, rigidly disciplined bodies of men, unable to move faster than their supply trains and often incapable of bringing campaigns to a decisive conclusion. Furthermore, European finance still could not indefinitely support armies in the field. Largely for

20. As noted by Sorel, *L'Europe et la révolution française*, I, 30–33.

these reasons, the coalition of Austria, Russia, and France, which planned the Seven Years' War with the hope of dismembering Prussia, retreated from the field in 1762–63 with nothing to show for the campaign but financial exhaustion. Similarly, Joseph II in 1784 abandoned his plans to acquire Bavaria in the face of Frederick's resistance without even fighting a battle.

In other ways, too, the history of the late eighteenth century suggests that the new ideas of natural law, uniform treatment of subjects by their sovereign, an end to old feudal privileges and restrictions upon economic activity, impartial justice, and career open to talent did not necessarily reflect European social and political realities. Under pressure from reformers, many of the supposed anachronisms derided by philosophes and pamphleteers showed that they retained considerable vitality and that monarchs tampered with them at their peril. Joseph II found virtually no constituency for his various reforms and eventually faced revolts in Belgium, Galicia, and Hungary.[21] Turgot's ambitious reform program failed to win acceptance in France, where the aristocracy tenaciously defended its principles and virtually no one appreciated the freeing of the grain trade. T. C. W. Blanning has more recently argued that the ecclesiastical principalities of western Germany were as enlightened as many secular states, and that they were by no means doomed to an imminent demise.[22] In Prussia the new civil code—a monument to enlightenment rationalism commissioned by Frederick the Great—coexisted with serfdom and a fully functioning seigneurial system in the countryside. An intellectual consensus prevailed at the upper reaches of European society from London to St. Petersburg, but the practicality of the new ideas remained questionable.

The idea of career open to talent did have a wide constituency within Europe, but it was not necessarily destined to change the ways in which governments actually behaved. A favorite idea of enlightenment philosophers, career open to talent was supported by monarchs such as Joseph II and became a major demand of the Third Estate in the French Revolution. Rising new men, however, often had their eyes upon traditional careers in the military and the highest levels of the state. The "bourgeois revolution," writes

21. Mitrofanov, *Joseph II*, pp. 223–224.
22. T. C. W. Blanning, *The French Revolution in Germany: Occupation and Resistance in the Rhineland, 1792–1802* (Oxford, 1983), pp. 33–47.

Louis Bergeron, was "a determined and successful attempt . . . to break down the barrier of legal orders that blocked upward social mobility into the highest echelons, and to destroy 'ministerial despotism,' the final version of monarchical absolutism. It was a demand for infusing into the directing elites, substantially enlarged and enriched, a new social content in which the only passport would be a combination of fortune and ability."[23] As events would shortly show, a new elite could be as expansionist as an older one. Both older and newer officials, moreover, regarded office as a source of personal profit. Officials of the most varied backgrounds continued to regard public office as the easiest means of making their fortune, and quite a few, including Mirabeau in France, Thugut in Austria, and numerous eighteenth-century Englishmen, were frankly corrupt.[24]

Beginning in 1787, a crisis of the French state combined with the new ideology of state power, the erosion of the legitimacy of the old regime, and the rise of a new and ambitious class of men to produce a new era of general war in Europe. New elites reached positions of power at a moment when expansion had become the business of the state, and Europe's territorial arrangements were increasingly becoming delegitimized. Men as diverse as the Prussian Hardenberg, the low-born Austrian Thugut, the Frenchman Dumouriez, the one-time English cabin-boy Nelson, the tsar Alexander of Russia, and the Corsican Napoleon Bonaparte took advantage of the collapse of the old regime to make their fortunes in spectacular fashion. The seductive power of new ideas tempted the rulers of Europe to new heights of ambition, but the resources of European society could not in the long run satisfy them. In the end, the revolutionary and Napoleonic era simply continued the consolidation of European states, while bequeathing new political and intellectual problems to subsequent generations.

Sources and Consequences of the Wars of the French Revolution

The French Revolution embodied many separate ideological currents and goals. On the one hand, it undertook numerous re-

23. Louis Bergeron, *France under Napoleon* (Princeton, 1981), p. 134.

24. On the situation in England, see above all George Otto Trevelyan, *The Early History of Charles James Fox* (New York, 1880), pp. 61–101.

forms—equality before the law, the free circulation of property and goods, free trade, religious toleration, the confiscation of church lands, and the removal of occupational barriers—similar in nature to the reforms of contemporary enlightened despots in central and eastern Europe. On the other, it witnessed the emergence of a democratic movement analogous to those in Britain, Holland, parts of Belgium, and the United States, and eventually endorsed the principle of universal male suffrage.[1] Influential Marxist historians have argued that the revolution reflected the interests of a new, rising class, the industrial bourgeoisie,[2] and that under the Jacobins the revolution in 1793–94 became a social revolution aimed at the redistribution of wealth as well as political power.[3] More recently a new school, led by François Furet, has argued for a return to a more intellectual and political interpretation similar to that introduced more than one hundred years ago by Alexis de Tocqueville.[4]

I shall touch on these debates in discussing the impact of the French revolution upon European international politics. Within three years of the calling of the Estates General, France had become involved in a major war, and beginning in 1792 the war led French troops into Belgium (1792–93 and 1794–1799), Holland (1795), Germany (1794–1799), Italy (1796–1798), Switzerland (1798), and even Egypt (1798). The French republic eventually annexed Belgium and the Rhineland and set up new republics in Holland, Switzerland , and various parts of Italy. I shall investigate the sources and consequences of the wars of the French revolution by focusing upon the following questions:

(1) Did the French revolutionaries, beginning in 1792, unleash and pursue the war with the intent of spreading revolutionary principles, and how did French expansion affect revolutionary movements within neighboring countries?

(2) What were the political and social effects of the wars of the 1790s, both in France and in the rest of Europe?

1. This of course is stressed by R. R. Palmer, *The Age of the Democratic Revolution: A Political History of Europe and America, 1760–1800,* 2 vols. (Princeton, 1959–1964).

2. This is stated most succinctly by Albert Soboul, *A Short History of the French Revolution* (Berkeley, 1977).

3. Albert Mathiez, *The French Revolution* (New York, 1964), and Georges Lefèbvre, *The French Revolution,* 2 vols. (New York, 1964), II, 39–136, make classic statements of this argument.

4. See François Furet, *Interpreting the French Revolution* (Cambridge, 1981).

(3) Did the European powers embark upon war against the French primarily in order to crush the revolution, or did they do so for other reasons?

The first question bears upon the issue of the Atlantic Revolution, a concept proposed by Jacques Godechot and R. R. Palmer, and more recently subjected to a measured attack by Simon Schama and a scathing polemic by T. C. W. Blanning.[5] Certainly Blanning and Schama make it quite difficult to see French expansion and the creation of sister republics as fundamentally the outcome of a generalized European revolutionary process. They have, however, based their arguments mainly upon developments within occupied territories, especially the Rhineland and Holland. We must therefore ask how their findings might also relate to the origins of the war within France.

The initial French decision for expansion in 1791–92 seems to have been taken for a mixture of political and ideological reasons.[6] Although revolutionary opinion as reflected in the cahiers of 1789 and the policy of the Constituent Assembly showed no aggressive impulses, by late 1791 the government was thinking seriously about war. The major issues before the Legislative Assembly in the latter half of 1791 included the proper attitude to take toward the king, who had effectively discredited himself by trying to flee the country; the question of continuing the revolution, which divided the Jacobin club; and the proper attitude to take toward the noble émigrés outside France and the foreign powers who were threatening to intervene. The faction known to history as the Girondins, led by Brissot, Vergniaud, and Roland, and allied to General Dumouriez, began advocating a war against Austria in late 1791. While arguing, in rhetoric typical of the revolution since its onset, that the Austrian government, the émigrés, refractory priests, and other domestic enemies were conspiring against the

5. Jacques Godechot, *La grande nation: L'expansion révolutionnaire de la France dans le monde de 1789 à 1799*, 2 vols. (Paris, 1956), actually takes a balanced view of the effects of French expansion, and Palmer, *Age of Democratic Revolution*, is also more mindful of the role of French armies in the revolutionary process than Blanning sometimes seems to suggest. For the attacks, see Blanning, *French Revolution in Germany*, pp. 11–13, and Simon Schama, *Patriots and Liberators* (New York, 1977), pp. 1–57.

6. This question has been treated most recently by Simon Schama, *Citizens: A Chronicle of the French Revolution* (New York, 1989); T. C. W. Blanning, *The Origins of the French Revolutionary Wars* (New York, 1986); Marcel Reinhard, *La chute de la royauté* (Paris, 1969); and M. J. Sydenham, *The Girondins* (London, 1961). Earlier works by Lefèbvre, Mathiez, Aulard, and Sorel remain important.

revolution, they also seemed to believe that a war would help consolidate the revolution by forcing the king and his party unequivocally to reveal their attitude toward it. At the same time, some elements around the throne believed that war would enable the king to reestablish his authority, either through impressive victories of his own, or with the help of the victorious foreign powers. They were opposed by Robespierre, who argued that France could not fight until the revolution had been consolidated, and who doubted that the revolution could be successfully exported.[7] The Girondins combined their official goals with their own worldly ambitions. Dumouriez, in particular—a low-born officer of the army who had seized upon the revolution as an opportunity to make his fortune—hoped to lead French troops into Belgium, where he planned to set himself up as a semi-autonomous monarch. He was only the first to entertain such plans.

The use of war to increase the prestige of the government was entirely traditional, but ideological goals rapidly emerged as well. The Girondins argued that they were fighting an international conspiracy against liberty, including European princes, and after the overthrow of Louis XVI in August 1792, the revolutionary government proclaimed its intention of liberating the peoples of Europe. The Convention adopted on November 19, 1792, a decree promising help to all peoples wishing to regain their liberty. Targets for this appeal included the Belgian Vonckists, who had fought an unsuccessful revolution against Joseph II in 1789–90; the Dutch Patriots, whose revolt against the old Dutch oligarchy had been defeated by Prussian troops in 1787–88; and smaller groups of German Jacobins.[8] As it turned out, however, political and ideological motivations for expansion gave way almost immediately to financial ones. Beginning in 1792, the revolutionary governments sought not only political but also financial salvation in expansion abroad. The financial crisis which had begun the revolution had not abated; it had become worse. As we shall see, only the exploitation of a whole series of territories kept the revolutionary governments alive. Expansion emerged as the solution to the financial crisis which the revolution had helped to produce. The

7. Schama, *Citizens*, pp. 591–597; Reinhard, *La chute de la royauté*, pp. 244–257; Sydenham, *Girondins*, pp. 101–107.

8. On these revolts, see Henri Pirenne, *Histoire de la Belgique*, V, 460–557; Schama, *Patriots and Liberators*, pp. 64–135; and Blanning, *French Revolution in Germany*, pp. 255–264.

vision of revolutionary brotherhood fell victim to the needs of the revolutionary state.

The political crisis which the Girondins hoped to resolve by beginning the war was only a part of a larger crisis of the French state. The revolutionary governments never successfully resolved the financial problem they faced. The Estates General had been called essentially to deal with the financial problems which had accumulated under the old regime, not least because of France's involvement in the American Revolution. Significantly, a relatively recent study of late eighteenth-century French finance suggests that the financial crisis of 1787 was more political and social than economic. J. F. Bosher argues that the crisis reflected not a long-term disequilibrium in French government finances but rather a temporary crisis occasioned by the bankruptcy of several key government financiers. Traditionally the government had dealt with temporary crises by arraigning the financiers as scapegoats, but by this time the financiers had become too prominent socially for this remedy to be adopted. Largely as a result, the French minister Calonne and his successors Brienne and Necker tried instead to use the crisis as the occasion for far-reaching reforms, eventually leading to the calling of the Estates General.[9] Lynn Hunt argues similarly that it was the old regime's political culture, rather than its economic structure, which led the crisis to take the form that it did, while John Brewer has also concluded that the French tax system was a political catastrophe more than a financial one.[10]

In any case, the deputies of the Constituent and Legislative Assemblies instituted drastic new measures to reform French finances and pay off the state debt. Reflecting the principles of the Enlightenment, they overhauled the tax system, relying primarily on a new, equitably apportioned series of direct taxes, and decided to pay off the state debt by nationalizing and selling off church lands. Both steps reflected the reforming spirit of the age, and neither was a revolutionary novelty. Joseph II had already undertaken similar reforms in Austria, and within France the idea of nationalizing church property had long been in the air.[11] Both measures, however, failed disastrously. The new taxes were extremely diffi-

9. J. F. Bosher, *French Finances, 1770–1795* (Cambridge, 1970), pp. 183–196.

10. Lynn Hunt, *Politics, Culture, and Class in the French Revolution* (Berkeley, 1984), pp. 221–222; Brewer, *Sinews of Power*, pp. 126–134.

11. Marcel Marion, *Histoire financière de la France depuis 1715*, 6 vols. (Paris, 1914–1931), II, 39–69.

cult to put in place, and revenues had fallen severely by 1791. The government began relying almost completely upon *assignats*, or paper money, issued by the Caisse de l'Extraordinaire. Theoretically backed by clerical lands, or *biens nationaux*, these bills multiplied so rapidly that they began to depreciate in value by 1792, ultimately enabling the purchasers of church lands to pay off their debts at a fraction of their value.[12] The government already needed money very badly at the time the war began.

It seems quite clear that the Girondins, who held power in the last few months of 1792, already intended to use conquests to ease their financial problems. Thus the Convention decree of November 19, 1792, was followed within a month by another decree, of December 15, providing for the destruction of the whole social, political, and economic apparatus of the old regime in occupied territories. The elucidation of the decree by Pierre Cambon made clear that the property of the ruling princes and the church would be expropriated and sold once again as *biens nationaux*, while *assignats* would circulate at full value. As it turned out, application of this decree was limited, both because of military reverses in the spring of 1793 and because Dumouriez, in Belgium, hoped to win the allegiance of the population by treating them relatively leniently. In the meantime, however, War Minister Lazare Carnot, one of the most important statesmen of the revolution, had defined the foreign policy of the republic in terms worthy of Frederick the Great. "Every political act," he told the Convention of February 14, "is legitimate, so long as it is required by the welfare of the state," and "every act which harms the interest of another without being absolutely necessary it itself unjust." France might annex territory either because the people involved had given their approval, or because the territory was vital to French security. Between November and March of 1793 the Convention annexed Savoy, Nice, Belgium, and various German territories.[13] At the same time the revolutionary government freed the new French armies from the restraints of the eighteenth century. Living off the land, which the old regime armies had generally forbidden, now became a patriotic duty.

Taking office in June of 1793, Robespierre's Jacobin dictatorship continued to live by requisitions, forced loans, and *assignats*, and

12. Ibid., pp. 176–257, 295–361.
13. Blanning, *French Revolution and Germany*, pp. 64–69.

by the spring of 1794 the government was spending more than five times its revenue every month.[14] Although Robespierre did not believe in annexations, he ordered the fullest possible exploitation of occupied territories. The army, which the revolutionary governments had been unable to pay, now began looking after itself, collecting 10 million francs in specie from the Palatinate in the fall of 1793. Such sums, however, could hardly bail France out of its financial crisis, and Cambon, now a member of the Committee of Public Safety, warned in the spring of 1794 that France must have victory that year.[15] But before victory could finally be won, the Thermidorian reaction overthrew Robespierre and the Jacobins.

Under the Thermidorians and the Directory, who took power after Robespierre's fall in the summer of 1794, the exploitation of occupied territories became even more important to French politics. The new elite—drawn from the moderate party in the Convention and reflecting the views of the Girondins—embodied the fusion of old regime officials and newer elements which Napoleon later drew upon.[16] Survivors of several violent revolutions in opinion, the new men distinguished themselves by their ambition and political caution. Having learned to fear the lower classes, the new government instituted a severely limited representative system with safeguards against any sudden changes of personnel. Its policy of separation of church and state, combined with official religious toleration, was more popular than the Jacobin attack upon Christianity, although it lost much of the credit gained thereby by continuing to insist upon the observance of the revolutionary calendar.[17] As the rest of Europe rapidly realized, the Directors wanted nothing more than to regain the status of a normal European state, with reformed, but not revolutionary, institutions.

The Directors also returned to a traditional, if ambitious, foreign policy. Led by the Alsatian Jean François Reubell, who took the lead in foreign affairs, they hoped to reach a peace which would guarantee the so-called natural frontiers, the Rhine and the Alps. Reubell argued for these acquisitions on entirely traditional

14. Marion, *Histoire financière*, III, 179.
15. Ibid., pp. 171–210.
16. Thus the five original Directors included three old regime army officers, the bourgeois Carnot and Letourneur and the noble Barras; the Girondin La Reveillière, son of a notary; and the Montagnard Reubell.
17. See Georges Lefèbvre, *The Thermidorians and the Directory* (New York, 1964).

grounds. France, he believed, was entitled to them as compensation for the new Prussian, Russian, and Austrian acquisitions at the expense of Poland. The coalition, he argued, had sought "to destroy all equilibrium, partition Poland, steal the islands and subsequently dismember the territory of France." France needed the Rhineland "to reestablish the equilibrium upon which its security depends."[18]

But the Directors—like the Thermidorians before them—also had to continue an expansionist policy for financial reasons. During the five months from September 1794 through January 1795, receipts totaled 266 million francs and expenses 1.734 million. *Assignats* fell to less than one-tenth of their nominal value. Although the Directory tried numerous financial expedients and in 1796 paid off two-thirds of the state debt in worthless *assignats*, only in its last year (1798–99) did the Directory significantly increase its revenue.[19] Beginning in 1794, the revolutionary governments systematically used expansion to try to fill the gap, thereby putting an end to their hopes of winning the allegiance of the oppressed peoples of Europe. Their policies alienated revolutionaries within neighboring countries. They also increased the authority of French generals, upon whom they came to depend both for financial help and political authority.

The exploitation of occupied territories may be described sequentially. Belgium, which the French armies reentered in 1794, yielded between 50 and 70 million francs in cash during the next few years, of which 30 million reached France.[20] The money theoretically came from levies upon the church, nobles, émigrés, and rich hostages, but pillage was so general that the populace began to long for annexation, if only to escape from a permanent state of emergency. Although the Vonckist party had welcomed Dumouriez in 1792, only a tiny minority of sans-culottes supported the new regime for very long. French attacks upon the church and confiscation of church property were especially unpopular. The French constitution of 1795 decreed the annexation of Belgium, and in 1796 the French extended the reforms of the revolution throughout the new Belgian departments. These reforms—simi-

---

18. Raymond Guyot, *Le directoire et la paix de l'Europe: Des traités de Bâle à la deuxième coalition* (Paris, 1911), pp. 108–123.

19. Marion, *Histoire financière*, III, 256–286, and IV, 59–64, 112–169.

20. Ibid., III, 171–210.

lar to the earlier measures of Joseph II—aroused little enthusiasm.[21]

The next big windfall came from Holland, which the French armies occupied in 1795. Here again the French could initially call upon an established revolutionary party, the Patriots, who had overthrown the stadholder in 1787, only to be defeated by Prussian intervention. Like the French in the early 1790s, the Dutch revolutionaries were divided between the Patriot leaders, who wanted to restore what they regarded as the traditional constitutional balance, and a democratic minority who wanted a unitary state. The French government—now firmly in the hands of moderates—supported the former. Eventually a new Dutch national assembly—elected, like the new French legislature, by a restricted suffrage—wrote a constitution quite similar to the French constitution of 1795, which was in turn rejected by the Dutch people. In the meanime, the French treated the new Batavian republic as conquered territory. The French army continued to live off the land, and the peace treaty signed in May 1795 imposed an indemnity of 100 million florins. As the Committee of Public Safety had explained to Sièyes and Reubell, who negotiated the treaty, specie from the Batavian republic was necessary to keep the French armies in Germany alive.[22] The Dutch also incurred a continuing obligation to maintain 25,000 French troops, costing 10–12 million guilders (about 20–24 million French francs) a year—an obligation which they had to fulfill whether the troops remained in the Netherlands or not. The new Dutch government, already saddled with a huge debt, ran large deficits during the late 1790s as a result. "Time and again," writes Simon Schama, "the historian is forced to the conclusion that the war which made the Dutch revolution possible also supplied the limiting conditions of its chances of fulfillment."[23]

Meanwhile two French armies plundered the Rhineland, but attempts to turn Germany into another reliable source of income were less successful. The French armies in Germany received no regular income from France, and the officers, returning to the practices of the early seventeenth century, apparently encouraged the troops to pillage at will. It is obviously impossible even to estimate how much was collected in this way between 1794 and 1797, but

21. Godechot, *La grande nation*, II, 545–550; Pirenne, *Histoire de la Belgique*, VI, 57–120.
22. Marion, *Histoire financière*, III, 337–338.
23. Schama, *Patriots and Liberators*, pp. 192–270, 354–409.

the behavior of the French completely alienated the population and discredited the minority of German Jacobins who collaborated with the occupation. Here, too, French attacks upon the church were most unpopular.[24] During 1795–1797 the French armies tried to collect 17 million francs in cash from the left bank of the Rhine and 40 million from right bank princes as indemnities, but the left bank yielded only about 4.5 million and the right bank had to be evacuated before much had been collected. Godechot estimates that Germany yielded a total of about 20 million francs between 1792 and 1795.[25]

If 1794 was the year of Belgium and 1795 was the year of the Netherlands, 1796 was the year of Italy. The Directors authorized Bonaparte's invasion of Italy partly to secure a bargaining counter in peace talks with the Austrians, but it quickly became the largest source of cash yet developed. (The Dutch indemnity was gone by the middle of 1796.)[26] Italian revolutionaries, including Michael Buonarotti, hoped at first that the French army would enable them to revolutionize Italy, but Buonarotti's involvement in Babeuf's Conspiracy of Equals in early 1796 put an end to these plans. The Directors, who intended to bargain northern Italy away in exchange for Belgium and the Rhineland in peace talks, ordered the fullest possible exploitation of the country.[27] During 1796 a series of levies upon northern Italian princes, towns, and the province of Lombardy yielded a total of about 45 million francs in specie, of which perhaps half went to France. The French civilian commissioners confiscated numerous art treasures as well, while the army and its furnishers continued to live off the land. The commissioners sometimes took hostages to ensure payments, and several local revolts occurred. During 1797 the war spread into Venice and the papal states, and Italy yielded about another 15 million francs.[28] When the Cisalpine republic was formed in northern Italy in 1797, it obligated itself to pay the French 1.5 million francs every month.

The invasion of Switzerland in 1798, undertaken in cooperation with two Swiss patriots, Ochs and La Harpe, aimed from the beginning at finding money to pay for the invasion of southern Italy

24. Blanning, *French Revolution in Germany*, pp. 83–134, 207–285.

25. Godechot, *La grande nation*, II, 551–556.

26. Guyot, *Le directoire et la paix*, pp. 157–170; Godechot, *La grande nation*, II, 551–560.

27. Jacques Godechot, *Les commissaires aux armées sous le directoire*, 2 vols. (Paris, 1937), I, 237–280.

28. Ibid., pp. 564–573.

and Egypt. It yielded about 15 million francs, mostly from urban treasuries, of which 3 million went to Bonaparte's Egyptian expedition, only 1 million back to Paris, and the rest to support the army in Switzerland itself. Cash ran out early the next year and the army had to begin requisitioning, and the unitary Helvetic republic installed by Ochs and La Harpe failed to win the support of the people.[29]

Expansion, obviously, had bred more expansion. The French had failed to develop a steady revenue base either in France or in occupied territories. Having tried and failed to solve the debt crisis by confiscating French church lands, the revolutionary governments had supported their armies and themselves by confiscating capital abroad. Between 1792 and 1799 they collected approximately 360 million francs from occupied territories but without solving the domestic financial crisis.[30] These policies could not continue indefinitely. The French were living on capital in the occupied territories, just as they had at home.

In the occupied territories the social and political effects of the French revolutionary occupation were decidedly mixed. The Belgians, annexed in 1795, continued to resent the French attacks upon the church. They generally refused to buy church lands put on the market as *biens nationaux*, and when in the spring of 1797 they took part in national elections, they chose anti-French candidates, most of whom were purged not long after.[31] In the Rhineland only a small minority of Jacobins remained faithful to the French, and although the French theoretically abolished all feudal dues, they continued to collect many of them.[32] In northern Italy few feudal rights still existed, while southern Italy was not occupied long enough to show many effects. The Cisalpine republic had to make over much of its *biens nationaux* to the French government to pay its debts, and the French in turn handed many of them over to provisioners of the armies.[33] Periodic insurrections

29. Godechot, *La grande nation*, II, 560–564.

30. The estimate is from ibid., p. 565.

31. Pirenne, *Histoire de la Belgique*, VI, 72–120; see also L. de Lanzac de Laborie, *La domination française en Belgique*, vol. 1 (Paris, 1895), pp. 99–272.

32. Blanning, *French Revolution in Germany*, pp. 135–167; R. Dufraisse, "Les départements réunis de la rive gauche du Rhin (1797–1815)," in R. Devleeshouwer, ed., *Les pays sous domination française* (Paris, 1968), pp. 37–77. *Biens nationaux* did not go on sale in Germany until 1803.

33. Albert Soboul, "Napoléon et l'Italie ou la révolution manquée," in Devleeshouwer, ed., *Les pays sous domination française*, pp. 78–91; Pasquale Villani, "Wirtschaftliche Folgen der Säkularisierung in Italien—Eine Umwälzung im Grundbesitz?" in Armgard

broke out throughout the occupied territories, usually provoked by pillage or conscription.[34]

Revolutionary expansion had dramatic political consequences within France as well. European states had used war to strengthen themselves since 1659, and the French government in 1791 had begun the war to strengthen itself as well. Now, however, the inability of the Thermidorians and the Directory firmly to establish either their financial position or their political leadership enabled generals to achieve positions comparable to that of Wallenstein in the 1620s and 1630s. Beginning in 1795, generals emerged as critical sources of funds, and by 1797 the Directors had begun relying upon them to secure political authority. The generals made fortunes, conducted diplomacy, set up their own vassal states in occupied territory, and ultimately assumed responsibility for the survival of the republic. Men like Dumouriez, Jean Championnet, Jean Moreau, Louis Hoche, and Napoleon Bonaparte, emerged as the archtypal "new men" of the revolutionary era. Using the revolution to ascend to the highest councils of government, they took advantage of the downfall of the old regime to make their fortunes. Eventually the new elite joined with the princes of eastern Europe to undertake the most far-reaching territorial and political adjustments in European history.

The rise of the generals reflects some of the most important social consequences of the French revolution and the revolutionary wars. The political chaos of the 1790s enabled the cleverest, most ambitious politicians to rise to the top, and we have seen that by the time of the Directory power was distributed among figures of varying social origins and political backgrounds. The scholarship of recent decades has probably underestimated the role of ambition, as opposed to ideology or class interest, during most of the French revolution. For the Girondins, Bonaparte, and the politicians of the Directory, social mobility was as much a personal as an ideological goal. Robespierre and Saint-Just, with their emphasis upon virtue, their vision of a France of smallholders and shopkeepers, and their personal incorruptibility, obviously represented an entirely different way of thinking, but contemporaries recognized them as exceptional, and they held power for only one year.

---

von Reden-Dohna, ed., *Deutschland und Italien im Zeitalter Napoleons* (Wiesbaden, 1979), pp. 171–189.

34. Blanning, *French Revolution in Germany,* pp. 331–336.

Significantly, theirs was also the only revolutionary government that renounced territorial expansion.[35] The leading figures of the late 1790s aimed more at doing well than doing good. This applies not only to frankly corrupt figures like Barras and Talleyrand but also to men like Reubell and Bonaparte, who used their positions to advance their own clienteles. The raising of armies on an unprecedented scale and the invasion of the Low Countries, Germany, Italy, and Switzerland opened up enormous professional opportunities for soldiers. And from the beginning of the revolution, soldiers developed impressive political pretensions. Dumouriez, who had hoped to become the protector of an independent Belgium, found many imitators. Numerous other generals strove for political, economic, and diplomatic responsibilities within the conquered territories, including Hoche, Moreau, and Pichegru in Germany, and Brune, Championnet, and above all Bonaparte in Italy.[36]

The pattern of civil-military relations under the revolution had emerged before 1796. After disastrous experiences with Dumouriez and Lafayette, both of whom defected to the coalition, the Convention and the Committee of Public Safety had exercised the tightest possible control over the conduct of the armies. During the turbulent year 1795, however, the Thermidorians had to call on the army for political purposes.[37] The Directors elected late that year intended to control the military, and they appointed commissioners for that purpose. As Godechot has shown, during 1796 the commissioners struggled with the generals for control of the occupied territories, often with considerable success.[38]

The generals themselves—especially Bonaparte—proved diffi-

35. It is noteworthy that Georges Lefebvre, who together with Mathiez did so much to restore Robespierre's reputation, often implies that the corruption of figures like Talleyrand and Barras, which he notes with unconcealed contempt, lessens their historical significance. Lefebvre will always remain a great historian, but it seems unlikely that future historians will continue to endorse this verdict. It was the incorruptibility of Robespierre which contemporaries found so unusual.

36. The generals' activities may be followed in the two most important works on the politics of the Directory: Guyot, *Le directoire et la paix de l'Europe*, and Godechot, *Les commissaires aux armées*.

37. Godechot, *Les commissaires aux armées*, I, 27–37.

38. Sorel, in the fifth volume of his work, argued that while Napoleon and the other generals worked for the glory of France, the Directors and their commissioners worked solely for their own welfare. Both Guyot and Godechot explode this myth. See Geyl, *Napoleon, For and Against*, pp. 258–269.

cult to control. Bonaparte took his first step toward independent authority in the spring of 1796, when after his brilliant victory at Lodi he announced that his army would be paid in specie. As Godechot argues, this step—taken while the other French armies were receiving worthless *assignats*—turned the soldiers into his own mercenaries and meant, in effect, that they would have to stay in Italy until there was enough specie in France to pay them off.[39] During 1796 Bonaparte also defied the Directory by conducting diplomatic talks with various Italian princes, although the Directory's commissioners, Saliceti and Gareau, generally managed to keep their hands in as well. Similar problems arose in Germany. In Italy both Bonaparte and the civilian commissioners established connections with Italian Jacobins, connections which the Directory, shaken by the Babeuf episode, disliked. Conflicts between generals and commissioners in both Germany and Italy grew in the latter half of 1796, largely, it seems, because there simply was not enough money to satisfy everyone's public and private needs.[40]

The generals' stock rose in late 1796, when the Directors, disheartened by the failure of peace talks with Britain and coming under pressure from royalists, suppressed most of the commissioners. But the real turning point came in April 1797, when Bonaparte negotiated the preliminary peace with Austria at Leoben. From the beginning of the Italian campaign the directors—led by Reubell—opposed territorial acquisitions within Italy.[41] They intended instead to trade their Italian gains for the left bank of the Rhine. Bonaparte, however, had apparently decided to keep his own power base in northern Italy, and the Leoben agreement specified that France would retain Lombardy, while not insisting upon the Rhine frontier. In Paris Reubell opposed the terms, but all France desperately wanted peace, and the Directory was shaken by the results of the elections of the very same month, which had returned a royalist majority to the legislature. The preliminaries were approved. Bonaparte proceeded to establish the Cisalpine republic in northern Italy during the summer of 1797 and helped turn Genoa into the Ligurian republic. His rival Hoche, worried

39. *Les commissaires aux armées*, I, 297.
40. Ibid., pp. 517–562.
41. The creation of the small Cispadane republic, which both Napoleon and the commissioners supported, was a small exception to this policy.

that the Rhineland might be surrendered, thought seriously about creating a Rhineland republic in return.

Bonaparte and the other generals emerged as the political arbiters both of France and the occupied territories in the fall of 1797. During the summer the struggle between the Directory and the new, royalist councils threatened to produce a restoration and made it impossible to conclude final peace terms with Austria or with Britain. Reubell, La Reveillière, and Barras decided to call in the generals to purge the councils and save the domestic achievements and foreign conquests of the revolution. The coup d'état of 18 Fructidor, in which Bonaparte played a leading role, was the result. The final peace with Austria followed but promised no end to the crisis.

During the next two years the Directory intermittently talked peace with Britain, but it also extended the war into southern Italy and Egypt, ultimately bringing about the formation of the Second Coalition. Domestic political crises continued, and the army remained the arbiter of political disputes both in France and in the sister republics.

By the late 1790s, relatively conservative and relatively democratic or "Jacobin" parties had emerged not only within France, but also in the Netherlands, Cisalpania, and Switzerland. In some cases these divisions were becoming more factional than ideological. Alphonse Aulard, whose political history of the revolution remains extremely important, noted that the Jacobins who won an election victory in France in the spring of 1798 had no apparent program other than the replacement of the existing government.[42] The army, acting with the Directory, controlled the oscillation back and forth between these two groups.[43]

The Fructidor coup of September 1797 deprived large numbers of royalist deputies of their seats in the legislative councils. It was applauded by the French Jacobins. Shortly thereafter, Dutch radical democrats persuaded the Directory to replace the French am-

---

42. Alphonse Aulard, *The French Revolution: A Political History*, vol. 4 (New York, 1965), pp. 89–132. Had the Directory been able to provide for a regular alternation of the civilian government in response to the results of elections, it might have saved Europe a great deal of trouble.

43. Here I am following one of the most remarkable chapters of Godechot, *La grande nation*, II, 451–476. Blanning, *French Revolution in Germany*, p. 330, argues that "the inspired invention of the satellite republic" enabled the French to capitalize on old conflicts in Holland, Switzerland, and northern Italy to create pro-French parties.

bassador in Batavia with their friend Charles Delacroix, and in January 1798 the democrats arranged the arrest of many of their opponents within the legislature and decided to rewrite the Batavian constitution. In April the Jacobins of the Cisalpine republic, whom Bonaparte had disdained in setting up the new government in the previous year, persuaded the French government and the French general Brune to authorize a similar purge. Significantly, in both the Batavian and the Cisalpine republics, the reigning government had been having difficulty fulfilling the financial exigencies of the French. The last of this series of coups took place in June 1798 in Switzerland, where Reubell's son-in-law Rapinat, the Directory's commissioner, installed the democrat Ochs after the government began complaining about French requisitions.

By this time, however, the political pendulum had already swung rightward within France. The elections of May 1798 favored the Jacobins, and the Directory, acting on its own this time, unilaterally excluded many of the new members in the coup of Floréal. In Holland, where the democrats in April had just rigged an election themselves, a Dutch general, Daendels, traveled to Paris after Floréal, returned to the Netherlands with increased prestige, and in June entered the Dutch assembly and took several Directors into custody.[44] According to Godechot, both Bonaparte and General Joubert were impressed by the ease of the operation. The Directory sent Charles Trouvé as ambassador to Cisalpania to counteract the Italian Jacobins' propaganda in favor of Italian unity, and in August he reduced the size of the legislature and removed a few directors. This coup, however, was short-lived. The Directory's moves coincided with new attempts to reign in the generals, many of whom had carried out too much propaganda for its taste, and the generals began striking back. They removed conservative governments in Genoa in August, in Rome in September, and in Cisalpania, once again, in October, as General Brune undid Trouvé's work. The Directory replaced Brune with Joubert, who emerged as a patron of the Jacobins. When Joubert left Italy in December 1798, a new ambassador restored the moderates once more.

The Jacobins now benefited not only from their links to some of the generals but also from a new series of French military setbacks, which always tended to favor the revolution's most extreme parti-

---

44. These coups are also discussed by Schama, *Patriots and Liberators*, pp. 271–353.

sans. Neapolitan Jacobins seized power in May 1799, and the French Jacobins won another victory in the spring elections. In June they managed to force out three directors. General Brune, in Holland, meditated a new coup on behalf of the democrats there, but it did not take place. In France, the factional struggle continued.

The coup d'état of 18 Brumaire (November 9, 1799), in which Sièyes and Barras brought Bonaparte to power as first consul and did away with the constitution of 1795, obviously climaxed a long series of power struggles between civilian and military leaders and between Jacobins and moderates. Only later did it become clear that Bonaparte's accession had brought Europe into a new era. We must now attempt to understand the significance of two related developments: the spread of the revolution from France into the sister republics, and the destruction of the French republic by a general, Napoleon Bonaparte, who soon instituted an entirely different sort of regime.

Without going as far as T. C. W. Blanning, who stigmatizes R. R. Palmer and Jacques Godechot as purveyors of high cold war propaganda, one may nonetheless legitimately conclude that the model of the Atlantic or democratic revolution hardly accounts for the spread of French ideas, institutions, and armies through western and southern Europe between 1792 and 1799. Revolutionary parties of varying strength and political coloration did, indeed, exist in Belgium and Holland, where they had been strong enough to make revolutions of their own, and in Germany and Italy, where they were much, much weaker. There seems no reason why twentieth-century democrats should not look to them for inspiration. The spread of French institutions, however, was propelled by the needs of the French revolutionary governments, which drove the armies across France's borders and kept them there to find sustenance. The rapacity of the armies—which was partly a function of the needs of the revolutionary governments—rapidly alienated the population, and led to numerous outbreaks of armed resistance.[45] The French confiscated church property in much of the occupied territories for the same reason as in France: to raise money. The constitutions of the sister republics generally followed the model of the French constitution of 1795 rather closely,[46] just as

45. As Blanning stresses: see *French Revolution in Germany*, pp. 317–336.
46. Godechot, *La grande nation*, II, 418–440.

their political struggles closely followed similar struggles within France. The work the French carried out in the occupied territories resembles the work of territorial consolidation and political reform which many other European princes had already undertaken or were about to undertake.

The rise of the generals, and more particularly of Bonaparte, reflects the failure of the French revolutionary governments to put their authority on a firm basis. In part, as we have seen, this problem was financial. The financial system of the old regime collapsed during the early years of the revolution, and successive governments failed to put anything effective in its place until about 1798. The civilians depended on the army every bit as much as the Emperor Ferdinand II had depended upon Wallenstein. The generals would not have achieved the position that they did after Fructidor, however, had the civilian politicians been able to make their authority respected.[47] Having destroyed the authority of the king and the church, the revolutionary governments failed to evolve a new pattern of legitimacy.[48]

Lynn Hunt has recently argued that the revolutionaries' failure to establish their authority owed a good deal to the nature of their principles, which drew so heavily upon the Enlightenment. The ideology of the revolution emphasized a single democratic community and instinctively opposed political factions and institutionalized struggles for power. The Directors, relying upon the generals, simply staged coups whenever one faction became too powerful, and in so doing undermined the ideology of republicanism from within.[49] Going further, one might suggest that the Enlightenment's emphasis upon uniformity, reason, and the united action of state and society predisposed late eighteenth-century Europe toward authoritarian solutions. In any event, Bonaparte's triumph reflected both the financial and political bankruptcy of the revolutionary regime.

47. Ranke, in the last pages of his *Geschichte Wallensteins*, explicitly compares Napoleon and Wallenstein, arguing that Napoleon triumphed because he had only revolutionaries to overcome, while Wallenstein could not defeat legitimate princes. The key difference between them consisted in the role they played, not in the legitimacy of their opponents. Ferdinand II needed Wallenstein to continue expansion within Germany, but the general was no longer necessary to preserve his authority within his own domains and could therefore be dispensed with. The Directors would probably have been able to deal successfully with the generals had they been masters of the situation within France.

48. The collapse of royal authority was of course mainly the fault of the king himself.

49. Hunt, *Politics, Culture, and Class*, pp. 224–229.

The business of government in the late eighteenth century focused upon the suppression of the old regime at home and expansion abroad. The wars of the French revolution gave French generals unprecedented opportunities to engage in these enterprises, and one French revolutionary general, albeit of Corsican descent, now emerged as the leading political figure of his age. Bonaparte began by applying the lessons he had learned in Italy to France itself. He succeeded in stabilizing the situation in France and resumed expansion for reasons of his own.

Like the French revolutionary governments, the other states of Europe took advantage of the crisis of the 1790s to strengthen their own power. Their response to the revolution generally reflected the expansionist principles of the late eighteenth century, rather than any concerted, ideologically motivated effort to defeat the principles of the revolution and restore the old regime. With very rare exceptions, they measured the success of their involvement in the revolutionary turmoil according to the territorial gain they could secure.[50] And in Germany, in particular, princes used the wars of the revolution to increase their territory and reduce domestic obstacles to their authority.

The political crisis in France began at a particularly tense moment in European politics. A new war in 1787 between Austria and Turkey brought an Austro-Russian alliance into play, opening up the possibility of the partition of the European domains of the Ottoman empire. At the same time, the Prussian government of Frederick William II, count von Herzberg, and the duke of Brunswick developed an even more ambitious scheme to divide the Ottoman empire and reapportion much of Poland among the three eastern powers. They also seriously considered an all-out war with Austria to establish Prussian supremacy within Germany. Prussia was busy subduing the Patriot revolution in Holland with Britain's cooperation during 1787, and the revolution against Joseph II in Belgium broke out in the next year. Catherine the Great, meanwhile, had determined to seize more of Poland and move her frontier to the Dneistr River. The Prussians attempted to forestall these plans—or at least to make sure that they would not be excluded

---

50. This is essentially the conclusion of Blanning, *Origins of the French Revolutionary Wars*, esp. pp. 120–123, 128–129.

from them—by making their own treaty of alliance with Poland in 1790. At Reichenbach during the summer of 1790 the eastern powers discussed various far-reaching schemes but ultimately decided upon a status quo peace among Austria, Russia, and Turkey after Frederick William II lost his nerve. Catherine the Great, displeased with the Reichenbach settlement, continued to seek a new partition of Poland. The British prime minister William Pitt the Younger—the only European statesman pursuing a status quo policy—tried in early 1791 to organize a league to force Catherine to back down, but Parliament failed to support this risky policy.[51]

The course of the French Revolution became involved with European politics as a result of the policies of Louis XVI and Marie Antoinette, who in early 1791 had sounded out her brother, Leopold II of Austria, regarding the possibility of Austrian intervention to reestablish the power of the king. "Nothing for nothing," replied the French ambassador in Vienna, succinctly stating the motto of the diplomacy of the old regime; any powers that intervened would demand compensation.[52] Leopold II did make some demarches to protect the personal safety of the royal couple, but he shunned the French émigrés who offered him their help and refused to begin war with France simply out of the goodness of his heart. The pretext for his intervention disappeared in December 1791, when Louis XVI apparently reconciled himself to the revolution.[53] And despite the increasingly warlike posture of the Legislative Assembly, Leopold II resisted drastic action against the French until his death on March 1, 1792.

In Poland, meanwhile, a revolution had created a new constitution, turning the state into a hereditary monarchy in an attempt to forestall Catherine the Great's designs. Catherine now persuaded the Prussians to join in a new partition, and the Prussians, in turn, encouraged the Austrians to seek compensation at the expense of France. When the French assembly declared war on the emperor in late March of 1792, the Prussians joined in. Vienna agreed in

51. Good accounts of these Byzantine proceedings can be found in Robert Howard Lord, *The Second Partition of Poland* (Cambridge, Mass., 1915), pp. 95–152, and J. H. Clapham, "Pitt's First Decade," in *The Cambridge History of British Foreign Policy*, vol. 1 (reprint, New York, 1970), pp. 170–208. A more recent summary is Blanning, *Origins of the French Revolutionary Wars*, pp. 36–62.

52. Marcel Reinhard, *La chute de la royauté*, pp. 27–28.

53. Karl A. Roider, *Baron Thugut and Austria's Response to the French Revolution* (Princeton, 1987), pp. 91–92.

principle to a new partition of Poland, and the Prussians indicated that the emperor might at long last exchange Belgium for Bavaria.[54] While the Austrians and Prussians invaded France, the Russians invaded Poland.

In 1951, surveying some of the literature on the origins of the war of 1792, Georges Lefèbvre approvingly quoted several European writers who divided the blame between the Girondins and the eastern powers, but he added, "It is strange that in discussing this point the authors attribute to the coalition powers only the traditional preoccupation with power, without ever introducing the motive of a passionate desire to crush the Revolution—a desire that the interests of their political and social dominance inspired in Europe's kings and aristocrats."[55] But Lefèbvre himself could not cite any specific evidence to support this view. The only European monarch then arguing seriously that the revolution posed a European danger was Catherine, and everyone recognized that she wanted simply to occupy the other powers in the west and leave herself free to deal with Poland. The nature of Austro-Prussian policy was stated far more clearly by Robert Lord in 1915:

> Without attempting to trace here all the ways in which the conflict in the West affected the fate of Poland, it is incumbent to point out the chief form which that interaction took. Vastly different as were the pretexts for the two wars—since France was being attacked for turning a monarchy into a republic, and Poland for converting a republic into a monarchy—nevertheless, the diplomacy of the predatory Powers succeeded in finding a common formula to justify the two utterly contradictory enterprises, and in establishing a subtle connection between them. Both were ranged in the category of "counter-revolutions," benevolently undertaken by the three allied Courts in the interests of order, stability and the general tranquility of Europe. Both were integral parts of a great common work; although for the sake of an equitable division of labor, the intervention in the West was entrusted to Austria and Prussia alone, while that in the East was reserved for for Catherine. Once this insidious theory was established, the deduction was obvious. Pooling the stakes, the three Powers would soon be pooling the profits. What was invested in one quarter could be recouped in the other.[56]

The acquisitive spirit dominated Prussian and Austrian policy throughout the 1790s. The Prussians, who never took their eyes off

54. Ibid., pp. 95–96.
55. Lefèbvre, *French Revolution*, I, 223.
56. Lord, *Second Partition of Poland*, p. 281.

of developments in Poland, yielded the field to the French at Valmy in September 1792. While demanding the largest possible subsidy from the British, they carried out their part of the second partition and lost interest in the campaign in the west entirely in the spring of 1794, when the remainder of Poland revolted.[57] In the spring of 1795 the Prussians became the first major power to make peace with the French republic, secretly agreeing in principle to cede their territories west of the Rhine in exchange for compensation at the expense of German ecclesiastical states. The Treaty of Basel also pledged to maintain the neutrality of all northern Germany, including Hanover, a possession of the British king. The French Revolution had received a generally favorable reception in Prussia, where it was regarded as a rationalization of the state similar to that of Frederick William I and Frederick the Great, and the neutrality policy remained generally popular for about ten years.[58]

Even after the execution of Louis XVI, European governments took more interest in territorial changes than in ideological threats. The second partition of Poland in the spring of 1793, which assigned huge portions of Poland to Prussia and Russia, made far more of an impression upon Vienna than developments in France. Count Philip Cobenzl, the Austrian chancellor, stated that the partition "changes the whole European system . . . The French revolution is child's play in comparison to the importance of this event." Apparently agreeing, the emperor Francis I dismissed him in March 1793, replacing him with Baron Thugut. "A parvenu who had risen by immense industry, intelligence, and some less creditable means," writes Lord, "in his outlook upon life, his aims and methods, his political morality, he represented only too faithfully the sordid, cynical, unprincipled eighteenth century at its worst. As a diplomat of the old school, familiar with the tricks of the trade,he believed that territorial aggrandizement was the Alpha and Omega of statecraft, and that all means were hallowed by that end."[59] Thugut initially proposed that Austria and Prussia parti-

57. See John M. Sherwig, *Guineas and Gunpowder: British Foreign Aid in the Wars with France, 1793–1815* (Cambridge, Mass., 1969), pp. 21–53.

58. See O. Tschirsch, *Geschichte der öffentlichen Meinung in Preussens Friedensjahrzehnt vom Baseler Frieden bis zum Zusammenbruch des Staates* (Weimar, 1933).

59. Lord, *Second Partition of Poland*, pp. 405–406. Roider, *Baron Thugut, passim.*, tries to refute this passage by showing that Thugut did fear the long-term political effects of the French Revolution. His own evidence shows that Thugut had no interest in maintaining the European status quo and consistently sought new acquisitions for Austria; see for instance pp. 132–135.

tion most of the German Rhineland, compensating the German ecclesiastical princes elsewhere,[60] and he tried unsuccessfully during the next two years to arrange the Belgium-Bavaria exchange. He consoled himself and his masters partially in 1795 by securing a share of the third partition of Poland, but Bonaparte's victories in Italy represented a new setback. In the Peace of Campo Formio in 1797 Thugut accepted Bonaparte's offer of the Venetian republic but complained bitterly that the last six years had still weakened Austria in relation to France and Prussia. He might have preferred to fight on, but the Hapsburg domains were exhausted.[61]

Alone among the powers of the First Coalition, the British entered the war to restore the status quo ante. The British government did not initially join the coalition in early 1792, but by the fall the prime minister William Pitt the Younger seems to have become alarmed by the growth of English Jacobinism, the Convention decrees on the liberation of foreign territories, the invasion of Belgium, the opening of the Scheldt, and the French decision to attack Holland.[62] A French occupation of Holland, whose South African colonies controlled the sea route to the Far East, would potentially threaten communications with India—a point which had already led the British government to support Prussian intervention in Holland against a French-backed revolution in 1787. Two other key British figures, Foreign Secretary George Grenville and King George III, conceived a violent ideological hatred for the revolution and tended to argue that it must be destroyed, but they too decided upon war only after Holland was threatened.[63]

The British, then, entered the war in early 1793 but had great difficulty persuading the allies to accept their war aims. They especially wanted Belgium to remain in Austrian hands and were most disappointed to find that Thugut preferred to exchange it for Bavaria. With the coalition in disarray, the British employed their traditional strategy of seizing French (and, after 1795, Dutch) possessions overseas. By 1797 the war had become extremely unpopular, and after a financial crisis and naval mutinies, the government seriously contemplated a peace with France, even at the cost

60. Roider, *Baron Thugut*, pp. 127–128.

61. Ibid., pp. 243–261; Eduard Wertheimer, *Geschichte Österreichs und Ungarns im ersten Jahrzehnt des 19 Jahrhunderts*, 2 vols. (Leipzig, 1884–1890), I, 17–33.

62. J. Holland Rose, *William Pitt and the Great War* (London, 1911), pp. 55–74.

63. Blanning, *Origins of the French Revolutionary Wars*, pp. 131–142.

of acknowledging the Rhine frontier and the acquisition of Belgium. Talks failed, however, and the British remained at war until 1802.[64]

The only major European sovereign to oppose the French upon ideological grounds was the Russian tsar Paul, who succeeded Catherine in February 1796. Highly unstable, he at one time declared against his mother's whole policy of territorial aggrandizement and even discussed the restoration of Poland. He soon began planning the formation of a chivalric order to combat the revolution, however, and entered the war against the French in 1798 both to restore the Knights of Malta and to stop French encroachments in the eastern Mediterranean. After Thugut joined the Second Coalition in early 1798, Paul quarreled with him over the fate of various northern Italian principalities. Thugut wanted them for Austria, while Paul hoped to restore them to their original sovereigns. The erratic Paul ultimately decided that the coalition had betrayed him and became friendly to Bonaparte in 1801.[65]

The goals of all the major European governments were reflected in the peace treaties which Napoleon Bonaparte, who became first consul in late 1799, managed to conclude with all the coalition partners, including the British, by 1802. The wars of the 1790s had accelerated the trends of the old regime. They had extended France, Austria, and Britain to the limit of their resources. All three nations had had to resort to paper money to continue them, and all three had seen that paper lose some of its value.[66] At the same time, all major European states had made significant territorial acquisitions. When the British finally made peace in 1802, the Addington ministry justified the terms on the basis of the acquisition of Ceylon and Trinidad. Russia had grown enormously at the expense of Poland, Prussia had done the same and acquired new German territories, and even the Austrians had compensated themselves for the loss of Belgium and Lombardy with large acquisitions of Polish territory, Venice, and Salzburg. The French had

64. See Rose, *William Pitt and the Great War,* and Guyot, *Le directoire et la paix de l'Europe,* pp. 372–475, on the peace talks.

65. Andrei Lobanov-Rostovsky, *Russia and Europe, 1789–1825* (New York, 1968), pp. 15–67.

66. I have already discussed the French *assignats.* The Austrians also made enormous use of paper money during the 1790s, and the Bank of England, which financed the war by discounting British treasury bills, had to suspend specie redemption of its notes in 1797.

conquered the frontier of the Rhine and the Alps, and enjoyed a predominant influence in the Batavian, Helvetic, and reconstituted Cisalpine republics.

Both major and minor princes had also swept away some of the domestic barriers to the growth of their power. The most dramatic changes took place in Germany. As compensation for the Rhine frontier, which Napoleon definitively secured in 1802, the German princes received the right to secularize ecclesiastical lands within their borders and mediatize most of the ecclesiastical principalities and free cities. These changes had long been in the air; Frederick the Great had put forth such ideas more than once. In pamphlet campaigns justifying the dispossession of ecclesiastical princes, the secular rulers argued that they had bankrupted themselves in the war against the French for the sake of the common defense. They also argued variously that the Rhineland electors had helped provoke the war, and that the new, purer religion of the nineteenth century should divorce itself from the state.[67] A *Reichsdeputation*, or committee of the *Reichstag*, theoretically divided the territories, but the key figures in the drawing up of the *Reichsdeputationshauptschluss* were the representative of Tsar Alexander I and Talleyrand, who turned a handsome profit from his role as arbiter.[68] The biggest winners were Prussia, Baden, Bavaria, Württemberg, Hesse-Darmstadt, and Nassau, but the Hapsburgs also took their part, receiving the bishopric of Salzburg.

Another imperial institution, the free imperial knights, had already come under attack. The king of Prussia had acquired Anspach and Bayreuth in 1791 and had immediately begun contesting the right of the imperial knights within these territories to regard themselves as independent vassals of the emperor. In October 1795—after the Peace of Basel, but before the Austrians had consented to any changes in the laws of the empire—the Prussian government simply decreed that henceforth the knights would be treated as subjects. When the imperial Reichshofrath upheld the knights' pretensions in 1797, the Prussians simply ignored it. After the Peace of Lunéville and the *Reichsdeputationshauptschluss*, a number of other German princes followed suit. Once again the

67. See Epstein, *Genesis of German Conservatism*, pp. 595–625.

68. For an extended description of the process, see K. Th. Heigel, *Deutsche Geschichte vom Tode Friedrichs d. Gr. bis zur Auflösung des alten Reiches*, vol. 2 (Stuttgart, 1911), pp. 380–448.

knights contested this step, and this time the conflict was not fi-nally settled until after another war.[69]

In France, meanwhile, Bonaparte was rapidly moving to eradi-cate the more radical vestiges of the revolution and establish his authority on a more traditional basis. The Concordat with the pope in 1801 allowed the Catholic church to regain a protected and priv-ileged position in France, which contributed to domestic tranquil-ity in France and in annexed territories such as Belgium and the Rhineland. The proclamation of Bonaparte as first consul for life in 1802 was another significant, conservative step, and more old re-gime nobles returned to France. Perhaps most significant, the do-mestic finances of the French government had finally begun to re-cover; the budget for the year X (1801–2) was balanced.[70]

The revolutionary wars, in short, had continued the pattern of change introduced by the first partition of Poland in 1772. All the European governments, both revolutionary and traditional, had used the wars to extend their domains and reduce or eliminate sur-viving feudal institutions and privileges. The *Reichsdeputations-hauptschluss* exemplified the process. The ideas of the Enlighten-ment, as interpreted by enlightened despots, had transformed the map. Although in the climate of the time one could hardly have expected a long period of peace, Europeans still might have con-cluded that no new general war was likely for some time. This, however, was not to be. Bonaparte was destined to overturn not only the peace but the entire European equilibrium. The reasons lie in his personality, which epitomized the spirit of the age, and in the nature of the system that he intended to establish.

The Napoleonic Era

I have distinguished four major influences upon international pol-itics in the revolutionary era: the glorification of the expansion of states; the erosion of the legitimacy of the territorial and social ar-rangements of the old regime; the financial needs of the French revolutionary governments; and the rise of ambitious new men, eager to take advantage of the opportunities offered by the situa-tion. All of these factors continued to play an enormous role in

69. Epstein, *Genesis of German Conservatism*, pp. 619–637.
70. Marion, *Histoire financière*, IV, 237–240.

European politics from 1799 through 1815, modified in significant respects by the extraordinary figure of Napoleon Bonaparte, who took advantage of these trends to achieve his own particular purposes. In the end he emerged not only as the prototypical man of the era, but also as the man who pushed its assumptions to their *reductio ad absurdum*.[1]

After one brief period of peace, the European war resumed in 1803 with Britain's renewed attack upon France. The Anglo-French war lasted without interruption until 1814 (and resumed, of course, when Napoleon returned from Elba in 1815), while Napoleon (as he should be called after becoming emperor in 1804) began and ended a long series of campaigns upon the Continent. Militarily he built upon some innovations of the French revolutionary armies, enabling him to bring several campaigns to rapid, spectacular conclusions, including particularly his 1805 and 1809 campaigns against Austria and the 1806 campaign against Prussia. He did this largely by dispensing with supply trains, thereby increasing his troops' mobility, and by concentrating his forces for decisive battles whenever possible.[2]

At the same time, Napoleon owed much of his success to energetic diplomacy. Clearly conscious of the danger of prolonged war, he generally sought in his campaigns to win a quick victory, to reach a peace agreement, and to demobilize his troops. The success of his political-military strategy also owed a great deal to the realism of his Austrian, Prussian, and Russian opponents, who were willing to make a quick peace and risk their chances of recovery on some future conflict. In short, he concentrated upon the most efficient use of armed force for political ends, reflecting the rationalism of his age, and inspiring Clausewitz's great work. His strategy depended to a large extent upon the maintenance of the

1. With the exception of a few stimulating monographs cited below, recent decades have contributed relatively little to the literature of the Napoleonic period. The best single work undoubtedly remains Georges Lefèbvre, *Napoleon* (6th ed., Paris, 1969), although its combination of a traditional narrative approach and a Marxist perspective makes it difficult reading. Felix Markham, *Napoleon* (New York, 1963), gives a fine introduction in English. Louis Bergeron, *France under Napoleon*, is most welcome for its fresh approach, albeit within a relatively limited framework. Also essential is Pieter Geyl, *Napoleon, For and Against*, a brilliant summary of most of the literature, including many very stimulating contributions by the author himself.

2. Gunther E. Rothenberg, *The Art of Warfare in the Age of Napoleon* (Bloomington, 1978), pp. 126–158.

authority of other states, with whom he could reach advantageous peace treaties. He came to grief when he destroyed traditional authority in Spain and had to try to subdue a united people.

Napoleon, like Wallenstein and Louis XIV, was the embodiment of the spirit of his age. The phenomenon of Napoleon Bonaparte arose from his own context as naturally as the Renaissance popes or the great nineteenth-century captains of industry arose from theirs. An era which glorified the internal and external role of the state, denied the legitimacy of numerous long-standing territorial and social arrangements, and broke down barriers to advancement into the political and social elite offered unparalleled opportunities to a brilliant general with unlimited energy, enormous ambition, and an unusual capacity for both abstract and practical thought. The conditions of the late 1790s had favored the rise of generals, and indeed, Napoleon had several military rivals for political power. Upon assuming power, he found the transformation of French institutions still incomplete, and he eagerly assumed the task of finishing it. Temperamentally unsuited to peace, he continued to profit by the unsettled state of Europe, often with the help of his fellow rulers' ambitions. Taking advantage of his military superiority, he at one point reduced virtually the entire European Continent to a collection of vassals and allies. He sought to remake the European economy and control the trade of virtually the entire world. I shall first look briefly at the ways in which the power of European states continued to grow during his rule, before discussing the motives for his expansion and the reasons for his eventual collapse.

The Growth of European State Power

Domestically, Napoleon's goals resembled those of the enlightened despots. Feudal restrictions upon property should be abolished; opportunities should be opened to the middle classes; church property should be confiscated, and the church paid by the state; taxes should be regularized; and the administration should supervise and encourage economic life. Any resistance to authority should be suppressed immediately and bloodily. As Tocqueville argued so brilliantly more than one hundred years ago, Napoleon threw out the libertarian aspects of the French Revolution while pushing forward the social and administrative changes already inaugurated under the old regime. In some ways, indeed, he undid the work of the revolution. Under the Concordat the church lost its economic power and independence but retained an important role among the masses, who Napoleon believed needed its care. Later he could not resist the temptation to use the propaganda opportunities offered by the church on his own behalf.[3] Like Frederick, he sought to order the whole life of society for the good of the state—and at the summit of the state he placed the army.

These changes were part of a general European phenomenon. Most European sovereigns used the Napoleonic period to strengthen their position vis-à-vis both their subjects and each other. Their willingness to reorganize Europe matched Napoleon's, in many instances, and they played an equally large role in the political transformations of the age. This took place most strikingly in Germany, where the consolidation of princely power begun in the late 1790s continued. Thus in 1804, when Austria joined England and Russia in the Third Coalition, Napoleon managed with a mixture of threats and blandishments to turn Bavaria, Baden, and Württemberg into allies. After the defeat of Austria he rewarded them with the end of the Holy Roman Empire, full territorial sovereignty, new territorial gains, and the freedom to treat former imperial knights simply as subjects.[4] In 1806 he formed the Confederation of the Rhine from sixteen German states. All incurred obligations to provide specific numbers of troops, but all retained full sovereignty.[5] Napoleon could treat legitimate rulers quite generously if they allied themselves with him, although he could also deal very harshly with those like King Frederick William III of Prussia or the duke of Brunswick who opposed him.

No systematic study of the lesser German states during the Napoleonic period has ever been written, but the major developments within the confederation obviously favored the princes. Most of the new sovereigns simply began collecting the revenues of the church lands they had confiscated under the *Reichsdeputationshauptschluss*. A few western and southern states introduced

3. Thus Geyl, *Napoleon, For and Against*, pp. 119–120, quotes the count of Hausonville on the new catechism Napoleon tried to institute, which praised the God-given blessings of his rule.

4. Eberhard Weis, "Napoleon und der Rheinbund," in Reden-Dohna, ed., *Deutschland und Italien*, pp. 57–80; Epstein, *Genesis of German Conservatism*, pp. 638–671.

5. E. Hölzle, "Das napoleonische Staatssystem in Deutschland," *Historische Zeitschrift*, 148 (1933): 277–293.

the Napoleonic Code, but hedged it about with restrictions protecting various legal and economic patrimonial rights.[6] Only in Bavaria, where King Max Joseph and his minister Montgelas had long planned an extensive program of enlightened reforms, did the government make a serious attempt to transform the social or legal structure. The Bavarian government, about which we know the most, maintained throughout the period a firm attitude of *raison d'état*. Montgelas in 1813 convinced the king to desert Napoleon; as he later wrote, "the interests of his state were his only compass." "Hitherto unknown remarks of Montgelas in different years," reports a leading authority on Bavaria, "show that despite his sympathy for France and wonder at Bonaparte's genius, the Minister never believed that Napoleon could maintain his hegemony in Europe for more than a decade or a little more. But Montgelas and his most important colleagues also knew very well that they must use this brief period to expand and round off their state outwardly and to modernize it inwardly."[7]

The Prussian state also maintained the principle of *raison d'état* throughout the Napoleonic period, but also tried in 1813–14 to exploit nascent German nationalism. Hardenberg, who became foreign minister in 1804, regarded "the glory and expansion of the Prussian monarchy" as the aim of his policy. He regarded Napoleon as a perfectly satisfactory diplomatic partner and sought to annex Franconia, Hanover, and the Hanseatic cities. In 1805 he acquired Hanover in exchange for neutrality in the War of the Third Coalition.[8] Eventually unsettled by the creation of the Confederation of the Rhine and by Napoleon's refusal to strike a new and advantageous territorial bargain, the Prussians declared war in September 1806, only to see their army destroyed in the following month at Jena. After the catastrophe of the Treaty of Tilsit, which cost Prussia all of its western possessions and much of its recently acquired Polish territory, Baron Stein sought briefly to put through sweeping social and economic reforms, but he went too far for the Prussian establishment.[9] Forced to enter the war with

6. Elisabeth Fehrenbach, "Die Einfluss Frankreichs auf das Verwaltungssystem Deutschlands," in Reden-Dohna, ed., *Deutschland und Italien*, pp. 23–39.

7. Eberhard Weis, "Bayem und Frankrich in der Zeit des Konsulats und des ersten Empire (1799–1815)," *Historische Zeitschrift*, 237, no. 3 (December 1983): 559–595.

8. Karl Hansing, *Hardenberg und die dritte Koalition* (Berlin, 1899), pp. 9, 90–99.

9. R. C. Raack, *The Fall of Stein* (Cambridge, Mass., 1965).

Russia at Napoleon's side, the Prussians abandoned him in 1813 and went to the peace conference in Vienna determined to realize Frederick the Great's old dream, the acquisition of Saxony. They emerged with the Rhineland as a consolation prize.

During the first few years of Napoleon's rule even the Austrians collaborated in the dismantling of the old regime. Not only did they take part in the secularization of church lands—a process, indeed, which Joseph II had already begun—but they also created the title of emperor of Austria and Hungary in 1804, clearly foreshadowing the disappearance of the Holy Roman Empire. Domestically, however, the old regime remained as resistant in Austria as in Prussia. Even after the disastrous War of the Third Coalition, a number of Joseph II's old officials failed to secure agreement to any significant domestic reforms.[10] Instead the Austrian government tried to arrange a new partition of the Ottoman empire in late 1807, but nothing came of these discussions. Two years later, inspired by the Spanish insurrection, they sought to set all Germany aflame and overthrow French domination but were once again defeated at Wagram. Again rejecting a scheme of enlightened reform,[11] the emperor and Metternich embarked frankly upon a policy of collaboration. The initiative for the marriage of Napoleon and Marie Louise, as we now know, came from the Austrians.[12] The Austrians collaborated faithfully until 1813, carefully choosing their moment to switch sides and turn against Napoleon. At the peace conference they did not scruple to regain Venice, which of course had been independent until 1797, and resumed the old struggle with Prussia for influence within Germany.

Alexander I of Russia, no less than Napoleon, believed that he had a great destiny in European affairs, and he pursued that destiny both in opposition to Napoleon and, for four years beginning in 1807, in alliance with him. On two occasions, first during the *Reichsdeputation's* deliberations over the future of Germany and later at Tilsit, the two men jointly supervised the reorganization of Germany, and after 1807 their governments discussed the partition of the Ottoman empire. This alliance, like many of Napoleon's other ones, eventually collapsed because of Napoleon's insatiability, and especially because of his insistence that while Alexander

10. Wertheimer, *Geschichte Oesterreichs*, II, 5–46.
11. Ibid., p. 55.
12. Markham, *Napoleon*, p. 185.

might receive Constantinople, he must get the Dardanelles.[13]
Alone among the great powers, the British consistently fought Napoleon from 1803 through 1815, but we shall see that they, too, did so largely because war was good business for them.

With the threat of democratic revolution extinguished, international politics in the Napoleonic era reverted to the pattern of the late eighteenth century, but on a far grander scale. With virtually all restrictions upon the redesign of the European map now eliminated, the great work of statecraft proceeded at an advanced pace. Yet the Napoleonic era is also distinguished for its failure ever to reach even a temporary equilibrium. The process of expansion went on and on, initiated time and again by Napoleon himself. Expansion had three principal sources—temperamental, economic, and social—all of them, in the context of the time, insatiable, and therefore destined to drive the emperor forward and, in the end, to bring about his ultimate collapse.

The Sources of Napoleonic Expansion

Napoleon embodied the spirit of the eighteenth century. He exemplified the creative statesman, earlier personified by Frederick the Great and Joseph II. He eagerly undertook not only the reorganization of French institutions in the wake of the revolution but also the transformation of the institutions of most of Europe. Never was there more work to be done, or a man more willing to do it. He labored indefatigably, and his correspondence shows that almost no detail was too small to escape his attention. His activities, indeed, seem to stem from an utterly inexhaustible energy, a force of its own which sought out new challenges and opportunities as soon as old ones had been dealt with. His own temperament, in short, was in itself a major source of European international conflict from 1803 through 1815, and deserves some detailed attention.

Napoleon's personality has intrigued and inspired several prominent historians. "Incessantly," wrote Gabriel Hanotaux, a biographer of Richelieu as well as a former foreign minister of France, Napoleon "keeps his eye and compasses on the map. His imagination is active all the time and works even in the abstract, if only

13. Vernon J. Puryear, *Napoleon and the Dardanelles* (Berkeley, 1951).

to keep himself in training and exercise the elasticity and easiness of his reflexes. This complete immersion in his task is the ratio of his being, it is the whole of his life . . . This enjoyment of action, this passion for its results, this hunt for an ever more exalted and unattainable prey, this excitement felt in the mastering of life, of the past, and of the future, of the world, with powers infinitely extended, in short, this super-human existence, strains the spring till it breaks." And indeed, as Hanotaux noted, in administrative matters as well as in foreign policy Napoleon's projects frequently outran reality. "The plans," he wrote, "are invariably impressive on paper. Some get carried into execution, but how many are abandoned for lack of means! . . . This, the greatest defect of all that can mar a man of action, the maladjustment between the imagination and reality, is to ruin him."[14]

The same point, though with specific reference to foreign policy, was made by the historian Pierre Muret, who in a 1913 review discussed various recent and highly specific arguments regarding the goals of Napoleon's foreign policy. After successively disposing of various arguments that Napoleon's *real* aim had involved the East, the natural frontiers, or the creation of a new Roman empire, Muret led up to his own conclusion by supposing, for the sake of argument, that Napoleon had been victorious in the Russian campaign of 1812.

[He] would, in that case, not only have occupied Constantinople but have thrown back the Russians for good and all towards the north in Asia. That is to say, he would have restored Poland, he might even have taken away the Baltic provinces. Suppose further that, as a result of the establishment of Napoleonic domination over the whole European continent, England was compelled to make peace. Would not Napoleon then have thought of India where he did actually plan more than once to strike at the English? Once in control of Constantinople and of India, would he have suffered the continued existence of the Persian Empire, another territory with which he had already meddled, in 1806 and 1807? What would have become of the old Spanish colonial empire? Since we are now launched on the wide waters of supposition, I am beginning to wonder whether we are justified in saying that Napoleon would have halted in Constantinople or at the eastern basin of the Mediterranean, or at the Atlantic coast . . . What does all this mean if not that it is im-

14. Hanotaux quoted in Geyl, *Napoleon, For and Against,* pp. 407, 414.

possible to confine the Napoleonic dream and to draw an arbitrary limit which his ambitions would not have crossed?

Had this policy an aim? Was there a great Napoleonic plan capable of definition? To speak of an aim is to speak of choice, is to speak of subjecting all other objects to a definite plan of disciplined activity. Now Napoleon . . . has never been able to choose. He has carried on, simultaneously, and in all directions, the most varied enterprises . . . Napoleon could never bring himself to sacrifice certain ambitions for the better success of others. No mind was ever less capable of understanding the necessity of compromises.[15]

And even the Marxist Lefèbvre, at the end of a long and penetrating discussion, ultimately explained Napoleon's foreign policy by "the heroic attraction of danger, the magic seduction of the dream, the irresistible impulse of the temperament."[16]

These observations are significant not simply because of their perspicacity, or because of the particular historical importance or interest of Napoleon's personality. More significant, this aspect of Napoleon's character has a close relation to the prevailing intellectual climate of the time, and to certain even broader currents in modern Western history. His behavior, to begin with, recalls some of the maxims of Frederick the Great, which as we have seen condemned statesmen to a life of perpetual work and struggle, and states and peoples to continual war. In his own case, Frederick did not by any means feel that he had completed the work of Prussian expansion—and indeed, based upon the maxims I have already quoted, it seems impossible to imagine that it could have been completed. Napoleon, of course, lived in a far more fluid age, and thanks to changes in military strategy and tactics which he himself helped to introduce, he disposed of greater resources. These material factors enabled him to go much further than Frederick ever dreamed of doing. Yet at the same time, positing the problem from a more general point of view, one may easily conclude that the maxims of reason of state, the rationalist faith in human progress, and the more general contemporary feeling that virtually nothing was impossible clearly helped to produce a statesman whose ambition would literally know no limits save those of the globe itself.

15. Muret quoted in ibid., pp. 324–325.
16. See ibid., p. 438.

Even this formulation may state the problem too narrowly. Napoleon's almost constant dedication to the task at hand—a quality he shared with Frederick and with Joseph II—has about it some of that middle-class devotion to a transcendental aim which Max Weber saw in the spirit of capitalism. Napoleon's endless quest of territorial gain and administrative reform embodies the pursuit of earthly, yet transcendental and ultimately unreachable goals which has played such a key role in the last two centuries of Western history. I will return to these issues at the end of this section, but first we must look at the economic and social bases of Napoleonic expansion, in order to understand how they, as well as his temperament, made it impossible for him ever to stop.

Napoleon, of course, inherited a tradition of expansion for economic reasons from the revolutionary governments. One of the most important tasks facing him when he became first consul in 1799, of course, was the stabilization of the finances of the French government. The recovery of France's domestic finances under Napoleon was indeed remarkable, although not, perhaps, quite so remarkable as Marcel Marion, an *academicien* and conservative admirer of Napoleon, would have us believe. To some extent, Napoleon took advantage of improvements that had begun under the Directory, but even in the first year of the Consulate (1799–1800) domestic revenue increased dramatically, to about 527 million francs.[17] Direct taxes, which had produced almost nothing, began bringing in at least 250 million francs annually, while the receipts from indirect taxes and state monopolies grew steadily under the empire. Revenues ultimately reached 684 million francs in the year XIII (1804–5), 772 million in 1808, 795 million in 1810, and about 954 million in 1811.[18] But despite all this progress, only once, during the year of peace in 1802–3, did Napoleon truly balance his budget. Political considerations, furthermore, inclined Napoleon to rule out the more popular contemporary solutions to the problem of deficits from the start. With the experience of the old regime and the revolutionary governments fresh in his mind, he refused to resort either to paper money or to large-scale loans. The circulation of the notes of the Bank of France was rigidly curtailed.[19] In

17. Marion, *Histoire financière*, IV, 170–215.
18. Ibid., p. 322.
19. Jean Gabillard, "Le financement des guerres napoléoniennes," *Revue Economique*, 4 (1953): 549–553.

addition, he never tried to raise direct taxes; indeed, he apparently manipulated the domestic tax burden so as to make newly annexed departments pay more than their share, to the benefit of pre-1789 France.[20] Thus, like his predecessors, he ultimately found the solution to his financial problems in conquest. War, not loans or taxes, provided the means with which Napoleon balanced his budget.

Napoleon seems to have *hoped* that by instituting reforms within occupied territory and encouraging them among his allies, he could increase current income sufficiently to support most or all of his permanent military establishment. And indeed, virtually all of his allies and newly created satellites undertook either to provide France with subsidies or to maintain troops for the benefit of the alliance. Thus Spain in 1803–4 (year XI) apparently paid about 69 million francs, and in 1804 undertook to pay France 6 million francs per month.[21] The Dutch never lost their obligation to maintain 25,000 French troops either inside or outside their country, and Napoleon forced them to spend heavily on war against the British after 1803, as well.[22] The kingdom of Italy, created in 1804, paid France about 30 million francs per year, and its army grew progressively from 23,000 in 1805 to 90,000 in 1813. Naples also eventually incurred obligations to support some French troops and maintain about 20,000 men.[23] Finally, all the German states of the Confederation of the Rhine obligated themselves to maintain specific contingents of troops. Their total came to about 125,000 by 1808.[24] The grand duchy of Warsaw—created in 1807—had to devote about two-thirds of its budget to military expenditures.[25]

In theory, of course, the administrative reforms undertaken by Napoleon and his satellites should have provided the revenues necessary to support these troops, while their economic and social reforms stimulated their economies and increased revenue even

20. Marion, *Histoire financière*, IV, 309.

21. Ibid., pp. 325–330; Lefèbvre, *Napoleon*, p. 174.

22. Schama, *Patriots and Liberators*, pp. 433–454.

23. Marion, *Histoire financière*, IV, 325–332; Owen Connelly, *Napoleon's Satellite Kingdoms* (New York, 1965), pp. 51, 70, 103. Naples incurred this obligation after 1808, under Joachim Murat; Joseph Bonaparte had actually persuaded Napoleon to support the French occupation army himself.

24. Eberhard Weis, "Napoleon und der Rheinbund," in Reden-Dohna, ed., *Deutschland und Italien*, pp. 57–80.

25. Monika Sendowska-Gluck, "Le duché de Varsovie,"in *Occupants-Occupés, 1792–1815* (Brussels, 1969), pp. 391–402.

more. Even without attempting to treat these enormous subjects systematically, we may note that these reforms rarely went very far, and that revenues rarely increased rapidly enough. The Napoleonic Code was introduced in its entirety in only two satellite states, the kingdom of Italy and the kingdom of Westphalia. In Naples and in the Rhineland German states it was adopted only with major modifications, allowing various seigneurial property arrangements to continue.[26] Nor did sales of national properties provide governments with much additional revenue. Thus in both the kingdom of Italy and that of Naples many of the sales went to liquidate the state debt, just as they had in France.[27] We shall also see that in much of Germany Napoleon reserved large parts of these domains for his own use.

Napoleon's dissatisfaction with the contributions of allied and occupied territories suggests that he was trying to maintain a larger military and administrative apparatus than European society could bear. He never believed that either the Netherlands or Spain was paying as much as it could, and he turned both countries over to his brothers with the hope of getting more. The results were disappointing in Holland and disastrous in Spain, where a rebellion became a critical drain upon his resources. In any case, Napoleon never came close to relying upon regular annual revenues to support his projects.

It is clear that from 1804 until 1812 Napoleon followed the practice of the Directory before him: relying on indemnities collected from defeated states to maintain his own army, pay for his campaigns, and balance the budget within France. These indemnities supplied him with critically needed infusions of specie, which enabled his armies to live, allowed him to pay the debts he incurred during mobilization, and met the deficit in the French budget.[28]

26. See Elisabeth Fehrenbach, "Der Einfluss Frankreichs," pp. 23–39; Connelly, *Napoleon's Satellite Kingdoms*, pp. 41–43, 77–78, 111–112.

27. Pasquale Villani, "Wirtschaftliche Folgen der Säkularisierung in Italien," pp. 171–190, and Christopher Dipper, "Wirtschaftsgeschichte der Säkularisation in Deutschland (1803–13)," in Reden-Dohna, ed., *Deutschland und Italien*, pp. 123–170.

28. Gabillard, "Le financement des guerres napoléoniennes," p. 560, notes that since Napoleon refused to float loans, he forced contractors and provisioners to advance needed supplies without paying them. Only by collecting an indemnity could he pay them off. During the first few years of his reign he also seems to have paid off contractors and provisioners with grants of national properties in the Rhineland and in Italy. See Villani, "Wirtschaftliche Folgen der Säkularisierung in Italien," and Dipper, "Wirtschaftsgeschichte der Säkularisation in Deutschland."

After war resumed in 1803, Napoleon seems to have needed a large windfall almost every year. In 1804 the sale of Louisiana to the United States realized 50 million francs, raised by discounting American bonds in London and Amsterdam. A year later, Napoleon established the Domaine Extraordinaire, which supervised the collection of contributions and indemnities in occupied territories.[29] The campaign of 1805–6 and the defeat of Austria allowed Napoleon to raise a total of 75 million francs, of which 27 million were spent in Germany and 48 million returned to France. The campaigns in Prussia and Poland from 1806 through 1808 raised about 482 million francs, of which 281 million returned to France. The campaign against Austria in 1809 raised a further 164 million, of which 88 million returned to France. In the course of these six years, these various indemnities (and the sale of Louisiana) had provided the French treasury with 482 million francs, or about 80 million francs per year—that is, about 10 to 15 percent of annual revenue. In the meantime, the amounts spent within occupied territories allowed Napoleon to maintain his armies.[30]

This system, obviously, condemned Napoleon indefinitely to seek new prizes abroad. Each campaign was like another turn of the roulette wheel, which, if it did not bring him more good fortune, would start him down the road to bankruptcy. The beginning of the end was the campaign in Spain—undertaken after the Spanish people revolted against the deposition of the Bourbons—which immediately became a drain on French resources. During 1808–9 it cost the French 300 million francs in specie, and its costs subsequently rose.[31] The Russian campaign of 1812 led to utter disaster. Far more expensive to prepare than any previous venture, it left Napoleon deeply indebted to his contractors and provisioners, and brought no return whatever. The subsequent collapse of Napoleon's credit, which had always depended upon victories and indemnities, played a major role in the collapse of the empire.[32]

The Napoleonic wars had another economic dimension as well:

29. See Henri de Grimoüard, "Les origines du domaine extraordinaire: Le receveur géneral des contributions de la grande armée, ses attributions, ses comptes, 1805–1810," *Revue des Questions Historiques*, 83 (January 1908): 160–192.

30. For breakdowns of these figures, see de Grimoüard, "Les origines du domaine extraordinaire," pp. 166, 172, 186.

31. Connelly, *Napoleon's Satellite Kingdoms*, pp. 241–242, 251.

32. Gabillard, "Le financement des guerres napoléoniennes," pp. 562–563.

the struggle for the control of European trade between Britain and France. This conflict—a continuation of the mercantilist wars of the seventeenth and eighteenth centuries—sheds more light upon changes in the nature of international politics and economics. The conflict culminated in attempts by the British and French to reorder the trade of the whole world for their own benefit.[33] It also illuminates the motives that led the British to wage their twelve-year war against Napoleon.

The wartime economic policies of both the British and the French reflected the mercantilist principles of the era of enlightened despotism. These principles, appropriate to an era of slow economic growth, implied that the commerce of one country could increase only at the expense of others. In France they had received powerful reinforcement from the impact of the Anglo-French Commercial Treaty of 1786, which had worked to the disadvantage of French industry.[34] During the 1790s the British and the French tried to use the war to exclude each other's commerce from the widest possible area, while regulating or expropriating neutral commerce with the enemy. Many Frenchmen already believed that Britain might be ruined by denying her outlets for her exports, and, by extension, the specie which London needed to carry out the war. As for the British, they tried to regulate trade between the French colonies and France. British privateers and naval ships, which seized large numbers of French and neutral cargoes in the course of their blockade of France, did not do so in order to starve the French out. Instead, they were encouraged to sell the goods on the Continent themselves, thus ensuring that the British would reap the profits of this trade, while specie drained out of France.[35]

The Franco-British economic struggle began during the brief period of peace in 1802–3. Alone among the European powers, the British regarded exports as critical to their economic health, and Napoleon had not the slightest intention of opening the Continent to British trade. With the reestablishment of the French Caribbean empire and the annexation of Piedmont, he began working to re-

33. Eli F. Heckscher, *The Continental System: An Economic Interpretation* (London, 1922), and François Crouzet, *L'économie britannique et le blocus continental (1806–1813)*, 2 vols. (Paris, 1958), are the basic sources on the economic war.

34. Heckscher, *Continental System*, pp. 13–25. The cahiers of 1789 showed tremendous resentment against this treaty.

35. Ibid., pp. 30–58.

build French colonial commerce and to reorganize European commerce in ways which would favor French industry.[36] The British, whose exports rose during 1802 but began to fall again the next year, declared war once again in 1803 partly for commercial reasons.

French and British attempts to use the war to improve their economic and financial status reached their climax beginning with Napoleon's Berlin Decree of 1806, which began the establishment of the Continental System to outlaw British trade with Europe. Napoleon, characteristically, seems to have pursued several contradictory purposes at once, and his success is therefore difficult to estimate. On the one hand, he clearly wanted, insofar as possible, to give French industry a Continental monopoly, with corresponding benefits for French economic life and imperial finances. Although the effects of his economic policies have never been systematically studied, these efforts seem to have met with some success. The French cotton industry, in particular, grew during this period, although in contrast the great Atlantic trade was wrecked by the British blockade. The steady increase in the yield of indirect taxes suggests that the French economy as a whole, while still overwhelmingly traditional, did grow.[37] The cotton industry sometimes suffered, however, from a shortage of raw materials stemming from the exclusion of British trade—a problem which persuaded Napoleon in 1810 to license imports of colonial goods, including cotton. And as we have seen, French revenue did *not* increase enough to enable Napoleon to support his rule without further conquests.

The Continental System also tried to raise money by profiting from British trade. Napoleon did not always insist upon the exclusion or destruction of British goods; he frequently authorized their resale, provided the profits went into French hands. But this system was extremely difficult to implement, and many French officials—including some of Napoleon's leading generals—found it more convenient simply to tolerate smuggling in return for a cut of the profits. Nor was it possible to secure enthusiastic cooperation from satellites like Holland and Naples or from the Hanseatic cities, who depended on foreign trade for their livelihood. Thus in

36. Lefèbvre, *Napoleon*, pp. 154–161.
37. Bergeron, *France under Napoleon*, pp. 159ff.

1810 Napoleon went over to a system of licenses for overseas imports, applying a 40 percent duty to colonial goods while continuing to exclude British manufactures. At the same time, he began bluntly demanding that his officials turn over part of their profits to him.[38] No one has attempted to assess the profits realized by the French government from these measures.

In addition to stimulating French industry and profiting from the control of imports into Europe, Napoleon intended the Continental System to bring Britain to its knees by drowning the British Isles in goods and draining them of specie. To analyze the success of these measures, we must turn to the British side and examine British motives for carrying on the war.

Like the other European powers, the British sought territorial gains from the war. London made some small gains as a result of the Peace of Amiens and eventually emerged from the war in 1815 having added Ceylon and the Cape of Good Hope to the empire. Commercial motives, however, played a key role in the British struggle against Napoleon. Alone among the European powers, the British already believed that their trade was vital to their prosperity—and as long as Napoleon remained in power on the Continent, their trade stood to benefit from war. Trade had grown during the 1790s. British exports, valued at £24 million in 1792, had fallen to £20 million in 1793, but thereafter risen steadily, peaking at £41 million in 1802. Napoleon in 1802–3 had refused to conclude a commercial treaty with the British, and in 1803 exports fell to £31 million, only to begin rising again after the resumption of war.[39] In 1806, when peace with Britain was once again seriously discussed, Napoleon privately proclaimed his intention to continue his prohibitions against British goods.[40] The British might legitimately have concluded, as they apparently did, that peace with Napoleon must spell their ruin. In the meantime, they managed to keep their exports at a satisfactorily high level.

Napoleon's Continental System did have serious effects upon British trade. Twice, from July of 1807 through July 1808, and again from 1810 until the Russian campaign of 1812, Napoleon made a concerted effort to enforce the system, and both times he met with

38. Heckscher, *Continental System*, pp. 157–161, 187–220.

39. Figures are from J. Holland Rose, *William Pitt and the Great War* (London, 1911), p. 571, and Crouzet, *L'économie brittanique*, II, 883.

40. Heckscher, *Continental System*, p. 79.

considerable success. During these periods, British exports to Europe fell drastically, and total British exports declined slightly in 1807–8 and very significantly in 1810–11.[41] These declines, however, were only temporary. Despite both the Continental System and intermittent restrictions upon British exports to the United States, the average exports of British goods in the years 1804–1812 exceeded the total for the peacetime year 1802.[42] Not only did the British frequently succeed in evading Napoleon's prohibitions through smuggling, but they also took advantage of Napoleon's invasion of Spain to open up the trade of the Spanish colonies. Showing impressive initiative, British merchants scoured the globe in search of new outlets. They thereby staved off economic disaster until Napoleon's Spanish and Russian adventures led to his collapse.[43]

This was not all. As we have seen, British naval ships and privateers had made great fortunes out of the confiscation of French and neutral commerce since the beginning of war in 1793—and so, apparently, had the officials of the admiralty courts who awarded their prizes. In response to Napoleon's decrees, the British Orders in Council of 1807 claimed the right to regulate all trade between the Americas and the Continent—that is, to require all neutral ships carrying on such trade to pay duty on their cargoes in British ports and to confiscate them if they failed to do so. The orders made any neutral ship attempting to trade with Europe fair game for British privateers. Indeed, it seems that the navy, the admiralty courts, and many members of the British government were drawing considerable profits from the regulation of neutral commerce.[44] Not only did the war fail to cripple British commerce, it also enriched important members of the British ruling class.

41. The latter decline—by far the more serious—was only partly due to French restrictions. It also reflected a European-wide crisis of overproduction, perhaps the first in European history, which struck the French hard as well.

42. Crouzet, L'économie britannique, II, 885.

43. In his conclusion (esp. II, 853–863) Crouzet argues that the invasions of Spain and Russia, indeed, doomed the blockade, and suggests that it might have been successful had Napoleon avoided these capital errors. While this may be true, we must still note other reasons which made it impossible for Napoleon to avoid these adventures, including the temperamental and financial factors I have already discussed.

44. Thus Henry Adams, History of the United States during the Administration of Thomas Jefferson, bk. 4 (New York, 1890), pp. 94–97. Adams, whose work remains extremely valuable, gives some intriguing evidence for this contention but does not investigate it thoroughly. Certainly it would make for a fascinating study.

So it was that in January 1808, in the midst of one of the periods in which the enforcement of the Continental System was most effective, a member of the government could proclaim that war, "the curse of every other nation, had to Great Britain been a comparative blessing." Britain had "gained everything and lost nothing": its trade flourished, British wealth multiplied, Britain's rivals had been eliminated from the seas, and no combination could threaten British maritime supremacy.[45] Of course this was something of an exaggeration. The war imposed serious strains upon the British, and they could hardly have known, either in 1793 or in 1803, that they would definitely be able to stand them. Government revenue rose from £18 million in 1792 to £27 million in 1798, £41 million in 1802, £69 million in 1809, and £78 million in 1814. Expenditure during the same period rose from £17 million to £113 million, and the national debt trebled.[46] The British paid tens of millions of pounds in subsidies to their allies during the Napoleonic wars, much of it, though not all, in specie. Total borrowing from 1798 through 1815 totaled £654 million.[47] The British financed the war mainly with note issues by the Bank of England, and with the exception of brief crises in 1797 and 1810, confidence in these notes remained sufficiently high. The British, in short, found that their economy was strong enough to support their war expenditures, and British lenders never lost confidence in the government.

The traditional view of Britain's role in the Napoleonic wars— that of the lonely bastion of the European balance of power, financing its Continental allies and gradually wearing down the emperor by virtue of its economic strength—needs some revision. In fact, the subsidies which the British provided to the Austrians in 1800, to Austria and several minor powers in 1805–6, to Russia in 1806–7, to Prussia in 1807, and to Austria in 1809, did *not* hurt Napoleon. If anything, they helped him, since they encouraged the other Continental powers to take the field against him, allowing him to defeat them and secure territorial concessions and indemnities.[48] Nor is it clear that the British blockade did critical harm to

45. Denis Gray, *Spencer Perceval: The Evangelical Prime Minister, 1762–1812* (Manchester, 1963), p. 143.

46. B. R. Mitchell, ed., *European Historical Statistics* (New York, 1975), pp. 697, 707–708.

47. John M. Sherwig, *Guineas and Gunpowder: British Foreign Aid in the Wars with France, 1793–1815* (Cambridge, Mass., 1969), *passim;* Denis Gray, *Spencer Perceval*, p. 390.

48. Sherwig, *Guineas and Gunpower,* pp. 97–215, details all these transactions, without necessarily reaching this conclusion.

the French economy.[49] The British campaign in the Iberian peninsula did drain Napoleon's resources substantially, but the campaign would not have occurred without the rising of the Spanish people, and it was not decisive. While British money also helped put together the last, victorious coalition against Napoleon, the emperor's own temperament, economic needs, and social goals actually brought about his collapse, by driving him ever forward until the catastrophes of Spain and Russia. Had he been able to restrain himself, he could have reached rather generous compromise peace agreements with the British on several occasions.

War remained more profitable for the British economy than peace with Napoleon—certainly for British exporters, and possibly for British lenders, whose loans paid higher interest, in all probability, than any peacetime opportunities. In this sense, British policy was every bit as mercantilist, and far more successful, than the economic imperialism of Napoleon. Like the French and other Continental European states, the British carried on the war partly because it benefited them to do so. The war left the international community and the international economy at the mercy of armed force. The British government and the British navy took advantage of the situation every bit as fully as Napoleon and his armies, and showed the same willingness to violate the rights of neutrals like the United States, even at the risk of war.

The last motive for Napoleonic expansion is perhaps the most interesting, and certainly the least studied. It is now clear that Napoleon intended to create and endow a new European elite, and that he needed continual territorial expansion for this purpose.

Napoleon Bonaparte was undoubtedly the most notable beneficiary of that great principle of the Enlightenment, career open to talent. Although his own origins were far from modest—his father was, after all, a Corsican nobleman who had played a role of some consequence in Corsican politics—he nonetheless needed the revolution to enable him to rise even to the command of an army, much less to the position of chief of state or emperor of most of Europe. He clearly did not, moreover, regard himself as unique, and as emperor he encouraged others to emulate his spectacular

49. Gabillard, "Le financement des guerres napoléoniennes," pp. 568–569, notes that France enjoyed tremendous prosperity from 1807 through 1810, and that the economic crisis which followed affected Britain as well as the Continent.

rise. The system of mobility which he tried to institutionalize had significant consequences for international politics.

Unlike the revolutionaries of the French Constituent Assembly, who abolished titles of nobility at a relatively early stage of the revolution,[50] Napoleon believed in social mobility within a traditional context and wanted to reward men of distinction with titles and endowments. He reestablished hereditary monarchy in 1804, and gradually reestablished nobility between 1806 and 1808.[51] The new nobility combined that part of the old nobility that wished to cooperate with the regime with Napoleon's own new creations. This fusion is also reflected in both of Napoleon's two marriages. Josephine was the widow of a French noble—albeit one with revolutionary sympathies—and Marie Louise came from one of the oldest ruling houses in Europe. As emperor, Napoleon encouraged other such marriages as well. All told, 22.5 percent of the Napoleonic nobility came from the old nobility, 59 percent from the middle classes, and 19.5 percent from the people.

More significant for our purposes are the kinds of men Napoleon favored for his new creations and the ways in which he chose to reward them. By far the largest single group of Napoleonic nobles came from the military—a full 59 percent. Most favored of all were the marshals, who became the richest single social group in France. Next in importance were other high civil servants, who accounted for 22 percent of his creations, while the commercial and industrial classes accounted for just one-half of 1 percent.[52] Napoleon consistently regarded the army as the backbone of his rule. During his campaigns, he made the prompt payment of his armies and his civil servants his highest financial priority.[53] It is not surprising, therefore, that he regarded his generals and marshals as the group most deserving of reward. It seems, too, that the military consistently provided the easiest channel for advancement from the top to the bottom. Most nobles of popular origin undoubtedly rose through the military, and Napoleon's marshals included several men, such as his brother-in-law Murat, whose origins could hardly have been more modest.

---

50. See Patrice Higonnet, *Class, Ideology, and the Rights of Nobles during the French Revolution* (Oxford, 1981), pp. 57–72.

51. Bergeron, *France under Napoleon*, pp. 63–71.

52. Ibid., pp. 63–158. "Other notables" made up 17 percent of his creations, while 1.5 percent were "talented."

53. Gabillard, "Le financement des guerres napoléoniennes," p. 560.

A system which places the military atop the social pyramid and which encourages talented men to seek their fortune in the officer corps can hardly fail to encourage frequent military adventures, both to provide new opportunities for distinction and to legitimize the military's preeminent position. Napoleon himself, at a fairly early but critical juncture of his rule, suggested bluntly that he needed frequent wars to assure his legitimacy. "Believe me," he remarked in the spring of 1802, "a First Consul in no way resembles divine right kings . . . They profit from tradition, which is for us an obstacle. Hated by her neighbors, forced simultaneously to contain various classes of ill-wishers at home and to prevail upon so many enemies abroad, the French state needs brilliant deeds, and, in consequence, war. It must be the first of all states or perish. In our situation I regard any conclusion of peace as a short truce and feel myself, during my term in office, destined to fight almost without interruption."[54] Such ideas in themselves inevitably predisposed Napoleon toward conflict, but the ways in which he decided to reward his new elite were perhaps even more important. He granted his most faithful followers the highest rewards European society had to offer: sovereignty, income, and land. These rewards could be secured only by further conquests.

The domestic and international political turmoil of the late eighteenth and early nineteenth centuries offered generals, admirals, and politicians tremendous opportunities to distinguish themselves, and Napoleon was only one of many who aimed to use those opportunities to become a head of state. Well before the French Revolution, Stanislas Poniatowski, a Polish count, had used his love affair with Catherine the Great to help secure the kingship of Poland. During the 1790s the French generals Dumouriez and Hoche schemed to become sovereign in Belgium or in a projected Rhineland republic. Later, Manuel Godoy, the favorite of King Charles IV and Queen Louisa of Spain, aspired to become a territorial prince, and Napoleon in 1807 agreed to make him the ruler of part of the soon-to-be partitioned kingdom of Portugal. Military glory also became a stepping stone to political power in America and Great Britain. George Washington became the first American president, while Arthur Wellesley capitalized upon his military success against Napoleon to become first a duke

---

54. Martin Phillipson, "La paix d'Amiens et la politique générale de Napoléon I," *Revue Historique*, 76 (1901): 76.

and, later, prime minister—an almost unprecedented development in English history. Another contemporary of Napoleon's, Alexander Hamilton, also dreamed in the late 1790s of leading an
expedition into the Spanish-American empire that would increase
the territory of the United States and presumably make him a leading candidate for president as well. Hamilton well understood the
nature of the age in which he lived, and when his plans collapsed
in 1799, he lamented that " 'the Chapter of extraordinary events
which characterize the present wonderful epoch' was not to include the name of Alexander Hamilton writ large across the history of Latin America."[55] A few years later, Aaron Burr tried, with
foreign support, to set himself up as the head of a new American
republic on the shores of the Gulf of Mexico.

Here as in so many other aspects of contemporary politics, however, Napoleon thoroughly institutionalized the spirit of the age.
Sovereignty became the ultimate reward for distinction within Napoleon's empire. Most of Napoleon's grants of sovereignty, of
course, went to his own relations. Three of his brothers became
kings, and his stepson Eugene de Beauharnais became viceroy of
the kingdom of Italy. In addition, Joseph in 1808 gave way as king
of Naples to Napoleon's marshal and brother-in-law, Joachim
Murat, who had previously served as grand duke of Berg, and
Marshal Jean-Baptiste Bernadotte became king of Sweden. Napoleon also created some new Italian princes with some sovereign
rights in Italy in 1806, although he eventually abandoned this experiment. Many other new dynasties might have been founded
had plans for the conquest of Russia and the Ottoman empire—
not to speak of Persia, India, and the Spanish colonies—ever
reached fruition.

Sovereignty was only the highest reward; beneath it came income and land. And these favors, too, as we now know thanks to
a remarkable work by Helmut Berding,[56] Napoleon organized and
distributed on a massive scale.

This critical aspect of Napoleonic social policy emerged after the
conclusion of the Treaty of Tilsit in 1807, when Napoleon created
two new states, the kingdom of Westphalia, whose throne went to

55. John C. Miller, *Alexander Hamilton and the Growth of the New Nation* (New York,
1959), p. 504.

56. Helmut Berding, *Napoleonische Herrschafts- und Gesellschaftspolitik im Königreich
Westphalen, 1807–13* (Göttingen, 1973).

his brother Jerome, and the grand duchy of Warsaw, which he gave to the king of Saxony. The kingdom of Westphalia—created out of previously Prussian lands in northwest Germany, and eventually including Hanover as well—was designed as a model Napoleonic state. It received a unitary constitution and was the only German state to adopt the Napoleonic Code in its entirety. At the same time, however, Napoleon reserved roughly half of the old royal domain within Westphalia, as well as large properties in the grand duchy of Warsaw and in other parts of Germany, for an entirely different purpose. These lands became part of the Domaine Extraordinaire, the same institution which supervised the collection and disbursement of contributions within occupied territories. There, totally free of any outside supervision, they were used by Napoleon himself to create *majorats*, or hereditary endowments for his new nobility.

Napoleon needed new income to reward his army, from the marshals at the top to the invalids and war widows at the bottom. He was determined to establish his new nobility upon a firm basis of landed wealth. The various grades of Napoleonic nobility required property yielding a specified annual income in order to make their titles hereditary, and Napoleon himself, a convinced physiocrat, wanted that income to be landed. This emerged most definitely when his brother Jerome, protesting that the imperial reservation of so much of the royal domains would make it impossible for him to put Westphalian finances upon a sound footing, suggested that Napoleon re-cede the land back to him in exchange for promises to pay the emperor the income. The emperor refused. "These lands," he replied, "belong to my generals, who conquered your kingdom; this is an engagement I have given them and which nothing can make me betray."[57] Napoleon might have preferred to endow his favorites with French lands, but no French lands were readily available, and he obviously did not want to risk the political consequences of a new round of confiscations within France.[58]

Napoleon personally supervised the endowment of these *majorats* from properties vested in the Domaine Extraordinaire. These properties included domainal income from Westphalia, Hanover, the grand duchy of Warsaw, several minor German states, Brabant

57. Ibid., p. 28.
58. Ibid., pp. 53–72.

in the Netherlands, the Tyrol, some properties within the Rhine departments, and the "octroi du Rhin," altogether totalling approximately 300 million francs within Germany. An additional capital of about 110 million francs in Italy included reserved domainal income, the properties of the Knights of Malta, and the "Mont de Milan," a fund Napoleon had reserved out of the income of the kingdom of Italy. Napoleon also invested about 50 million francs in cash in French canal shares and in loans to the cities of Paris and Bordeaux and the Bordeaux vineyards, and distributed the income from these shares to common soldiers and their widows, while reserving the domainal income for higher officers.[59] The largest endowments went to generals, of whom more than 90 percent—897 out of 956—received grants. All told the generals received more than half of the approximately 29.6 million francs of yearly income which Napoleon passed out.[60]

As Berding points out, the reservation of properties for hereditary noble endowments flatly contradicted the professed principles of Napoleonic administration, which held that all land, and all landholders, must be treated equally. This contradiction led to bitter disputes between Napoleon and his vassal rulers in Westphalia and the grand duchy of Warsaw, especially since Napoleon sometimes insisted that his reserved domains be exempted from local taxation or from social and economic reforms. King Jerome, whose financial position had been rendered impossible by these policies, finally yielded to his brother in 1811 after Napoleon had threatened to replace him with Marshal Davout.[61]

Like France's inadequate finances, this system inevitably promoted further expansion. Despite his investments in French canals, Napoleon was generally compensating his followers not out of the proceeds of economic growth, but rather out of the existing capital of Europe. More compensation could only come from new land. Here again, just as in the realm of economics and finance, we encounter the *reductio ad absurdum* of Napoleonic policy: that it re-

59. De Grimoüard, "Les origines du domaine extraordinaire," pp. 185, 187.
60. Berding, *Napoleonische Herrschafts- und Gesellschaftspolitik*, pp. 55–72.
61. Ibid., pp. 31–52; see also Monika Sendowska-Gluck, "Le duché de Varsovie," pp. 391–402. Sendowska-Gluck notes that the Prussians had also used state and church land to endow officers and bureaucrats after the second partition of Poland, and adds that in the grand duchy, for some reason, Napoleon eventually agreed that the reserved domains *would* pay taxes.

quired continuing expansion to fulfill its social requirements, as well as its economic ones. Not only Napoleon's temperament, but also the imperatives of his economic and social policies, condemned him to new wars. In this sense, too, he was destined to continue expanding either until he was finally defeated, or until he reached the ends of the earth.

In several ways, indeed, Napoleon's eventual defeat shows how he pushed the principles of his age to an illogical conclusion. Napoleon's successes depended upon his ability to win decisive military victories, to make quick peace treaties with his enemies, and to reward both his allies, such as the minor German princes, and his subordinates. His difficulties began in 1808, when the Spanish *people* revolted after he deposed the Spanish Bourbons and installed his brother Joseph as king. He could neither end the insurrection nor draw more revenue from Spain, especially after the British sent an expeditionary force to Spain to help the rebels. In the same way the Russians in 1812 refused even to discuss peace despite several military defeats and the loss of Moscow, and Napoleon's army disintegrated.

By 1812, moreover, Napoleon had no important allies left. As late as 1807, when he made peace with Alexander at Tilsit, he had been able to offer territorial gains to at least one other Continental power, but by 1812 all of them had suffered from his defeats, even if both Prussia and Austria were nominally allies in the campaign against Russia. During the revolutionary era and the 1800s, the European states had pursued parallel expansion. By this time, however, Napoleon was monopolizing the benefits of expansion for his own marshals and soldiers, even challenging the sovereignty of his own satellites in order to provide for them. The German states therefore found it quite natural to turn against Napoleon during 1813. To defeat him, moreover, they adopted some of the expedients of the French revolutionary governments: the opening of their armies to middle-class officers, appeals to national feeling, and the *levée en masse*. Conscription in Prussia, applied on an unprecedented scale, helped raise the army that defeated Napoleon at Leipzig in October 1813.[62]

Napoleon's use of expansion to reward his subordinates also

---

62. Friedrich Meinecke, *The Age of German Liberation, 1795–1815* (Berkeley, 1977), pp. 12–21.

helps explain one of the most puzzling aspects of his diplomacy: his refusal, during most of 1813, to make peace upon relatively generous terms, including the maintenance of the Rhine frontier for France. In theory, as so many French historians have pointed out, he might easily have retained these gains and thereby given himself or his successors a chance of defending them in the future—although as Geyl noted whether the French could have retained the left bank of the Rhine in the coming age of nationalism is a very open question.[63] Yet Napoleon's withdrawal from most of the rest of Germany, which the allies demanded, would probably have meant the return of many of the properties he had reserved for his subordinates, thereby undermining the basis of his whole political system.

From a broader historical perspective, Napoleon's attempts to create and endow a new ruling elite also suggest that the rationalism of the late eighteenth century—like the Counter-Reformation in Germany in the early seventeenth—had simply become an excuse for the redistribution of wealth and property to a new military elite. And indeed, he carried out this redistribution—temporary though it turned out to be—on a far more sweeping scale than Wallenstein and his contemporaries ever could, partly because the new rationalist principles could be applied so much more broadly, without regard for either historical tradition or the religion of the inhabitants. Sound administration on supposedly impartial principles, he obviously felt, would secure the allegiance of European peoples, regardless of their religion or nationality.[64] In the meantime, he felt absolutely free—like Philip II or Wallenstein—to *distribute* sovereignty over various territories, and the revenues which flowed from them, according to principles which were entirely traditional, and dubiously rational. Thus, he obviously found it quite natural that family should share his success from the beginning of his career, and that they should furnish Europe with a new ruling dynasty, however inadequate to the task of governing some of them proved to be.[65] And the other men he chose to reward did

63. Both Edouard Driault and Georges Lefèbvre made this argument. See Geyl, *Napoleon, For and Against*, pp. 304–306.

64. Geyl, *Napoleon, For and Against*, develops this point at length; see for example p. 188.

65. Ibid., pp. 177–209, for a very entertaining discussion of this problem based on the works of Frédéric Masson.

not pass competitive examinations in writing, but were those who fought with him upon the battlefield. In this sense his policies seem to reflect the values of the feudal aristocracy of medieval Europe more closely than those of the Enlightenment.

Here, too, Napoleon reflected the spirit of the age. His fellow European sovereigns did not object in principle to the establishment of this new dynasty and considered leaving it in place, in France at least, even after they had clearly secured the upper hand militarily in 1813–14. By and large, European society, while increasingly accepting the idea of career open to talent, interpreted it simply as the opening up of the traditional aristocracy, rather than its abolition. And war remained the highest calling of the newer aristocracy, just as it had been since the founding of the old. To achieve more social and political stability, Europe needed new outlets for the ambition which the Enlightenment had unleashed, and these Napoleon did not provide.

Napoleon's collapse ended his attempts to endow a new European ruling elite, and restored or enlarged the domains of many of the dynasties he had dispossessed or reduced. The indemnity imposed upon France at Vienna, moreover, roughly equaled the indemnities he had collected after his victorious campaigns.[66] The military, political, diplomatic, and economic tools available to Napoleon had failed to establish his empire over all Europe. But the experience of the years 1789–1815 had transformed the European map, European political institutions, and European ways of thinking.

Rationalism and History

The revolutionary and Napoleonic period, as Tocqueville noted specifically with respect to France, tended mainly to eliminate most vestiges of feudal political power and strengthen the authority of centralized states. Despite the rhetoric of universal freedom, equality before the law, the rights of national communities to rule themselves, and representative institutions, in practice, both revolutionary governments and existing European states used such principles simply to justify the growth of their own power, particularly at the expense of older institutions such as the church,

66. See de Grimoüard, "Les origines du domaine extraordinaire," pp.190–191.

towns, and independent fiefdoms, and to expand their territories. When the war was over the victorious powers made no effort to restore these institutions or to surrender their own territorial gains. Several of the German princes of the Confederation of the Rhine were confirmed as kings, and Prussia simply took over the left bank of the Rhine from France. The three hundred jurisdictions of the Holy Roman Empire had been reduced to about thirty independent states. In Italy, Austria not only regained Lombardy but kept Venice as well.

On the whole these decades simply intensified the practices of the era of enlightened despotism. Armed with the ideas of the Enlightenment as well as larger armies, European states continued their expansion and their attempts to impose a more uniform, regular authority over their subjects and territories. The rule of reason, however, could not in the long run be the basis for the organization of a European state system, since it could not confer legitimacy upon any particular territorial arrangements. To have maintained the idea that expansion was justified simply by its success and that any enlightened ruler was entitled to any territory he could conquer ultimately would have condemned Europe to perpetual war. In practice, this principle died quickly. The Congress of Vienna restored the principle of dynastic or historic legitimacy—although the congress's decisions often violated it. Within a few more decades that principle gave way to the the idea of nationalism, which rapidly became the new organizing principle of European international politics. Nationalism had played only an occasional role in the revolutionary and Napoleonic era. Both the French revolutionary governments in the 1790s and some of the German states during the last stages of the war against Napoleon had made some use of it, but German and Italian nationalists were almost completely disappointed by the outcome of the Napoleonic wars. Significantly, Napoleon himself had no sympathy or understanding for the idea whatever. Only later did it become critical to European international politics.

But although it tended in practice simply to intensify the practices of the old regime, the revolutionary and Napoleonic era had a variety of profound long-term consequences. After this era, the European aristocracy—including the princely houses—ceased to be a major source of European conflict. Although the nobility continued to dominate the officer corps throughout Europe for another century after 1815, and soldiers found wars to fight on other continents, neither they nor their monarchs exerted any consistent pressure for war in Europe. The behavior of the ruling princes in the years 1815–1848 suggests that they regarded both war and the mobilization of their peoples as too dangerous to risk. Metternich, in particular, who remained in power throughout that period, tried in the 1820s to organize European military force to fight revolution, rather than to resume the competition among states.[1] Monarchical solidarity generally prevailed during the revolutions of 1848 as well, and although some kings and aristocrats in Piedmont and Prussia learned in the 1850s and 1860s to exploit middle-class national movements, their wars were brief and infrequent.

Fortunately for Europe, the rising middle class also turned to other occupations. We have seen that in the late eighteenth and early nineteenth centuries, the principle of career open to talent applied above all to service in the government and the military. Napoleon and his subordinates tried to use war to establish themselves as a new ruling elite. Napoleon attacked the problems of war and administration with an obsessive creative energy highly characteristic of the emerging middle class. The Napoleonic era, however, illustrates the unfortunate consequences of focusing these energies upon international politics. Napoleon's activities were also based upon the illusion that government reform and a mercantilist state could create enough wealth to satisfy the enormous ambitions which the Enlightenment had unleashed. In fact, in the years 1792–1815 the ruling European elite was still pouring its energies into an activity which destroyed more wealth than it created.

With social barriers to advancement crumbling, Europe desperately needed a new outlet for the ambition of the middle class. The most important outlet that eventually emerged was the industrial revolution, which allowed men to make their fortune in ways which were not necessarily socially destructive and which might even be socially useful. Temperamentally Napoleon's real successors were the great nineteenth-century captains of industry, who in the long run changed the face of Europe and the Western world far more than he. It is of course hardly a coincidence that the in-

1. Henry A. Kissinger, *A World Restored: The Politics of Conservatism in a Revolutionary Age* (New York, 1968), pp. 191–311.

dustrial revolution occurred in roughly the era I have been discussing. The same intellectual and demographic changes which unleashed international conflict also promoted technical progress and mass production. Still, we leave the revolutionary and Napoleonic period with the feeling that the emergence of new roads to wealth and power was a most fortunate development for Western society. The industrial revolution eventually created new sources of conflict in international politics, but in the short run it provided a partial solution for the problem of modern ambition by enormously increasing the opportunities available in Western society. Another outlet that emerged later in the nineteenth century was increased imperialism in the tropics, which I shall examine in connection with the coming of the two world wars.

The political and intellectual heritage of the Enlightenment and the revolutionary period has remained enormously influential during the nineteenth and twentieth centuries. The long-term impact of the ideas of the era reflects to a remarkable degree the critical duality of the French Revolution itself: its emphasis upon liberty, equality, and fraternity on the one hand, and its tendency to strengthen the state on the other. Looking back over the last two centuries, it is difficult to identify a more powerful or influential image than that of a national community coming together to reshape its destiny. Even Tocqueville, still the single most perspicacious critic of the revolution, who understood so well how it had strengthened the state and endangered liberty, was inspired by the spectacle of 1789, "that rapturous year of bright enthusiasm, heroic courage, lofty ideals—untempered, we must grant, by the reality of experience: a historic date of glorious memory to which the thoughts of men will turn with admiration and respect long after those who witnessed its achievement, and we ourselves, have passed away."[2]

Near the end of his life, in his unfinished study of the revolution, he went even further.

> A great enterprise was really opening. Its magnitude, its beauty, its risks were now visible. This great sight gripped and enraptured the imagination of the whole French people. In the presence of this immense design there was a moment when thousands of individuals completely forgot their particular interests to dream only of the common achievements.

2. Tocqueville, *The Old Regime and the French Revolution*, p. 208.

This lasted but for a moment, but that moment was perhaps unexampled in the history of any other people.[3]

Somewhat more sympathetic to the French Revolution, Immanuel Kant anticipated its legacy in equally prophetic terms:

The revolution of an ingenious people which we have lived to see, may succeed or fail. It may be filled with such calamities and atrocities that a righteous man, even if he could be sure to carry it out luckily, never would decide to repeat the experiment at such a high price. In spite of all this such a revolution finds, in the minds of all spectators, a sympathy very near to enthusiasm . . . Such a phenomenon in the history of mankind can never be forgotten; because it proves that in human nature there exists an inclination to the better which no politician ever could have been able to predict by summing up the course of former events.[4]

Despite the Romantic movement of the early nineteenth century and various other attempts to revive a more conservative approach to politics, the ideas of equality, natural rights, and progress have generally strengthened their hold upon the Western imagination during the last two centuries. Even more influential has been the image of man using his reason to reshape his destiny. Western civilization has generally adopted the two beliefs which François Furet identifies as the bedrock of revolutionary consciousness: that "there is no human misfortune not amenable to a political solution," and that "since everything can be known and changed, there is a perfect fit between action, knowledge, and morality."[5] Man's belief in his ability to reshape his destiny is probably the single most enduring legacy of the eighteenth century, and we shall find that it is the key to an understanding of the two world wars.

The appeal of these ideas, however, must also be weighed against the actual effects of attempts to implement them. Because the vast majority of twentieth-century Western historians—including both the Atlanticists and the Marxists—have shared the professed hopes of the French Revolution, most twentieth-century treatments of the period have been fundamentally optimistic. Several very recent studies of the French Revolution emphasizing its violence and cruelty suggest that its interpretation is entering a

---

3. Alexis de Tocqueville, "The European Revolution," in John Lukacs, ed. *"The European Revolution" and Correspondence with Gobineau* (New York, 1959), p. 85.

4. Kant quoted in Ernst Cassirer, *Myth of the State* (New Haven, 1946), p. 178.

5. Furet, *Interpreting the French Revolution*, p. 25.

new phase. New treatments of the civil war in the Vendée, the role of revolutionary armies, and of the revolution as a whole have asked whether the practice of the revolution truly reflected its principles, or rather introduced new horrors to modern politics.[6] The significance of the revolution, in short, has been called into question once more. The resulting debate involves fundamental issues in western civilization.

To enter fully into this debate here would carry us well beyond the subject of this book. With respect to the impact of warfare, however, one can easily argue that many past treatments have been partially blinded by identification with the revolutionary spirit. Whereas most historians treat the Thirty Years' War as tragic and essentially meaningless, very few have written about the era of the French Revolution and Napoleon without endorsing at least to some degree the principles the French claimed to be fighting for. This certainly applies to both the Marxists and the Atlanticists, who dominated the field during the middle decades of the twentieth century. Yet both contemporary testimony and some recent historiography suggest that our cultural prejudices have given us an anachronistic view of the revolutionary period, and that to the people of Europe its impact was often similar to the Thirty Years' War. "Husbands and fathers, whose wives and daughters had been raped often before their eyes, were inspired to castrate the Frenchmen alive and then to butcher them as one would butcher hogs," an eyewitness wrote of the retreat of French armies from the Rhineland in 1796.[7] Goya's Los desastres give a similar picture of French campaigns in Spain.[8] And if the same cruelties were perpetrated in the late eighteenth century as in the early seventeenth, we must ask whether historians have overemphasized the significance of the different ideas of the two eras. We have already seen that it is difficult to distinguish the redistribution of power and property which Napoleon tried to carry out from the earlier efforts of Wallenstein and Gustav Adolf. The emergence of new principles could not, in and of themselves, change the character and consequences of international conflict.[9]

6. Reynald Secher, Le génocide franco-français: La Vendée-vengée (2d ed., Paris, 1988); Richard Cobb, The People's Armies: The Armées Révolutionaires, Instrument of the Terror in the Departments (New Haven, 1987); Schama, Citizens. Although these books have been written from three different perspectives, all of them highlight revolutionary violence.

7. Quoted in Roidan, Baron Thugut, p. 224.

8. See also Geoffrey Best, War and Society in Revolutionary Europe, pp. 99–107.

9. Certainly this is the implication of Blanning, French Revolution in Germany.

The Enlightenment has had an even more lasting impact on practitioners and historians of European international conflict. The Enlightenment vision of the state and the classic eighteenth-century view of international politics has been adopted by many distinguished politicians and historians. The appeal of such ideas to statesmen is natural enough. A theory which regards the expansion of the power of the state both as natural and desirable, which assigns to society the role simply of supporting the statesman, and which thereby claims for the statesman an exemption from many (if not all) of the traditional rules of civilized behavior can hardly fail to appeal to the ambitious, energetic individuals who seem destined to attain political power in every age, and to the scribes which every age finds to glorify them. Such a model also assumes—following Frederick the Great—that war is an inevitable aspect of international politics, that it remains the supreme test of every national community, and that states and societies must therefore subordinate every other goal to the need to fight and win wars. In recent years such views have been put forward as a guide for diplomacy and strategy by no less a figure than Henry Kissinger, while Richard Nixon has suggested that "national security"—a rough American synonymn for "reason of state"—frees the American president of all constitutional limitations.[10] Many see in the state the transcendental values that had previously been claimed by the church, and its representatives therefore claim prerogatives and exemptions at least as sweeping as those who formerly claimed to speak to heaven.

What is perhaps more surprising is the appeal of an Enlightenment model of international politics to professional historians. Ranke himself referred to states as ideas of God,[11] and many subsequent historians accepted their transcendental claims quite uncritically. Many nineteenth- and twentieth-century historians of international conflict also treated expansion and war as natural processes, whose participants' motives require no more explanation than those of parasites and antibodies, or of athletes trying to win games of skill. This tendency has allowed numerous historians simply to identify with their favorite statesmen, or to follow the eighteenth-century practice of exalting statesmanship as

10. See Stanley Hoffmann, "The Case of Dr. Kissinger," *New York Review of Books*, December 6, 1979, esp. pp. 21–25. For Nixon's belief, see David Frost, *I Gave Them a Sword* (New York, 1978), pp. 183–184.

11. Meinecke, *Historism*, p. 506.

the highest calling without necessarily asking what purpose it serves.[12] It has also contributed to the equally widespread tendency to view the whole of modern European history as the story of the growth of the power of the state and to exaggerate the rapidity with which state power has grown—a tendency that has seriously distorted many treatments of the sixteenth and seventeenth centuries. During the last few decades many historians of the twentieth century have tried to pay more attention to the domestic political context of international relations—albeit with mixed results—but the eighteenth-century model still survives. The most recent general treatment of modern European international conflict, Paul Kennedy's *Rise and Fall of the Great Powers*, relies almost entirely upon an Enlightenment model of both domestic and international politics. It implicitly treats war simply as a natural occurrence among states, views the task of government as the organization of the resources of the nation, and generally downplays the whole question of why wars take place.[13]

In the late eighteenth and early nineteenth centuries, the new rationalism simply legitimized the ambitions of the older and newer ruling elites, whose appetites actually exceeded the available resources just as surely as those of the colonels who raised regiments in the Thirty Years' War. During the rest of the nineteenth century the idea of expansion for its own sake lost ground in European politics, but two new ideas with even greater potential significance became important. The idea of nationalism called for the division and consolidation of Europe into ethnically homogeneous states, while imperialism encouraged the new industrial powers to build economically self-sufficient empires. Although both of these ideas were rational in theory, neither had a firm basis in reality. Still, Europeans in the twentieth century eventually tried to apply them with a zeal worthy of Robespierre and Saint-Just. The era of the two world wars witnessed new attempts to transform European society according to abstract principles, with tragic and horrifying consequences.

12. Striking examples of these tendencies include William Langer's treatment of Bismarck in his *European Alliances and Alignments, 1871–1890* (New York, 1931), and Henry Kissinger's *A World Restored*.

13. As Kennedy remarks in his introduction, his book "is not centrally concerned with general theories about the *causes* of war, and whether they are likely to be brought about by 'rising' or 'falling' great powers" (*Rise and Fall of the Great Powers*, p. xxi).

4   The Era of the Two World Wars

Above all, we ought never to forget that nowadays
no war can be declared unless a whole people is
convinced that such a war is necessary and just. A
war, lightly provoked, even if it were fought successfully, would have a bad effect on the country;
while if it ended in defeat, it might entail the fall of
the dynasty. History shows us that every great war
is followed by a period of liberalism, since a people
demands compensation for the sacrifices and effort
war has entailed. But any war which ends in a defeat obliges the dynasty that declared it to make
concessions which before would have seemed un-
heard of.

—Bernard von Bülow, 1908

European Politics in the Late Nineteenth and Early Twentieth Centuries

European society, economic life, and politics changed fundamentally during the long, only rarely interrupted period of European
peace from 1815 through 1914. These changes brought to the fore
the two major issues that led to the enormously destructive conflicts of the years 1914–1945—the problem of imperialism and economic self-sufficiency, which took on a new aspect as a result of
the industrial revolution, and the idea of nationalism, which eventually overthrew the political structure of central and eastern Europe. To understand the impact of these issues, we must first look
briefly at the new forms of politics which emerged in almost all of
Europe during the late nineteenth and early twentieth centuries.
A series of political, intellectual, economic, and social changes radically altered the roles played by European politicians within their
societies and conditioned their responses to the issues of imperialism, nationalism, and war.

While European politics in the late nineteenth century remained essentially a struggle for power among a closed society of ambitious men, both the theoretical justifications for their exercise of power and their relationship to their constituents had changed more since 1815 than in the preceding three centuries. In an age of specialization and professionalization, politics too had become a profession. The modern politician sought power primarily for its own sake, rather than to achieve broader social or economic goals. In France, Britain, and Italy the political game was played almost exclusively by professionals. Successful careers depended upon cultivating relationships with powerful older members of the House of Commons or the Chamber of Deputies, as well as upon building a national reputation while holding ministerial office. In France and Italy the insularity of political life, in which shifting coalitions of politicians continually shuffled and reshuffled the spoils of office, had become a standing national joke.[1] In Britain, recent studies have shown how even the gravest national political crises reduced themselves to struggles and shifting alliances among political factions, both within and between the two major parties.[2] In Germany, Austria-Hungary, and Russia political intrigue still revolved around monarchs and courts, and political leadership still depended largely upon the good will of monarchs and the influence of their intimates.[3] A politician's success depended upon his standing within a restricted political milieu.

What changed fundamentally during the nineteenth century was the theoretical basis for political power and the nature of the relationship between the rulers and the ruled. As constitutional rule spread across Europe—finally reaching even Russia in 1905[4]—European rulers and politicians could no longer claim to

1. On France, see Theodore Zeldin, *France, 1848–1945*, vol. I *Ambition, Love, and Politics* (Oxford, 1973), pp. 570–604, and for a contemporary view, Robert de Jouvenel, *La république des camarades* (Paris, 1914). On Italian politics, see A. William Salomone, *Italy in the Giolittian Era: Italian Democracy in the Making 1900–1914* (Philadelphia, 1945).

2. The interesting, detailed study of the Home Rule crisis of 1885–86 by A. B. Cooke and John Vincent, *The Governing Passion: Cabinet Government and Party Politics in Britain, 1885–86* (New York, 1974), stresses that even the advent of household suffrage had not prevented British politicians from dealing with great national questions within their own very parochial framework. The same point emerges from Robert J. Scally, *The Origins of the Lloyd George Coalition: The Politics of Social-Imperialism, 1900–1918* (Princeton, 1975).

3. See Isabell V. Hull, *The Entourage of Kaiser Wilhelm II, 1888–1918* (New York, 1982), esp. pp. 76–105.

4. Actually the last European territory to receive a constitution was Bosnia-Herzegovina, after its annexation by Austria-Hungary in 1908.

rule according to their own interests, or even, as in the late eighteenth century, in the interests of the state itself. Instead, they increasingly acknowledged their role as servants of the general welfare, ultimately responsible for the well-being of the whole society, and guarantors of their peoples' basic rights.[5] This change complicated their job enormously. The development of literacy and improved communication, the acceleration of economic growth, the spread of poverty in the midst of wealth (the so-called social question), the decline of religious belief, and above all the general belief in human progress encouraged the growth of expectations which governments inevitably found difficult to satisfy.

The modern political process, moreover, did not simply respond to new expectations, but also created them. Whereas a politician's success within his narrow political milieu depended largely upon personal relationships, his standing among the public at large required that he draw attention to himself. And government and opposition politicians could most easily attract attention by claiming to have identified an evil threatening the survival of the body politic, and arguing that they and they alone could remove it. This tactic was especially pronounced within parliamentary regimes that allowed politicians to reach the top of the political ladder. Men like Jules Ferry, Joseph Chamberlain, Emile Combes, and David Lloyd George used issues like lay education, urban poverty, the separation of church and state, and old age pensions to achieve national prominence, often turning from one favorite issue to another in response to changing circumstances without losing any of their oratorical fervor.[6] Because of the spread of literacy, political success also depended to a great extent upon the careful management of public opinion and the press.[7]

In recent decades, an exaggerated emphasis upon modern poli-

---

5. This role was even acknowledged by the Russian autocrat Nicholas II in his manifesto of October 17, 1905, although Nicholas subsequently undermined these principles. See Geoffrey A. Hosking, *The Russian Constitutional Experiment: Government and Duma, 1907–1914* (Cambridge, 1973), pp. 8–9.

6. In the words of Peter Clarke, discussing British elections, "The argument was about power. To some extent the politicians were asking for support on their own terms: and to some extent they were seeking votes on any terms. The 'issues' of an election reflect this tension." *Lancashire and the New Liberalism* (Cambridge, 1971), p. 343.

7. This enormously important aspect of modern politics has regrettably been left almost untouched by contemporary historians, although a few have noted the importance which politicians gave the press. See for example Paul Kennedy, *The Rise of the Anglo-German Antagonism, 1860–1914* (London, 1980), pp. 364–369.

tics as class struggle has obscured the role which late nineteenth-century politicians actually played. Many recent historians of modern European politics have treated European governments primarily as representatives of particular class interests, and argued that the nature of European governments and the course of their development was determined by the presence or absence of a successful "bourgeois revolution," usually said to have occurred in France between 1789 and 1815 and in England between 1832 and 1867, while failing to occur in Germany until 1918.[8] Others have seen the political history of Europe in the late nineteenth and early twentieth centuries as a struggle between traditional agrarian groups and heavy industrialists anxious to maintain the socio-politico-economic status quo on the one hand, and middle-class democrats and working-class socialists whose objectives ranged from full political democracy to socialist revolution on the other. More significantly for our purposes, this literature has also argued that conservative elites frequently used international crises and war to maintain or expand their power.[9] But most European politicians did not behave or see themselves primarily as representatives of any particular class, and such analyses cannot satisfactorily explain international politics in the first half of the twentieth century.

Certainly classes continued to struggle for political power. The concept of a bourgeois *political* revolution remains useful if it is defined simply as the seizure of national political power by middle-class politicians. Under this definition, we may note that a bourgeois revolution had been completed in France in 1877, after which aristocrats had almost no involvement in parliamentary politics;[10] that it was quite incomplete in Britain until at least the 1920s, since the old landed families still provided most of the leadership of

8. See David Blackbourn and Geoff Eley, *Peculiarities of German History: Bourgeois Society and Politics in Nineteenth-Century Germany* (New York, 1984), pp. 1–61, for a good discussion of this tendency and its limitations.

9. The most notable exponents of such a view are Arno J. Mayer, both in *The Persistence of the Old Regime* (New York, 1981) and *The Politics and Diplomacy of Peacemaking* (Princeton, 1969), and Hans-Ulrich Wehler, "Probleme der Imperialismus," in *Krisenherde des Kaiserreiches, 1871–1914* (Göttingen, 1971). The enormously influential Fritz Fischer took a similar line with respect to Germany in *War of Illusions: German Politics from 1911 to 1914* (New York, 1975), as did V. R. Berghahn, *Germany and the Approach of War in 1914* (New York, 1973).

10. Daniel Halévy, *La république des ducs* (Paris, 1937).

both major parties until the First World War; and that the upper middle classes generally dominated political life in the kingdom of Italy. In Germany, by contrast, the nobility almost entirely monopolized ministerial positions in the imperial and Prussian governments right through the First World War, and the same was true in Russia and in Austria-Hungary. In general, however, European political leaders faced essentially the same problems and dealt with them in essentially the same ways regardless of their social origins or how their political system enabled them to secure power. With the partial exceptions of Russia and Hungary, whose political systems were still designed to maintain aristocratic supremacy, European political leaders increasingly played a mediating role among classes, political parties, and economic interest groups.

Thus, as David Blackbourn and Geoff Eley have suggested, the social origins of the political leadership do not seem decisively to have determined the ways in which European governments handled the contemporary domestic and international issues with which virtually all of them had to deal. Despite differences in political institutions among European states, Eley suggests, "the respective stability of those states depended on the breadth, popularity, and cohesion of their social base, and the relative adequacy of their institutional apparatuses for organizing the necessary degree of consensus among both dominant and subordinate classes. And there is no reason why authoritarian features *per se* should render them totally disabled for this purpose."[11] Indeed, any late nineteenth-century European government faced essentially the same problem: maintaining the confidence of a citizenry which was increasingly divided economically, socially, and politically. Politicians in office did not and indeed could not approach domestic or international political problems simply as representatives of one particular social group. Whatever their personal beliefs, they had at least to claim to speak for the whole society.

The need to maintain the confidence of the nation was institutionalized by the government's obligations to national legislatures, whose composition mirrored the growing complexity of their societies. Although in Germany and eastern Europe the government was not chosen from or by the legislature, by 1914 every European

11. Blackbourn and Eley, *Peculiarities of German History,* p. 141.

government had to maintain a working majority within an elected parliament in order to carry on the essential business of the state.[12] Governments formally responsible to elected legislatures relied upon coalitions of varying degrees of formal cohesiveness or duration to remain in office, while governments independent of their legislatures, such as the government of imperial Germany, could remain in power by securing the support of different parties on different issues.[13] Under the circumstances, no government could survive based upon the support of only one or two leading social groups—and the leaders of imperial Germany, in particular, understood this very well.[14]

The task of European governments was now infinitely more complex than the protection of one or two leading social groups. Every government had to deal with the apparently irreconcilable demands of different social groups, economic interests, government bureaucracies, and social and political activists, all of whom had developed effective new ways of making their views known and pressuring the political system. Every European society included agricultural and industrial interests, some of which usually favored protection against foreign competition while others opposed it; an industrial working class, whose demands ranged from improved working conditions and the recognition of trade union rights all the way to the overthrow of the existing society and government and its replacement by social democracy; and well-established churches, who sought to maintain their role in education against the claims of unbelievers who wanted to use education to promote secularization. In addition, many European countries included large populations with different ethnic origins, religions, and languages, many of whom dreamed of redrawing

12. Once again, however, we must note that in Hungary and Russia the franchise had been manipulated to assure the domination of the aristocracy and the dominant national group; see below, pp. 312–313.

13. Despite the tendency to label British politics as a two-party system, it is a fact that from 1885 until 1914 only one government—the Liberal government of 1906–1909—actually relied upon a majority from a single party.

14. Thus although Bülow and Bethmann-Hollweg, the last two prewar imperial chancellors, came from the Prussian aristocracy, both complained bitterly about the narrowly selfish stance of the German Conservative party. See David E. Kaiser, "Germany and the Origins of the First World War," *Journal of Modern History*, 55 (September 1983): 458–460.

the map of Europe and creating their own national states. These groups all disposed of authors, journalists, political activists, and sometimes whole political parties who stated their claims in dramatic and extreme fashion. In an age of growing specialization and professionalization, Europe's ruling politicians assumed one of the most difficult tasks of all: the task of reconciling these opposing interests and ideas and maintaining the confidence of these heterogeneous societies in their governments.

Ideological conflicts on a variety of fronts had become quite serious by 1900. European politicians, journalists, intellectuals, and political activists frequently put forth extreme opposed positions on a variety of national issues. Catholic monarchists in France, republicans in Italy, socialists in Germany, various Slavic politicians in Austria-Hungary, and Kadets in Russia all called for a radical reorientation of national political, social, and economic life. In an era of rapid social and economic change, many observers felt that changes had proceeded too rapidly while others argued that they had not gone far enough. But European governments generally maintained a national consensus which allowed both old regime and revolutionary ideas—most notably typified by the Catholic church on the one hand, and socialism on the other—to coexist. They could do so partly because the actual effects of government intervention in society remained limited until 1914.

One might easily argue that many European governments managed to keep opposing constituencies satisfied by endorsing fairly revolutionary rhetoric but leaving reality essentially untouched. With respect to the issues of religion, education, the social question, and tariffs, politicians in and out of office often used sweeping language and proposed drastic changes in national life in an effort to win votes. In general, however, the actual effects of legislation and administrative action remained slight. This reflected not only the limited resources of European states, which disposed of only a small portion of their country's gross national product, but also the continuing strength of existing institutions. Thus in the France of the Third Republic no issue aroused more fervor than the proper role of the Catholic church, and from 1902 to 1905 Emile Combes waged a determined campaign against it. Yet recent studies have shown that his government's most extreme measures, including the supposed abolition of religious orders, did not achieve their goals in practice, and that the church conserved much of its position.[15] The same fate befell Bismarck's *Kulturkampf* in Germany, which did much less harm to the Catholic church than he and his liberal supporters had hoped.[16] In Great Britain the emotional issue of temperance resolved itself in practice into fairly trivial restrictions upon brewers and public houses. Protective tariffs, which most Continental countries imposed in response to economic distress during the so-called Great Depression (1872–1890), did relatively little to affect international trade, which expanded rapidly from the late 1890s until 1914.

Socialism, which developed a significant electoral base in Britain, France, Germany, and Italy before 1914, theoretically posed a serious threat to the whole structure of European politics and society and, as already noted, several contemporary authors have argued that pre-1914 European politics revolved around the need to meet this threat. But however seriously both socialist and antisocialist politicians may have taken socialism's revolutionary potential, the political systems of the major prewar European industrial powers managed to integrate their socialist parties into their national political systems quite successfully. In Britain the Liberals adopted several of the Labour party's most important demands in the late 1890s, and the Labour party easily became their coalition partner in 1909.[17] In France Socialists were generally too divided to have a consistent impact upon policy, and several leading Socialist politicians found it convenient to drop their Socialist affiliation in order to assume ministerial office.[18] And even in Germany, the Social Democratic Party (SPD), after becoming in 1912 the largest party in the Reichstag, voted with the government on critical financial questions, while opposing the expansion of the army. Despite the lack of a legal road to power within the constitution of imperial Germany, true revolutionaries remained a very small minority within the SPD.[19] During the interwar period, Socialist par-

15. Zeldin, *France, 1848–1945*, I, 686–698.

16. Ronald J. Ross, "Enforcing the Kulturkampf in the Bismarckian State and the Limits of Coercion in Imperial Germany," *Journal of Modern History*, 56, no. 3 (September 1984): 456–482.

17. Clarke, *Lancashire and the New Liberalism*, pp. 311–340, discusses the two parties' growing collaboration.

18. Zeldin, *France, 1848–1945*, I, 745–787.

19. Carl Schorske, *German Social Democracy, 1905–17* (New York, 1955).

ties led governing coalitions in every major European country, signaling a new step in their integration into the body politic.

Perhaps socialism did not become revolutionary partly because European political systems all recognized the importance of the social question and took some legislative steps to deal with it. Despite their vastly differing constitutional positions, the governments of Britain, France, and Germany had all established social insurance—including sickness, accident, and old age insurance—and given trade unions some legal protection by 1914.[20] The same three countries established unemployment insurance within a relatively short period in the 1920s, and both Germany and France briefly instituted the eight-hour day in the interwar period, only to abandon it shortly thereafter.[21] At the same time, European societies had difficulty reconciling their demands upon their governments with their willingness to support them financially. By 1910, a gap was rapidly emerging between the cost of the services that government was expected to provide and the taxes that society was willing to pay. The British, French, and German governments all increased social and military expenditures in the ten years before 1914, and all of them underwent severe political crises involving the need to increase taxes. The British government, which alone of the three managed consistently to balance its budget, needed two general elections and a major constitutional change to resolve its crisis, while neither the French nor the German government had managed to bring taxation in line with expenditure by the time of the war.[22] The demands of various interest groups for public support—demands which ambitious politicians inevitably sought to meet—clearly tended to outrun society's willingness to pay increased taxes.

Despite this problem, European governments successfully maintained the confidence of their peoples in the late nineteenth

20. Zeldin, France, 1848–1945, I, 665–671, shows that France did not lag as far behind as is commonly supposed, although France did not have effective old-age pensions until after the First World War.

21. A useful survey of comparative social insurance policy is Peter A. Köhler and Hans F. Zacher, eds. (in collaboration with Martin Partington), The Evolution of Social Insurance, 1881–1981: Studies of Germany, France, Great Britain, Austria, and Switzerland (New York, 1982).

22. For a useful contemporary analysis, see A. Landry and B. Nogaro, La crise des finances publiques en France, en Angleterre, en Allemagne (Paris, 1914).

and early twentieth centuries as long as they remained at peace. The experience of 1914–1918, however, showed that war posed new, virtually impossible problems for modern governments, leading in central and eastern Europe to revolution, the collapse of traditional political and social arrangements, and eventually to the emergence of totalitarian regimes. For these reasons the long-term impact of the two world wars—despite the comparatively limited duration of the fighting—has been significantly greater than that of any earlier era of general European conflict.

In some ways modern wartime governments have disposed of advantages relative to the monarchs of the old regime. Their economies have provided them with unprecedented resources, and the size of the armies they fielded increased roughly by an order of magnitude from the Napoleonic period to the First World War. Modern financial instruments, and the confidence of modern investors, enabled them to borrow money more quickly and more easily and to draw upon future resources on a scale that would have dazzled even Philip II. The institution of universal conscription has enabled them to draw, at little cost, upon virtually the whole adult male population, and the problem of the obedience of the troops, so troubling in the sixteenth and seventeenth centuries, has only rarely become serious in the twentieth. Above all, twentieth-century governments have benefited, especially in the early stages of conflicts, from one of the essential beliefs of modern politics: that governments fight wars on behalf of the whole people, and that the people share an enormous stake in the outcome. But this belief has also made wars extremely difficult to stop, and has in the long run posed insoluble problems for the governments that fight them.

We have seen that from the sixteenth to the early nineteenth centuries European war generally remained the business of the European ruling elite. In the late sixteenth and early seventeenth centuries conflicts within the aristocratic elite made war endemic, while in the era of Louis XIV and in the revolutionary and Napoleonic era the elite, led by the European monarchies, began and concluded wars as it suited them, and thereby found it relatively easy to accept setbacks and stalemates. By the twentieth century, however, war had become an aberration, and one which imposed new, unique demands upon the whole society. Speaking for their peoples, governments demanded extraordinary rewards for unprecedented national sacrifices. During both of the world wars, indeed, European governments pledged to their constituents an outcome which would prevent such a catastrophe from ever taking place again. Specifically, they sought either the total defeat and subjugation of the enemy, or a reorganization of the European and world community that would make war impossible—two goals which they proved unable to achieve.[23]

This, however, was not all. The peculiar tragedy of the twentieth century lies not simply in the demands of modern warfare upon governments but also in the two issues that gave rise to the two world wars: the issue of imperialism and economic self-sufficiency in the industrial era, and the principle of nationality. These issues reflect beliefs that won considerable, though not total, acceptance in the nineteenth and twentieth centuries: the belief that industrial states, to secure their full independence, required a self-sufficient economic unit under their political control, and the belief that all European nationalities deserved to rule themselves and ideally to form their own nation-states. Like the social question in domestic politics, these beliefs became part of the context of European politics in the late nineteenth century. While the idea of imperialism generally appealed most strongly to intellectuals and publicists, the idea of nationalism appealed to a much broader spectrum of society, even in relatively less developed areas of central and eastern Europe. Both the outbreak of the two world wars and the aims of the warring nations grew directly out of these two ideas.

Much of the tragedy of twentieth-century politics—and much of the theory and practice of totalitarianism—stem from the failure of these two beliefs to reflect reality. The unprecedented economic growth of the late nineteenth and early twentieth centuries took place within an increasingly *international* economic environment in which complete economic independence had become impossible for any European state. In addition, the population of central and eastern Europe was extraordinarily heterogeneous, and homogeneous national states could be formed only by expelling or murdering literally millions of people. Governments had either to reconcile these ideas with existing realities by making some symbolic or partial concessions to them, or to try to transform reality accord-

23. Similar points have been raised by George F. Kennan, *The Fateful Alliance: France, Russia, and the Coming of the First World War* (New York, 1984), pp. 254–257.

ing to these ideas. In the first half of the twentieth century, traditional and democratically elected European governments failed to accomplish the former task, and totalitarian governments attempted the latter one.

As long as Europe remained at peace, governments generally managed to handle the problems posed by these beliefs without making any thoroughgoing attempt to apply them in practice. The governments of the industrial powers of western Europe assured their peoples that they had annexed their fair share of African and Asian territory, while the empires of eastern Europe tried to contain nationalist movements with a mixture of concession and repression. During the First World War, however, imperialism and nationalism rapidly became the basis for the combatants' war aims. The warring nations planned the realization of their most extreme imperialist and nationalist aims, however visionary or inappropriate to the real problems of Europe they might be. Then, because the war dislocated the world economy and inevitably created new nationalist conflicts, these issues persisted during the 1920s and 1930s, eventually finding their ultimate expression in National Socialism, and their final, horrible implementation in the Second World War. Although in theory Europe in the first half of the twentieth century fought in pursuit of rational objectives, in practice the disparity between the objectives and reality had never been greater. The result was destruction and suffering on an unprecedented scale.

European Imperialism and Economic Prosperity, 1880–1914

European imperialism in the late nineteenth and early twentieth centuries reflected the demands of modern politics. Imperialism was not a carefully calculated strategy, conceived by bankers and executed by their allies within governments, to secure necessary outlets for investment capital, as several early theorists argued.[1] A brief survey of European patterns of investment shows that the new acquisitions of the decades before the First World War absorbed very little European investment. Nor was imperialism a

---

1. Most notably J. A. Hobson, *Imperialism: A Study* (London, 1902), and V. I. Lenin, *Imperialism: The Highest Stage of Capitalism* (St. Petersburg, 1917).

clever means by which aristocratic and upper middle-class elites tried to woo the masses away from socialism. Though imperialism remained generally popular before 1914, and although some politicians did regard it as a useful means of uniting different economic classes, it never fulfilled the short-term economic, social, or political roles which Hans-Ulrich Wehler and William Appleman Williams have claimed for it.[2] Rather, European politicians annexed large territories and staked out spheres of influence in the late nineteenth and early twentieth centuries mainly in response to factors beyond their control: the breakdown of informal arrangements in the tropics, moves by other powers, and initiatives by soldiers and administrators in existing colonies. They did so because the climate of public opinion increasingly seemed to require it, and because the costs of acting were usually small.

This interpretation, clearly, owes a good deal to relatively recent theories of peripheral and informal imperialism, most notably those of D. K. Fieldhouse, and Ronald Robinson and John Gallagher.[3] Crises at the periphery, rather than careful planning within European capitals, accounted for much of the imperial expansion of the late nineteenth century. In citing these theorists, however, one must try to correct some common misapprehensions of their arguments. Although Robinson and Gallagher's interpretation is often thought of as non-economic, neither they nor Fieldhouse actually deny the importance of economic factors in European involvement in the tropics. Robinson and Gallagher's whole theory of the imperialism of free trade presumes a British interest in the tropics during most of the nineteenth century, and *Africa and the Victorians* seems merely to argue that the economic importance of these territories did not *increase* beginning in 1880 or so. Fieldhouse, who deals with the point more specifically, notes that while the European powers' economic involvement in newly annexed territories remained small in European terms, its impact at the periphery was large enough to cause substantial social and political

2. Hans-Ulrich Wehler, *Bismarck und der Imperialismus* (Cologne, 1970); William Appleman Williams, *The Tragedy of American Diplomacy* (New York, 1962).

3. D. K. Fieldhouse, *Economics and Empire, 1880–1914* (2d ed., London, 1984), and Ronald Robinson and Jack Gallagher (with Alice Denny), *Africa and the Victorians: The Climax of Imperialism in the Dark Continent* (New York, 1961). See also John Gallagher and Ronald Robinson, "The Imperialism of Free Trade," *Economic History Review*, 2d ser., 6, no. 1 (1953): 1–15.

convulsions.[4] Fundamentally, the growth of the world economy lay behind European involvement in the tropics in the late nineteenth century, just as it had ever since the time of Columbus and Vasco da Gama. Imperialism increased largely because the world economy was growing.

European politicians, however, did not carry out annexations or delimit spheres of influence in pursuit of any thoroughgoing economic strategy—much less because they were personally interested in colonial trade and investment. It is becoming more and more difficult to identify sincere imperialists among the European statesmen of the late nineteenth century. Research has shown that even such a leader as Jules Ferry showed no interest whatever in colonies during most of his career. To be sure, popular views of the future of their national economies undoubtedly did influence politicians, and they often claimed that annexations and spheres of influence would protect their countries against severe fluctuations in the years ahead. For much of the period 1880–1914 (and especially until the early 1900s) the economic climate was quite uncertain, and colonies, like tariffs, could be touted as a useful form of economic insurance. But these arguments usually represented useful justifications after the fact.

Politicians rarely initiated expansion of their own free will. Instead, they simply responded to three kinds of initiatives at the periphery. First, as Robinson, Gallagher, and Fieldhouse have emphasized, existing or increasing European economic involvement often brought about local crises which undermined existing informal arrangements. The bankruptcy of the Egyptian government and subsequent nationalist revolution of 1881, leading to the Anglo-French occupation of the country, remains the classic case of such a breakdown. Second, soldiers, sailors, administrators, and adventurers, acting either from existing colonies or within unclaimed territory, independently tried to push their domains beyond existing frontiers and then asked their governments to back them up. Outstanding players of this game included Cecil Rhodes and Alfred Milner in South Africa, Captain Jean Baptiste Marchand and General Hubert Lyautey in West and North Africa, and Karl Peters in East Africa. Finally, European nations continually had to respond to the initiatives of other powers, which them-

4. Fieldhouse, *Economics and Empire*, esp. pp. 84–87, 450–477.

selves had been unable to avoid a breakdown in informal arrangements or an aggressive imperialist initiative at the periphery. Like a major strike, a new report on public health, or the spread of a new social theory, such developments demanded some decision from European politicians and governments.

Politicians and diplomats developed their standard response to such crises during the 1880s and used it, by and large, right up until 1914. Briefly, when crises arose, European governments negotiated settlements which usually gave something to all involved parties, without allowing a monopoly to any one. The typical African partition treaty of the 1880s or 1890s gave all its parties new political acquisitions, while promising equal treatment to the commerce of every one. In so doing governments often disappointed their own most dedicated imperialists, but they evidently convinced the bulk of public opinion that their nation's interests had been adequately safeguarded. The extraordinary benefits of imperial acquisitions promised by the colonizers themselves never materialized, but politicians could nonetheless claim that they had secured *potentially* valuable territories. In the meantime, the costs of imperialism remained remarkably low. Annexations and delimited spheres of interest represented the simplest responses to the changes at the periphery which the growth of the world economy was bringing about, and for the most part pre-1914 governments carried them out without overextending themselves or becoming involved in unnecessary and costly conflict with each other.

The experience of all the major European imperial powers followed this pattern. Britain, of course, already possessed a large empire when the era of the new imperialism began, but the empire had not served much of a political function during the middle decades of the nineteenth century. More than anyone else, Benjamin Disraeli reintroduced the mystique of empire into British politics, both by proclaiming Queen Victoria the empress of India and by emphasizing Russian threats to the British empire. The opposition Liberals initially protested Disraeli's aggressive jingoism and reaffirmed their gospel of an empire of self-governing territories, but when they returned to office in 1880, they soon found themselves prisoners of the transportation revolution and Britain's foreign financial interests. A revolt in Egypt faced Gladstone with the choice of intervening or risking the fall of the Suez Canal into unfriendly hands, with all that might portend for communications with India. Forsaking this risk, Gladstone intervened and soon found himself unable to disengage.[5]

Since so much of late nineteenth-century British imperialism related to communications with India, it should be noted that India represented a real and increasing economic asset. In 1880, India was second only to the United States as a British trading partner and as an outlet for British capital investment.[6] India's relative importance as a field for investment declined between 1880 and 1914, but by 1914 India was the only major trading partner with which the United Kingdom ran a consistent current-account surplus, a surplus which occasionally reached £20 million in the years before 1914. The government of India also transferred sterling to Britain annually to cover the "home charges"—various payments to Britain regarded as compensation for the benevolent favor of British rule, which by 1914 amounted to another £20 million per year. The largest single item in the home charges, and a steadily increasing one, was pensions to retired Anglo-Indian officials.[7] Thus, India provided approximately one-fifth of Britain's pre-1914 positive overall balance of payments and supported an appreciable fragment of the professional middle class. Whether or not most British politicians knew these figures, virtually all of them accepted the unquestioned importance of India to the British nation—all the more easily, perhaps, because the government of India was almost completely self-supporting. Both Conservative and Liberal governments also allowed the government of India considerable freedom of action in defending against real or potential threats to its frontiers, with the result that its influence spread into Afghanistan, Baluchistan, and Burma during the last decades of the nineteenth century.[8]

The need to protect communications with India, as well as the need to protect existing trading interests against competition, be-

5. The early history of imperialist and anti-imperialist slogans may be followed in Richard Koebner and Helmut Dan Schmidt, *Imperialism: The Story and Significance of a Political Word, 1840–1960* (Cambridge, 1964), pp. 107–165.

6. Robinson and Gallagher, *Africa and the Victorians*, pp. 76–159; for the figures on India, see p. 6.

7. On these charges, see Vera Anstey, *The Economic Development of India* (4th ed., London, 1952), pp. 333–334; trade figures are from B. R. Mitchell, *European Historical Statistics, 1750–1970* (New York, 1975), p. 573.

8. Bernard Porter, *The Lion's Share: A Short History of British Imperialism, 1850–1970* (New York, 1975), pp. 84–88.

came the standard rationale for the British occupation or annexation of large parts of Africa between 1881 and the fall of the Liberal government in 1895. The government preferred to charter companies to rule these areas but often had to step in itself after companies had failed. British diplomacy, moreover, consistently showed itself quite willing to meet the claims of other powers provided that the government could claim that essential British interests had been safeguarded.[9] By the early 1890s the security of the Nile valley had become the keystone of British African policy, and the British jealously kept their hands on the Nile watershed while continuing to make large concessions elsewhere. They also generally insisted that partition treaties guarantee all nations equal commercial access to the territories in question. The British government in this period declined to adopt a whole-hearted imperialist platform. Thus, in 1890 Lord Salisbury in the Heligoland-Zanzibar agreement with Germany signed away the dream of a British Cape-to-Cairo railway without a qualm, trenchantly dealing with its poor economic possibilities and massive strategic disadvantages in a speech to the House of Lords. Salisbury in this period expressed a good deal of skepticism toward the whole process of imperial expansion, whereas Gladstone, who remained the leader of the Liberal party, continued to view it as a regrettable but occasional necessity.[10]

Several factors increased British interest in imperialism during the 1890s. Since the 1880s, various British publicists and leading politicians had spread the idea of imperial federation, by which they generally meant a closer union of Britain and the self-governing settler colonies.[11] Both politicians and the informed public spoke increasingly of a worldwide struggle among the leading white races for the control of territory and resources, and committed British imperialists argued that only a united empire could meet the threats posed by the French, Germans, Russians, and North Americans. Britain's emerging relative economic decline,

9. Most notably at the Berlin Congo Conference of 1884 and in the Anglo-French agreement of 1899. Disraeli had set a similar example in 1878, when he did concede the Russians substantial gains against the Turks after securing Cyprus for Britain.

10. Robinson and Gallagher, *Africa and the Victorians*, esp. pp. 163–176, 296; Lady Gwendolyn Cecil, *Life of Robert, Marquis of Salisbury*, vol. 4 (London, 1932), pp. 222–228.

11. Koebner and Schmidt, *Imperialism*, pp. 166–195. Both Lord Roseberry, Liberal prime minister in 1894, and Joseph Chamberlain, the colonial secretary and Unionist leader in Salisbury's subsequent government, adhered to this movement.

the spread of protectionism in the other industrial countries, and Britain's increasing diplomatic isolation added to these anxieties.[12]

Largely under the influence of Colonial Secretary Joseph Chamberlain, the British government in the years 1898–1903 adopted much of the program of the most active imperialists for the first time. Although Chamberlain, like Ferry, had not always been interested in the empire, he had not only become a convinced imperialist but had also invested (and lost) a large sum of money in the economic development of the Bahamas in the early 1890s.[13] Oddly, the government now began talking more about the commercial benefits of the empire—just at the time when world trade was beginning a rapid new expansion.[14] In some parts of the world Salisbury refused to bow to imperialist pressure. When the Russian government became more aggressive in Manchuria in 1898, he insisted upon handling Russia the same way he had handled France in Africa: by giving something (in this case Port Arthur and Manchurian railway rights) to the Russians in exchange for recognition of British rights in the Yangtze valley. Salisbury's failure to defend British interests more aggressively occasionally received some severe press criticism.[15] In the meantime, Chamberlain pushed unsuccessfully for sweeping schemes of colonial economic development, increased the budget of the Colonial Office somewhat, and used the considerable freedom of action Salisbury found it prudent to allow him to try to change the direction of British diplomacy. In South Africa, where Chamberlain and not the Foreign Office controlled British policy, his dealings with more extreme imperialists on the scene led to war.

The South African war eventually demonstrated the costs of more serious economic imperialism—that is, of trying to secure economically significant areas with armed force. The British attempt to secure British hegemony over the Transvaal reflected almost all of the economic motives to which imperialism is traditionally ascribed. The prime movers in the attempt to overthrow the

---

12. Porter, *Lion's Share*, pp. 119–151.

13. J. L. Garvin, *The Life of Joseph Chamberlain*, vol. 2 (London, 1933), pp. 487–500. The enterprise, a sisal plantation, was managed by Chamberlain's son Neville. It lost £50,000 of Chamberlain's own money, and a good deal more invested by partners.

14. Koebner and Schmidt, *Imperialism*, pp. 206–208.

15. J. A. S. Grenville, *Lord Salisbury and Foreign Policy: The Close of the Nineteenth Century* (London, 1964), pp. 130–147.

Transvaal were the Randlords, Cecil Rhodes and Alfred Beit, who wanted to combine their enormous wealth with more political power. The influx of foreigners (Uitlanders) into the Transvaal after the gold rush—many of them British—became their excuse for political intrigue. In 1895, Rhodes talked Joseph Chamberlain into at least allowing the Jameson raid, Rhodes's attempt to bring down the Transvaal through what would now be termed "covert action." The raid ended disastrously when a planned Uitlander rising failed to take place after Jameson crossed the Transvaal border, but Rhodes and Chamberlain managed to conceal their part in it.[16]

Having barely escaped from the Jameson debacle with his political life, Chamberlain might have preferred to leave South Africa well enough alone. But the new British high commissioner in the Cape Colony, Alfred Milner, who had helped administer the British occupation of Egypt, believed absolutely in the need to create a much stronger federation of Britain and the white settler colonies, in which South Africa would play a critical part. Rather than foment a rising among the Uitlanders, Milner in early 1899 forced Transvaal president Paul Krueger to discuss the political rights of the Uitlanders with him. In London both Chamberlain and Salisbury wanted merely to score a dramatic political triumph by securing gains on the Uitlanders' behalf, but Milner had determined upon war. His clever tactics, helped by the slow communications between South Africa and London, allowed him to provoke Krueger to send an ultimatum and attack the British before London realized that he had wanted war all along.[17]

From 1880 until 1899, the territories annexed by Great Britain and the other European imperial powers had generally consisted of tropical, relatively poor territories, whose population lacked any effective means of defense. The Boer War showed how much more financially and politically expensive the subjugation of a determined and moderately armed population could be. The Boers won impressive initial successes, demonstrating Britain's military unpreparedness, and stubbornly held out for three years of effective guerilla warfare. To subdue them the British eventually employed new and cruel methods that shocked much of the British public and angered the rest of Europe. The British eventually

16. Thomas Pakenham, *The Boer War* (New York, 1975), pp. 18–22. Pakenham implicitly compares the raid to Watergate, but it resembles the Bay of Pigs far more closely.

17. Pakenham, *Boer War*, pp. 40–124.

herded a large part of the population into concentration camps, while writers like J. H. Hobson claimed, not without some truth, that the whole war had been fought on behalf of the Randlords.

The war was a short-term political success and helped the Unionists win the "Khaki" election of 1900 impressively.[18] But it cost £200 million—about twice the prewar annual government revenue—and showed how difficult the defense of Britain's far-flung imperial interests might be. It also achieved relatively few of the original British objectives. Because British immigration into South Africa remained low, Milner's dream of a British-dominated South Africa never came into being. To make peace with the Boers the government had to abandon the pretext of defending the rights of the black native population, which Chamberlain had claimed to be defending. The Randlords now found themselves short of labor to work their gold mines, and when Milner encouraged them to import Chinese laborers to fill the gap, the resulting scandal led to Milner's resignation and became a potent campaign issue for the Liberals in 1906.[19]

After the Boer War the British took no more armed imperialist initiatives before 1914. They generally continued to settle colonial disputes with other powers by mutual agreement whenever possible. Only once, in 1902, did they attempt to defend an imperial outpost by making an alliance, and the Anglo-Japanese alliance of that year was written so as to become effective only if one of the partners were attacked by *two* other powers.[20] They made a vague agreement with Germany regarding the future of China in 1900; adjusted African, Asian, and North American claims with the French in 1904; settled Persian, Tibetan, and Afghan questions with the Russians in 1907; made a new hypothetical agreement to partition the Portuguese colonies with the Germans in 1913; and settled the Anatolian railway question with the Germans in June 1914. The crushing defeat of the Unionists in 1906, when they campaigned on a program of tariff reform and imperial preference, put an end to schemes for increased economic or political union of the British empire.

Despite the enormous expansion of the British empire in the

18. Clarke, *Lancashire and the New Liberalism*, pp. 366–369.
19. Pakenham, *Boer War*, pp. 607–613.
20. Ian H. Nish, *The Anglo-Japanese Alliance: The Diplomacy of Two Island Empires, 1894–1907* (London, 1966), pp. 204–245.

years before 1914, *no* government ever really met the extreme demands of British imperialists, including imperial federation and tariff preference, conscription, and preparation for an inevitable war. As Paul Kennedy has pointed out, the private and public writings of leading British imperialists after the Boer War show tremendous frustration. They had long realized that not only Liberals like Asquith and Grey, but also traditional Conservatives like Salisbury, simply did not share their apocalyptic view of the future and the requirements which it imposed upon the present.[21] While the Conservative leadership became more imperialist in the years immediately before the war—driven, perhaps, by the loss of three successive elections—neither the government nor the country seems to have accepted the extreme, social Darwinist view of the imperialists until well after the First World War had begun.

The entente with France of 1904, which began as a settlement of long-standing colonial differences in several continents, became something more after the German government challenged its provisions relating to Morocco. Elements within the Admiralty and the Foreign Office, who already saw Germany as the main threat to the British empire, eagerly sprang to France's defense, and the Moroccan crisis eventually led to staff talks and the exchange of letters in 1912 between Paul Cambon and Grey promising consultations in the event of a threat to peace.[22] The British, however, never contemplated a major European war to increase their empire in the decade before 1914. No serious political figure questioned the need for the empire, but Britain remained willing, as always, to negotiate any new disputes that might arise.

France also expanded an existing empire in the late nineteenth century. The French government began expanding some of its enclaves along the West African coast in the 1870s and acquired a right to Tunisia at the 1878 Congress of Berlin, in compensation for Britain's occupation of Cyprus.[23] Jules Ferry, who found himself in office as premier when the Tunisian question came to a head a few years later, was a leading middle-class politician who had never

21. Kennedy, *Rise of the Anglo-German Antagonism*, pp. 361–385.

22. Samuel R. Williamson, Jr., *The Politics of Grand Strategy: Britain and France Prepare for War, 1904–14* (Cambridge, Mass., 1969).

23. On the West African initiatives, see C. W. Newbury and A. S. Kanya-Forster, "French Policy and the Origins of the Scramble for Africa," *Journal of African History*, 10, no. 2 (1969): 253–276.

shown much interest in France's overseas possessions. In 1881, he reluctantly allowed himself to be persuaded to undertake an expedition into Tunisia and the establishment of a French protectorate—steps which aroused the opposition of much of the Chamber of Deputies. In succeeding years, Ferry took credit for a good deal of French expansion in West and Central Africa, and in his second ministry, from 1883 through 1885, he made imperialism the centerpiece of his program.[24] Despite his lack of previous interest in colonies, Ferry began trumpeting imperialism as the great task of France's future, suggesting that colonies would provide essential markets and outlets for capital, and that an imperial mission might compensate France for the loss of Alsace-Lorraine. At the Berlin Congo Conference of 1884, Ferry secured recognition of French protectorates on the right bank of the Congo and in West Africa. He did not, however, convert the French chamber wholeheartedly to imperialism, and when French troops in Tonkin lost a battle, the deputies used this as an excuse to overthrow him.[25] On the whole the French Chamber of Deputies never became as imperialist as the German Reichstag or the British House of Commons.

French imperialists in the 1880s and 1890s gradually grouped themselves together into the *parti colonial*, an interlocking group of societies composed largely of officers, civil servants, businessmen, journalists, and politicians who by accident of birth or economic interest or for psychological reasons had developed an enthusiasm for French colonies.[26] Their influence grew but never became dominant. In 1889 their leader, Eugene Etienne, a deputy from Oran, became undersecretary of state for the colonies in the ministry of commerce, and three years later Etienne became vice president of

24. Thomas F. Power, Jr., *Jules Ferry and the Renaissance of French Imperialism* (New York, 1944).

25. Ibid., pp. 190–192; William L. Langer, *European Alliances and Alignments, 1871–1890* (New York, 1931), pp. 286–287; Gilbert Ziebura, "Interne Faktoren des französischen Hochimperialismus, 1871–1914," in Wolfgang Mommsen, ed., *Die moderne Imperialismus* (Stuttgart, 1971), pp. 85–104; James J. Cooke, *New French Imperialism, 1880–1910: The Third Republic and Colonial Expansion* (Hampden, Conn., 1973), pp. 13–24.

26. The best analysis is by Christopher M. Andrew and A. S. Kanya-Forster, *The Climax of French Imperial Expansion, 1914–24* (Stanford, 1981), pp. 9–32; Andrew and Kanya-Forster's interpretation does not seem to me seriously threatened by L. Abrams and D. J. Miller, "Who Were the French Colonialists? A Reassessment of the *Parti Colonial*, 1890–1914." *Historical Journal*, 19, no. 3 (1976): 685–725; see their reply in the same journal, pp. 981–1000.

the chamber. In 1894 the new ministry of the colonies was created, and the imperialist Théophile Delcassé became its first minister. Gabriel Hanotaux, another believer in French expansion, directed the Quai d'Orsay for most of the period 1894–1898.

With enough soldiers on the scene in Africa and important strongholds within the French government, the French imperialists had ample opportunity to expand their field of activity. With some encouragement from Delcassé and Hanotaux, they pushed deeper into the interior of Africa but ultimately failed to commit the government to their most cherished dream: control of the upper Nile valley, which would have given them both a lever against the British in Egypt and the possibility of a unified French Africa spanning the continent from east to west. The climax of French imperial enterprise, the Marchand mission to Fashoda, was authorized when Hanotaux was briefly absent from the Quai d'Orsay in 1895. Hanotaux, knowing Salisbury's determination to control the Nile, feared the consequences of the mission but did not dare recall it. By the time Marchand reached Fashoda in the summer of 1898, just before Lord Kitchener's victorious armies advancing through the Sudan, even the colonial party itself realized that the French government would have to concede the Nile valley to the British. War seemed to threaten at one point, as the Dreyfus case made it difficult for Paris to make the necessary concessions to the British, but Delcassé and Salisbury eventually settled matters peacefully. No one, in short, was willing to go to war over the Nile valley.[27]

The same mixture of local imperialist initiative, guarded government encouragement, and divided parliamentary opinion determined the course of French expansion into Morocco. Etienne and the rest of the African colonial party made Morocco their next target after Fashoda, and they hoped that border problems with Algeria would encourage French intervention. Delcassé made Morocco the centerpiece of his diplomatic strategy and carefully reached agreements with Italy, Spain, and finally, in 1904, Britain, which satisfied these potential opponents of a French presence in Morocco. Yet in 1905, when the first French moves aroused the opposition of the Germans, Delcassé's numerous opponents within the chamber managed to overthrow him for having brought

27. Cooke, *New French Imperialism*, pp. 52–68, 81–97; Roger Glenn Brown, *Fashoda Reconsidered: The Impact of Domestic Politics on French Policy in Africa, 1893–1898* (Baltimore, 1970).

France to the brink of war. Imperialism, clearly, had never achieved the popularity in France that it had won in Britain or Germany. No foreign minister would ever have lost his position from excessive zeal in either of those countries.[28]

After Delcassé's fall, the French conceded economic rights in Morocco to other powers at the Algeciras Conference of 1906 and in a further Franco-German agreement in early 1909. The Fez expedition that precipitated the Agadir crisis of 1911 was also undertaken without proper authorization from Paris, and the premier, Joseph Caillaux, insisted upon settling the crisis diplomatically. Caillaux's cession of a large tract of the French Congo to the Germans in return for a protectorate over Morocco angered the colonial party, but the chamber ratified it.[29]

Since the 1880s, a relatively small body of French imperialists had kept the African pot boiling, and French governments had backed them up, insofar as they could do so in agreement with foreign powers. The French government had also staked out its own shares of the planned Chinese and Turkish railway networks. The new annexations showed that France was keeping pace with the other imperialist powers, but they had brought France relatively little economic benefit. The French colonies took only about 10 percent of French exports, and their trade with foreign countries was growing more quickly in the years before 1914 than their trade with France.[30] By 1914 less than 10 percent of total French foreign investments had been placed in French colonies, while the whole rest of Africa and Asia accounted for slightly more than an additional 10 percent.[31] On the whole imperialism seems to have played far less of a role in French politics than in British or German. After Ferry, no leading French political figure adopted imperialism wholeheartedly, and it never became a critical issue in French general elections. By 1914 the French government had no major outstanding colonial claims.

The German imperial experience shows a most interesting inter-

28. Cooke, New French Imperialism, pp. 107–117; Christopher Andrew, Théophile Delcassé and the Making of the Entente Cordiale, pp. 136–157, 180–215, 255–301.

29. Cooke, New French Imperialism, pp. 137–145.

30. Winfried Baumgart, Imperialism: The Idea and Reality of Britsh and French Colonial Expansion, 1880–1914 (New York, 1982), pp. 112–135; Henri Brunschwig, French Colonialism, 1871–1914: Myths and Realities (New York, 1964), pp. 94–96.

31. Baumgart, Imperialism, p. 128.

action between the government and its constituencies. By 1884 Bismarck made imperialism one element of his foreign policy, and after 1897 his successors made it the centerpiece of theirs. Public interest in imperialism and other forms of *Weltpolitik* (world policy) seems to have grown quite steadily in the German empire. Unfortunately for the German government, Germany had begun its career as an imperialist power too late to catch up with the British or French. From 1884 until 1914 the German government followed essentially the same strategy as London or Paris: it attempted to secure for Germany a reasonable share of newly annexed territories and spheres of influence, while taking account of the rights and interests of other governments. The government encountered serious difficulties because the realities of the international situation did not allow it to secure enough to satisfy its various imperialist constituencies, and eventually the highest authorities themselves decided that German imperialism was worth a general war.

Well before the German government entered the colonial scramble in 1884, two separate strains of German imperialism had begun to make themselves heard: economic imperialists or advocates of *Weltpolitik* who saw colonies simply as one means of promoting German industrial development, and spokesmen for new *Lebensraum*, or living space, who stressed the need for colonies for German peasant settlement but actually wanted only to preserve a useful set of agrarian myths.[32] Thus, when Bismarck adopted colonialism himself in 1884 and began staking small German claims in various parts of Africa and the Pacific, imperialist constituencies already existed and naturally greeted this new policy with enthusiasm. Bismarck also used the colonial issue rather cleverly to divide the National Liberal party, most of which still opposed colonialism, as well as to create a brief Franco-German colonial entente in opposition to the British and, perhaps, to tie the hands of the Anglophile crown prince Frederick. Colonialism did help him create a new governing majority in the Reichstag, but Bismarck never became a full-fledged convert to it. He insisted that chartered companies administer the new colonies to try to spare the imperial government any expense, and he lost interest in colonies within a

---

32. This is the thesis of Woodruff Smith's extremely useful book, *The Ideological Origins of Nazi Imperialism* (New York, 1986), pp. 41–82. Similar studies for Great Britain and France would be invaluable; interestingly enough, Akira Iriye has noted a similar split in Japanese opinion.

relatively short time, particularly after the chartered companies failed.[33]

Bismarck's immediate successors, the Caprivi and Hohenlohe governments, did little to further German colonial expansion. Caprivi openly expressed his distaste for colonies, and his exchange of Zanzibar for Heligoland in 1890 enraged many German imperialists. Although Caprivi did believe that Germany had to improve its foreign trade position, he sought to do so with trade treaties in central Europe rather than with new colonies.[34] But in 1897, the government, led by Bernhard von Bülow and Alfred von Tirpitz, officially adopted world policy (*Weltpolitik*), and a new era in imperial history began.[35]

World policy, as Woodruff Smith has recently argued, was not a social or economic strategy but a political one. Its adoption in 1897, together with a new series of unrelated political concessions to various constituencies, enabled the government to overcome a serious political crisis by forming a new coalition in the Reichstag and reconciling the emperor, who supported world policy wholeheartedly, and the south German states, who were rapidly losing confidence in his leadership. World policy—the protection and extension of German economic interests abroad through the encouragement of German trade, the acquisition of German colonies, and the construction of a great German navy—did appeal very strongly to certain German liberals who wanted it to encourage a common national endeavor. Among the parties it immediately won the assent of the National Liberals, who wanted to promote

33. The best brief surveys of Bismarck's colonial initiatives are in Smith, *Nazi Imperialism*, pp. 32–40, and Hartmut Pogge von Strandmann, "Domestic Origins of Germany's Colonial Expansion under Bismarck," *Past and Present*, 42 (February 1969): 140–169. The interpretation of Wehler, *Bismarck und der Imperialismus*, has not won many converts. In *Nazi Imperialism* Smith argues that Bismarck used imperialism to try to overcome German social and political fragmentation—the same argument he uses more generally to explain the new imperialism in *European Imperialism in the Nineteenth and Twentieth Centuries*. While some liberal politicians, such as Gustav Stresemann, undoubtedly did believe that imperialism could fulfill this function, it seems to me that Bismarck never really wanted to overcome German fragmentation, and simply used imperialism—as he had earlier used the *Kulturkampf* and tariffs—to form a new coalition of several constituencies.

34. J. Alden Nichols, *Germany without Bismarck: The Caprivi Era, 1890–94* (Cambridge, Mass., 1958), pp. 102–103, 138–153.

35. To avoid confusion I shall use "world policy" to refer to the broadly imperialist stance taken by the imperial government and reserve *Weltpolitik* for the specific form of German imperialism identified by Woodruff Smith.

industrial exports; the Conservatives, who officially supported settlement colonies which they claimed would preserve the German peasant ethos; and the Catholic Center, which agreed to support it in exchange for concessions on social policy. Yet it does not seem that the German ministers who adopted the policy really expected it to accomplish very much. Bülow used the acquisition of Pacific islands and Chinese concessions to show that the imperial government was providing for Germany's future, but he did not take the economic value of these gains very seriously. As for Tirpitz, he seems more and more clearly to have regarded world policy as the best excuse for building a large navy, rather than seeing the navy as necessary to pursue world policy.[36]

World policy had serious international political consequences almost from the start. It effectively ruled out any wide-ranging Anglo-German settlement or alliance, since Tirpitz could justify the construction of his battleships only on the grounds of Britain's potential hostility.[37] But the Bülow government pursued it quite cautiously, generally confining itself, like London and Paris, to trying to show the German people that their country was securing its proper share of colonial prizes. Thus in 1897 Bülow annexed Kiaochow, which became the center of a German sphere of influence in China, and in 1898 he concluded the Anglo-German agreement guaranteeing a loan to Portugal, which provided for a partition of the Portuguese colonies should Lisbon go bankrupt. He also continued to support German trade, investment, and settlement in Turkey and labored mightily to secure an international agreement on the construction of the Berlin-Bagdad railway.[38] After France began to move into Morocco in 1905, Bülow demanded that German interests receive proper consideration and concluded the 1906 and 1909 agreements that protected German economic enterprise in Morocco. During the first Moroccan crisis, however, he made it quite clear that he did not believe that an issue like Morocco was worth a war, or that public opinion thought so either.

36. On these points, see especially Smith, *Nazi Imperialism*, pp. 44–82, and Kaiser, "Germany and the Origins of the First World War," 442–474, which includes a fuller summary of the literature on the adoption of *Weltpolitik*.

37. As I have argued elsewhere, however, he consistently shrank from actual hostilities with Britain; see Kaiser, "Germany and the Origins of the First World War."

38. Edward Meade Earle, *Turkey, the Great Powers, and the Bagdad Railway: A Study in Economic Imperialism* (reprint ed., New York, 1966), esp. pp. 120–142.

Imperialism remained popular. In 1906, Bülow used a controversy over the brutal war against the Herreros then taking place in Southwest Africa to score an impressive triumph in Reichstag elections. By 1908, however, Búlow was beginning to doubt that world policy, and particularly the navy that was supposed to support it, was worth its increasing cost. Deeply concerned by the large and growing imperial deficit, he argued in a letter to Friedrich von Holstein that the money borrowed for the imperial navy would yield much bigger diplomatic dividends if it could be invested abroad instead.[39] The financial problem proved too much for him. He resigned in 1909 after the Reichstag had rejected his proposed inheritance tax.

As time went on, the government found it harder and harder to satisfy German public opinion, all the more because the split between the ideas of *Weltpolitik* and *Lebensraum* continued. Since 1898, *Weltpolitik* had developed a strong constituency within the bureaucracies of the German Colonial and Foreign Offices. But supporters of settlement colonies for *Lebensraum*, who included the Free Conservative party and the Pan-German League, disliked the policies of *Weltpolitiker* like Bernhard Dernburg, the colonial secretary from 1906 through 1910, who developed East African railways but did little to promote German agrarian colonial settlement.

The German political system also contributed to the government's problems—not because the government feared socialism, but because the system did not allow middle-class imperialists ever to hold real political power. Whereas in Britain and France some of the most forward imperialists occasionally secured power over policy, and thereby learned how their demands had to be moderated to conform to physical and political realities, in Germany the lack of responsible, representative government encouraged pressure groups and parties to remain as intransigent as possible. Middle-class politicians like Gustav Stresemann, who resented their exclusion from power, argued that the Junkers who controlled the government could not speak for Germany's real interests. Others, like Max Weber and Friedrich Naumann, believed that imperialism could unite all sectors of German society by giving them a new task

39. Kaiser, "Germany and the Origins of the First World War," pp. 454–455.

as challenging and as exciting as the earlier unification of Germany.[40]

The second Moroccan crisis of 1911 showed how difficult the government's position had become. The crisis was the work of Foreign Secretary Alfred von Kiderlen-Wächter, a convinced *Weltpolitiker*, who wanted to exchange Morocco for the French Congo, which in turn would enable the Germans to construct Mittelafrika, a large, rich central African domain to provide raw materials and markets for German industry. Although Kiderlen brought Germany and France to the brink of war, Bethmann and the emperor eventually decided to end this crisis, like its 1905–6 predecessor, through negotiation, and Germany secured only a part of the French Congo. The settlement pleased almost no one. Advocates of *Lebensraum*, who had designated Morocco as an area for German settlement, regarded it as a betrayal, while supporters of *Weltpolitik* in the Reichstag, led by Stresemann, attacked Germany's compensation as inadequate, and therefore as additional proof that the noblemen of the Wilhelmstrasse could not be trusted with Germany's future.[41]

The government, though finding it harder and harder to please those who took imperialism seriously, persevered. The new chancellor, Theobald von Bethmann-Hollweg, completed a new, albeit hypothetical, agreement with Britain to partition the Portuguese colonies in 1913, and finally finished the negotiations for the Bagdad railway in July 1914. Both Bethmann and the new colonial secretary, Wilhelm Solf, wanted to make Central Africa a focus of German expansion, and British Foreign Secretary Sir Edward Grey intermittently encouraged them with talk of partitioning the Belgian Congo.[42] Bethmann had not scored any truly dramatic successes by 1914, but the German economy continued to thrive. The government's position was far from hopeless; in many ways, in-

---

40. Smith, *Nazi Imperialism*, p. 47. Stresemann argued in 1908 that colonial and naval issues could secure the support of thousands of voters whom economic questions would always tend to divide. See Theodor Eschenburg, *Das Kaiserreich am Scheideweg: Basserman, Bülow und der Block* (Berlin, 1929), p. 117.

41. Smith, *Nazi Imperialism*, pp. 134–140.

42. Jacques Willequet, "Anglo-German Rivalry in Belgian and Portuguese Africa?" in Prosser Gifford and Wm. Roger Louis, eds., *Britain and Germany in Africa: Imperial Rivalry and Colonial Rule* (New Haven, 1967), pp. 245–273, gives an excellent account of these complex maneuvers.

deed, Bethmann had managed to strengthen his position between 1912 and 1914.[43] Yet Germany and Europe found themselves on the verge of a catastrophe, not because the chancellor could no longer cope with the German imperialists, but because he himself had adopted some of their most critical beliefs.

The experience of the Russian government, which took a somewhat reckless approach toward imperialism in East Asia in the 1890s and early 1900s, is another example of the dangers of imperialism. Russia's more reckless course undoubtedly owed something to the nature of the Russian government, which differed fundamentally from those of western and central Europe. Not only was the Russian government before 1905 a theoretical autocracy which did not even make any pretense of mediating among various constituencies, but it also suffered from extremely unclear lines of authority, and in particular from unique problems in civil-military relations. Russian army officers, who held many high government positions, rarely recognized the authority of the civilian government and often used their independence to carry out expansion upon Russia's southern and eastern frontiers.[44] The separation of public and private spheres of interest, moreover, seems hardly to have been recognized in Russia. The government heavily subsidized imperialist ventures in the Far East, which became another means of support for the court nobility. These ventures led Russia into a disastrous war with Japan in 1904, partly because of the anarchy which prevailed at the highest levels of the Russian government, and partly, according to the most recent study of the conflict, because the Russians simply did not believe that the Japanese would fight and hence failed to recognize the need to reach a settlement with them.[45] Not only did the Japanese soundly defeat the Russians, but the war also shattered Russia's political structure and forced the government into drastic concessions. The government settled outstanding colonial questions with Britain soon after its recovery, in 1907. Its experience, like the Boer War, showed that it behooved governments not to take imperialism too seriously.

43. See Kaiser, "Germany and the Origins of the First World War," pp. 461–462.

44. See B. H. Sumner, *Russia and the Balkans* (Oxford, 1937), a magnificent discussion of the crisis of the 1870s, and Andrew Malozemoff, *Russian Far Eastern Policy, 1881–1904, with Special Emphasis on the Causes of the Russo-Japanese War* (Berkeley, 1958).

45. Ian Nish, *The Origins of the Russo-Japanese War* (London, 1985), pp. 238–257.

The outburst of Western imperialism in the decades before the First World War stemmed from the increasing economic involvement of the industrial nations in the tropics, the consequent breakdown of many tropical political structures, and the requirements of modern European politics. Imperialists in the tropics and at home argued that the economic interests at stake in Africa and Asia required an active policy by their home governments, and the governments, for the most part, did not dispute this.[46] As time went on, a more general corollary to the economic argument emerged: that the European nations had embarked upon a great mission of development and civilization, and that every self-respecting nation must play an appropriate part in this grand enterprise. More dangerous was the social Darwinist extension of this view, which saw European imperialism as the prelude to a worldwide military struggle that would establish a new balance of power for generations to come. These ideas aroused considerable interest in the decades before 1914, but the actual experience of those years did not bear them out. The historical record shows quite clearly that the new imperialism had only a limited economic impact, and that the spread of imperialism had not generally increased the danger of war.

The actual economic significance of imperialism—or rather the lack of it—is a crucial issue in understanding its influence upon the outbreak of the First World War. Imperialists frequently argued that colonies would provide export markets, areas for investment, and sources of raw materials. But the historical record shows that while the European nations undoubtedly did need export markets, areas for capital investment, and sources of raw materials in the late nineteenth and early twentieth centuries, formal imperialism did very little to meet any of these needs.

Exports played an important role in the economic growth which Europe experienced in the years 1890–1913, especially for Germany. German, British, and French exports all increased more rapidly than national output as a whole during that period.[47] Imperial acquisitions, however, had a small part in these increases of ex-

46. Nor, of course, did the government of the United States, whose experience with imperialism beginning in the 1890s has many Continental parallels.

47. Mitchell, *European Historical Statistics*, pp. 490–497, 781–790. No French figures for gross national product are available for most of this period.

ports. The British empire's share of British exports did grow from about 25 percent in 1890 to about 37 percent in 1913, but 31 percent of this share went to Australia, Canada, India, New Zealand, and South Africa, and only 6 percent to other colonies.[48] The French colonies took only about 10 percent of French exports, and their trade with foreign countries was growing more quickly in the years before 1914 than their trade with France.[49] Germany's few colonies took a trivial proportion of German exports, and the entire continents of Africa and Asia took less than 10 percent of German exports in 1913.[50]

The export of capital was at least as important to European economic development. Merchandise exports alone never paid for Europe's purchases from the rest of the world. Thirty years ago Albert Imlah showed that in the British case, exports had generally failed to pay for imports even in the first half of the nineteenth century, much less in the second.[51] In the latter part of the century the same was true for France, Germany, and virtually every other European country. The British, French, and Germans all covered substantial current-account deficits with a consistent surplus on "invisibles"—shipping and railway income, insurance, and, above all, income from foreign investments. Thus in 1913, when British exports totaled £635 million, the British invisible surplus reached £317 million. The German invisible surplus in that year was 10 million Reichsmarks, or about one-fifth the value of German exports, while the French showed an invisible surplus of 2–3 billion francs compared to exports of about 7 billion francs.[52] In all three cases, these surpluses more than made up for substantial annual deficits on current account.

Since most of the invisible surplus came from interest on foreign capital investments, Lenin and Hobson were not wrong to suggest that the European powers depended upon foreign investment opportunities—but they were wrong to link this dependence with imperialist annexations in the decades before 1914. As Herbert Feis

48. Great Britain, Board of Trade, *Statistical Abstract of the United Kingdom, 1913, 1921–34* (London, 1936), pp. 358–359.

49. Baumgart, *Imperialism*, pp. 112–135; Brunschwig, *French Colonialism*, pp. 94–96.

50. *Statistisches Jahrbuch für das deutschen Reiches, 1913* (Berlin, 1914), pp. 253–254.

51. Albert H. Imlah, *Economic Elements in the Pax Britannica* (Cambridge, Mass., 1958), pp. 40–41.

52. Mitchell, *European Historical Statistics*, pp. 490–497, 818–819; Albert Sauvy, *Histoire économique de la France entre les deux guerres*, vol. 3 (Paris, 1984), p. 406.

showed several decades ago, investments went overwhelmingly into other parts of Europe, the Americas, and the settler colonies of the British empire, not to the newly annexed territories of Africa or the new spheres of influence in Asia. Of the 47 percent of British investments in 1914 that were held within the British empire, less than 10 percent could be found within new African or Asian acquisitions; and of the remaining 53 percent, only slightly more than 10 percent were held within Africa and Asia. The Dominions, India, and the Americas accounted for more than three-fourths of British capital investment.[53] The French empire was far less important as an outlet for French capital. French colonies in 1914 accounted for less than 10 percent of total French investment, while the whole rest of Africa and Asia accounted for slightly more than an additional 10 percent.[54] Of the somewhat smaller total of German foreign investments, approximately 15 percent had gone into Africa and Asia, including Germany's colonies.[55]

The new imperial acquisitions of the late nineteenth century, in short, contributed little to Europe's economic prosperity. Under the circumstances, we should hardly be surprised to find that governments rarely undertook annexations or claimed spheres of influence *in response* to either bankers or trading interests. With respect to trade, both the British and German governments seem quite definitely to have assumed an obligation to support their own traders in cases where other governments were already involved. With respect to finance, European governments and banks generally preferred, in the years before 1914, to share both the risks and profits of loans in Africa and Asia. They consistently pursued this strategy in Turkey, and eventually adopted it in China, where competition for concessions and loans had for a time been most intense. Occasionally banking interests even protested when their own government seemed to be claiming an exclusive interest in some part of the world. Such claims, as the Deutsche Bank noted with respect to professed German government designs

53. Herbert Feis, *Europe, the World's Banker, 1870–1914* (reprint ed., New York, 1964), p. 23. Lance E. Davis and Robert A. Huttenback, *Mammon and the Pursuit of Empire: The Political Economy of British Imperialism, 1860–1912* (Cambridge, 1986), have also argued that investment in the empire was relatively unprofitable; see pp. 30–110.

54. Feis, *Europe, the World's Banker*, p. 51.

55. Ibid., p. 74. Feis estimates total British investments in 1914 at £3.763 billion, French at 45 billion francs (24 to the pound, thus less than 2 billion), and German at 23.5 billion Reichsmarks (about 19 to the pound, thus a little more than one billion).

upon Turkey as a German hinterland, only made international co-operation harder to secure.[56]

If prewar governments still found it more expedient to continue acquiring colonies ánd spheres of influence before 1914 despite their lack of economic benefits, they did so because colonies, although they brought in very little, cost even less. Colonial expenditures remained a minor item even in the relatively modest budgets of European central governments before 1914. On the eve of the First World War, the colonial budget of the French government totaled about 100 million francs annually—roughly 2 percent of the total expenditure of the French government.[57] The German government spent less than 1 percent of its budget on colonial administration.[58] Since the government of India was more than self-supporting, the British empire cost Britain surprisingly little as well. As long as the occupying powers had only poorly armed native populations with which to deal, colonies would remain inexpensive. The Boer War, however, showed how much the conquest of unfriendly territory could cost—and the costs of an all-out struggle among the European powers, as the British recognized in the wake of the Boer War, would undoubtedly be much higher. Frequently, imperialism imposed enormous costs upon subject populations, including lethal forced labor in parts of tropical Africa and brutal wars to pacify native populations, most notably in Southwest Africa. But these costs aroused relatively little concern among the European public.

On the whole, furthermore, European political leaders rejected the idea that imperialism must lead either to sharper economic competition or to war. They differed from imperialists like Max Weber, who expected trade eventually to be confined within economically homogeneous units, or from Cecil Rhodes, Alfred Mil-

56. On these points see Earle, *Bagdad Railway*, pp. 120–121; D. C. M. Platt, *Finance, Trade, and Politics in British Foreign Policy, 1815–1914* (Oxford, 1968), pp. 294–304; and Raymond Poidevin, *Les relations économiques et financières entre la France et l'Allemagne de 1898 à 1914* (Paris, 1969), esp. pp. 36–86, 286–312, 318–343, 458–510, 541–586. At certain times political considerations did make cooperation impossible, notably in 1903, when British public opinion forced London to abandon collaboration with the Germans regarding the Bagdad railway, and after 1911, when the Agadir crisis put an end to Franco-German cooperation.

57. Brunschwig, *French Colonialism*, pp. 135–138, gives figures and further states, without any justification, that they show colonies to have been "expensive." Mitchell's figures for total French government expenditure (*European Historical Statistics*, p. 700) put the question in proper perspective.

58. *Statistisches Jahrbuch, 1913*, pp. 351–354.

ner, and Theodore Roosevelt, who believed not only in the inevitability but also in the desirability of worldwide struggle. Indeed, anyone who took the trouble actually to investigate international economic developments in the decades before the war found that the beneficial interactions among the economies of the various European imperialist powers far outweighed rivalries within certain sectors. They also found that major domestic interests regarded the possibility of general European war with horror.[59]

Although European politicians may not have known exactly how little economic value the new colonies had for their nations as a whole, their handling of imperial questions suggests that they understood that there was plenty of territory to go around. The rivalry for colonies, they sensed, was essentially a political question—a question of convincing domestic constituencies that their governments took sufficient account of their national interests. Rather than regard their competition for colonies as a matter of life and death, they generally acted almost exactly in the spirit epitomized by Lord Salisbury's famous speech of May 4, 1898.

> You may roughly divide the nations of the world as the living and the dying . . . the weak states are becoming weaker and the strong states are becoming stronger . . . *For one reason or another—from the necessities of politics or under the pretext of philanthropy—the living nations will gradually encroach on the territory of the dying, and the seed and causes of conflict amongst civilized nations will speedily appear.* Of course, it is not to be supposed that any one nation of the living nations will be allowed to have the profitable monopoly of curing or cutting up these unfortunate patients, and the controversy is as to who shall have the privilege of doing so, and in what measure he shall do it. These things may introduce causes of fatal difference between the great nations whose mighty armies stand opposed threatening each other. These are the dangers which I think threaten us in the period that is coming on.[60]

Only at first glance does this formulation seem to reflect social Darwinism. Although Salisbury (wrongly) foresaw the complete

---

59. On German-British relations, see the excellent discussion by Paul Kennedy, *Rise of the Anglo-German Antagonism*, pp. 291–305; as I have argued elsewhere, the impressive data presented by Kennedy sharply contradicts his conclusion that "the most profound cause" of Anglo-German antagonism was economic. Poidevin, *Relations économiques et financières, passim*, develops the same point regarding France and Germany, but points out that relations were worsening from 1911 through 1914.

60. Langer, *The Diplomacy of Imperialism, 1890–1902* (New York, 1951), p. 505; Grenville, *Lord Salisbury and Foreign Policy*, pp. 166–167, emphasis added.

demise of the Turkish, Chinese, and perhaps Portuguese empires, he did *not* believe that a death struggle among the major European states must accompany it. While war undoubtedly *threatened* as a result of these enormous changes, careful diplomacy could regulate the distribution of spoils so as to avoid it. And this was the policy followed not only by Salisbury but by every major European government, almost without exception, between 1880 and 1914. The number and complexity of the agreements European diplomats and politicians arranged during these years is almost as impressive as the extent of territory they partitioned. This, surely, was the golden age of European diplomacy—largely, of course, because non-Europeans were absorbing its costs.

During the years 1910–1914 the international climate became considerably harsher, leading to larger armament budgets in all the major countries and calls for stronger and more effective government action to safeguard national security economically, socially, and militarily. Social Darwinist views of the world seem to have undergone a revival at this time, and their popularity at least reached the level of the late 1890s.[61] The major European governments, however, generally continued their policy of accommodation, carefully handling a series of Balkan crises in 1912–13 and continuing to negotiate on colonial questions. War, as we shall see, had little to offer the industrial European nations. What they truly required was, first, continuing access for their trade and capital to various rapidly developing areas in the non-European and non-colonial world, including Russia and North and South America and, second, the absence of a major war, whose economic consequences might be vast. The British government certainly understood this,[62] and for the most part other governments did as well. Economic competition before 1914 had proved beneficial to all and injurious to none.

In July 1914, however, the illusion of imperialism took hold of the German government and helped unleash the First World War.

61. Thus Bethmann's government came under pressure from the Pan-German and Conservative "Fronde," while social imperialism made gains within both of the major British parties, and the "National Revival" became more important in France. See Roger Chickering, *We Who Feel Most German: A Cultural Study of the Pan-German League, 1886–1914* (Boston, 1984); Scally, *Origins of the Lloyd George Coalition;* Eugen Weber, *The Nationalist Revival in France, 1905–1914* (Berkeley, 1959).

62. See for example the concluding remarks of Platt, *British Foreign Policy,* pp. 353–368.

But imperialism alone would not have had this effect. To understand the outbreak of the war we must examine the second great issue of late nineteenth- and early twentieth-century politics: the impact of nationalism in general, and the growth of national movements in eastern and southeastern Europe in particular.

The Impact of Nationalism and the Outbreak of the First World War

The idea of nationalism—"a state of mind, permeating the large majority of a people and claiming to permeate all its members," which "recognizes the nation-state as the ideal form of political organization and the nationality as the source of creative cultural energy and of economic well-being"—had begun to influence European politics in the late eighteenth century and had transformed the map of central Europe during the nineteenth.[1] As we have seen, nationalism became politically important at the time of the French Revolution, but the national movements of the revolutionary period generally found themselves co-opted by governments. By 1815 the idea had spread through much of Europe. Some provisions of the European settlement at the Congress of Vienna—most notably the creation of the German confederation and the provision that Poles within Austria, Prussia, and Russia should receive "national representation and national institutions adapted to the kind of political existence each of the three governments to which they belong will judge useful and correct to grant them"—implicitly endorsed the principle of nationality, but virtually nothing happened to further it in practice.[2] During the nineteenth century national movements grew in strength in virtually every part of Europe, and the issue of the rights of nationalities became increasingly intertwined with the issue of popular and representative government.

1. This definition, from Hans Kohn, *The Idea of Nationalism: A Study in its Origins and Political Background* (New York, 1944), p. 16, seems to me the most useful for an analysis of twentieth-century European politics. Other definitions have been collected by Boyd C. Shafer, *Faces of Nationalism: New Realities and Old Myths* (New York, 1972), pp. 3–8. The question of the source of the emotional and political power of nationalism, while absolutely critical to the understanding of modern politics, would carry us well beyond the scope of this book.

2. Hannah Alice Strauss, *The Attitude of the Congress of Vienna toward Nationalism in Germany, Italy, and Poland* (New York, 1949), esp. p. 144.

In western and central Europe, popular national uprisings seldom managed to prevail against established authority. The Belgian uprising of 1830 did create a new state—although not a national state—but popular uprisings in Germany, Italy, and Hungary failed to achieve any lasting results in 1848–49.[3] During the next two decades, however, the governments of Prussia and Sardinia (Piedmont) used the nationality principle, combined with war and diplomacy, to establish German and Italian national states. These dynasties also managed to reconcile a certain measure of representative government with the maintenance of their authority. Most other European governments tolerated Prussian and Piedmontese expansion, often because they hoped to gain something themselves from the rearrangement of Europe. And although the new German state, in particular, was far from a pure national state, national states composed most of western Europe by 1871, with the major exception of the United Kingdom of Great Britain and Ireland. The emergence of national states, of course, was closely related to the growing identification of the interests of the state with those of its people, which as we have seen had become a fundamental principle of European politics by 1900.

The situation remained very different, of course, within the three eastern empires of Austria-Hungary, Russia, and Turkey. While the ruling houses of Prussia and Sardinia had managed to use national movements to their own advantage, the eastern empires could not adopt the nationality principle without abandoning much of their domains. National movements of various kinds arose in eastern Europe throughout the nineteenth and early twentieth centuries. In the Russian empire, the Poles rose in 1830 and 1863, while the Finns, who had lost much of their autonomy in the 1890s, regained some of it during the Russian revolution of 1905. Both Magyars and Czechs demanded sweeping concessions from the Austrian empire in 1848, and the Magyars secured the establishment of the Dual Monarchy in 1867.[4] The Turks had to contend with armed risings in Serbia during the Napoleonic period, in Greece beginning in 1821, in Rumania in the 1820s, in Bosnia, Herzegovina, and Bulgaria during the late 1870s, and in Ar-

3. A convenient summary of these developments is William Langer, *The Revolutions of 1848* (New York, 1969).
4. Following a common practice, I am using "Magyars" to refer to ethnic Hungarians.

menia and Macedonia in the 1890s. Helped by the decay of the Ottoman empire and the difficult terrain of the Balkan peninsula, the Serbs and the Greeks won autonomy and independence, respectively, in the first half of the nineteenth century, and the Rumanians won autonomy after the Crimean War.[5]

As the century wore on, a series of diplomatic crises gradually established nationalism as a guiding principle in European diplomacy. For a variety of reasons, European governments frequently took an active interest in national movements outside their own borders, treated them as subjects of general European concern, and recognized certain rights of subject peoples. Western European opinion often supported national rights in principle and agitated for either autonomy or independence for those who lacked them, while central and eastern European empires began using nationalist movements for their own political and strategic advantage. British opinion strongly favored the rights of European nationalities, and British governments supported independence movements in Greece and Poland with varying degrees of effectiveness and enthusiasm.[6] Later, under Gladstone, the Liberal party turned the rights of the Balkan Christian subjects of the Ottoman empire into a major campaign issue in the late 1870s,[7] and supported the rights of the Armenians during the 1890s. Gladstone adopted similar ideas closer to home in 1885, when he endorsed Home Rule for Ireland, a proposal which the Liberal party continued to support and intermittently attempted to implement right up until 1914. In France the empire of Napoleon III also expressed some guarded support for Polish nationalism and claimed a kind of protectorate over the Christian subjects of the sultan, but governments of the Third Republic took a much more restrained line towards eastern European nationalities problems.

The European powers tried more systematically to control the growth of Balkan nationalism during the Balkan crisis of 1875–1878 and the Congress of Berlin. While creating a small new autonomous Bulgaria, the European concert left the Ottoman empire in

5. See Barbara Jelavich, *History of the Balkans*, 2 vols. (New York, 1983), vol. 1, for the most recent account of Balkan developments.
6. John Howard Gleason, *The Genesis of Russophobia in Great Britain* (Cambridge, Mass., 1950), pp. 107–134; R. C. Leslie, *Reform and Insurrection in Russian Poland, 1856–1865* (London, 1963).
7. R. W. Seton-Watson, *Disraeli, Gladstone, and the Eastern Question* (London, 1962).

control of Eastern Rumelia and Macedonia. In addition, Austria-Hungary tried to protect against Serbian nationalism by occupying Bosnia-Herzegovina—Turkish territory inhabited largely by Serbs—and the sanjak of Novibazaar. The powers expected Serbia to become an Austrian client and Bulgaria a Russian one. The Treaty of Berlin also imposed vague obligations upon the sultan to undertake reforms among his Christian subjects. Bulgaria's pursuit of an independent course and its unification with Eastern Rumelia in 1885 signaled an increasingly independent spirit among the new Balkan governments.[8]

During the rest of the nineteenth century the powers continued to intervene on behalf of the Christian subjects of the Ottoman sultan. In 1878 they forced the Porte to grant some autonomy to the Greek population of Crete, and in 1894–95 the Russian, French, and British governments interceded in Constantinople on behalf of the sultan's Armenian subjects but failed to prevent a massacre of 100,000–200,000 Armenians.[9] Vienna and St. Petersburg agreed in 1897 and 1903 jointly to monitor developments in Macedonia, which Greeks, Serbs, and Bulgars all claimed for their national heritage. Making a virtue of necessity, then, the concert of Europe was endorsing the erosion of Ottoman authority in Europe in favor of either autonomy or independence for its non-Turkish subjects. Paralleling their attitude toward overseas expansion, the European governments tried to regulate these changes in ways that would protect each of their particular interests.[10]

Thus from 1815 until about 1900 the national idea had won many significant victories in central and eastern Europe without leading to a general European conflagration. The powers had tolerated both the creation of Germany and Italy (largely, though not exclusively, at the expense of minor dynasties) and the establishment of small new national monarchies in the Balkans. Despite these changes, nationalities questions became far *more* troublesome, and potentially far more explosive, in the two decades be-

8. Sumner, *Russia and the Balkans, 1870–1880.*

9. Richard G. Hovannisian, "The Historical Dimensions of the Armenian Question, 1878–1923," in Hovannisian, ed., *The Armenian Genocide in Perspective* (New Brunswick, 1986), pp. 19–42.

10. Developments in the Balkans may be followed in M. S. Anderson, *The Eastern Question, 1774–1923* (New York, 1966); Raymond Pearson, *National Minorities in Eastern Europe, 1848–1945* (New York, 1983); and Jelavich, *History of the Balkans,* I, 329–376, and II, 13–50.

fore 1914. Even in western Europe, where ethnic and religious minorities had achieved full legal equality, their status remained a matter of sharp debate. Various French right-wing publicists and politicians denied that Jews or Protestants could become sincere Frenchmen,[11] and in Great Britain the possibility of Home Rule for Ireland became after 1911 the most contentious issue in British politics. In central and eastern Europe, serious issues had developed with respect to the internal rights of minorities in the German, Austro-Hungarian, and Ottoman empires and as a result of the autonomous expansionist aims of the new Balkan states.

The empires of central and eastern Europe were relying more and more upon nationalism to strengthen their authority but without reconciling their subject nationalities to their rule. Although the German government in 1911 finally gave Alsace-Lorraine a measure of self-government,[12] the two provinces remained under military rule. In the east the German government waged a determined but unsuccessful campaign to reduce the size and economic power of the Polish population of West Prussia, Posen, and Silesia, including legislation allowing for the confiscation of Polish estates and attempts to restrict the use of the Polish language in schools.[13] Extreme imperialists such as the leadership of the Pan-German League still hoped for a further expansion of the German empire, especially in the east. Some extremists had already suggested that new nationality conflicts might be avoided simply by "evacuating" any non-German peoples whom the Reich might acquire, and the Pan-German League had even toyed with the expulsion of Jews from Germany.[14] The leadership of the German government, however, had drawn the opposite conclusion. Like Bismarck, both Bülow and Bethmann believed that Germany could not assimilate any more foreign elements and rejected further Continental expansion on those grounds.[15]

11. Ernst Nolte, *Three Faces of Fascism: Action Française, Italian Fascism, National Socialism* (New York, 1969), pp. 51–192.

12. David Schoenbaum, *Zabern 1913: Consensus Politics in Imperial Germany* (London, 1982), pp. 71–94.

13. William W. Hagen, *Germans, Poles, and Jews: The Nationality Conflict in the Prussian East, 1772–1914* (Chicago, 1980), pp. 159–207.

14. Imanuel Geiss, *Die Polnischen Grenzstreifen, 1914–1918: Ein Beitrag zur deutschen Kriegzielpolitik im Ersten Weltkrieg* (Lübeck, 1960), pp. 41–43; Henry Cord Meyer, *Mitteleuropa in German Thought and Action, 1815–1945* (The Hague, 1955), pp. 107–108; Chickering, *We Who Feel Most German*, pp. 243–245.

15. Kaiser, "Germany and the Origins of the First World War," pp. 455–456.

In Russia the nationalities question had an intimate connection with the more general question of popular rights and representative government. The tsarist government, which had no intention of granting either one even to the Russian people, tightened its grip on its many millions of minority subjects severely in the decades before the First World War. In Poland and Finland, which theoretically possessed considerable autonomy and which had actually enjoyed substantial control over their own affairs during parts of the nineteenth century, the Russian government revoked some existing concessions and pressed for the use of the Russian language in government and education. Russian also became the language of schools and universities in the Baltic states during the 1880s, undermining the rights of Baltic Germans and of the Baltic peasantry. Throughout these areas the government also tried to increase the wealth and power of the Russian Orthodox church. Lastly, Russia's huge Jewish community—by far the largest in the world—was refused even the option of Russification and assimilation. Confined to the overcrowded pale of settlement and subject to periodic pogroms, Russian Jews increasingly looked to immigration to America, Zionism, or revolutionary socialism to achieve basic rights.

Like the Russian people, the subject nationalities won some important political concessions during the revolution of 1905, including representation in the Duma. But the Russian authorities seem to have decided that equal rights for nationalities would make it impossible to preserve the power of the Russian aristocracy. The new electoral law instituted by coup d'état in 1907 reduced the representation of non-Russians to token levels, and the government also revoked some recent concessions to the Jews. "The State Duma must be Russian in spirit, the other nationalities ought not and shall not be represented in numbers giving them the power to have the deciding voice on purely Russian issues," the new edict read. The state and right-wing parties counted upon Russification to bring most minorities into national life. Not surprisingly, minorities played a vastly disproportionate part in the Russian revolutionary movement.[16]

Austria-Hungary, of course, faced the most serious nationalities

16. Violet Conolly, "The 'Nationalities Question' in the Last Phase of Tsardom," in Erwin Oberländer et al., eds., *Russia Enters the Twentieth Century, 1894–1917* (New York, 1971), pp. 152–181; Hosking, *Russian Constitutional Experiment*, pp. 215–222; Pearson, *National Minorities*, pp. 66–83; Adam Ulam, *Russia's Failed Revolutions* (New York, 1981),

problem.[17] After being threatened with the loss of much of its territory and power in 1848–49, the Hapsburg dynasty imposed the most rigid, bureaucratic control over the whole empire that it had ever enjoyed, eliminating even the long-standing privileges of the Magyar nobility in Hungary. In 1867, however, after the Hapsburgs' defeat by Prussia and the loss of some Italian territories, the Austrian empire became Austria-Hungary, and the Magyars won the right to rule their half of the empire. Essentially, the German-Austrian nobility now shared the task of ruling over its Rumanian and Slavic nationalities with the Magyars.[18] Rather than a pure bureaucratic and military empire like Russia, Austria-Hungary was now a state of nationalities in which some nationalities were privileged to rule over others.[19]

In the decades before the First World War, the Austrian and Hungarian approaches to the nationalities question increasingly diverged. In Hungary the Magyars pursued policies similar to those of the Russians. The Croats enjoyed some local autonomy, but the Magyars refused to concede national political rights either to the middle class (much of which was German or Jewish) or to its subject nationalities, including Croats, Serbs, and Rumanians. The suffrage was manipulated to keep the entire lower house in Magyar hands, and the nobility dominated almost every area of Hungarian life. Political debate within Hungary asked not whether minorities should receive greater rights but rather whether the Magyars should secede from the Dual Monarchy altogether to safeguard their ruling position. Stefan Tisza, the prewar prime minister of Hungary, hoped to solve the nationalities problem simply by the Magyarization of the entire population, which the government tried to encourage by establishing Magyar schools throughout its territory.[20]

---

pp. 197–208; Edward Thaden et al., *Russification in the Baltic Provinces and Finland, 1885–1914* (Princeton, 1981), esp. pp. 54–87, 179–183, 382–447.

17. Both this problem and its enormous influence upon European politics are treated at length in Lawrence Lafore, *The Long Fuse: An Interpretation of the Origins of the First World War* (Philadelphia and New York, 1965).

18. The Poles also enjoyed a somewhat privileged status in Galicia, where they ruled over Ruthenian (Ukrainian) peasants.

19. Arthur J. May, *The Hapsburg Monarchy, 1867–1914* (Cambridge, Mass., 1951), is the best general survey. It should be noted (see pp. 33–36) that the talks with Hungarian leaders that led to the *Ausgleich* had begun before the war with Prussia.

20. Oscar Jászi, *The Dissolution of the Hapsburg Monarchy* (Chicago, 1929), pp. 298–343; May, *Hapsburg Monarchy*, pp. 343–385.

The Austrian government, by contrast, tried sincerely to give both the middle and working classes and the non-German nationalities the maximum political rights consistent with the maintenance of the authority of the ruling nobility. In Bohemia the government tried at various times to treat Germans and Czechs more equally, but its measures generally struck the Germans as too egalitarian without satisfying the Czechs. In 1907, the government granted manhood suffrage throughout Austria, and although a majority of deputies were still reserved for the Germans—who made up just 36 percent of the population—discontent among Austrian minorities seems to have ebbed somewhat as a result. But the granting of these rights hardly brought national conflicts to an end. In much of Austria—and especially in Bohemia—national antagonisms seemed to be irreconcilable and frequently paralyzed both local and national parliamentary institutions. Language rights which the Czechs demanded in the name of equality, such as a requirement that public officials in mixed areas speak Czech as well as German, seemed to the Germans to condemn them to inferiority, since they, unlike the Czechs, rarely learned their neighbors' language.[21] Austrian sections of the Pan-German League actually hoped for the dissolution of the monarchy and the union of its German territories with the German empire, while many other German Austrians hoped simply to regain their political and social supremacy. No idle fantasy, this policy had the support of the heir apparent, Archduke Francis Ferdinand, who intended to implement it in both halves of the Dual Monarchy when he ascended the throne. The Dual Monarchy's problems, he believed, stemmed from its concessions to the Magyars in 1867, which had excited the jealousy of the other minorities. While waiting impatiently for his uncle Francis Joseph's death, Francis Ferdinand carefully laid plans to break the Magyars' power by decreeing universal suffrage in Hungary immediately upon his accession. This accomplished, he intended to reestablish the complete preeminence of the Germans throughout the empire and eventually to regain the lost Italian territories as well.[22]

21. May, *Hapsburg Monarchy*, pp. 322–342; see also Jászi, *Dissolution of the Hapsburg Monarchy*, pp. 284–297, arguing that Austria had made significant strides toward reconciling its nationalities before the war.

22. Vladimir Dedijer, *The Road to Sarajevo* (New York, 1967), pp. 118–141, shows very clearly that Francis Ferdinand had rejected the trialist solution to the Austro-Hungarian problem—that is, the creation of a third, Slavic kingdom—and that he had planned to return to absolute rule.

All in all, the Hohenzollern, Hapsburg, and Romanov empires managed to keep their internal nationalities problems under control. They found themselves much less able to control the nationalist foreign policies of the Balkan states formed out of the Ottoman empire during the nineteenth century. The agitation of these new Piedmonts faced the eastern empires with a series of crises from the 1890s to the outbreak of the First World War.

Greece, Serbia, Bulgaria, and Rumania all emerged from the Congress of Berlin dissatisfied with their territorial extent, and their pretensions led to conflicts of increasing severity beginning in the 1890s. Bulgaria managed to unite itself with Eastern Rumelia in 1885. Within Greece, the National Society, which included many Greek officers, agitated for union with Macedonia and Crete, and the Greek government declared war on the Turks in 1897 after a rebellion in Crete had proclaimed union. The Turks defeated the Greeks, but the intervention of the powers saved the Greek mainland and granted Crete autonomy.[23] In Serbia, army officers assassinated the Austro-Hungarian client King Milan Obrenovich in 1903, and his successor, Peter Karageorgevich, abandoned the old friendship with Vienna. At about the same time, Greeks, Bulgarians, Serbs, and Rumanians all sponsored propaganda and armed revolt in Macedonia, which included some ethnic brethren of all these nations within itself. Austria-Hungary and Russia, however, agreed to maintain the territorial status quo in Macedonia in 1897, and in 1903, Vienna and St. Petersburg presented the sultan with a list of reforms he must impose within Macedonia. The powers, then, were trying once again to administer peaceful change within the Ottoman empire, but the reform program seems to have made the nationality conflict even worse.[24]

Curiously enough, the nationalist impulse which finally upset the post-1885 territorial status quo came not from any of the Balkan states but from the Turks. Officers of the Turkish army in Macedonia staged the Young Turk Revolt in 1908. Hoping to maintain Turkish preeminence within a newly democratic empire, they announced constitutional rule and called elections to a parliament throughout the Ottoman empire. They apparently dreamed of regaining effective control over both autonomous Bulgaria and the

23. Jelavich, *History of the Balkans*, II, 42–43.
24. Ibid., pp. 89–95; Douglas Dakin, *The Unification of Greece* (New York, 1972), pp. 169–170.

provinces of Bosnia-Herzegovina, which the Austro-Hungarian government had occupied and administered since 1878.[25]

The changes in Turkey forced the Austro-Hungarian government to reconsider its position in Bosnia-Herzegovina, which had suddenly become literally the only territory in Europe which did not enjoy at least formal constitutional government. Fearing that Austria-Hungary's occupation might be called into question, the common foreign minister, Aehrenthal, decided to annex the two provinces.[26] When Vienna announced the annexation, Bulgaria seized upon the occasion to declare its independence.

The annexation shocked Serbian nationalists, who had hoped eventually to add Bosnia-Herzegovina to Serbia, and the Serbian government claimed compensation. The Russian government, which now fancied itself as Serbia's patron, supported the demand. Serbia's demands faced Vienna with a peculiar dilemma. The Austrian military wanted to attack the Serbs, the Magyar government of Hungary opposed any further addition of new Slavs to the monarchy, and Francis Ferdinand wanted to delay the resolution of the Serbian question until after he came to the throne.[27] The Vienna government, backed by Berlin, contented itself with an ultimatum to the Serbian and Russian governments that forced the Serbs to abandon their demand for compensation.

Revolts in Turkish Albania beginning in 1910, and Italy's attack on Turkish Tripoli in 1911, led to a new Balkan crisis.[28] Alarmed by Turkey's closure of the Black Sea straits, the Russian government, led by Foreign Minister Sergei Sazonov, tried to create an alliance

25. Ernest Edmondson Ramsaur, Jr., *The Young Turks: Prelude to the Revolution of 1908* (Princeton, 1957), pp. 147–148.

26. While this interpretation of Aehrenthal's motives differs from both Luigi Albertini, *The Origins of the War of 1914*, 3 vols. (London, 1952–1957), and Bernadotte Schmitt, *The Annexation of Bosnia* (Cambridge, 1937), key contemporary documents clearly state that Aehrenthal wanted to *withdraw* the Austrian garrison from its exposed position in the sanjak of Novibazaar, where he feared it might become embroiled in rebellion, and to annex Bosnia-Herzegovina to compensate for the loss of prestige involved in the withdrawal and to enable Austria to grant the two provinces a constitution and autonomy. See Aehrenthal's memorandum of August 7, 1908, and the Common Council Protocol of August 18, in Ludwig Bittner et al., eds., *Öesterreich-Ungarns Aussenpolitik von der Bösnischen Krise 1908 bis zum Kriegsausbruch 1914*, vol. 1 (Vienna, 1930), nos. 29, 40.

27. Albertini, *Origins of the War of 1914*, I, 273–276, summarizes Austro-Hungarian opinion on this question.

28. We may note that Italy's designs on Tripoli, which had been linked by agreement to France's assumption of a protectorate over Morocco, provide an obvious link between the imperialism of the European powers and the nationality conflicts of the Balkans—a link which eventually provoked the outbreak of a general European war.

of Turkey and the Balkan states to safeguard its access to the Mediterranean from the Black Sea. When Turkey declined the offer, Serbia and Bulgaria took advantage of the Russian initiative to make an alliance against Turkey, including a plan for the partition of the remainder of European Turkey.[29] All the major European governments tried to stave off the war by imposing new reforms upon the Turks, but the Balkan states—including Greece, Rumania, and Montenegro, as well as Bulgaria and Serbia—attacked Turkey in late 1912. They won a spectacular series of victories and almost drove the Turks completely out of Europe.[30]

During the period of the two Balkan wars (1912–13),[31] the European powers continued to cooperate in an attempt to make sure new territorial changes did not impinge upon their interests, and the Balkan states themselves yielded, when necessary, to the great powers' demands. The Austro-Hungarian government and its new foreign minister, Count Berchtold, tried to deal with this outburst of nationalism by creating a new client state of Albania while playing the remaining Balkan powers off against one another. Acting with the support of all the major European powers—including Russia—Vienna insisted upon the creation of a new Albanian state so as to deny Serbia access to the Adriatic. Vienna succeeded because all the powers wanted jointly to regulate the outcome of the wars in a way which did not seem too favorable to any of the contestants, and because the Serbian government itself, although it forced Vienna in October 1913 to issue an ultimatum to force its troops out of territory allocated to Albania, had no wish to come to a conflict with Austria-Hungary. Vienna also planned to contain Serbia by organizing the rest of the Balkan states, including Bulgaria, Greece, and Rumania, against it.[32] Balkan nationalism, however, was increasingly escaping from the control not only of

29. Edward C. Thaden, *Russia and the Balkan Alliance of 1912* (Princeton, 1965).

30. Albertini, *Origins of the War of 1914*, I, 364–432, summarizes these developments well. Ernst C. Helmreich, *The Diplomacy of the Balkan Wars* (Cambridge, Mass., 1938), gives the fullest account and quite definitely shows (pp. 151–164) that although some lesser Russian military and civilian officials welcomed the Balkan attack, Russian Premier Kokovstov and Foreign Minister Sazonov opposed it.

31. The second Balkan war began in late June 1913, when Bulgaria, dissatisfied with its own gains at the expense of Turkey, attacked Serbia and Greece, who were joined in turn by Rumania. This war led to Bulgaria's defeat.

32. In practice the various relationships between great powers on the one hand and Balkan states on the other had become fantastically complicated—for example, while Russia and Austria-Hungary supported Bulgarian claims against Greece, France and Germany took the opposite side; see Albertini, *Origins of the War of 1914*, I, 448–478.

the great powers but also of the Balkan governments. And in the long run, the conflict between Balkan nationalism and Austria-Hungary was irreconcilable.

Although the crisis that ushered in a new era of general war in July 1914 eventually involved imperialism as well as nationalism, it began as another episode in the confrontation between Serbia and Austria-Hungary. This crisis reflected the growth of Serbian nationalism to the point where it threatened its own government, as well as Austria-Hungary. In 1909, after the Serbian government bowed to the Austro-Hungarian ultimatum requiring that it accept the annexation of Bosnia-Herzegovina, some of the military officers who had murdered King Milan Obrenovich founded the secret society Union or Death, more commonly known as the Black Hand. Led by Dragutin Dimitrievich (known as Colonel Apis) the secret society agitated against the government's cautious foreign policy in its journal—entitled, significantly, *Piedmont*—and called for the formation of a greater Serbian empire. The Serbian army's victories in the Balkan wars increased the prestige of both itself and Colonel Apis, and the civil authorities barely managed to win a tremendous struggle for power with the army in newly occupied Macedonia.[33]

Similar situations had arisen in other Balkan states as well. The Bulgarian and Greek governments had had to contend for many years with army officers and irregular groups who sought to make up for their government's lack of nationalist zeal by fomenting risings in Macedonia and Crete.[34] Balkan governments, forced by the requirements of diplomacy not to espouse their peoples' national claims publicly, continually found themselves under pressure from more extreme groups, who frequently resorted to violence at home and within *irredenta* to promote their aims. Since the Second World War the world has encountered many other examples of this phenomenon among newly emerging states, suggesting that nationalism has often been stronger than loyalty to constituted authority.

Greek and Bulgarian nationalism, unlike Serbian, did not

33. The whole remarkable story is told in Dedijer's extraordinary book, *The Road to Sarajevo*, pp. 371–388.

34. Richard A. Crampton, *Bulgaria, 1878–1918: A History* (New York, 1983), pp. 229–241, 270–294, 321–322; Dakin, *Unification of Greece*, pp. 149–175.

threaten Austria-Hungary, but in the wake of the Balkan wars a new threat was emerging from Rumania. The Rumanian king Carol was most friendly to Germany, and Rumania had secretly been a member of the Triple Alliance since 1883. But when in late 1913 the Austro-Hungarian government tried to strengthen its diplomatic position by asking the Rumanian government publicly to recognize this obligation, the king bluntly replied that the plight of the Rumanians within Hungary made this impossible.[35]

The crisis that led to the outbreak of the First World War began when Colonel Apis authorized one of his collaborators to provide a group of young Bosnian revolutionaries with bombs and revolvers to assassinate the Austrian archduke Francis Ferdinand at Sarajevo, the Bosnian capital, on June 28, 1914.[36] While the students hoped to provoke rebellion in Bosnia by performing a spectacular act of tyrannicide, Apis feared that Francis Ferdinand might make it far more difficult for Serbia to realize its entire nationalist program by turning the Dual Monarchy into a Triple Monarchy with a South Slav kingdom.[37] The Serbian government discovered the plot after the conspirators had crossed back into Bosnia but was unable to stop it.[38] Francis Ferdinand was going to Sarajevo to reaffirm the authority of his dynasty in Bosnia-Herzegovina by making an impressive display of his royal person. The same wish led him to continue his program even after a first assassination attempt had narrowly failed.

The assassination of the archduke, which the Austro-Hungarian government quickly traced to elements within Serbia (although not to Apis and Union or Death, of whose existence Vienna was evidently unaware), immediately impressed the Vienna government as a further Pan-Serb challenge to its authority, all the more so since the deed did ignite the revolutionary demonstrations in Bosnia which its perpetrators had sought. When on July 7 the Austro-Hungarian Council of Ministers met to discuss the situation, Foreign Minister Berchtold proposed a war against Serbia in addition to "a number of internal measures which the critical state

35. Albertini, *Origins of the War of 1914*, I, 497–501.
36. Dedijer, *Road to Sarajevo*, p. 393.
37. Although as we have seen Francis Ferdinand had long since abandoned trialism, his advisers encouraged the idea that he believed in it for tactical reasons. Dedijer, *Road to Sarajevo*, pp. 134–135.
38. Ibid., pp. 388–395.

of Bosnia has made desirable . . . The Governor in Bosnia and Herzegovina declares," he added later, "that it is his belief that no successful measures could be applied in the interior of these provinces
unless we deal Serbia a forcible stroke first." [39] Significantly, when
the Hungarian premier Tisza, who wanted to avoid war, argued
that Rumania was now unfriendly and likely to attack as well,
Berchtold replied that such a danger would increase if more time
were allowed to pass. The government, he felt, must deal a decisive blow to Balkan nationalism. He persuaded his colleagues to
give the Serbs an ultimatum that would include unacceptable demands, to be followed almost at once by an armed attack. The ultimatum was delivered on July 23, with a time limit of only forty-
eight hours.

Berchtold probably assessed the long-run threat to the Dual
Monarchy correctly. The events of the years 1878–1914 show that
Balkan nationalism would most probably have continued to increase in strength, and that further confrontations between
Austria-Hungary and Serbia—as well, perhaps, as new conflicts
with Rumania—must logically have been expected. Alternatively,
had Francis Ferdinand come to the throne and carried out his coup
d'état against the Magyars in Hungary, the resulting civil war
would probably have spread beyond Austria-Hungary's borders.
The Vienna government, in short, would most probably have had
to reach the decision that it reached in July 1914 at some point or
other in the future. The course of the July crisis shows quite clearly
that had the Austro-Hungarian leaders agreed to submit the dispute with Serbia to European arbitration, they could have obtained
considerable satisfaction in the short run. Yet they were probably
correct to assume that such a victory would last no longer than
those of 1909 and 1913. The Austro-Hungarian government was
based upon, and by its nature could only be based upon, the principle of arbitrary dynastic authority. To survive it had to show that
it could back that authority effectively by force.

Although the Russian government had little real affection for
Serbia, which had caused it more than enough trouble during the
Balkan wars, its concern both for the Black Sea straits and its gen-
eral diplomatic prestige did not allow it to let Vienna deal unilater-

---

39. Imanuel Geiss, *July 1914: The Outbreak of the First World War—Selected Documents*
(New York, 1967), pp. 80–83.

ally with Serbia. Thus, Foreign Minister Sazonov made it quite clear during the crisis that Austria-Hungary might chastise Serbia severely provided that it recognized its dispute as a European question, but he also initially advised the Serbian government to reject at least parts of the Austrian ultimatum and advocated mobilization of the Russian army and war should Vienna persist in its course.[40]

The growth of nationalism in southeastern Europe, then, triggered the July crisis. The crisis might have turned out very differently, however, had the German government not decided to use it to realize its own unrelated imperialist goals. When the Austrian count Hoyos visited Berlin in the first week of July, the German chancellor, Bethmann-Hollweg, saw that the crisis could lead to a trial of strength between Germany and Austria-Hungary on the one hand, and France, Russia, and possibly Great Britain on the other. He also decided, based upon considerations of imperialism, that the time for a trial of strength had come.

Since taking power in 1909, Bethmann had become increasingly concerned with the progress of German imperialism. On the surface, his handling of colonial questions since 1909 resembles his predecessor Bülow's. Bethmann had undertaken talks with Britain regarding the partition of the Portuguese colonies and the Bagdad railway, successfully settling the latter question on the eve of the war. In 1911 he had secured compensation for Germany in the Congo region when France assumed a protectorate over Morocco. Yet whereas Bülow never seems to have believed wholeheartedly in the *need* for colonies, Bethmann's policies suggest that he had fallen for the imperialist rhetoric that had become so common in Germany, and that he really believed Germany needed a much larger empire to survive, even if war would be necessary to secure it. He was quite close to the Colonial Office, which already had far-reaching plans for Central Africa. And although he had worked hard to secure an entente with Great Britain, he had also tried to

40. On July 27, the Austrian ambassador Szápáry reported, Sazonov told him that "he had no feelings for the Balkan Slavs. They were actually a heavy burden on Russia and we could hardly imagine how much trouble they had already given Russia. [Vienna's] aims as described by me were perfectly legitimate but he thought the way we had chosen to attain them not the safest." Albertini, *Origins of the War of 1914*, II, 404–405. The Russian advice to the Serbs to reject the ultimatum has been relatively recently revealed: see Gale Stokes, "The Serbian Documents from 1914: A Preview," listed in *Journal of Modern History*, 48, no. 3 (September 1976): iii.

improve Germany's military position so as to make it possible for Germany either to extort or force France and Russia to make important colonial concessions.

Bethmann's intentions on this point, indeed, are clearly reflected both in his diplomatic posture and in the important military reforms which he put through. During Anglo-German talks on naval limitation, Bethmann had insisted that Britain promise to remain neutral in a Continental war—a promise that would enormously improve Germany's chances against France or Russia in a war over Central Africa or Asia Minor, where Bethmann believed that Germany "must expand."[41] In addition, while trying to limit naval expansion, he substantially increased the strength of the German army. Bethmann's confidant and press liaison, Kurt Riezler, specifically argued that the army would enable Germany to coerce France in his pseudonymous book, *Grundzüge der Weltpolitik in der Gegenwart,* which was published in 1914.[42] Bethmann further believed that Germany's chances to achieve an empire were slipping away, and that the growth of Russian power would make Germany's position impossible within a few years. Since 1911 German opinion had divided sharply over the desirability of war. On the one hand, the Pan-Germans, whose views found expression in their leader Heinrich Class's popular pseudonymous book, *Wenn Ich der Kaiser wär,* believed in its necessity, while on the other hand a pseudonymous Foreign Office pamphlet, *Deutsche Weltpolitik und Kein Krieg,* definitely rejected it. Significantly, Riezler took an ambiguous middle position in *Grunzüge der Weltpolitik in der Gegenwart,* arguing that while war was not essential to German happiness, it *might* be necessary. This was the position Bethmann took during the July Crisis.[43]

German political and business circles seem to have discussed the probable onset of war around the middle of July 1914, before the Austro-Hungarian ultimatum had been delivered. They planned to defeat France and claim several of its colonies—includ-

---

41. Konrad Jarausch, *The Enigmatic Chancellor: Bethmann Hollweg and the Hubris of Imperial Germany* (New Haven, 1973), p. 110.

42. Wayne C. Thompson, *In the Eye of the Storm: Kurt Riezler and the Crises of Modern Germany* (Iowa, 1980), pp. 50–51.

43. On these books, see Fritz Fischer, *War of Illusions: German Policies, 1911–1914* (New York, 1975), pp. 245–246, 261–263, 266, and Thompson, *In the Eye of the Storm*, pp. 42–59.

ing, quite possibly, Morocco—as an indemnity. The shipping magnate Albert Ballin discussed such a plan in London on July 25, and Bethmann himself outlined these peace terms on July 29, when he tried to secure British neutrality at the height of the crisis.[44] In the meantime, Bethmann steadfastly backed up Austria's refusal to treat its quarrel with Serbia as a European question. Well before the Austrian ultimatum had been written, he had decided that the crisis must end either with a diplomatic collapse for the Franco-Russian alliance, or with war. "If war comes from the east," he told Riezler on July 8, "so that we must fight for Austria-Hungary and not Austria-Hungary for us, then we have a chance of winning. If war does not come, if the Tsar does not want it or a dismayed France counsels peace, then we have a chance to divide the entente over this question."[45] On the night of July 29–30, when it seemed that the German and Austrian governments might be blamed for the war, and that he might lose the support of the German people, Bethmann briefly panicked, but on July 31, when he learned of the Russian mobilization, he immediately proceeded to begin the conflict, rightly believing that the German people would support him.

The German and Austrian governments bear the responsibility for the war because they, and they alone, found the existing European situation intolerable and risked war to overturn it. While the French, Russian, and British governments willingly faced the war, they would have been happy to settle the crisis within the existing diplomatic framework and had no immediate aims of their own which threatened the security of the German and Austrian empires. Moreover, whereas the Austrian government had some reason for believing that its survival might be at stake, the German government, tragically, had none. We have seen that Germany's lack of extensive overseas holdings had in no way impeded its economic development, and nothing suggests that colonies were becoming more necessary in 1914. But Bethmann lacked enough realism to appreciate the essentially symbolic importance of overseas acquisitions, or enough cynicism or skill to continue trying to satisfy German public opinion with minor successes, which had

44. Kaiser, "Germany and the Origins of the First World War," pp. 467–468.

45. Kurt Riezler, *Tagebücher, Aufsätze, Dokumente*, ed. Karl Dietrich Erdmann (Göttingen, 1972), pp. 183–184.

failed to help the government much during the second Moroccan crisis.

Attempts to blame the outbreak of the war upon military planning, miscalculation, or misunderstanding do not take sufficient account of political and diplomatic realities. The Russian decision for a general mobilization on July 30, which led in turn to the German general mobilization and declarations of war on France and Russia on August 1, and the Schlieffen Plan, which forced Germany to begin the war with an attack upon Belgium and France, reflected the political aims of the governments involved and of their opponents. Russia mobilized against both Germany and Austria-Hungary because Sazonov had become convinced that Vienna was determined to deal unilaterally with Serbia and that Berlin would stand behind Vienna. He was right on both counts. The Schlieffen Plan reflected the German desire to use the war to defeat both France and Russia, and to secure a much larger empire at their expense. Bethmann was not interested in a simple defensive war against Russia—although for a moment the emperor William II, who always shrank from war in a crisis, did show some interest in such a solution.

Bethmann has a reputation for idealism. His idealism was real enough, but it did not help either him or his nation in 1914. He did not believe that war would help defeat Social Democracy, but he had stated publicly in February 1912 that the German people had "a deep longing . . . for aims worth fighting for." Now, in order to make Germany a world power, he was willing to execute this "leap in the dark," his "most difficult duty."[46] Another German chancellor might also have fallen victim to contemporary imperialist and social Darwinist rhetoric, but it was Bethmann who did so. He therefore left himself open, as Gerald Feldman has suggested, to the accusation of having shared the illusions of the society which he was supposed to govern.[47] The result was a war which left both Berlin and the other major European governments as well with the impossible task not only of bringing the war to a successful conclusion, but also of making gains which might enable them to justify the enormous costs of the conflict to their own people. Their in-

46. Fischer, *War of Illusions*, p. 104; Riezler, *Tagebücher*, p. 185.
47. Gerald D. Feldman, *Army, Industry, and Labor in Germany, 1914–1918* (Princeton, 1966), p. 145.

ability to fulfill this hopeless task determined the subsequent course of European history.

The First World War

War and Politics, 1914–1918: The Problem of Victory

The First World War made demands upon European governments which they simply could not meet. After the illusion of a quick victory vanished in late 1914, governments found themselves in an inescapable dilemma. They could only retain the confidence of their peoples by winning a complete victory over their opponents, but they lacked the means necessary to bring such a victory about. Forced by the war to make unprecedented demands upon their constituents, governments adopted grandiose war aims in an attempt to justify these enormous sacrifices. Inevitably, given the contemporary political and intellectual climate, these aims were based upon the ideas of imperialism and nationalism. War aims became even more sweeping as the strain of the war brought down governments in eastern Europe and Asia, thereby opening up new possibilities for formal and informal imperialism. The end of the war and its aftermath, however, exposed the essential fallacy behind the conflict. While the governments that had failed to win the war collapsed entirely, the winners found that victory could not possibly compensate their peoples for their sacrifices.

Despite many private reservations, the governments that embarked upon the first general European conflict of the modern political era generally refused to accept anything less than total victory over their opponents. Confronted during the first year of the war by neutral proposals for a compromise peace, the belligerent governments uniformly replied that any generally acceptable terms would be immediately rejected by their peoples. Within another year they refused to discuss a peace that would deprive them of substantial gains at all.[1] Although no one has systematically investigated the source of the belief in essential victory, the course of

---

1. See the reports of Colonel House to Woodrow Wilson in February and March 1915, in Charles Seymour, ed., *The Intimate Papers of Colonel House,* 4 vols. (Boston, 1926–1928), I, 380–383, 402–403, and his reports of a year later, II, 137–148, 163–165. The

the war suggests that politicians understood the political climate correctly. In Britain, France, Italy, Russia, and Germany, successive civilian governments that failed to win the war fell from power, usually giving way to administrations that promised to fight more aggressively. A series of defeats led to revolution in Russia, and by mid-1917, important elements within the British, French, and Italian governments had all concluded that defeat would probably overturn their regimes as well.[2] A little more than a year later, this fate actually befell the ruling regimes of Turkey, Austria-Hungary, and Germany. Nowhere did the war strengthen the traditional order, as a few conservatives had hoped it might. Instead, it everywhere undermined confidence in existing institutions, forced governments to make unprecedented concessions to labor, and, as Bethmann had predicted, fostered the growth of social democracy and toppled many thrones.

The victory which governments strove for proved militarily impossible to achieve. After the initial war of movement on the western front came to an end late in 1914, trench lines and machine guns made decisive battles almost impossible. Military authorities, whose prestige would also depend largely upon the conclusion of the conflict, never gave up hope of total victory, but never managed to secure it. On the eastern front both the Germans and the Russians occasionally scored some impressive tactical successes, but never managed to destroy the opposing forces. In the west lines remained essentially frozen until 1918, and even then neither the Germans nor the Allies managed to break through enemy lines and achieve a decisive military victory.[3] European governments, having generally ruled out diplomacy as a means of settling the conflict, had no choice but to assemble more and more men and equipment, readying their armies for periodic offensives which only increased loss of life. The strain of the fighting eventually pushed soldiers beyond the limits of obedience. As John Keegan has pointed out, the troops of almost all the major European ar-

---

Allies in the spring of 1916 rejected Wilson's offer to try to mediate a peace on relatively favorable terms, backed by a threat of American intervention: see Ernest R. May, *The World War and American Isolation, 1914–1917* (Cambridge, Mass., 1959), pp. 352–360.

2. Paul Guinn, *British Strategy and Politics, 1914 to 1918* (Oxford, 1965), pp. 240–251.

3. Jehuda L. Wallach. *The Dogma of the Battle of Annihilation: The Theories of Clausewitz and Schlieffen and Their Impact on the German Conduct of Two World Wars* (Westport, Conn., 1986), pp. 165–166, 188–189.

mies refused to fight at least once during the war, generally at the moment when their total number of men killed in battle equaled the number of infantry in the field.[4]

Frustrated by their generals' and admirals' failure to achieve victory, civilian leaders tried to exert more control over military policy, but without much success. As early as 1915, leading British and French politicians had begun to doubt the wisdom of pouring more men into the western front, and by early 1917 both the British and the French governments suspected that total victory might not be possible. But instead of seeking peace, the British and French undertook military operations in the Mediterranean—at Salonika and the Dardanelles—from which they expected critical political benefits. When these operations failed both militarily and politically, they reluctantly agreed to new, even costlier offensives on the western front in 1916 and 1917, with disastrous results.

Paradoxically, despite repeated military failures, military leaders seem to have enjoyed a better reputation among the civilian population than politicians, and the idea of total victory remained politically popular despite the military stalemate. Politicians therefore treated their generals quite gingerly. In France, Aristide Briand managed to edge General Joffre out of the Supreme Command in late 1916, but after Briand's fall from power the Ribot government swallowed its objections to the Nivelle offensive in the spring of 1917. After that offensive led to mutinies in much of the French army, Marshal Pétain and Premier Painlevé agreed to remain on the defensive until large American forces arrived. Clemenceau, who became premier in November 1917, proclaimed a policy of total war but did not order any new offensives until the German army had clearly exhausted itself in the summer of 1918.[5]

A recent study of British strategy and war aims highlights the British response to this dilemma.[6] Although the British govern-

---

4. John Keegan, *The Face of Battle: A Study of Agincourt, Waterloo, and the Somme* (New York, 1976), pp. 270–271. Keegan gives an excellent overview of land warfare in the First World War.

5. Jere Clemens King, *Generals and Politicians: Conflict between France's High Command, Parliament, and Government, 1914–18* (Berkeley, 1951), pp. 115–170. The interplay of strategy and politics in France still deserves more detailed study. The problem was more complicated there than in Britain or perhaps even in Germany, since anticlerical Republican politicians regarded most generals as Catholic, monarchist, and dangerous to the regime.

6. David French, *British Strategy and War Aims, 1914–1916* (London, 1986).

ment called from the beginning of the war for the overthrow of the existing government of Germany, it planned to take advantage of its economic strength and initial lack of a large army to let its allies do the bulk of the fighting, at least until the Central Powers were exhausted. As early as 1915, the Liberal cabinet ordered the Dardanelles expedition as an alternative to western offensives, but failed to push it through to a successful conclusion. Even in the fall of 1915, they hoped that the war would not last through 1916, and that Kitchener's new army could apply the coup de grace to the Germans. But the failure of the Dardanelles campaign and German successes in the east, which threatened to knock the Russians out of the war, forced the British to agree to the Somme offensive in the summer of 1916 despite dubious prospects for success. Even after the Somme disaster, the press and the public apparently still hoped for a complete victory, and Lloyd George talked himself into power in late 1916 as the advocate of a "knock-out blow." Once in power he showed much more skepticism toward the possibility of a victory on the western front, but he reluctantly agreed to a new offensive in the fall of 1917 under the pressure of submarine warfare and air raids upon England. The Paaschandaele offensive, which failed disastrously, typified the predicament that all civilian governments faced as a result of their commitment to complete victory. "Perhaps one must deplore, not the War Cabinet's lack of political courage," Paul Guinn has written, "but rather their understandable reluctance to veto an operation which of course just *might* succeed, uniquely because of their own doubts."[7]

Nowhere, however, did the civilian government fail more disastrously to control events than in Germany. Bethmann's situation was more difficult than that of his French and British counterparts for several reasons: the greater prestige and constitutional authority enjoyed by the military and naval leaders, Germany's commitment to extravagant war aims, and, perhaps more than anything else, the fairly steady stream of German victories between 1914 and the summer of 1918, which suggested that victory might be just around the corner. Bethmann knew as early as 1915 that total victory had become quite unlikely, and he also knew that unrestricted submarine warfare—the only major remaining untried military option—would probably bring the United States into the

7. Guinn, *British Strategy and Politics*, pp. 243–253.

war and doom Germany.[8] Yet the parties, the people, the emperor, and Bethmann himself reacted to two years of losses by ousting War Minister von Falkenhayn, who had also doubted the possibility of total victory, and replacing him with the enormously popular Hindenburg and Ludendorff, who would try anything to achieve it.[9] Not long after, in early 1917, Bethmann reluctantly assented to the introduction of unrestricted submarine warfare—partly, perhaps, because he simply wanted to remain in office, but also because, as he well knew, only complete victory could possibly satisfy the ambitions of the parties, industry, the military and naval staffs, and the German people.

Military and civilian leaders also tried to win the war through economic mobilization. After the stalemate on the western front developed, British and German military authorities began to argue that superior production of munitions could produce victory. Both the British and the Germans apparently preferred to accept their generals' excuse for failure—that munition production was inadequate—than to believe that the military authorities simply did not know how to win the war, or that decisive victory was not possible. In Britain the military leadership blamed the failure of their spring 1915 offensive on a shortage of shells and brought about the formation of the First Coalition and the accession of Lloyd George as minister of munitions. A vast expansion of the armaments industry enabled the British to expend huge amounts of ammunition during the Somme offensive of 1916, but without success. Nonetheless, as Gerd Hardach has pointed out, the German High Command, led by Ludendorff, began arguing at the same time that increased German armaments production could lead to victory and called for a "Hindenburg Program" to raise production of steel and munitions. The government adopted the program after Falkenhayn's dismissal in late 1916, even though German transport and supplies of raw materials seemed clearly unable to meet its requirements. The program had serious internal economic consequences during 1917 and 1918, but the High Command continued to argue that full economic mobilization held the key to victory almost until the end of the war.[10]

8. Jarausch, *Enigmatic Chancellor*, pp. 264–307.
9. See esp. Feldman, *Army, Industry, and Labor*, pp. 141–145.
10. Gerd Hardach, *The First World War, 1914–18* (Berkeley, 1977), pp. 55–73, 77–96.

The economic demands of the first general European conflict of the industrial era outran Europe's productive and financial capacities. The increases in German arms production led to coal shortages, serious transportation bottlenecks, and serious skilled labor shortages. In German agriculture, shortages of labor and equipment, combined with the Allied blockade, caused rations of most foodstuffs to drop to between 50 and 10 percent of prewar consumption levels.[11] The British substantially increased food production and decreased imports, but the French had vastly to increase imports to avoid severe food shortages, at a considerable cost in foreign exchange.[12] Because of the German occupation of northwestern France, French heavy industrial production dropped severely, thereby increasing French dependence on foreign trade. Another effect of the war was the rise of new national industries to replace foreign imports, such as German dyestuffs or Chilean nitrates, which had become unavailable because of the war.[13]

On the whole, the Germans kept their armies in the field by a combination of drastic cuts in civilian consumption and huge domestic borrowing, while the British and French imported many essential goods and raised critical loans overseas, especially, of course, in the United States. The British had exhausted their credit at the moment of American entry into the war in April 1917. By the time of the armistice, all the governments involved had incurred unprecedented financial liabilities—debts which could never be paid out of normal resources, and which the major powers therefore planned to liquidate with indemnities from their defeated opponents. These problems had enormous consequences after the war and helped bring about the Second World War.

Hamstrung by military realities, yet under tremendous pressure to control events and bring the war to a successful conclusion, European governments adopted a variety of other expedients without much success. Diplomacy, which they rejected as a means of settling the war, focused on attempts to win it. Both sides bid shamelessly for the support of neutral countries like Turkey, Italy, Greece, Bulgaria, Rumania, and even Mexico, and although most of these states eventually entered the war, none of them contrib-

11. Ibid., p. 119. By the end of the war only potatoes and sugar were rationed at more than half their prewar consumption levels.
12. Ibid., pp. 123–133.
13. Ibid., pp. 77–91, both for basic facts and references to individual monographs.

uted much to victory. Since in many cases the military value of these new allies was obviously low, one suspects that the governments who enticed them into the war simply used their entry to boost morale. In addition, the Allies in particular promised each other enormous gains in order to persuade them to continue the fighting—even though, in retrospect, it seems quite doubtful that any of them needed so much persuading. The British and the French promised the Turkish straits to Russia, the Adriatic coast to Italy, Transylvania to Rumania, and large parts of Asiatic Turkey to each other.[14]

By 1917 the strain of the war had become too great for one government to bear. In Russia, where the government had failed abysmally either to prosecute the war successfully or to manage the wartime economy, the prestige of tsarism had collapsed completely by early 1917. Mutinies in St. Petersburg in February led to a revolutionary coup d'état by the Duma and the Soviet of Workers' Deputies. These two bodies formed the Provisional Government and forced the tsar to abdicate in March. The foreign minister, the liberal Paul Miliukov, still supported most of the tsarist government's war aims, but the Petrograd Soviet immediately began pressing for quick general peace without annexations or indemnities, and Miliukov had to resign in May. The Provisional Government hoped that the international Socialist movement might force the various allied and enemy governments to agree to a peace without annexations or indemnities, but neither the Allies nor the Germans would agree to these demands. The Provisional Government's failure to end the war contributed mightily to its downfall in November.[15] The Bolshevik government, which initially counted upon world revolution to end the war, refused in early 1918 to accept the harsh terms of peace offered by the Central Powers, but after the Germans had resumed their advance, Lenin insisted upon accepting the Brest-Litovsk peace, which stripped the new government of the Baltic provinces and the Ukraine.

The Austro-Hungarian government also feared for the consequences of an indefinite war, and in the spring of 1917 the new

14. Horst Günther Linke, *Das zarische Russland und der erste Weltkrieg: Diplomatie und Kriegsziele 1914–17* (Munich, 1982), argues convincingly that the danger of tsarist Russia dropping out of the war, which made its allies so forthcoming with respect to war aims, never really existed before the March 1917 revolution.

15. Rex A. Wade, *The Russian Search for Peace, February–October 1917* (Stanford, 1969).

emperor Charles made a secret and dramatic peace overture to the French government. The British and French decided not to respond after the Italian government refused to drop its territorial demands upon Austria-Hungary. When Clemenceau revealed the approach one year later, Charles immediately reaffirmed his loyalty to the German alliance.[16]

The drive for victory reflected a promise which every major government made to its people: that the peace terms must make any recurrence of the conflict—which every government, of course, blamed upon its enemies—absolutely impossible. The same determination to establish a new basis for peace lay behind an entirely different kind of war aim. As the war went on, socialists and liberals increasingly voiced the hope that peace would lead to a more just and peaceful international order based on general disarmament, an end to trade barriers, and perhaps a new world organization. Although many Europeans adopted these views independently, only the American government based its program of war aims upon them, and President Wilson, of course, became the symbol of the proposed new order during 1918.[17] Wilson's ideas, however, did not command universal support even in the United States, where the Republican opposition, like the other Allied governments, stood for total victory and a harsh peace. Such ideas, in any case, were not necessarily *alternatives* to complete victory. Within the Allied powers, proponents of these ideas often argued that the war must also end with the destruction of "Prussian militarism" and the creation of a peaceful Germany.[18]

In late 1918, Wilson's Fourteen Points, combined with the deterioration in Germany's military and economic position, helped bring the war to a close without a decisive military victory. Late in September 1918, just as Bulgaria was signing an armistice with the Allies, Ludendorff realized that Germany might be defeated and advised William II to appoint a liberal civilian government to ne-

16. Z. A. B. Zeman, *The Gentlemen Negotiators: A Diplomatic History of the First World War* (New York, 1971), pp. 121–161.

17. The best survey of the spread of internationalism is probably Arno J. Mayer, *Political Origins of the New Diplomacy, 1917–1918* (New Haven, 1959). Stevenson, *French War Aims*, pp. 11–25, and V. H. Rothwell, *British War Aims and Peace Diplomacy, 1914–1918* (London, 1971), pp. 210–213, note the independent development of such ideas in France and Britain.

18. See Arno Mayer, *The Politics and Diplomacy of Peacemaking: Containment and Counterrevolution at Versailles, 1918–1919* (New York, 1967), pp. 55–61.

gotiate an armistice with Wilson. The strategy worked, and Colonel House persuaded the Allies to grant an armistice that would leave the German empire intact. The French government insisted upon the occupation of the German Rhineland but gave up the dream of total victory, partly because the four-year quest for it had left the French in a state of complete financial dependence on the United States. Even the British and French generals also agreed to the armistice; only the American Pershing called for a fight to the finish.[19]

Having admitted its failure to win the war, the German High Command now provoked the German revolution by trying to reverse itself at the last moment. The German government's request for an armistice in October was an obvious admission of defeat, but Ludendorff wanted an armistice that would enable the German army to resume fighting if the Allies proposed unacceptable peace terms. The military authorities therefore urged the government to refuse the harsh Allied terms. The resulting delay provoked the German revolution, as the German people, led by sailors and soldiers, demanded the removal of the regime which had failed to win the war and now seemed unable to conclude it. The imperial regime's confession of impotence had doomed it to share the fate of the Russian and Austro-Hungarian empires. The fear of all the European regimes, that only victory could redeem them in the eyes of their own people, had proven true.[20] The war, which had become a test of political endurance, ended with the collapse of the German empire.

Imperialism, Nationalism, and War Aims

Although total victory rapidly became a *sine qua non* for all the major contestants in the war, it was not a *ne plus ultra*. As the conflict dragged on, all the powers formulated ambitious programs of war aims to be put into effect when victory was won. Inevitably, these

---

19. These developments are well covered by Stevenson, *French War Aims*, pp. 110–132.

20. Arthur Rosenberg, *Imperial Germany: The Birth of the German Republic, 1871–1918* (Oxford, 1931), pp. 241–274. Rosenberg himself clearly shared the German people's anger at the imperial regime's failure to win the war. Though himself a revolutionary Socialist, he supported the government's decision to enter the war but complained bitterly (pp. 73–80) that its antiquated structure doomed the German people.

aims revolved around the issues of imperialism and nationalism that had dominated international politics during the four decades before the war. Every major contestant sought both to increase its empire and to extend the application of the principle of nationality to help itself and hurt its enemies.

The war naturally favored the growth of imperialism. Not only did imperialist predictions of a worldwide struggle for planetary resources seem to have come true, but imperialists also had very definite war aims. Colonial societies counted upon the war to realize their fondest dreams, and European governments, desperate to make gains that would justify the sacrifices of their peoples, adopted extreme positions more easily than they had before 1914. The war raised imperialists to positions of greater power in virtually every participating government. The war also encouraged the growth of projects for economic self-sufficiency, particularly because of the disruption of the world economy. Meanwhile, the collapse of the governments of Russia, Turkey, and Austria-Hungary opened up vast new territories for expansion—an opportunity which the Germans and the Allies successively tried to exploit.

In the meantime, the war led not only to the most far-reaching triumphs of European nationalism to date but also to the emergence of some of nationalism's most frightening potential consequences. National questions within the major belligerent powers became much more serious during the war. Thus the British government, pleading the excuse of the war, delayed Irish Home Rule, leading to armed risings within Ireland. The central and eastern European empires also tried to clamp down. We have seen that the authoritarian states of Europe—with the partial exception of Austria—had increasingly adopted extreme nationalism as a basis for their rule in the decades before the war. This tendency became more pronounced upon the outbreak of the war, which the German and Russian governments proclaimed to be a struggle between Teutons and Slavs. To secure their power, elements within the eastern empires adopted new and sometimes horrifying strategies to strengthen their dominant nationalities against minorities, both within their homelands and within territories which they planned to annex. Some of these measures set precedents for even more extraordinary measures during the Second World War.

Virtually every European government tried to turn the nationality principle to its own advantage. The major powers blessed the claims of national groups within enemy territories, while planning to establish their direct or indirect rule over foreign nationals in territory they hoped to acquire. The powers struggled torturously to reconcile the well-known difficulty of ruling foreign subjects with their territorial claims. In the end, the powers' general endorsement of the idea of nationalism combined with the successive collapse of the authority of the Russian, Austro-Hungarian, and German empires to redraw the map of central and eastern Europe.

To Germany the war seemed to offer the opportunity to achieve the world power status it had coveted in the years before 1914. Only with difficulty, however, could the government develop a program of achievable war aims. Bethmann, who vainly tried to keep the discussion of war aims under control until his fall in July 1917, well understood the dilemmas of Germany's position, all the more so because he knew better than most that complete victory was not likely. Indeed, had the chancellor analyzed Germany's international position as acutely before July 1914 as he did afterward, the war might not have taken place.

Literally from the moment of the outbreak of the war, the chancellor faced a variety of constituencies determined to use the war to revolutionize Germany's international position. The High Command, the navy, the Pan-Germans, the Colonial Office, industrialists, and almost all of the political parties supported different programs of expansion, most of which included the retention of considerable control over Belgium, the annexation of parts of northern France, frontier changes in the east at the expense of Poland, and a large, unified Central African empire. To realize this program they counted upon a complete victory over all Germany's enemies, including Britain. While many of these constituencies disagreed violently over Germany's domestic political future, they all expected Germany to derive a large profit from the war.[21]

Bethmann avoided any precise statement of his war aims but he certainly intended to maintain thorough German control of Belgium, to annex the Longwy-Briey basin from France, and to expand somewhat into Russian Poland. But he privately stated again and again that Germany's experience to date showed how difficult the assimilation of foreigners had become, and that actual annexa-

21. Hans Wilhelm Gatzke, *Germany's Drive to the West: A Study of Germany's Western War Aims during the First World War* (Baltimore, 1950), pp. 7–62, summarizes German opinion in the early stages of the war.

tions must be kept to a minimum. He himself put more stock in the ideas of leading *Weltpolitiker* like Albert Ballin, Walter Rathenau, Hans Delbrück, and Colonial Secretary Wilhelm Solf. Like Bethmann, these men regretted the conflict with Britain and intermittently hoped for a separate Anglo-German peace. To assure Germany's economic future, they planned to create a united Central African empire at the expense of France, Belgium, Portugal—and, in more optimistic moments, the British as well—and to create a huge protected market in central Europe, including Germany, Austria-Hungary, Belgium, a newly recreated Poland, the smaller Balkan states, and possibly France. Such programs, of course, carried the name of "Mitteleuropa."[22]

The whole war aims controversy shows not only how the divisions within German political life became worse because of the war but also how difficult it had become to make major territorial additions to a modern state without disturbing various delicate balances. Thus, the Pan-Germans' extravagant plans for annexation must have involved either the subjugation or the evacuation of millions of non-Germans, or their incorporation as Reich citizens, which Bethmann knew could only create new political problems. The Mitteleuropa plan—which to its most important advocate, Friedrich Naumann, would involve an economic union of free central and eastern European peoples—angered the Junkers and Prussian civil servants, who feared competition from central European agricultural products.[23] Plans for Mitteleuropa, moreover, assumed that some form of Allied blockade would continue to restrict Germany's access to world markets after the war—but prewar trade figures showed clearly that central European markets could not possibly have compensated for the loss of British and American markets. Indeed, even *during* the war Bethmann opposed the immediate establishment of a central European economic federation because it might make it more difficult to continue Germany's essential trade with neutrals![24]

Bethmann stuck tenaciously to his colonial aims. Thus in early 1916, in an official reply to secret Belgian feelers for a separate peace, the German government made it quite clear that it would

22. Meyer, *Mitteleuropa*, pp. 194–290; Jarausch, *Enigmatic Chancellor*, pp. 185–229.
23. Jarausch, *Enigmatic Chancellor*, pp. 185–229.
24. Fritz Fischer, *Germany's Aims in the First World War* (London, 1967), pp. 201–202.

insist upon an economic agreement that would completely open the Belgian Congo to German exploitation; this accomplished, "it will not matter very much whether the Congo belongs to Belgium or passes to Germany."[25] Bethmann's reply to Wilson's mediation proposals of December 1916 called for "guarantees" for Germany in Belgium, changes in the German-French and German-Polish frontiers, and "restitution of colonies in the form of an agreement which would give Germany colonies adequate for her population and economic interest"—a claim that could be interpreted to mean that Germany needed a larger empire than either France or Britain. (Significantly, the German note also demanded an end to wartime trade restrictions and "reasonable treaties of commerce," suggesting that the chancellor realized that prosperity depended upon the restoration of world trade.) By this time, Solf at the Colonial Office had concluded that "since the Congo and the Portuguese colonies would not at first bring anything in," Germany must acquire some more profitable French colonies in North Africa as well.[26] Five months later, in a rare public statement of government policy, which clearly alluded to a future compromise peace with Britain, Solf once again claimed Angola, Mozambique, and part of the Congo, but he offered to cede Southwest Africa to Britain—an obvious attempt to revive the bargain which Bethmann had tried and failed to conclude with London from 1911 to 1914.[27] Since Bethmann planned to disappoint the extreme right both by limiting formal annexations to a minimum and by making major concessions to the left in domestic policy, he simply *had* to try to realize the colonial programs which parties like the National Liberals and the Center supported. Britain, however, would not have agreed either to a vastly enlarged German empire or to the kind of "guarantees" which Bethmann had in mind for Belgium. Under the circumstances, it is not really surprising that Bethmann in early 1917 finally bowed to the will of the navy, the Supreme Command, and the emperor and agreed to submarine warfare. The German nation, its imperialist dreams now sealed with blood, would ob-

25. Ibid., p. 224.

26. Gatzke, *Germany's Drive to the West*, pp. 139–144, and Fischer, *Germany's Aims*, pp. 317–318. Similar aims had emerged when Bethmann asked interested ministries for their war aims somewhat earlier, before issuing his own invitation to the entente to begin peace negotiations; Fischer, *Germany's Aims*, pp. 313–322.

27. Fischer, *Germany's Aims*, pp. 359–360.

viously have regarded any achievable peace as a complete betrayal as long as any hope of victory remained. The chancellor, who had done much to spread imperialist beliefs and still shared more than a few of them, had to agree to submarine warfare as long as it offered the slimmest hope of complete victory.[28]

Bethmann's fall in July 1917 stemmed from the impossibility of satisfying the various German factions, whose appetites had all increased during the war. Despite his acquiescence in submarine warfare, the High Command still rightly mistrusted his position on war aims, as did Stresemann's National Liberals and, for different reasons, Erzberger of the Center, who felt that the U-boat campaign had to be abandoned to make peace. So it was that after a center-left coalition passed a resolution calling for a peace without "forced annexations of territory and political, economic, or financial oppressions," the High Command used Bethmann's failure to prevent the resolution as the pretext for his dismissal. His attempts at compromise had become impossible.[29]

In late 1917, the collapse of Russia and the November revolution enabled the High Command and two new chancellors, Michaelis and Hertling, to implement a policy not dissimilar to Bethmann's throughout eastern Europe: the establishment of German hegemony through the creation of vassal states, including Poland, Finland, the Baltic region, the Ukraine, the Don basin, and the Caucasus. During 1918 both the High Command and elements of the civilian bureaucracy worked very carefully to secure German political and economic hegemony over this entire area, even at the expense of good relations with Austria-Hungary or Turkey.[30] Germany had effectively secured a new political and economic hinterland in eastern Europe.

This, however, was not enough. Rather than attempt to make peace in the west, the High Command tried once more for total victory and maintained demands for the annexation of Longwy-Briey, the reduction of Belgium to vassal status, and the annexation of vast territories in Central Africa.[31] During the last year of the war the government tried to satisfy the Conservatives and the High Command by sticking to its maximum war aims program, while trying to appease the center and left by proceeding with a

28. Jarausch, *Engimatic Chancellor*, pp. 295–302.
29. Ibid., p. 373; Mayer, *Political Origins of the New Diplomacy*, pp. 128–135.
30. Fischer, *Germany's Aims*, pp. 510–586.
31. Ibid., pp. 475–608.

limited reform of the unequal Prussian suffrage. Only the impending collapse of the German army in the fall of 1918 led to a change in policy.

The German government's sweeping plans for annexations inevitably raised very difficult nationalities problems. Bethmann, as we have seen, had to respect the annexationist demands of the High Command and the Pan-Germans, who planned to take large parts of Belgium, France, Poland, and Russia and to rule their populations dictatorially or simply drive out non-German elements and resettle them. But while the chancellor himself wanted to alter Germany's military and economic boundaries both in the east and in the west, he opposed incorporating large new numbers of non-Germans within the empire because he knew that they would be new divisive elements. In public Bethmann made some dramatic gestures toward the Pan-German position, both by labeling the conflict as a struggle between Teutons and Slavs and by referring to the Belgian Flemings as German peoples who must not once again be abandoned to "Latinization." Privately, however, he laid more complex plans for Belgium, Poland, and the Russian Baltic provinces in order to secure the benefits of annexation without its drawbacks.

Thus in Belgium, the "guarantees" which Bethmann consistently argued that Germany would require always included naval and military bases, economic union, and control of the Belgian railways. Under one program drawn up by two of his closest collaborators, Belgium would have adopted Germany's currency, tariffs, taxes, and social legislation and given up its army, while Germany continued to rule the territory militarily. This ingenious proposal, which may have been inspired by German difficulties in Alsace-Lorraine, would essentially have laid all the duties of imperial citizenship upon the Belgian population while withholding all of the corresponding rights.[32] The imperial government also planned a similar form of "autonomy" for Poland and for the Russian Baltic provinces, where the Germans would retain military and economic control while yielding some local political rights.[33]

32. Gatzke, *Germany's Drive to the West*, pp. 13–14.

33. Fischer, *Germany's Aims*, pp. 260–279, 450–472; Jarausch, *Enigmatic Chancellor*, pp. 185–229. Despite the enormous controversy in Germany over Fischer's aims, nothing in the work of his major antagonist, Gerhard Ritter, *The Sword and the Sceptre: The Problem of Militarism in Germany*, vols. 3–4 (Coral Gables, 1972), really refutes this picture of German aims.

Vienna and Berlin proclaimed the creation of an independent Poland in November 1916, but their hopes for a large Polish volunteer army did not materialize.[34]

On one major point Bethmann adopted the radical demands of the Pan-Germans and the German military. Emperor William II wanted to clear territory annexed from France and Belgium for settlement by German war veterans. Although Bethmann rejected those demands, in the east he adopted similar schemes developed by the Pan-Germans and the *Ostmarkverein* and supported by numerous professors and industrialists. The German High Command was determined to eliminate the Polish salient which had allowed the Russians to threaten to cut off East Prussia at the outset of the war by annexing a "frontier strip" of substantial dimensions. Everyone involved realized, however, that to annex the Polish population would simply strengthen Polish elements in Silesia, Posen, and West Prussia, who would long for union with whatever Poland emerged from the war. As a result, the scheme adopted in principle by the government called for the removal of the Polish and Jewish population of the frontier strip, followed by resettlement of the area with Germans.[35] Unfortunately, as the promoters of prewar schemes for internal colonization in the east had already discovered, the German people had apparently lost their pioneer spirit, or rather taken it to North and South America. A different solution emerged: the first contingent of new settlers would come from the German minority in Russia, whom the tsarist government had dispossessed. To realize these strategic goals without jeopardizing the German empire's national character, Bethmann was willing to resort to the movement of populations, at least on a limited basis. The military successfully insisted upon this policy after his fall.[36]

The German government also brazenly demanded that its ally

---

34. May, *The Passing of the Hapsburg Monarchy, 1914–1918*, 2 vols. (Philadelphia, 1966), I, 154–169; Fischer, *Germany's Aims*, pp. 236–246.

35. Geiss, *Die Polnischen Grenzstreifen*, esp. pp. 41–95.

36. Bethmann did not initially believe that the whole population could be cleared, but the High Command seems to have planned on substantial evacuations and pushed through its policy in July 1918. Geiss, *Die Polnischen Grenzstreifen*, pp. 91–95, 117–147. Proof that Bethmann sincerely believed in these plans comes from his discussions with Austrian leaders, in which he insisted that part of the restored kingdom of Congress Poland must be set aside to make room for the expelled population from the frontier strip. See for example Ritter, *Sword and Sceptre*, III, 105–106.

Austria-Hungary strengthen the position both of the Germans and the Magyars within its territories. During the war several leading German officials discussed the possibility of an *Anschluss* of Austro-Germans with the empire should the Central Powers lose the conflict, and in the last three weeks of the war, as Austria-Hungary clearly began to break up, General Ludendorff toyed with the idea of a military expedition to bring the Austro-Germans into the German empire. Developments within Germany made this impossible, but the extreme nationalism bred by the war survived into the 1920s and 1930s.[37]

The Russian government also pursued sweeping war aims, and encountered similar problems regarding the rights of nationalities. The Russians hoped to add both Austrian and Prussian portions of Poland to their empire and to expand at Turkish expense, both in Constantinople and the Caucasus. They also planned to transform the internal structure of Austria-Hungary to strengthen the Slavs.[38] But while encouraging the hopes of some foreign minorities, the government resorted to an even harsher nationalities policy within Russia. The grand duke Nicholai Nicholaevich, commander-in-chief of the Russian army, issued a manifesto promising the Poles of Germany and Austria-Hungary union with their brethren, and another one promising the liberation of all the Slavs living within Austria-Hungary.[39] The Polish proclamation inaugurated a tremendous struggle in St. Petersburg between moderates who wanted to give the Poles more rights and conservatives who wanted to deprive the proclamation of any meaning. On the Turkish front, a Russian general promised to create an autonomous Armenia, and similarly aroused those who feared the effect of such a step upon Russian's Armenian minority. Meanwhile, the Jewish and German minorities within Russia suffered heavily from new measures. In the first year of the war, Russian generals, taking advantage of their authority within military areas, expelled the Jews from large parts of western Russia—the territories to which the law had previously confined them. This step caused untold suffering, but paradoxically allowed moderate civilians in the

---

37. Z. A. B. Zeman, *The Break-up of the Hapsburg Empire, 1914–1918: A Study in National and Social Revolution* (London, 1961), pp. 104, 148–150, 233–234; Peter Grupp, *Deutsche Außenpolitik im Schatten von Versailles, 1918–20* (Paderhorn, 1988), pp. 213–214.

38. Linke, *Das zarische Russland*, pp. 37–61.

39. Zeman, *Break-up of the Hapsburg Empire*, pp. 53, 64.

Council of Ministers to lift most of the old restrictions on Jewish residency.[40] The government also confiscated the land of German settlers, which the army authorities hoped to redistribute to Russian soldiers.[41] And in Eastern Galicia, the mostly Ukrainian-inhabited territory which the Russian army occupied in the first year of the war, the government instituted a wholly Russian administration and persecuted Ukrainian activists and Jews.[42]

After the Russian people abandoned the tsarist government in March 1917, national questions and war aims became critical issues for the new Provisional Government. While the Petrograd Soviet called for an immediate peace without annexations or indemnities and nationalist movements claimed independence in Finland and the Ukraine, the Provisional Government secretly adhered to tsarist war aims and tried to continue the war.[43] This of course increased the popularity of the anti-war Bolsheviks, who seized power in November 1917. Their immediate conclusion of an armistice with the Central Powers left a vacuum in the non-Russian borderlands which both the Central Powers and the Allies tried to fill.

The war aims discussion took a somewhat different course in Britain and France. The British and French governments managed to keep public discussion of their war aims under much tighter control than the German, partly because their people (though not, of course, their soldiers) suffered much less, and partly because they saw themselves as somewhat more satiated powers. But British and French imperialist constituencies gained ground as the war continued and eventually realized some cherished goals. The main proponents of further expansion had not changed. In Britain they included the self-governing colonies, especially in the southern hemisphere, and a small group of extremely vocal imperialist politicians who secured key positions during the war. In France the *parti colonial* seized upon the conflict, the threatened breakup of the Ottoman empire, and the need for major gains after the war to achieve some longstanding dreams. Both countries received

---

40. Discussions on this question may be followed in Michael Cherniavsky, *Prologue to Revolution: Notes of A. N. Iakhontov on the Secret Meetings of the Council of Ministers, 1915* (Englewood Cliffs, 1967), pp. 56–72.

41. Link, *Das zarische Russland*, pp. 61–73, 129–167, 206–226.

42. Adam Ulam *Russia's Failed Revolutions*, pp. 241–242.

43. Ibid., pp. 227–234.

substantial help from their empires during the war and enlarged them after it was over.

Great Britain entered the war with the fewest declared war aims but eventually added far more territory to its empire than any other power. Many new aims reflected the demands of the British empire. The governments of Canada, Australia, New Zealand, and the Union of South Africa all entered the conflict at once, but the price of assistance from the self-governing colonies was London's assent to their own imperialist schemes. The British government willingly paid that price. The South African government easily won London's assent to its annexation of Southwest Africa, while the Australians and New Zealanders successfully insisted upon retaining German New Guinea and Germany's South Pacific islands.[44] Meanwhile, India made an enormous contribution to the war, providing as many men as all the self-governing dominions combined, and effectively financing £367 million of the British war effort, or more than one-fourth of the amount that Britain borrowed from the United States.[45] Turkey's entry into the war also offered the British the opportunity to realize sweeping plans at the expense of the Ottoman empire. Having promised Constantinople to the Russians, the British staked out their own claims to Palestine and the Tigris and Euphrates valley in the Sykes-Picot agreement of 1916.[46]

Within the government, imperialists gained ground as frustration at the inconclusive course taken by the war grew. Since the era of Joseph Chamberlain, a mixed bag of tariff-reform Unionists and Liberal imperialists had continued to call for tariffs, national conscription, better public health, old age insurance, and the economic and institutional strengthening of Britain's ties with its empire.[47] The imperialists triumphed within the government late in 1916, when Lloyd George became prime minister, brought the politically active Alfred Milner into the cabinet, and eventually gave major roles to other leading imperialists such as Leopold Amery

44. Wm. Roger Louis, *Great Britain and Germany's Lost Colonies, 1914–1919* (Oxford, 1967), pp. 36–56.

45. Krishan G. Saini, "The Economic Aspects of India's Participation in the First World War," in DeWitt C. Ellinwood and S. D. Pradhan, eds., *India and World War I* (Columbia, Mo., 1978), pp. 144–153.

46. Jukka Nevakivi, *Britain, France, and the Arab Middle East, 1914–20* (London, 1969), pp. 13–44.

47. Scally, *Origins of the Lloyd George Coalition*, pp. 1–249.

and Lord Curzon. They brought a more determined cast of mind to the war and adopted a far more imperial strategy.

Thus, having become prime minister largely by demanding that the war end with a knock-out blow, Lloyd George gradually shifted Britain's military force from the western front to the Near and Middle East. No sooner had he taken office than he proposed a combined *anti-Austrian* offensive as the major Allied war effort for 1917. Although forced by developments beyond his control to agree to a further offensive on the western front late in 1917, Lloyd George in the following year began planning to withdraw troops from the western front, where he hoped to rely more on tanks and airplanes, while continuing the offensive against Turkey in the Middle East.[48] In the meantime, imperialists such as Milner, Curzon, and their disciples seized upon the opportunity to achieve two of the fondest dreams of prewar imperialism: the Cape-to-Cairo railway, which could be realized after the annexation of German East Africa, and "continuity of territory or of control between Egypt and India." Like some of their German counterparts, they also hoped to create a large preferential tariff unit to help survive in the competitive world economy which they expected to emerge from the war.[49]

In the dark winter of 1917–18, after the Bolshevik revolution and the beginning of the peace talks at Brest-Litovsk, Lloyd George toyed with the idea of reviving the pre-1914 European concert. A general imperialist peace could satisfy British, French, Italians, and Germans alike at the expense of the collapsing empires of the east, which now included Russia. Since the Allies could not defeat the Germans, Berlin might retain its newly won hegemonic position in eastern Europe, provided that it evacuated French, Belgian, Italian, and Serbian territories. The Allies would keep the German colonies (or at least most of them) and some new gains in Central Asia at the expense of the Turks and the Russians, which their own intervention in Russia hoped to secure. Lloyd George effectively intended to abandon the European balance of power in exchange

---

48. Guinn, *British Strategy and Politics*, pp. 209–263;

49. Louis, *Great Britain and Germany's Lost Colonies*, pp. 98–116; A. P. Thornton, *The Imperial Idea and Its Enemies: A Study in British Power* (New York, 1959), p. 188; Robert E. Bunselmayer, *The Cost of the War, 1914–1919: British Economic War Aims and the Origins of Reparation* (Hamden, Conn., 1975), pp. 21–51.

for new imperial gains.[50] He publicly outlined these terms on January 5, 1918, and disclaimed any intention of changing the German constitution. But the German government, encouraged by the collapse of Russia and unwilling to settle for less than total victory, prepared a new offensive on the western front again. As late as July 1918, the British still doubted the imminence of an Allied victory and planned to reduce their European forces further. The collapse of the Germans was a most welcome surprise. Curiously enough, the defeated German government soon revived the same fantasy: that the victors and vanquished alike might join in overthrowing the Bolsheviks and restoring the Russian economy, with gains for all.[51]

French war aims showed a remarkable similarity to German plans. Although the French took longer to develop their war aims, by 1916 a similar coalition of bureaucrats, soldiers, industrialists, and publicists argued for the same mix of "strategic rectification" of frontiers, annexation of enemy mineral resources, a large indemnity, a dominant position within Belgium, a larger empire, and a large preferential trade area. The entire French government and French public opinion, of course, expected the return of Alsace-Lorraine, but the General Staff and the Foreign Office also aimed from an early stage to detach the left bank of the Rhine from Germany proper and at the very least bring it into an alliance and a customs union with France. French industry, supported by the government, also planned to regain the Saar and secure deliveries of German coking coal as part of reparations. Meanwhile, the *parti colonial* worked diligently to secure a major share of Germany's colonies and to emerge with Syria—*la Syrie intégrale*, including Palestine—when the Ottoman empire was partitioned. The French empire made a major contribution to the war, providing 600,000 soldiers and about 184,000 workers during the conflict.

When Clemenceau took power in late 1917, he refused to discuss any war aim except victory. Perhaps because he himself could not foresee how the war would end, he never discussed peace terms even with his cabinet. After the armistice, however, he fol-

50. Guinn, *British Strategy and Politics*, pp. 274–278, 308–313; Michael Howard, *The Continental Commitment: The Dilemma of British Defense Policy in the Era of the Two World Wars* (London, 1972), pp. 59–73.

51. Grupp, *Deutsche Außenpolitik*, pp. 143–145.

lowed the lead of his General Staff and Foreign Office with respect to Germany. In addition, he accepted Foreign Office suggestions that France sponsor the creation of new pro-French states in eastern Europe, including a large Poland which would take considerable territory from Germany and establish a new European balance of power.[52] Like the Germans, the French believed that they could turn the successor states of the eastern empires into reliable allies and economic assets. In addition, although Clemenceau himself had never cared much about colonies, he realized more of the aims of the *parti colonial* than his own at the peace conference. France emerged from Versailles with most of Germany's West African empire, mandates in Lebanon, a much-reduced Syria, and renewed hopes that a strengthened empire might provide the key to France's future greatness. Like the British, the French found their colonial aims easier to achieve than their European goals.[53]

Although for most of the war the British and French made less diplomatic use of the nationality principle than the Central Powers, they eventually adopted it as the basis of the 1919 peace. Initially they had less to gain from it. Significantly, the French government, which hoped to move its military frontier to the Rhine, generally recognized that the nationality principle would make it impossible to annex the left bank of the Rhine as well as Alsace-Lorraine, and planned simply to create a French client state and military ally there.[54] In eastern Europe, the French government quickly endorsed Russian claims upon Prussian Poland and blessed the national aspirations of Polish expatriates after the Russian revolution of 1917.[55] But Paris and London generally opposed dismembering Austria-Hungary during the first three years of the war, both because they hoped for a separate peace and because they feared an *Anschluss* of the Austro-Germans with Germany. And despite extensive propaganda by Austro-Hungarian exiles in Great Britain, Lloyd George as late as January 1918 called only for "autonomy" for the subject races of Austria-Hungary. The American government went no further, and Wilson's Fourteen Points,

---

52. D. M. Stevenson, *French War Aims against Germany, 1914–19* (New York, 1982), esp. pp. 98–107.

53. Andrew and Kanya-Forster, *Climax of French Imperial Expansion*, pp. 137–236.

54. Stevenson, *French War Aims*, pp. 153–160, notes that Clemenceau, Marshal Foch, and President Poincaré actually entertained the hope that the Rhineland Germans might eventually *desire* incorporation into France.

55. Ibid., pp. 51–56, 87, 98.

which called only for autonomy for the Austro-Hungarian nation-alities, dismayed the Czechs and South Slavs.[56] With military victory quite uncertain, the Allies dared not foreclose the possibility of a separate peace with Vienna, but they had meanwhile made promises to Italy and Serbia that would make one very difficult to achieve.

Events in the spring of 1918 induced the Allies to change their policy. The German attack in March left the Allies in a most serious situation. In addition, the Austro-Hungarian foreign minister, Czernin, tried to rally his country by revealing that the Allies had been negotiating with Vienna for peace, and arguing that only defeatist and treacherous minorities within Austria-Hungary had led the Allies to abandon the talks. Clemenceau in return revealed that the emperor Charles had endorsed French claims to Alsace-Lorraine during peace talks, forcing Czernin to resign and Charles to reaffirm his solidarity with Germany. The American and British governments both concluded that Austria-Hungary, under the supremacy of the Germans and the Magyars, would certainly remain an ally of Germany after the war, and that a lasting peace therefore required its dismemberment. Thus in May 1918 the French, British, and American governments endorsed the national aspirations of the "Czecho-slovaks" and South Slavs, although British authorities preserved some ambiguity and remained divided over the future of Austria-Hungary right up to the end of the war.[57]

What actually liberated the nationalities of Austria-Hungary—like those of Russia—was the collapse of their authoritarian government. Although in the last month of war the Austrian government issued a manifesto which sought to meet the nationalities' demands, it could not go so far as to break up the kingdom of Hungary, which would be necessary to unite the Serbs and Croats in the south and the Czechs and Slovaks in the north. Minority politicians, who now knew of the diplomatic achievements of their national councils overseas, preferred to wait for the collapse of the monarchy. When the Czech national committee rose in Prague on

56. Victor S. Mamatey, *The United States and East Central Europe, 1914–1918: A Study in Wilsonian Diplomacy and Propaganda* (Princeton, 1957), pp. 153–232. Wilson did endorse the creation of an independent Poland.

57. Stevenson, *French War Aims*, pp. 28, 56–60, 106–108; Rothwell, *British War Aims*, pp. 148–149, 158, 245–249; Zeman, *Break-up of the Hapsburg Monarchy*, pp. 215–216; Mamatey, *United States and East Central Europe*, pp. 233–317.

October 28, 1918, the military governor did not dare resist. The Germans within Austria immediately began organizing their own state, which the Germans in Bohemia and Moravia hoped to join. In Hungary the government in late October gave way to a revolutionary Hungarian National Committee which finally promised the minorities self-determination within the existing Hungarian state. But this was not enough. A Rumanian army entered Transylvania, and Croatia eagerly embraced the victorious Serbs and Allies. As in Germany and Russia, the military defeat of the old regime led to its political collapse, and Socialists and national minorities stepped forth to fill the political vacuum.[58]

In an effort to undermine both German expansion in eastern Europe and the Bolshevik revolution in Russia, the Allies in 1918 followed the lead of the Germans and endorsed the national claims of the Balts, Finns, and Poles, hoping to build a bulwark against the Soviets. They also tried to encourage anti-Communist resistance within Russia but were less successful. The Allies' efforts suffered partly because they had to try to reconcile the irreconcilable claims of White Russians, who insisted on maintaining the territorial integrity of the old Russian empire, and of the non-Russian nationalities, who wanted independence. In early 1919, the French marshal Foch tried to persuade the Allied governments to begin an anti-Bolshevik crusade from Poland and Rumania, but with the armistice concluded the British refused to foot the bill. After the White forces were defeated in the Russian civil war, the Allies encouraged the more extreme aspirations of Poland and Rumania vis-à-vis Russia, with the result that Rumania acquired Bessarabia, and the Poles emerged from a war with the Bolsheviks with an eastern frontier considerably to the east of the "Curzon line," designed by the Allies at the Paris peace conference to define the limits of "indisputably Polish" territory.[59] And by sponsoring the successor states that emerged after the collapse of Austria-Hungary, London and Paris hoped to secure protected markets in southeastern Europe as well.

In 1917–18 the British also encouraged the national claims of some of the subject peoples of the Ottoman empire and endorsed Zionist aspirations for a "national home" in Palestine. British offi-

---

58. Zeman, *Break-up of the Hapsburg Monarchy*, pp. 217–245.

59. John M. Thompson, *Russia, Bolshevism, and the Versailles Peace* (Princeton, 1966), pp. 50–61, 178–192, 296–303, 316–346, 351–375.

cers in the Middle East had encouraged Arab nationalism, and the British government, effectively repudiating part of the Sykes-Picot agreement in 1918, vaguely promised that some Arab territory would become independent after the war.[60] Zionism also made great strides during the war. The Zionist movement before the First World War had achieved a relatively modest following in Austria-Hungary, Germany, France, Great Britain, and the United States, where many Jews still sought assimilation, but it had aroused enormous excitement within the Russian empire, where the largest numbers of Jews lived and where, as we have seen, their position was becoming more rather than less precarious. Like the subject nationalities of eastern Europe, the Zionists regarded the war as their great opportunity, because they could encourage both sides to bid for their support and because of Turkey's entry into the war. By 1917, important British figures, including Lloyd George, Alfred Milner, and the Middle Eastern specialist Sir Mark Sykes, had adopted the Zionist cause, not least because they could use Zionism as a lever in their continuing struggle with the French for postwar control of Palestine. After the March revolution in Russia and the American entry into the First World War, Zionism also became a means of enlisting the support of the Russian and American Jewish communities (though these were far from united on the subject) and a means of countering Russian and American demands for a "peace without annexations" that would leave Turkey intact.[61] The British War Cabinet finally issued the Balfour Declaration in October 1917, partly also in the mistaken belief that the German government might soon endorse Zionist claims. After the declaration had been issued, American, French, and Italian Zionists induced their governments to support it as well.[62]

At the peace conference, the new mandate system enabled the British and French to achieve their territorial claims south of Anatolia, and the Balfour Declaration was written into the British mandate for Palestine. But British, French, and Italian plans for the partition of Anatolia proper collapsed when the Turks, like the Russian Bolsheviks, successfully organized a new indigenous government. The victors' empires had become larger than ever, and

60. Nevakivi, *Britian, France, and the Arab Middle East*, pp. 45–67.

61. All these points are covered most effectively by Leonard Stein, *The Balfour Declaration* (London, 1961), pp. 117–146, 309–360.

62. Ibid., pp. 533–604.

they had performed important services during the war. In retrospect, however, the Turkish victory clearly foreshadowed the real long-term threat to European imperialism: the awakening of the colonized peoples, which posed a greater threat to the colonial powers than their struggles among themselves.

Not only the major powers emerged from the war with grandiose programs for expansion. The Italian government, which had joined the Allies in response to territorial promises in 1915, hoped to secure the undisputed mastery of the Adriatic and a substantial part of Asia Minor. The Belgian government prepared to annex Luxemburg and small but economically important parts of Germany.[63] The Balkan states, meanwhile, had taken advantage of the diplomatic and military needs of the major belligerents to secure the endorsement of their national claims. During the war the great powers readily endorsed any Balkan national claims against their enemies, while declining to make any concessions at their own expense. Thus in the first months of the war Rumania received pledges of Russian Bessarabia from the Central Powers and Austro-Hungarian Transylvania and Bukovina from Russia—both simply for remaining neutral. The Central Powers dangled Macedonia before Bulgaria—to whom the Allies, pledged to Serbia and solicitous of Rumania, had nothing to offer—and the Bulgarian government entered the war and received its reward in 1915, when Serbia was crushed and occupied. In the next year, after the successful Russian Brusilov offensive, the Rumanian government also decided to join the Allies in return for promises of Austro-Hungarian and Bulgarian territory, but suffered a series of military defeats against the Austro-Hungarians, Germans, and Bulgarians, and found themselves forced in 1918 to conclude a humiliating peace. The intrigues regarding Greece's role in the war were the most intricate of all. After Turkey had entered the war, the Entente Cordiale tried to bribe the Greek government with territory in Asia Minor, while at the same time suggesting that Greece secure Bulgaria's neutrality by making concessions in Macedonia. Complicated negotiations and a terrible struggle between the Greek king Constantine and the prime minister Venizelos led to an extraordinary situation in late 1915, when Allied troops landed at Salonika

63. René Albrecht-Carrié, *Italy at the Paris Peace Conference* (New York, 1938); Sally Marks, *Innocent Abroad: Belgium at the Paris Peace Conference of 1919* (Chapel Hill, 1981).

to fight the Bulgarians and Turks although Greece had not entered the war. After a revolution, Venizelos finally led Greece into the war in the summer of 1917, promising to unite all Greeks at last—including several million living in Asia Minor. After Bulgaria and Turkey collapsed, the Greeks secured the concession of largely Greek-inhabited territory around Smyrna, but failed to hold on to these gains in the struggle against the new Turkish republic.[64]

During the war, the Turks had adopted the most radical solution to a national minorities question seen to date. The Committee of Union and Progress—the so-called Young Turks—had come to power in 1908 proclaiming the equality of all Ottoman subjects regardless of race or religion. By the time of the Balkan wars, however, they had abandoned this principle and determined instead to rebuild the empire upon a basis of ethnic Turkish nationalism. Minorities such as the Greeks and Armenians they now regarded as fifth columns in conflicts against Greece or Russia. After the Balkan wars they had forced the Greek government to agree in principle to a large-scale exchange of Greeks from Asia Minor for Muslims from Macedonia.[65]

The Turks entered the First World War on the side of the Central Powers with the intention of uniting the Turkic peoples of Russia in a vast central Asian empire. After their initial winter campaign of 1914–15 against the Russians ended unsuccessfully, the Young Turks decided both to blame the defeat upon their Armenian minority—to whom the Russians had indeed offered a brighter future—and to solve the problem of the Armenian minority by exterminating the Armenians. The government disarmed the Armenians of Anatolia in 1915 and announced its decision to deport them to Mesopotamia. But the deportation was only a pretext: the Turks shot Armenian men and marched Armenian women and children into the mountains and the desert, where they starved to death. Between 1 and 1.5 million Armenians perished.[66] After the war, when the new Turkish nationalist movement under Mustapha Kemal successfully drove the Greeks out of Asia Minor, the

64. Dakin, *Unification of Greece*, pp. 201–228.
65. Ibid., p. 202.
66. Despite some attempts at revisionism by Turkophile historians, these facts are no longer in dispute. See Hovannisian, *Armenian Genocide in Perspective, passim;* Ulrich Trumpener, *Germany and the Ottoman Empire, 1914–1918* (Princeton, 1968), pp. 200–270; and Henry Morgenthau, *Ambassador Morgenthau's Story* (New York, 1918), pp. 274–363, which recounts conversations about the massacre with leading Turkish officials.

new government insisted upon a Greek-Turkish exchange of populations which enabled it to expel 1.5 million Greeks from Anatolia.[67] Here the nationalities question had entered a new phase.

The peace settlements of 1919–1922 enabled the victorious powers to achieve most of their imperialist aims and to redraw the map of Europe along lines which reflected both the principle of nationality and the strategic objective of weakening Germany and Soviet Russia. In southeastern Europe, formerly German- and Magyar-ruled areas of mixed nationality such as Transylvania, the Banat, Bohemia-Moravia, and the Tyrol invariably went to entente-sponsored claimants, including the Czechs, South Slavs, Rumanians, and Italians. On the rimland of the Soviet Union the Allies eventually endorsed the maximum Polish and Rumanian claims upon the Bolsheviks. The Allies also denied self-determination (although not self-rule) to the Germans of Austria and Danzig, whom they forcibly separated from the German empire; handed mixed German-Polish areas to the new Polish republic; returned Schleswig-Holstein to neutral Denmark; and gave Alsace-Lorraine to France without a plebiscite. The nationality principle won another victory in 1922, when a Conservative-dominated British government conceded Home Rule for Ireland, albeit upon terms which enabled it to claim that it had protected the rights of Protestant Irishmen in Ulster.

Partly because of the nationality principle, however, the Allies did not really achieve the overarching aim of making a new war impossible for the foreseeable future. Wilson and Lloyd George refused to allow the French to create a new client state on the left bank of the Rhine or annex the Saarland. Recognizing that the nationality principle made it impossible to guarantee French security through territorial acquisitions, the French government chose to rely upon alliances, the disarmament and reparations clauses of the Versailles Treaty, and perhaps the new League of Nations instead. These clauses—involving the almost complete demilitarization of Germany and the imposition of huge economic obligations—were the means by which the Allies sought to make a recurrence of the war impossible, along with the new league and

67. Dakin, *Unification of Greece*, pp. 242–243.

the general disarmament which they also promised eventually to undertake. Clemenceau apparently concluded that the maintenance of the alliance with Britain and the United States—without which France could never have won the war—was more important than the dismemberment of Germany. The subsequent history of the Ruhr occupation suggests that France might not have been able to achieve this goal anyway. The French suffered a cruel disappointment, however, when the American government failed to ratify the treaty and the promised new alliance collapsed.[68]

The long-term prospects for peace after the First World War depended largely upon the resolution of the problems of imperialism and economic self-sufficiency on the one hand, and nationalism on the other. In retrospect it is clear that the war created new, at least equally serious problems in these areas. The economic failure of wartime imperialism emerged in the years following the war. The annexation of foreign territories—which as we have seen had contributed little to European economic prosperity before the First World War—could not possibly solve the infinitely more serious economic problems which Europe faced as a result of the conflict. Although the British and French had added to their empires, the cost of the war had destroyed many of the foundations of the prosperous prewar world economy. The European powers had squandered their resources in the mindless pursuit of a victory which had not only proved impossible to achieve, but which could not in any case have made up for their wartime losses. The economic and political consequences of the debacle of 1914–1918 included further international turmoil, stagnation and depression, and new impulses toward imperialism.

The issue of nationalism, furthermore, was altered but not solved by the peace settlement. History and geography made any *complete* reorganization of Europe along national lines impossible. The creation of several new states reduced the presence of national minorities but could not eliminate it. While before the war no nationality had enjoyed a majority within Austria, Hungary, or Russia, after the war one nationality comprised well over half of the population of most of the new states, and nearly half of Czechoslovakia and Yugoslavia. Still, because of the continuing presence of

68. Stevenson, *French War Aims*, pp. 133–215.

mixed areas, almost one-third of the population of the successor states was composed of national minorities.[69]

Indeed, the peacemakers not only realized that minorities would remain but also concluded that their welfare must not simply be left in the hands of their new governments. The new states found themselves obliged to sign minorities treaties guaranteeing their minority subjects equal political, cultural, linguistic, and religious rights. This idea seems to have originated among Jewish leaders in the Allied countries, who wanted to guarantee the rights of the large Jewish community within Poland, and the smaller one within Rumania, which before 1914 had tried to avoid recognizing its Jews as citizens at all. German minorities in Poland, Lithuania, Rumania, and Yugoslavia also clamored for protection. The British government claimed that the treaties were designed to prepare for the assimilation of national minorities, but they also seemed to admit that national minorities would not be treated equally by the new states.[70] This assumption proved true.

The legitimacy of governments, moreover, had eroded as a result of the war. A renewal of popular confidence depended upon the successful reconstruction of European economies and societies—a reconstruction which had to overcome unprecedented obstacles. Already, in Russia, a traditional regime had given way as a result of the war to one founded upon the transformation of society according to ideological principles. In Germany, the failure of reconstruction led eventually to the emergence of another such regime—founded upon the most extreme principles of imperialism and nationalism, and willing to try to implement them in a new war.

The Failure of Reconstruction, 1919–1933

The Economic Consequences of the War

The First World War shattered prewar economic structures and left European governments with enormous economic problems. The warring governments had all borrowed heavily to pay for the war, and the Continental states had relied almost entirely upon loans

69. Pearson, *National Minorities in Eastern Europe*, pp. 148–149.
70. This point was made in striking fashion more than thirty years ago by Hannah Arendt, *The Origins of Totalitarianism* (2d ed., New York, 1958), pp. 271–275.

for their unprecedented expenditures. By 1917, all the major powers planned to try to restore their financial position by collecting indemnities from their defeated opponents—plans which the British and French governments tried to put into effect beginning in 1919. The war, however, had done much irreparable damage. The billions which had gone to finance it could not be replaced, and Continental governments eventually repudiated much or all of their war loan obligations through inflation, effectively acknowledging that several generations' worth of savings had been swallowed up by the war. The European powers had also accumulated large debts to the United States, while sizable amounts of foreign investment in eastern Europe and Asia had been wiped out, erasing much of the invisible surpluses with which the prewar European powers had paid for their imports. The war had grossly distorted worldwide patterns of production, creating significant surplus capacity both for primary products and industrial goods. This surplus depressed postwar economies both in Europe and overseas, reducing European exports and eventually reducing the return on remaining investments around the world. The war, moreover, had created new financial claims upon European states and vastly increased the European peoples' expectations of their governments. The European peoples now expected generous pensions, continuing prosperity, and the eight-hour day, as well as a reduction of the financial burdens imposed by the war. During the 1920s European governments struggled intermittently to restore a functioning world economy; during the 1930s they almost abandoned the attempt, and turned once again to various forms of imperialism as a substitute.

It is quite clear in retrospect that in their zeal to achieve victory, the European powers, especially the Germans, French, and Russians, completely disregarded their financial future. The German government, which in 1914 had an ordinary revenue of 2.47 billion Reichsmarks ($588 million), had increased its national debt by 137.2 billion Reichsmarks by the armistice. New taxes, which had provoked bitter political debates before 1914, had provided just 6 percent of the total cost of the war.[1] The French government, whose revenue totaled 5.092 billion francs in 1913 ($98 million),

---

1. Hardach, *First World War*, p. 155; Carl-Ludwig Holtfrerich, *The German Inflation, 1914–1923: Causes and Effects in International Perspective* (New York, 1986), p. 105.

increased its domestic debt by 134 billion francs by the end of 1919, while incurring foreign debts equivalent to 47 billion francs more.[2] The British government, which managed substantially to increase taxation during the war, still increased its domestic debt from £65 million to £6.085 billion. The British also incurred foreign debts of £1.35 billion, but balanced these with wartime loans to empire governments and foreign powers of £1.68 billion—over half a billion of those, unfortunately, to imperial Russia.[3] Nothing like this had ever happened before.

Predictably, all three powers had decided by the end of the war that the defeated powers must pay a large indemnity. The French, who for most of the war had pressed for postwar inter-Allied economic cooperation to help deal with reconstruction, began to focus their demands upon an indemnity sufficient to repair damages and pay for the cost of the war after the armistice, when it became clear that inter-Allied cooperation would not continue.[4] Lloyd George, who had to face the reality and the potential political consequences of Britain's financial position during the "Khaki" election campaign of November 1918, had publicly demanded that Germany pay for the entire cost of the war.[5] The Germans had also expected a large indemnity. William II in the spring of 1917 had envisioned the collection of perhaps $85 billion, compared to $33 billion which the Allies eventually assessed against Germany, and the German government exacted a substantial indemnity from the Russians after Brest-Litovsk.[6] Since the Allies won the war, they imposed reparations upon the Germans rather than the other way around, but the story might not have turned out much differently had the Germans been victorious.

We need not review the tortuous story of reparations negotiations from the Paris peace conference to the London conference of

2. Sauvy, *Histoire économique de la France*, III, 397, 395; Gaston Jèze and Henri Truchy, *The War Finance of France* (New Haven, 1927), p. 336.

3. F. W. Hirst and J. E. Allen, *British War Budgets* (New Haven, 1926), p. 244; F. W. Hirst, *The Consequences of the War to Great Britain* (New Haven, 1934), p. 251.

4. Stevenson, *French War Aims against Germany*, pp. 152–153.

5. Bunselmayer, *Cost of the War*, pp. 121–184.

6. Fischer, *Germany's Aims*, p. 354; Hardach, *First World War*, p. 234. The literature on German war aims gives few specific figures for indemnities, although Steven A. Schuker has noted that the banker Max Warburg had anticipated an indemnity of 50 billion gold Reichsmarks as early as November 1914; see Schuker, *The End of French Predominance in Europe: The Financial Crisis of 1924 and the Adoption of the Dawes Plan* (Chapel Hill, 1976), p. 182.

1924, which adopted the Dawes Plan. The politics of the reparations issue now seem quite clear. The German and the French governments faced an impossible combination of gigantic domestic debts, inflated currencies, and angry publics who rejected substantial increases in taxation. While French governments argued that only German reparations could solve their problems and German governments answered that reparations were crippling their economy, both preferred to continue increasing their short-term debt rather than raise taxes and attempt to stabilize their currencies. The reparations question, in short, enabled both governments to postpone the painful admission that their constituents would never retrieve the savings which had paid for the First World War.[7]

It is not surprising, given the political stakes involved for both sides, that reparations took so long to settle. In 1921 the French government effectively scaled down total claims from the original figure of 132 billion gold Reichsmarks to about half that much.[8] Although the Germans did transfer between 8 and 20 billion gold Reichsmarks worth of foreign investments, merchant shipping, and other deliveries in kind between 1919 and 1922, the German government still refused to make regular annual payments.[9] In late 1922 the French government, which regarded these payments as the only alternative to unacceptable tax increases, occupied the Ruhr with the help of the Belgians.

During the next one and a half years the French and German governments reached the limit of their respective powers of coercion and resistance. The French government agreed to a large additional reduction in reparations at the London conference of 1924 and renounced any further occupation of the Ruhr because it needed a large Anglo-American loan, and British and American bankers insisted upon these concessions. The German govern-

7. See Holtfrerich, *German Inflation*, pp. 125–155, and Schuker, *End of French Predominance*, pp. 3–56.

8. Schuker, *End of French Predominance*, pp. 14–15, argues persuasively that the 1921 London schedule, which included 82 billion Reichsmarks in "C" bonds which could not be realized for many years, effectively scaled down the total claim by that amount.

9. The total amount paid by the Germans remains a matter of considerable debate. While the Allied Reparations Commission put German payments at 8 billion Reichsmarks, the Germans claimed to have paid 52 billion, and British and American estimates put the total in the range of 20–28 billion. See Holtfrerich, *German Inflation*, pp. 137–155.

ment finally agreed to regular payments after months of hyper-inflation and the virtual collapse of the authority of the Weimar government.[10] The Dawes Plan, however, was followed by currency revaluation in both Germany and France. The revaluation of the Reichsmark in 1924 wiped out about 85 percent of the German state debt, as well as 75 percent of private debts.[11] Two years later the French government finally abandoned its dream of restoring the franc to its prewar gold parity and stabilized it at one-fifth of that value. The French and German governments had now acknowledged that the war had actually been financed by a massive capital levy.

The repudiation of war debts, however, had dealt with only one of the war's economic consequences. Others proved far less tractable, including the loss of much foreign investment and the distortion of worldwide production patterns.

Foreign investment, as we have seen, played a critical role in the growth of the European economies before 1914. The invisible surpluses enjoyed by all the major European powers had enabled them to pay off their current-account deficits and to increase their foreign investments, and therefore their imports, almost every year.[12] The war and postwar dislocations had enormously weakened the European investment position. The British and French had contracted substantial debts to the United States, although for Britain these debts had largely been compensated by Britain's own loans to other Allies. Furthermore, assets in large parts of the world had either disappeared completely, as in Russia, or lost a great deal of their value, as in the case of investment in southeastern Europe and the Ottoman empire. Thus France, whose prewar foreign investments had totaled about $8.7 billion, had lost perhaps $4 billion worth of foreign investments as a result of the war (including $1.9 billion in repudiated, privately held Russian debt), while contracting a total of $3.65 billion in debts to the British and Americans. The British had done much better, losing about $1.3 billion worth of foreign investments ($0.5 billion in Russian loans) out of a prewar total of more than $18 billion. Their loans to Allies other than Russia ($4.5 billion) also exceeded their debt to the

10. See especially Schuker, *End of French Predominance*, pp. 232–382, and Charles A. Maier, *Recasting Bourgeois Europe* (Princeton, 1975), pp. 293–387.

11. Holtfrerich, *German Inflation*, pp. 321–330.

12. See above, pp. 302–303.

United States ($3.7 billion). The Germans had suffered most heavily of all. The Allies had claimed their entire foreign investment portfolio ($5.6 billion) as reparations and confiscated their merchant fleet, which had provided a substantial share of their prewar invisible surplus.[13]

In the years immediately following the war, the French, British, and Italians tried to recoup some of their economic losses by establishing new markets for capital and for exports in the successor states of the Austro-Hungarian and Russian empires. Like the Germans in 1917–18, they all hoped to take advantage of their sponsorship of the new states, but the results proved disappointing. The British and French made large stabilization loans to the new states' central banks, while investors infiltrated southeastern European industry and exporters tried to displace the Germans. Export markets hardly materialized, however, and the new states continued to need foreign capital throughout the 1920s to cover current-account deficits and interest on existing loans.[14] Thus the imperialism of the First World War paid the victors' few economic dividends in eastern and southeastern Europe, and the German experience might easily have been similar had the Germans been victorious. Attempts led by Lloyd George to revive the Russian market also had only the most limited results.

The Europeans achieved a degree of economic stability from 1925 though 1928, of course, but substantial economic problems remained, as comparisons with the prewar period show. The British, French, and Italians recouped some of their wartime losses by collecting German reparations that more than covered their debt payments to the United States, while the Germans financed their reparations and their current-account deficit with the help of American capital. Yet in the year 1928 French income from foreign investments, measured in constant prices, was only about one-third of what it had been in 1913, while 95 percent of the German invisible surplus of 1.6 billion Reichsmarks in 1914 had disap-

---

13. See Hardach, *First World War*, pp. 148, 155, 289; Harold G. Moulton and Leo Pasvolsky, *War Debts and World Prosperity* (Washington, 1932), pp. 479–480. The French also sold some overseas investments and suffered substantial losses in the Ottoman empire and southeastern Europe.

14. These developments are summarized by György Ránki, *Economy and Foreign Policy: The Struggle of the Great Powers for Hegemony in the Danube Valley, 1919–1939* (New York, 1983), pp. 7–58.

peared when measured at constant prices. The British and Italian invisible surpluses had also declined somewhat at constant prices, while their visible deficits had substantially increased.[15] The reparations which the Allies collected from 1925 through 1930 left them with a small surplus after making their debt payments to the United States, but hardly made up for their losses in foreign capital, while adding an additional burden to the German position.

Since the European countries' invisible balances of payments had generally deteriorated while their current-account position had not much improved, they managed to maintain reasonable overall balances only with the help of large inflows of capital, especially from the United States. The Germans, whose position was clearly the most serious owing to the complete disappearance of their foreign investment, actually began receiving large sums of foreign currency in the early 1920s. Foreigners invested the equivalent of $1.9 billion in the Reichsmark, 1919–1922, apparently believing that the German currency must shortly begin to rise.[16] The flow resumed after the stabilization of the Reichsmark and reached a total of about $8.3 billion by the summer of 1930—more than half of it short-term. Since the Germans paid at most about $8 billion in reparations during this period, it seems clear that foreign capital did much to make up for the disappearance of Germany's foreign investments.[17]

The European powers, lastly, suffered the consequences of worldwide overproduction of both agricultural and industrial goods—a problem which also originated during the war, and which had become critical by 1930. Wartime interruption of trade, combined with the enormous needs of munitions production, had

15. Sauvy, *Histoire économique*, III, 349, 406; Mitchell, *European Historical Statistics*, pp. 738, 818–826.

16. Holtfrerich, *German Inflation*, pp. 285–287.

17. Figures are from Derek H. Aldcroft, *From Versailles to Wall Street, 1919–1929* (Berkeley, 1977), pp. 86, 255. Steven A. Schuker, *American "Reparations" to Germany, 1919–33: Implications for the Third-World Debt Crisis* (Princeton, 1988), pp. 14–46, shows quite clearly that Germany benefited massively from net capital transfers from 1919 through 1932, and that the Germans even managed to reconstitute a substantial foreign investment portfolio during this period. He also argues that the Germans could theoretically have maintained an export surplus sufficient to finance reparations. Although this may well be true theoretically, it must be noted once again that *no* European industrial country consistently ran a current-account surplus from the late nineteenth century through 1950. When the Brüning government did create such an export surplus during 1930–1932, dire political consequences resulted.

vastly increased world productive capacity in coal, heavy industry, chemicals, some other branches of manufacturing, and especially agriculture. Excess industrial capacity created long-term structural unemployment and downward pressure on industrial prices, even during the so-called boom years of the late 1920s. Wartime expansion of primary production led to worldwide surpluses of grain, sugar, rubber, and coffee by the late 1920s as well. These surpluses reduced the export earnings of many primary-producer countries—most notably, perhaps, in eastern Europe—and helped bring about the depression by in turn reducing exports to primary-producer countries.[18]

The economic consequences of the First World War, in short, can hardly be overestimated—and the same holds true, of course, for the political changes to which those economic consequences contributed. While the war wiped out large portions of European foreign investment and left the Europeans with huge new debts—therefore reducing or eliminating the invisible surpluses which had enabled them to grow before 1914—it also left behind substantial overproduction of industrial goods, leading to widespread structural unemployment and reduced export earnings. In addition, the massive wartime flow of capital from Europe to the United States led in the postwar period to massive American loans to Europe—and these loans turned the American economic downturn of 1928–29 into a European and worldwide catastrophe, since the United States recalled many of them after the stock market crash.[19] The industrial depression also wiped out the value of foreign industrial investments.

The war, then, had brought about the inflation of the early 1920s, the repudiation of wartime debt undertaken by most of the Continental powers, and the loss of large amounts of European overseas capital. These developments hurt the Europeans' trade balances badly, and left European governments—especially the German government—with extremely difficult political choices.

18. Aldcroft, *From Versailles to Wall Street*, pp. 200–212, 223–238. Aldcroft does not believe that the problems of primary producers were critical in bringing about the depression, however.

19. Summarizing existing literature, Aldcroft, *From Versailles to Wall Street*, pp. 271–284, notes that most interpretations now agree that the Depression began in the United States, while differing on the reasons for the American downturn. For our purposes, of course, its European consequences are more important than its precise American causes.

Beginning in 1928 the Europeans' dependence upon American capital, the Wall Street crash, and increasing worldwide overproduction of both agricultural and industrial goods apparently combined to bring about the Depression, which reduced international trade by about two-thirds and wiped out large new amounts of international capital investment. Without undertaking detailed economic analysis, one may reasonably ascribe most of these developments to the imperialism of the European powers as manifested by the First World War. More remarkably, most European governments undertook new imperialist initiatives of varying sorts in response to the depression.

The Renewal of Imperialism

We have seen that in the pre-1914 period, the idea of imperialism had grown along with the development of a healthy world economy, even though the two developments had little to do with each other. During the First World War, which seemed like exactly the kind of struggle for the world's means of subsistence that the imperialists had predicted, imperialism became the basis for war aims. For the most part, however, European governments during the 1920s focused upon the rebuilding of the world economy and the redistribution of the resources of the *industrialized* world involved in the reparations and war debt questions.

The Depression narrowed the options which governments faced. Ironically, although it was in many ways the outcome of the war, it led to a rebirth of European imperialism, partly because European governments had no other expedients to offer their impoverished constituents. Governments revived and implemented many of the old prewar economic arguments on behalf of imperialism—that colonies might provide privileged outlets for merchandise exports, capital investment, and even surplus population. And in Germany the Depression contributed to the rise of Hitler and the Nazis, who after 1933 not only asserted but also implemented the most extreme imperialist program of modern European history.

After the First World War raised many leading British imperialists to new positions of power, they took advantage of the empire's contribution to the war to begin realizing some of their most cherished projects. Thus in the spring of 1917 the new Imperial War

Cabinet had endorsed the principles of imperial preference and increased British emigration to the Dominions. The government also exempted the Dominions from the wartime McKenna duties on industrial goods—duties which in any event would have affected them very little. After the war, Milner's protégé Leopold Amery, who served under Milner at the Colonial Office from 1919 through 1921 and became colonial secretary himself in 1924, eventually endorsed subsidized emigration as a partial solution to the British unemployment problem, and in 1922 he persuaded the government to adopt such a scheme. During the late 1920s the government combined subsidized emigration with substantial capital outlays for imperial development, and tens of thousands of Britishers took advantage of the scheme until the economic collapse of the late 1920s, which affected Canada and Australasia badly.[20]

British governments discussed imperial tariff preference during the 1920s, but to make preferences effective, the British government would have had to impose tariffs upon the staple agricultural goods which the Dominions exported. With memories of 1906 still fresh, no government could impose food duties during the 1920s, as Stanley Baldwin discovered in 1923. The related questions of tariffs and imperial preference became more acute in late 1931, when a run on the pound brought down the Labour government. The National government that replaced it and went off the gold standard faced severe financial difficulties and a precarious balance of trade. Chancellor of the Exchequer Neville Chamberlain proposed a general 10 percent ad valorem tariff, which would also allow Britain to grant the Dominions preferential rates in return for preferences for British industrial goods. Over Foreign Office objections, the government adopted this program.[21]

At Ottawa in July and August of 1932, the leaders of the British government seemed determined to reach sweeping agreements, if only to secure, as Prime Minister Ramsay MacDonald put it, "the intangible but very important gain to sentiment and confidence (which might well extend far beyond the Empire) in the course of which the Empire had shown unity of purpose and had translated

20. Ian A. Drummond, *Imperial Economic Policy, 1917–1939: Studies in Expansion and Protection* (Toronto, 1974), pp. 23–144.

21. David E. Kaiser, *Economic Diplomacy and the Origins of the Second World War* (Princeton, 1980), pp. 83–86; Drummond, *Imperial Economic Policy*, pp. 177–184.

ideals into specific agreements."[22] British negotiators, moreover, faced a difficult problem. While for the most part they might satisfy the Dominions' demands by favoring the Dominions' agricultural products over *foreign* produce, they could benefit in return only if the Dominions made concessions that would impinge upon the Dominions' *home* industries. As a result—and because the British negotiators wanted so badly to reach agreement—London made much more specific and consequential concessions to the Dominions than they made in return. While the Dominions substantially increased their share of British imports during the period of the agreements (1932–1935), British exports to the Dominions grew only slightly.[23] The British also failed during the interwar years to shift much of the burden of imperial defense to the Dominions.[24]

The British government and the British nation, with less resources to dispose of both relatively and absolutely, put a substantially higher proportion of those resources into the British empire. By the late 1920s, when total British foreign investments had dropped a whole billion pounds below the 1914 figure, almost 60 percent of new investments were going into the empire, compared with 46 percent in the immediate prewar period.[25] In 1932, after the abandonment of the gold standard and the devaluation of the pound, the British government entirely reversed the policy of the last one hundred years or more and embargoed foreign lending.[26] Developments in defense policy mirrored these changes. The defense of the British empire, rather than the maintenance of the European balance of power, also remained the guiding principle of British foreign policy during the interwar period, reflecting the shift away from Continental commitments which Lloyd George had begun in 1917. Governments consistently refused to plan for any major commitment of British troops in defense of France until 1939.[27]

Although French imperialism during the interwar period has been much less studied, it is clear that the French also increased

22. Drummond, *Imperial Economic Policy*, pp. 222–223.
23. Ibid., pp. 279–289; Kaiser, *Economic Diplomacy*, p. 90.
24. Correlli Barnett, *The Collapse of British Power* (London, 1972), pp. 188–233.
25. Lowe, *Lion's Share*, pp. 260–261.
26. Gustav Schmidt, *The Politics and Economics of Appeasement: British Foreign Policy in the 1930s* (New York, 1986), p. 152–153.
27. Howard, *Continental Commitment*, pp. 96–130. Schuker, *End of French Predominance*, pp. 388–390, discusses the emergence of these views in the early 1920s.

the relative economic importance of their empire during the 1920s and 1930s. In the immediate aftermath of the First World War, Albert Sarraut, like Leopold Amery in Britain, pushed ambitious schemes for colonial development but could not find much money for his projects.[28] During the 1920s the French government took new steps to bring various parts of the French empire into a tariff union with France, and when in 1930 the government decided to regulate all imports with a quota system, it exempted the colonies from quotas. The French colonies' share in French trade increased enormously as a result.[29] The bulk of French foreign capital investment went into the French empire during the 1930s.[30] In 1938–39, when the French government had to decide whether or not to defend its allies in eastern Europe, some, though not all, of the French financial press argued that France's future lay in its empire, and that eastern Europe might be abandoned to the Germans.[31]

Imperialism also played a large and increasing role in the foreign policy of Italy, whose government had been taken over by Mussolini's Fascists in 1922. Mussolini, who had abandoned revolutionary socialism in favor of imperialism in the early stages of the First World War, had capitalized upon widespread discontent with the Italian government's failure to secure most of its ambitious war aims at the peace conference, and after coming to power he clearly dreamed of widespread gains in the Balkans, North Africa, and East Africa. Fascists and many more traditional conservatives agreed upon the need for expansion to meet the needs of Italy's rapidly increasing population, although the two groups differed on where to achieve it. The depression apparently stimulated Mussolini to greater activity, and he ordered plans for an attack on Ethiopia in late 1932.[32] His attack on Ethiopia in 1935 was designed

28. Jean Suret-Canale, French Colonialism in Tropical Africa, 1900–45 (New York, 1971), pp. 272–285.

29. Kaiser, Economic Diplomacy, pp. 201–203.

30. Alice Teichova, An Economic Background to Munich: International Business and Czechoslovakia, 1918–1938 (Cambridge, 1974), pp. 5–6.

31. René Girault, "La décision gouvernementale en politique extérieure," in René Rémond and Janine Bourdin, eds., Edouard Daladier, chef du gouvernement, avril 1938–septembre 1939 (Paris, 1977), p. 223.

32. Esmonde M. Robertson, Mussolini as Empire-Builder: Europe and Africa, 1932–36 (New York, 1977), pp. 1–6, 28–34. Robertson also argues (pp. 92–95) that Mussolini decided after the breakup of the disarmament conference in 1934 that he had better realize some of his plans at once.

to increase Italy's industrial and manpower base, and it succeeded militarily despite sanctions by the League of Nations.

Mussolini also intervened heavily in the Spanish Civil War for ideological and strategic reasons, and in the late 1930s Italy began rearming to try to take advantage of the approaching world crisis. Mussolini spoke of possible expansion in the Balkans, against France, and in North Africa, but he had to cope with the opposition of King Victor Emmanuel to a new general war. Mussolini's policies clearly drew upon long-standing imperialist traditions, as well as Fascist theories of autarky.[33] Although he hoped to profit from a new war, he had no intention of unleashing a general conflict on his own.[34]

The German government, which had lost its colonies and most of its military forces as a result of the First World War, could not so easily turn to imperialism in response to the onset of the Depression. During the period 1923–1929, Gustav Stresemann had tried to loosen the restrictions of the Versailles Treaty by agreement with the western powers—a process that culminated with their agreement to end the occupation of Germany in 1929. He had also done what he could to attract foreign capital and contribute to general economic prosperity. The Brüning government, however, which took power in 1930 after the financial burden of the Depression had toppled the Great Coalition, definitely abandoned this course. Brüning, whose deflationary policies imposed much greater sacrifices upon the German people than any previous Weimar government, apparently wanted to compensate for the hardships the Germans were experiencing with successes in foreign policy, including the end of reparations and the legalization of German rearmament.[35] Pursuing economic imperialism with the limited means at hand, Brüning in 1931 also tried to create a new economic hinterland for Germany in southeastern Europe, both by proposing an Austro-German customs union and by concluding preferential trade treaties with Hungary, Rumania, and Yugoslavia. For-

33. A James Gregor, *Italian Fascism and Developmental Dictatorship* (Princeton, 1979), pp. 138–139.

34. See also MacGregor Knox, *Mussolini Unleashed, 1939–1941: Politics and Strategy in Fascist Italy's Last War* (New York, 1982), pp. 3–43.

35. Schuker, American *"Reparations" to Germany* pp. 53–54; Edward Bennett, *German Rearmament and the West* (Princeton, 1979); and especially Krüger, *Der Außenpolitik der Republik von Weimar*, pp. 507–555. Franz Knipping, *Deutschland, Frankreich und das Ende der Locarno-Ära, 1928–1931* (Munich, 1987), takes a more skeptical view of Stresemann's eventual intentions.

eign Office officials hoped that these agreements would also help achieve the goal of revision of the German-Polish frontier.[36] But the customs union project—which the French government quite rightly interpreted as the beginning of an attempt to overturn the 1919 peace settlement—increased international tensions and led to withdrawal of foreign capital from Germany, making the economic situation even worse.

Unfortunately for Brüning, despite his successful liberation of Germany from the reparations burden in 1932, his new policies did not win him a secure position either among the voters or with President Hindenburg, upon whose support he relied for his deflationary decrees. Hindenburg dismissed Brüning in the spring of 1932, and the established parties continued losing ground to the Nazis and the Communists in the two Reichstag elections of that year.[37] The accession of Adolf Hitler as German chancellor ushered in a new era of European imperialism.

Nationality Problems, 1919–1933

Throughout this period nationality conflicts persisted, and in some cases worsened, within the new central and eastern European frontiers drawn after 1918. No new pattern of relationships among different peoples emerged in the successor states, each of which was dominated by one particular national group. Minorities did not enjoy language, cultural, and political rights in many instances, but even in Czechoslovakia, which had the best record, one language group, the Czechs, generally controlled national political power. The Serbs occupied a similar position in Yugoslavia. Meanwhile the Magyars in Transylvania—now Rumanian—and the Germans within Poland struggled to maintain their economic and language rights against determined attacks from the Rumanians and Poles.[38] Jews in eastern Europe also suffered extensive discrimination. In Hungary, Rumania, and Poland they became sub-

36. Kaiser, *Economic Diplomacy*, pp. 17–35.

37. Thomas Childers, *The Nazi Voter: The Social Foundations of Fascism in Germany, 1919–1933* (Chapel Hill, 1983), pp. 192–211. One older party, the DNVP, did gain votes in the second election.

38. Two surveys of the treatment of eastern European minorities between the wars are Stephan M. Horak et al., *Eastern European National Minorities, 1919–1980: A Handbook* (Littleton, Colo., 1985), and Pearson, *National Minorities in Eastern Europe*. On the crucial case of Czechoslovakia, see Johann Wolfgang Brügel, *Tscheschen und Deutsche, 1919–38* (Munich, 1967).

ject to various forms of legal discrimination during the 1920s and 1930s, both before and after the imposition of anti-Semitic laws within Germany. As early as 1936, the Polish government advocated a massive emigration of Jews from Poland, either to Palestine or possibly to Madagascar.[39]

The postwar minorities treaties and the League of Nations provided little help. Under the procedures developed by the league, minorities could address complaints directly to the secretary general of the league, but only a member of the league council could actually make a complaint the subject of a discussion. The Germans of eastern and southeastern Europe therefore lacked any advocate within the league until 1926, when Germany became a member, while the Jews could not count upon any member to take up their case. Within the council, the French government consistently backed the claims of its allies among the successor states, who protested intervention in their internal affairs, while the British representatives generally argued for assimilation as the solution to the problem of national minorities. The "Committees of Three" appointed by the secretary general to hear complaints sometimes put pressure upon governments to moderate their treatment of nationalities but almost never brought complaints before the full council.[40]

National minorities also fared increasingly poorly within the other new nation of the postwar world, the Soviet Union. The Bolsheviks began by encouraging national self-determination throughout the old Russian empire, but in practice the largely Russian Red Army had to retake many of the borderlands and overthrow middle-class nationalist regimes, most notably in the Ukraine. In addition, the increasing centralization of state and party authority throughout the USSR in the early years of the regime inevitably put more and more power in the hands of the Bolshevik leadership, most of whom were Russians. Despite the reservations of Lenin, who was campaigning against "Great Russian

---

39. Bela Vago and George L. Mosse, eds. *Jews and Non-Jews in Eastern Europe, 1918–1945* (Jerusalem, 1974); Antony Polonsky, *Politics in Independent Poland, 1921–1939* (Oxford, 1972), pp. 423–428, 465–470. The growth of racially exclusive and anti-Semitic nationalism has also been discussed in George L. Mosse, *Toward the Final Solution: A History of European Racism* (New York, 1978), esp. pp. 150–190.

40. Carole Fink, "Defender of Minorities: Germany in the League of Nations, 1926–1933," *Central European History*, 5, no. 4 (December 1972): 330–357.

chauvinism" at the time of his last illness, the constitution of the Soviet Union adopted in 1923 gave undisguised priority to the class question—that is, the need for the dictatorship of the proletariat and the Communist party—over the national question, or the proper relations among different national groups. Stalin, who supervised the establishment of the USSR, even managed to pack the Council of Nationalities, or second chamber of the legislature, with a substantial Russian majority.[41] During the late 1920s, he accused both the so-called Left and Right oppositions of nationalist deviations, and in the early 1930s show trials began, at which Stalin's opponents, including former Soviet prime minister Alexei Rykov and many non-Russian Communist leaders, were accused of plotting to sell various Soviet borderlands to foreign countries. The purges of 1936–1939 also took a heavy toll on non-Russian Communist leaders.[42] Despite its theoretical emphasis upon national equality, Stalin's regime was moving toward drastic solutions to some of its national questions.

Thus, the new central and eastern European governments had achieved at best only very tenuous accommodations with their national minorities by the mid-1930s, and the problem of the political organization of ethnically mixed areas of eastern Europe had not been solved. With the exceptions of Switzerland and Belgium, no Continental European government treated its national minorities as fully equal citizens. Many minorities clearly hoped to be reunited with their own national states, or, in the case of the Jews, to create their own national entity in Palestine. All European national minorities, moreover, had lost a critical safety valve in 1924, when the United States had virtually ended legal immigration. Indeed, both the wartime and postwar history of the United States show a heightened, more chauvinistic, and more exclusivist nationalism quite similar to concurrent developments in much of Europe.[43] By the mid 1930s, omens for the future of national minorities were generally poor. As long as peace lasted, European governments—like those before 1914—could probably cope with nationalist dis-

41. Richard Pipes, *The Formation of the Soviet Union: Communism and Nationalism, 1917–1923* (Cambridge, Mass., 1954), pp. 241–286; E. H. Carr, *The Bolshevik Revolution, 1917–1923*, vol. 1 (London, 1950), pp. 259–413.

42. Walter Kolarz, *Russia and Her Colonies* (3d ed., New York, 1953), pp. 9–13.

43. David M. Kennedy, *Over Here: The First World War and American Society* (New York, 1980), pp. 45–92; Robert A. Divine, *American Immigration Policy, 1924–32* (New Haven, 1957), pp. 1–25.

content. Should a new war occur, however, national claims would inevitably become the focus of war aims, while governments might easily be tempted to increase the homogeneity of their states.

Hitler and the Second World War

Adolf Hitler represented a new element in European domestic and international politics. On the surface, Hitler seemed in many ways to be a modern type of politician. Despite the many anti-modern aspects of Nazi political ideology and the violence of the Storm Troopers (SA), the Nazis had come to power mainly through modern political techniques of propaganda and electoral mobilization. Indeed, the most authoritative study of electoral politics in the Weimar republic has concluded that the Nazis amassed the largest electoral following in Germany in 1932 largely because they understood the techniques of modern electioneering better than their opponents.[1] Moreover, Hitler in power continued to manipulate domestic and foreign opinion very effectively, and in the early stages of his rule he often played a kind of mediating role among the military and civilian bureaucracies, economic interest groups, and organizations of the Nazi party.[2] In the long run, however, Hitler turned out to be not in any sense a typical modern politician, but rather the most extreme ideologue who has ever held power in a modern Western country. He determined to revolutionize Germany, Europe, and the world, and his collaborators zealously built new institutions with which to do so. His most extreme views dealt with precisely the two questions around which European international politics in the late nineteenth and early twentieth centuries had hitherto revolved: imperialism and nationalities questions.

Hitler's views on imperialism and economic self-sufficiency were not original. Research, indeed, has tended to show that the ideas of *Mein Kampf*, his unpublished second book, his 1936 memorandum on the Four Year Plan, and his musings at headquarters during the Second World War all had been current in German

---

1. Childers, *Nazi Voter, passim*.
2. This is perhaps most thoroughly covered by Martin Broszat, *Der Staat Hitlers: Grundlegung und Entwicklung seiner inneren Verfassung* (Munich, 1969), pp. 244–362.

right-wing political and academic circles since the late 1890s, and further study will probably show Hitler's beliefs to be entirely typical of radical German and Austrian nationalists.[3] Although Hitler knew little of the details of economics, he believed (wrongly) that Germany suffered from certain chronic long-term economic problems that imperialism, and imperialism alone, could solve. Germany's essential problem, he argued, was its lack of living space and inability to feed itself. Thus, after the German state had brought the Germans of Austria and Czechoslovakia within its borders, it would proceed to conquer eastern Europe, turn it into a German economic hinterland, and settle the Ukraine with agricultural colonists. While some eastern European peoples, such as the Balts, might possibly be Germanized, many others must be reduced to the status of colonized peoples or slaves. Hitler's program for eastern Europe as he described it before the seizure of power seemed to combine elements of Naumann's Mitteleuropa scheme and Ludendorff's plans for the Ukraine, although on one occasion he specifically denied these influences.[4] After coming to power, Hitler endorsed the need for eventual colonial expansion in tropical Africa.[5] He also believed along with the extreme imperialists of the pre-1914 period that war was not only a necessity but a positive benefit in modern society. And ultimately—after the conquest of a self-sufficient empire in eastern Europe—he expected worldwide military conflict against other powers, apparently including the British empire, the United States, and Japan.

Hitler's foreign and economic policy, like that of many German imperialists before and during the First World War, reflected the belief that the world would eventually be divided into huge, self-sufficient empires. The real solution to the economic problems of Germany and other European industrial nations lay in a free world economy, and most German governments before and after the First World War had generally recognized this. But in his unpublished second book, written in 1928, Hitler had flatly rejected world trade as a solution to Germany's problems on ideological

3. Karl-Dietrich Bracher, *The German Dictatorship: The Origins, Structure, and Effects of National Socialism* (New York, 1970), pp. 127–128.

4. Kaiser, *Economic Diplomacy*, pp. 60–62.

5. Klaus Hildebrand, *Vom Reich zum Weltreich: Hitler, NSDAP, und koloniale Frage, 1919–1945* (Munich, 1969).

grounds.[6] By the time he came to power in 1933, the German government and other major governments had already taken steps that reduced trade and tried to create protected markets. The Weimar government in 1931–32 had already frozen foreign assets in Germany to avoid complete financial collapse, and the German civilian economic bureaucracy, led by Hjalmar Schacht, began restructuring German trade along bilateral lines in 1933–34.[7]

Almost at once, however, Hitler began preparing for the war of conquest upon which he counted to establish Germany as a world power. By continuing to freeze foreign holdings in Germany, eliminating political democracy and financial accountability, and allowing Schacht to begin extensive government borrowing while rationing foreign exchange and controlling imports, Hitler and his collaborators managed to initiate large-scale rearmament despite the financial and foreign trade problems that had plagued the Weimar republic. Rearmament, combined with large, previously begun public works programs, rapidly reduced unemployment in Germany in the years 1933–1936, and although the German people suffered from shortages of many foodstuffs and consumer goods, Hitler undoubtedly benefited politically from the stimulation of the economy.

The real significance of the Nazi regime in European politics began to emerge in 1936. By March of that year, Hitler had not only achieved some rearmament but had also cast off the restrictions upon German sovereignty established by the Versailles Treaty. Shortly thereafter, he began a series of domestic and foreign moves designed to rearm much more heavily, redraw the map of central Europe, and eventually conquer a huge, self-sufficient empire. In so doing, he encountered the inevitable economic and political obstacles to a successful great war that Germany and the other European powers had faced during the First World War. The years 1936–1941 tell the story of Hitler's initially successful but ultimately disastrous attempt to overcome these obstacles by taking advantage of the structure of European politics. His tactics re-

---

6. He clung consistently to this belief throughout his career as chancellor, and during the war he frequently boasted that his refusal to rely upon export markets had lifted Germany out of the depression. See *Hitler's Secret Conversations, 1941–1944* (New York, 1953), pp. 35–36.

7. Kaiser, *Economic Diplomacy*, pp. 63–80, 130–136; James, *German Slump*, pp. 387–397.

volved around the three critical problems of European international politics in the first half of the twentieth century: the problem of economic self-sufficiency, the nationality problem, and the domestic political problems of general war.

The effects of German rearmament, and the related issue of war or peace, became controversial in the German government beginning in 1936. Until then, Schacht, as economics minister and Reichsbank president, had loyally carried out the expansion of the German economy through public works and rearmament while continuing to repudiate many of Germany's foreign obligations, and the Army High Command had welcomed rearmament and the expansion of the army. The nature of Hitler's policies became clearer in 1936, when the German economy faced a new crisis. Rearmament had stimulated demand for imported raw materials and foodstuffs, while diverting resources from export industries. Schacht argued that the time had come to slow rearmament and increase exports—in other words, to begin preparing for Germany's return to the world economy. He also seems to have believed that Germany could now secure the return of its lost colonies and the revision of the German-Polish frontier at an international conference, thus fully restoring its great-power status. Hitler, however, absolutely refused to slow down rearmament and entrusted Göring with the task of preparing the German economy and the German army for war in four years. He rejected both a return to the world economy and the satisfaction of Germany's colonial demands by peaceful means. Hitler was proud of having freed Germany, as he saw it, from dependence upon export markets, and he liked to boast about this during the war.[8] The Four Year Plan concentrated upon expanding heavy industrial capacity and developing synthetic substitutes for two critical imported raw materials, oil and rubber. To achieve these goals, Göring rapidly increased state ownership of the economy and reserved the maximum possible foreign exchange for imports of raw materials. Food shortages persisted, but the Germans avoided catastrophe by purchasing millions of tons of grain from southeastern European nations who lacked other markets and had to accept Reichsmarks for their goods.[9]

8. *Hitler's Secret Conversations*, pp. 35–36, 60–61.
9. Kaiser, *Economic Diplomacy*, pp. 153–169.

Hitler's memorandum on the Four Year Plan, together with *Mein Kampf* and his second book, leave no doubt that he always wanted to conquer living space in the east by fighting a great war.[10] He confirmed this again at the so-called Hossbach Conference of November 5, 1937.[11] At the conference Hitler discussed the possibility of absorbing Austria and Czechoslovakia in the near future—and thereby, he argued, helping to solve the problem of living space, partly by expelling some of the existing population of those countries—and also referred to the need for a great war in 1943–1945. He failed to persuade Generals Blomberg and Fritsch or Foreign Minister von Neurath, who doubted the possibility of a local war against Austria or Czechoslovakia.

Such doubts were widespread. After 1918, many German military leaders and diplomats had concluded that Germany must avoid another total war. During the 1920s and early 1930s, several important figures within the German General Staff had argued that Germany simply could not plan for a new war on the scale of 1914, and had groped for alternative strategies to achieve German national goals.[12] Chief of Staff Ludwig Beck and Foreign Office State Secretary Ernst von Weizsäcker argued during 1938 against a new conflict with Britain and France over Czechoslovakia. In a new war against Britain, France, and the Soviet Union, Weizsäcker argued on June 20, 1938, "the common loser with us would be the whole of Europe, the victors chiefly the non-European continents and the anti-social powers."[13] And despite the bold front that Hitler displayed at the Hossbach Conference and on other occasions, he shared these fears. To make Germany a world power, he had to overcome the obstacles that the First World War had revealed: Germany's diplomatic isolation, its restricted economic base, and the possibility—which Hitler never forgot—that the German people might turn against the government once again should it involve them in a prolonged war.[14]

10. The memorandum on the Four Year Plan is printed in *Documents on German Foreign Policy, 1918–1945, from the Archives of the German Foreign Ministry* (Washington, 1949–1966), series C, vol. 5, no. 490.

11. Ibid., D, I, no. 19.

12. See Michael Geyer, "German Strategy in the Age of Machine Warfare, 1914–1945," in Peter Paret, ed., *Makers of Modern Strategy from Machiavelli to the Nuclear Age* (Princeton, 1986), pp. 554–564, and Geyer's much longer *Aufrüstung oder Sicherheit: Die Reichswehr in der Krise der Machtpolitik, 1924–36* (Wiesbaden, 1980), esp. pp. 167–176.

13. See Kaiser, *Economic Diplomacy*, p. 222.

14. Albert Speer, *Inside the Third Reich* (New York, 1970), p. 281, makes one of the best statements of this point.

Initially, Hitler had hoped that clever alliance diplomacy might smooth his path. His writings had violently criticized the diplomacy of the German empire and cited the need for more effective alliances, specifically with Britain and Italy. By November 1937, the experience of the Ethiopian and Spanish civil wars, in which Britain had failed to offer effective opposition to Italy, had convinced him to opt for Italy over Britain.[15] But the Hossbach Conference showed that he had not convinced his senior military leaders and diplomats that he had developed a viable strategy. In order to stay on the course he had set, he had to overcome their opposition and to begin expansion despite Germany's diplomatic isolation and continuing lack of resources for a long war.

From early 1938 until the attack upon the Soviet Union in June 1941, Hitler overcame all these problems with a remarkable combination of careful diplomacy, intervention in the internal affairs of other countries, threats and intimidation, and rapid, spectacular blitzkriegs. In so doing, he temporarily overcame both his economic and domestic political problems. His first three successes were the *Anschluss* with Austria, in March 1938, the annexation of the Sudetenland in October 1938, and the destruction of Czechoslovakia in March 1939. His initial successes owed much to the principle of nationality, which he had exploited to undermine the governments of Austria and Czechoslovakia, and which the British and French now declined to oppose. By late 1937, Hitler's own success within Germany had strengthened National Socialism in Austria and German nationalism in Czechoslovakia tremendously. Austrian Nazis were nearing a major position within the Austrian government, and Konrad Henlein's Sudeten German party had emerged as the clear representative of Germans within Czechoslovakia.[16] As Hitler came to understand, neither the French nor the British were willing to fight to maintain the provisions of the peace settlement of 1919 that violated the nationality principle to Germany's disadvantage. They therefore acquiesced in the *Anschluss* and agreed to the transfer of the Sudetenland to Germany in September 1938 rather than risk a war. Hitler subsequently managed

15. Jonathan Wright and Paul Stafford, "Hitler, Britain, and the Hossbach Memorandum," *Militärgeschichtleiche Mitteilungen*, 42, no. 2 (1987): 77–123.

16. ". . . the status quo," writes Gerhard L. Weinberg, "especially in Austria, was crumbling steadily and could quite easily dissolve without the kind of overt international crisis in which any foreign power might usefully intervene." Weinberg, *The Foreign Policy of Hitler's Germany: Starting World War II, 1937–39* (Chicago, 1980), p. 284.

to destroy the remainder of Czechoslovakia by encouraging Slovak nationalism and Hungarian revisionism. Remarkably, all these changes took place under a facade of legality.

While recognizing in 1937–38 that Germany could not yet fight a prolonged war, Hitler tried to use what later came to be called brinkmanship, diplomacy, and limited local wars to carry out the first stage of his expansionist program. When his generals objected to the dangers of his policy toward Czechoslovakia during the summer of 1938, he replied that the British and the French would not intervene. More significantly, when he became convinced, on the very eve of his planned attack on Czechoslovakia, on September 28, that they probably *would* intervene—and when Mussolini declined to join him in a war and the German people seemed unenthusiastic—he called off the attack and contented himself with a diplomatic triumph at Munich.[17] Thus, although he had hoped to destroy Czechoslovakia in a short local war that would demonstrate Germany's new military might, he refused as yet to risk a conflict with Britain and France and settled the crisis diplomatically when war threatened.

Hitler occupied Prague in March 1939 and also secured another peaceful, quasi-legal victory in Memel. He then tried to negotiate with the Polish government for the return of Danzig and extraterritorial transportation across the Polish corridor. After the British and French promised to protect Poland against him, however, he decided to attack Poland. This, he knew, could well mean war with the western powers and therefore required more diplomatic preparation. He initially sought a tripartite alliance with Italy and Japan which would commit all three powers to fight in a war against France, Britain, and the Soviet Union. When the Japanese government refused to commit itself, Hitler came to terms with the Soviet Union instead.[18] After agreeing upon spheres of influence in Poland and the rest of eastern Europe with Stalin in the Nazi-Soviet

17. R. J. Overy's argument that Hitler was always planning for a long war rather than a short one, and therefore had no blitzkrieg strategy, has been overdrawn. While Hitler was apparently preparing for a huge war sometime during the 1940s, all his projected campaigns between 1938 and 1941—from the planned attack on Czechoslovakia to the attack on the Soviet Union—were based upon rapid success. See Weinberg, *Starting World War II*, pp. 18–24, and R. J. Overy, "Hitler's War and the German Economy: A Reinterpretation," *Economic History Review*, 2d ser., 35, no. 2 (May 1982): 272–291.

18. Weinberg, *Starting World War II*, pp. 600–611.

Pact, Hitler attacked Poland on September 1, 1939, despite the danger of British and French intervention.

The *Anschluss*, the annexation of the Sudetenland, the occupation of Prague, and the attack on Poland also solved many of Hitler's domestic economic and political problems. The outbreak of war in 1939 also reflected the consequences of Hitler's rearmament policies—consequences which turned his belief in the inadequacy of the German economic base into a self-fulfilling prophecy—and the political importance of foreign policy successes for his rule. Since the mid-1970s, a number of authors have argued that Hitler's decision for war reflected the growing economic crisis in Germany, which was making it impossible to continue rearmament at the current level under peacetime conditions.[19] A recent controversy suggests that agreement is growing at least on the economic importance of the attack upon Poland.[20] This means not that war was a real economic necessity for Germany, but rather that Hitler's belief in the need for German expansion had become a self-fulfilling prophecy because of the effects of accelerated rearmament. In particular, rearmament was hurting the German trade balance by increasing imports and diverting production from exports, and the German labor market was having trouble coping with the combined demands of rearmament, construction projects, and the rest of the economy.

Hans-Erich Volkmann has written the best analysis of the situation to date. As he showed in 1979, German heavy industrial capacity had reached its limits by 1937, and only increased in 1938 and 1939 because of the annexations of Austria, the Sudetenland, and Bohemia-Moravia.[21] Efforts to become self-sufficient in food

19. See Timothy W. Mason, "Innere Krise und Angriffskrieg, 1938/1939," in Friedrich Forstmeier and Hans-Erich Volkmann, eds., *Wirtschaft und Rüstung am Vorabend des Zweiten Weltkrieges* (Düsseldorf, 1975), pp. 158–188; see also Mason, *Sozialpolitik im dritten Reich: Arbeiterklasse und Volksgemeinschaft* (Opladen, 1977); Wilhelm Deist, *The Wehrmacht and German Rearmament* (Toronto, 1981), pp. 111–112; William Carr, "Wirtschaft, Rüstung und Politik am Vorabend des zweiten Weltkrieges," in Wolfgang Michalka, ed., *Nationalsozialistische Außenpolitik* (Darmstadt, 1978), pp. 451–454; Kaiser, *Economic Diplomacy*, pp. 281–282.

20. The controversy among Tim Mason, R. J. Overy, and myself, is in *Past and Present*, 122 (February 1989): 200–240. Despite some important continuing disagreements, all three participants agree that Hitler undertook the war against Poland largely for economic reasons, and that the war had favorable economic consequences.

21. The occupation of Bohemia and Moravia also enabled the army to equip several divisions with Czech equipment. See Deist, *The Wehrmacht and German Rearmament*, p. 89.

and raw materials, or to import them only from eastern European states that traded with Germany in Reichsmarks, had not succeeded, and demands for foreign exchange to pay for overseas imports remained high. German exports, moreover, were *falling* during 1939–despite a general upturn in the world economy—because so much productive capacity had been diverted to rearmament and public construction projects. German manufacturers were even losing orders for arms exports because of the enormous demands of rearmament. As Volkmann shows, Germany would clearly have run out of foreign exchange and goods with which to pay for exports within a few more months had the war not begun. Labor shortages had reached one million workers, and Göring had already made some attempts to control the use of labor throughout the German economy, with a view to restricting labor in nonessential areas.[22] It has been convincingly argued that the economic crisis grew partly out of the political anarchy characteristic of the Nazi regime, which in this case had allowed Hitler to approve separate, enormous expenditures for the navy, the Siegfried line of fortifications against France, and numerous public construction projects, without any governmental mechanism for assessing or resolving competing claims upon resources.[23]

During 1939 Hitler himself spoke of the immediate need to widen Germany's territorial base, and added—in agreement with military authorities—that although Germany was not yet ready for a long war, it could fight a short one. Furthermore—as Tim Mason has recently suggested—the new rearmament targets adopted by Hitler early in 1939 were so grandiose as to have required a major enlargement of the German economic base.[24] Elements within German industry—especially the chemical giant IG Farben and elements of heavy industry—carefully planned the reorganization of various sectors of the European economy before war began, and

22. Hans-Erich Volkmann, "Die NS-Wirstchaft in Vorbereitung des Krieges," in Militärgeschichtliche Forschungsamt, ed., *Ursachen und Voraussetzungen der deutschen Kriegspolitik: Das deutsche Reich und der zweite Weltkrieg*, vol. 1 (Stuttgart, 1979), pp. 177–370; see esp. pp. 190–198, 310–370.

23. Jost Dülffer, "Der Beginn des Krieges 1939: Hitler, die innere Krise und das Mächtesystem," *Geschichte und Gesellschaft*, 2, no. 4 (1976): 443–457.

24. "There is no possible way in which the armaments plans of 1939 could be even approximately fulfilled within Germany's boundaries of March 1939 and under the prevailing social and constitutional order." Mason, "Comments," *Past and Present*, 122 (1989): 217.

moved immediately to implement some of their plans (such as the adaptation of the heavy industry of Polish Silesia into the German war economy) as soon as the war made this possible.[25] Hitler himself had remarked during the Hossbach Conference that time would work against Germany economically, and according to one account, he told his generals on August 22, 1939, that "because of our restrictions [*Einschränkungen*, or bottlenecks] our economic situation is such that we can only hold out for a few more years. Göring can confirm this."[26] In attacking Poland, Hitler was choosing a strategy which Nazi economic theorists had put forward for years: a strategy of small, predatory wars to increase self-sufficiency.[27]

Hitler's diplomacy and military strategy from the summer of 1939 onward was also designed to secure necessary supplies of foodstuffs and raw materials. In the months before the outbreak of war, an unofficial study prepared by IG Farben had concluded that Germany needed the resources of the Soviet Union, as well as those of northern and eastern Europe, to withstand a blockade.[28] The Nazi-Soviet Pact included generous economic clauses that provided Germany with large immediate deliveries of food and raw materials in exchange for *future* deliveries of industrial goods and thus enabled Hitler to begin the war with some confidence.[29] Then, after the war began, German imports and exports suffered a sharp fall—largely because of Germany's inability to pay for imports—and the occupation of Denmark, Norway, and the Benelux countries was designed to put the resources of these countries at Germany's disposal.[30] Hitler also ordered the immediate attack

25. Waclaw Dlugoborski and Czeslaw Madjaczyk, "Ausbeutungssysteme in den besetzten Gebieten Polens und der UdSSR," in Friedrich Forstmeier and Hans Erich Volkmann, eds., *Kriegswirtschaft und Rüstung, 1939–1945* (Düsseldorf, 1971), pp. 384–400.

26. *Documents on German Foreign Policy*, D, VII, no. 172. Another account of this talk gives a different version of the remark, however, and refers to a period of ten to fifteen years. See Jeremy Noakes and Geoffrey Pridham, eds., *Documents on Nazism, 1919–45* (New York, 1975), p. 563.

27. Volkmann, "Die NS-Wirtschaft," pp. 190–198.

28. Kaiser, *Economic Diplomacy*, p. 278. Several other official and unofficial studies stressed that the resources of eastern Europe would not suffice to fight a war.

29. Of course, this inevitably put more pressure on German industry when *German* deliveries fell due, and thus tended to encourage an attack upon the Soviet Union.

30. Hans-Erich Volkmann, "NS-Außenhandel im geschlossenen Kriegswirtschaftsraum (1939–1941)," in Forstmeier and Volkmann, eds., *Kriegswirtschaft und Rüstung, 1939–1945*, pp. 92–101.

upon France partly because he believed that Germany's economic position would rapidly worsen relative to the Anglo-French allies, and partly because he feared continued dependence upon Soviet supplies.[31] The victory over France placed much larger resources of food, raw materials, arms, and labor at his disposal, but by 1941, the nations of southeastern Europe seemed less willing to meet Germany's needs, and Hitler worried more and more about dependence upon the Soviet Union. The war against the Soviets—undertaken with the help of some of the successor states—was designed to secure direct control of Soviet resources and to encourage the states of southeastern Europe to tailor their economies to the needs of war.[32] Like the previous attacks upon Poland and France, it also aimed at the immediate collapse of the Soviet government.

War immediately helped solve some of Germany's economic problems—especially the labor shortage—and eventually enabled the Germans to increase arms production most impressively. Planning for the use of prisoners of war in German agriculture began as early as January 1939, and the recruitment of Polish workers started within days of the attack. The use of Polish and then French prisoners of war on a massive scale more than made up for losses of German men to the military, at least until 1941.[33] Arms production during these three years increased far more rapidly than at any other time under the Nazi regime. The increase, moreover, was accomplished largely at the expense of domestic consumption, which dropped significantly, supporting Mason's claim that the war enabled the government to demand more from the civilian population.[34]

Hitler's diplomatic and military successes also solved two separate but closely related domestic political problems. They maintained the confidence of the German people in his leadership de-

31. Hans-Adolf Jacobsen, *Fall Gelb: Der Kampf um den deutschen Operationsplan zur Westoffensive 1940* (Wiesbaden, 1957), pp. 143–153; Jehuda L. Wallach, *The Dogma of the Battle of Annihilation: The Theories of Clausewitz and Schlieffen and Their Impact on the German Conduct of Two World Wars* (Westport, Conn., 1986), pp. 252–262.

32. Volkmann, "NS-Außenhandel," pp. 126–129.

33. Ian Kershaw, *Popular Opinion and Political Dissent in the Third Reich* (Oxford, 1983), pp. 281–288, discusses the impact of Polish workers upon the desperate Bavarian peasantry. See also Ulrich Herbert, *Fremdarbeiter: Politik und Praxis des "Ausländer-Einstatzes" in der Kriegswirtschaft des dritten Reiches* (Berlin and Bonn, 1985), pp. 66–67.

34. Overy, "Hitler's War and the German Economy," p. 283.

spite the sacrifices which he had imposed upon them, and they intimidated the high-level opposition which believed that Germany could not fight a new general war and which actually plotted Hitler's overthrow on two occasions during the early stages of expansion.

Several recent studies of popular opinion and social policy in the Third Reich seem to suggest that the popularity of the Nazi regime reached its peak around 1935 or 1936, just as unemployment ended and as the economic difficulties associated with rearmament—including continual shortages of consumer goods, labor shortages in agriculture, and upward pressure on wages—began to emerge. By 1938, economic problems in many sectors had become serious, and police and other sources reported increasing discontent.[35] Unless Hitler cut back on rearmament, all of these problems would get worse, not better—and far from reducing rearmament, Hitler was insisting that it be drastically increased once again, apparently to prepare for the great war he anticipated in several years. In this context, the political and economic significance of a series of crises and small wars becomes clear. Crisis and war provided some excuse for the hardships imposed upon the German people. A continuing stream of triumphs enormously enhanced Hitler's prestige, apparently encouraging the people to credit him with Germany's triumphs while blaming their hardships—and other unpopular aspects of Nazi policies—upon his subordinates. Meanwhile, expansion provided at least some short-term solutions to Germany's economic problems. As preparations for war increasingly disrupted the German economy, it behooved Hitler to show that these preparations would lead not to a repetition of the catastrophe of 1914–1918 but instead to the rapid expansion of German power and the eventual achievement of world-power status.

Two recent studies suggest that even before 1938, Hitler's foreign policy was extremely popular, and probably made up among the population for considerable economic hardship and other unpopular domestic moves. His more dramatic foreign policy successes from 1938 through 1940 had a tremendous effect upon his popularity at a time when hardships were becoming even

35. See Mason, *Arbeiterklasse und Volksgemeinschaft*, and two works by Ian Kershaw, *Popular Opinion and Political Dissent*, and *The "Hitler Myth": Image and Reality in the Third Reich* (Oxford, 1987).

greater.[36] While the outbreak of war in 1939 seems initially to have depressed the population, the victories over Poland, Norway, and France strengthened the emerging myth of Hitler's genius and raised his approval to new heights. Still, he apparently believed that the German people would simply not tolerate a long war. And while intelligence reports in early 1941 showed a high level of approval of Hitler among the populace at large, the people also expected a decisive stroke which would bring about peace. A continuing string of foreign policy and military successes had become something of a necessity. Any prolonged period of peace would surely have called into question the need for the further disruption of the economy.

Hitler's diplomatic and military successes also crippled the high-level opposition to his policies. The *Anschluss* put an end to the crisis inaugurated by the dismissal of Generals Blomberg and Fritsch and, indeed, may have been accelerated by that crisis.[37] The Munich agreement ended the first major conspiracy to overthrow Hitler, in which a number of generals and diplomats had planned to arrest him if a general war broke out.[38] The conspiracy revived in the winter of 1939–40, after the defeat of Poland and Hitler's insistence upon an immediate offensive against France,[39] but after Hitler's victories in western Europe it collapsed, not to revive until Germany was clearly losing the war. The Führer was well aware of the domestic political impact of these victories. As he made clear in August of 1939, every one of his dramatic foreign policy initiatives had been opposed by subordinates, but he had been proven right again and again.[40]

Despite his victories, however, Hitler in 1941 was still far from ready for the great war he anticipated. After the defeat of France,

36. See Marlis G. Steinert, *Hitler's War and the Germans: Public Mood and Attitude during the Second World War* (Athens, Ohio, 1977), pp. 1–132, and Kershaw, "Hitler Myth," pp. 121–160.

37. The crisis is covered most thoroughly in Harold C. Deutsch, *Hitler and His Generals: The Hidden Crisis, January–June 1938* (Minneapolis, 1974). On intrigues among the Nazis, see Hans Mommsen, "Ausnahmezustand als Herrschaftstechnik des NS-Regimes," in Manfred Funke, ed., *Hitler, Deutschland und die Mächte: Materialien zur Außenpolitik des Dritten Reiches* (Düsseldorf, 1976), pp. 30–45.

38. See Peter Hoffmann, *The History of the German Resistance, 1933–1945* (Cambridge, Mass., 1977), pp. 49–98.

39. Harold C. Deutsch, *The Conspiracy against Hitler in the Twilight War* (Minneapolis, 1968).

40. His remarks of August 22, 1939, are in Noakes and Pridham, eds., *Documents on Nazism*, pp. 564–565.

he seems to have hoped for a peace with Britain—perhaps one dictated by the weight of German air power—that would enable him once again to prepare for a large-scale war at some future date. But he failed either to defeat Britain or to coerce it into making peace, and the United States in late 1940 and early 1941 began rearming and providing generous assistance to Britain. Hitler then decided to undertake the conquest of the Soviet Union as soon as possible, in order to create his planned European empire before American rearmament had been completed. By this time he had convinced most of the old elites that they could safely pursue the goal of world power, and that a blitzkrieg could vanquish the Soviet Union at relatively little cost. Significantly, neither Hitler nor the German General Staff wanted to risk a long-term conflict *even with the Soviet Union*, but they had concluded that one would not be necessary. Operation Barbarossa anticipated the immediate collapse of the Soviet government as soon as the German army had defeated the Soviet army at the frontier.[41] Hitler and his generals essentially hoped to recreate the situation of mid-1918, when the almost complete disintegration of the Russian state had allowed the German government to begin setting forth a new network of political and economic relationships in the Ukraine, the Baltic, and the Caucasus.[42] Once the Soviets had collapsed, German arms production would shift to aircraft and ships, so as to defend the European empire against the Anglo-Americans and prepare for future conflict on a world scale.[43]

The failure of the blitzkrieg against the Soviets, whose authority held together despite crushing initial defeats, and the American entry in to the war in December 1941 left Hitler in exactly the situation that he had hoped to avoid: a long-term struggle with industrially superior powers.[44] Helped by the occupation of most of Eu-

---

41. All these points have been covered brilliantly by Andreas Hillgrüber, *Hitlers Strategie: Politik und Kriegführung, 1940–41* (Frankfurt, 1965), esp. pp. 352–388, 511–512.

42. The German High Command actually made plans for operations through the Caucasus to the Middle East in July 1941, on the assumption that the Soviets would have already been defeated. Significantly, Hitler often drew analogies between the German positions in the two world wars. See Hillgrüber, *Hitlers Strategie*, pp. 542–543, 553, 555.

43. Ibid., pp. 377–388.

44. "Once the strategy of the aggressors had failed [in early 1942]," Alan Milward writes, "the strategies of all the major combatants became aligned, and the most important element in each was production." Alan S. Milward, *War, Economy, and Society, 1939–1945* (Berkeley, 1977), p. 56.

rope, the German economy performed remarkably well from 1942 through most of 1944. An impressive system of inflated "occupation costs" and clearings gave the Germans an almost unlimited claim upon the resources of western Europe and enabled them to use western European agriculture, heavy industrial resources, and labor to raise production far above 1914–1918 levels. Their brutal methods in eastern Europe were less successful economically, but one author has found that the campaign in Russia was supported principally from Russian resources. With the help of more than seven million foreign workers, Germany raised production of heavy industrial products and munitions to new heights.[45] But the Germans could not match the British and Americans, and their production collapsed rapidly when they had to retreat from Russia and France in 1944–45. In retrospect, Hitler's whole strategy was doomed from the moment the Soviet regime failed to collapse in the summer of 1941.

Hitler's revolutionary foreign policy—designed to overturn the postwar European settlement—bore a marked resemblance to his domestic political strategy before and after his seizure of power. Both relied upon dramatic measures and announcements, dazzling displays of force, and a knack for seizing and keeping the initiative. Both also took advantage of structural weaknesses within contemporary domestic and international politics—weakness which resulted largely from the First World War—and of confusion, disunity, and paralysis among the opposition.[46] It is true, as Hans Mommsen in particular has suggested, that Hitler was personally lazy, that he himself principally played the role of a propagandist, and that his chronic failure ever to define clear lines of authority helped create a situation in which various different Nazi potentates competed to achieve both ideological and personal goals.[47] In the years 1937–1941, however, Hitler was not simply a weak mediator but also—at least in foreign policy—the prime mover. His diplomacy and strategy made Germany the master of

45. Ibid., pp. 71–81; for production figures, compare Hardach, First World War, p. 71. On the Russian campaign, see Alexander Dallin, German Rule in Russia, 1941–45: A Study in Occupation Politics (London, 1957), pp. 365–375.

46. This analogy has been strikingly drawn by Karl Dietrich Bracher. See Bracher, Wolfgang Sauer, and Gerhard Schulz, Die nationalsozialistische Machtergreifung: Studien zur Errichtung des totalitären Herrschaftssystems in Deutschland, 1933/34 (Cologne, 1962), pp. 232–241.

47. Mommsen, "Ausnahmezustand als Herschaftstechnik," passim.

central and western Europe, but without securing the territory that he counted on for future conflict on a world scale.

Because the other European powers were even more eager to avoid a new war than Hitler, the rearmament of Germany and Hitler's denunciation of the Versailles settlement beginning in 1933 posed extremely difficult problems for them. After 1918 the British government had recognized the virtual impossibility of financing and fighting another major war, and it initially solved the problem in 1919 by adopting the ten-year rule, which assumed that no such war would take place for at least ten years.[48] A recent study argues that British governments from 1919 onward feared that a peacetime arms race, let alone a major war, would set off a chain reaction of inflation and social conflict at home, which might have very serious consequences.[49] As late as December 1937, the chiefs of staff stated that they could not successfully fight Germany, Italy, and Japan at the same time, and bluntly recommended steps to reduce the number of Britain's potential enemies.[50]

The British public and some British officials had looked to the League of Nations to provide new mechanisms to settle international disputes, but the Manchurian and Ethiopian crises had dashed these hopes by 1936. Led by Neville Chamberlain, the British government tried to deal with the crises of 1938–39 by combining some rearmament with "appeasement," by which they meant the peaceful settlement of international disputes as an alternative to war.[51] As it ultimately emerged at Munich, appeasement meant the implementation of the Four Power Pact originally proposed by Mussolini in 1933—that is, the creation of a directorate of the great powers to revise the treaties of 1919. Almost a year earlier, Chamberlain had privately made clear that he anticipated changes in central Europe to meet German national claims, and that he would

48. Howard, *Continental Commitment*, pp. 77–79.

49. This is the premise of Schmidt, *Politics and Economics of Appeasement*. Although in my opinion Schmidt exaggerates policy makers' fear of an intensified class struggle should Britain decide to spend more upon arms, they were certainly motivated in their foreign policy by British financial weakness.

50. Howard, *Continental Commitment*, pp. 117–118.

51. As I have argued elsewhere, British appeasement can be understood only if one keeps in mind the actual meaning of the word—"pacification"—rather than the commonly ascribed meaning, "satiation," which undoubtedly stems from an association with "appetite." It is important to note in this connection that Chamberlain never spoke of the appeasement of Germany; rather, he spoke of the appeasement of Europe. See Kaiser, *Economic Diplomacy*, pp. 192–193.

try to bring those changes about peacefully—an intention which his colleague Lord Halifax had communicated to Hitler in November 1937.[52] This strategy was foreshadowed by the Hoare-Laval Pact of 1935, which had sought to avoid war with Italy by meeting Italian claims in Ethiopia halfway. After arranging the peaceable transfer of the Sudetenland to Germany in September 1938, Chamberlain and many other British policy makers were also willing to concede both the recognition of a special German economic position in eastern Europe and greater access to British empire markets as part of a general European settlement.[53] Chamberlain in early 1938 had also specifically offered Hitler a share of the Portuguese and Belgian colonies in Central Africa.[54] After Munich, a British government economic specialist discussed an economic rapprochement of the Munich powers with German authorities.[55] Rather than risk a ruinous war, appeasement sought to give the Germans some of the benefits of war without fighting, and Chamberlain was generally willing to satisfy German claims based upon the principle of nationality. In return, he wanted a German renunciation of force, and above all a disarmament agreement to end the arms race.

The appeasement policy, however, assumed (in public at least) that Hitler would confine himself to bringing ethnic Germans into the Reich,[56] and that he would not undertake *unilateral* initiatives. When Hitler broke up the remainder of Czechoslovakia and annexed half of it in March 1939, British opinion rebelled. Chamberlain had to make it clear that he would not tolerate further unilateral German moves, and that he would fight if Hitler attacked Poland or any other country. He did *not* commit himself to the territorial status quo. During 1939 British government figures made it known publicly and privately that they were willing to meet at

52. Ibid., pp. 193–194.

53. Schmidt, *Politics and Economics of Appeasement*, pp. 84–246.

54. On Chamberlain generally, see Kaiser, *Economic Diplomacy*, pp. 191–192; Keith Middlemas, *The Diplomacy of Illusion: The British Government and Germany, 1937–39* (London, 1972), pp. 110–116, 138–143, 155–156.

55. Kaiser, *Economic Diplomacy*, p. 287.

56. It is a noteworthy but much-neglected point that Chamberlain and Halifax, meeting with French ministers in late November 1938, discussed the possibility of German sponsorship of an independence movement in the Ukraine and agreed that they would do nothing to stop it. Kaiser, *Economic Diplomacy*, p. 261. This is an echo of Lloyd George's peace strategy in early 1918.

least some new German demands, provided that the Germans renounced coercion and showed peaceful intentions. They undoubtedly did so partly because their rearmament, which required a large increase in imports of raw materials and machine tools, had led to a deteriorating trade balance, a fall of the pound, and a Treasury warning that Britain might not be able to sustain military spending at the current level.[57] But Chamberlain knew after March 1939 that if Hitler made an armed move against Poland, Britain would have to go to war, and in September he did so.

Although we know much less about French government policy during the 1930s than about British, some recent studies have shown that Paris, like London, suffered from severe financial problems when it began rearming in response to Hitler's rise and the rearmament of Germany. These problems owed much to the First World War. As late as 1930–31, direct and indirect costs of war, including pensions and debt service, took up more than half the French budget. Revenue had caught up to expenditure only briefly in the late 1920s, and the French government was already running a substantial deficit during the early 1930s.[58] Rearmament began in 1935, under Laval, and sped up considerably in 1936, under the Popular Front government of Léon Blum. But French government revenues remained low, and the government financed rearmament out of loans. This tactic—combined with opposition in financial circles to the Popular Front government on political and social grounds—led to several financial crises in 1936–37, slowed rearmament, and eventually brought down the Blum government. Eventually, after two devaluations and the repeal of the eight-hour day in the fall of 1938, confidence in the government returned, and French rearmament began to reach impressive levels in 1939.[59]

Financial problems, however, had already had major effects on French foreign policy. The French authorities, like the British, understood that in any long war they must depend upon imports from overseas, which could be financed only if the Bank of France retained sufficient reserves. They estimated that the bank needed 50 million francs in gold at the outset of a war in order to finance

57. Ibid., pp. 308–309.
58. Robert Frankenstein, *Le pris du réarmement français (1935–1939)* (Paris, 1982), p. 96.
59. Ibid., esp. pp. 289–299.

the necessary imports—fully two and one-half times the bank's reserves in 1914!—and in the fall of 1938, at the time of Munich, the bank's reserves had fallen to 38 million. After the French and British had repudiated their First World War debts to the United States in 1932, American neutrality laws had made new loans to belligerents impossible. This must also have weighed heavily in Anglo-French planning for war. During the spring of 1938, moreover, both Premier Daladier and Foreign Minister Georges Bonnet had spoken to the German ambassador in Paris of their fears of the consequences of a new European war, which might destroy western European civilization and hand the Continent over to Bolshevism.[60] A year later the reserves had risen to 48 million, and this may well have encouraged the French government to risk war.[61]

The British and French governments continued to try to avoid the consequences of the First World War even after the outbreak of the Second in September 1939. They welcomed the phoney war, which did not require them to fight, and focused their planning upon peripheral military operations, including a wild scheme for the bombing of Germany's new ally, Soviet Russia.[62] The fall of France left the British government with the seemingly impossible problem of financing a new long war against Germany and finding a military strategy that could defeat Germany under far more unfavorable circumstances than in 1914–1918. Financially, the United States came to the rescue with lend-lease in early 1941, offering to finance the British war effort out of American resources and thereby allowing Britain to fight on without incurring a new war debt. Strategically, Winston Churchill throughout the war tried to continue the strategy of Mediterranean, Middle Eastern, and Balkan operations which Lloyd George had initiated in 1918. And at least until American entry into the war, as recent research has shown, he hoped that Britain might achieve victory by blockade and bombing, which in turn might bring about revolts in Nazi-occupied territory *and in Germany itself*—the same way in which the Allies had won the war in 1918.[63] Eventually, however, he had

60. Kaiser, *Economic Diplomacy*, p. 239.
61. Ibid., pp. 109–110.
62. Henri Michel, *The Second World War* (New York, 1975), pp. 59–64.
63. Robert H. Keyserling, "Die Deutsche Komponente in Churchills Strategie der nationalen Erhebungen, 1940–1942; Der Fall Otto Strasser," *Vierteljahreshefte für Zeitgeschichte*, 31, no. 4 (October 1983): pp. 614–645.

to yield the initiative to the American authorities and agree to landings in northern France. He found to his surprise that the British and Americans could in fact mount a successful land offensive against Germany in western Europe.[64]

The Soviet government also preferred to avoid war by cooperating with Hitler, rather than risk the consequences of a new conflict. Stalin's preference for the Nazi-Soviet Pact, over a pact with Britain and France that might have involved him in an immediate war with Hitler, suggested that he, like the western powers at Munich, preferred to regulate the course of German expansion rather than to oppose it. The pact, which created a common frontier between Germany and the Soviet Union, showed that both of these states had achieved a new status and now disposed of the territory between them in the way that late nineteenth-century governments had disposed of tropical Africa. Although our knowledge of internal Soviet politics is virtually nonexistent, we may hypothesize that the gains it brought to the Soviets—eventually including the incorporation of the Baltic states, Bessarabia, and substantial parts of Poland and Finland—gave Stalin even greater prestige. The generous economic concessions Stalin made as part of the pact suggest that he deeply feared Hitler, as do his attempts to maintain their friendship in the spring of 1941.[65] Stalin's refusal to believe in the possibility of a German attack and his nervous collapse when the attack occurred suggest that he, even more than Chamberlain or Bonnet, believed that a new war would mean complete disaster for him and for his regime. He eventually prevailed with the help of the Soviet people and Allied productive capacity.

The Second World War confirmed the lesson of the First: that no European power had the economic resources to compete with the economic might of the United States, which furnished most of the supplies for the Allied war effort against Germany and simultaneously defeated Japan as well. While the Germans, British, and Soviets each produced between 112,000 and 137,000 aircraft during the war, the United States built 300,000; while the Germans pro-

64. David E. Kaiser, "Churchill, Roosevelt, and the Limits of Power: A Review Essay," *International Security*, 10, no. 1 (Summer 1985): 209–212.

65. Hillgrüber, *Hitlers Strategie*, suggests that by the spring of 1941 Stalin realized that his position had weakened vis-à-vis Hitler, and that he would have to make new, important concessions. This seems to be the most sensible explanation of the Soviet dictator's behavior.

duced 45,000 tanks, the United States built 87,000 and the Soviets 103,000.[66] Although both the Soviet Union and the western Allies eventually learned to use the techniques of blitzkrieg to defeat the German armies and reconquer Europe, they consistently relied upon material superiority to win their victories.

Technologically the war introduced armored warfare and strategic bombing, both of which, in different ways, eased the political problems of modern warfare that had emerged during the First World War. Armored warfare turned land combat once again into a war of movement, enabling both sides to win decisive victories at different stages of the conflict. Strategic bombing did *not* initially have anywhere near the impact that many had predicted for it. It did not allow Hitler to coerce Great Britain into making peace in 1940–41, or enable the Allies to bomb the Germans into submission, or even—until very late in the war—to reduce German war production.[67] Bombing did, however, enable the warring governments to claim that they were bringing the war home to the enemy, and to inflict very great human and material losses while incurring relatively low casualties.[68] Bombing, Churchill told the British public in 1941, was making "the German people taste and gulp each month a sharper dose of the miseries they have showered among mankind."[69] The western Allies found bombing especially useful during the long period in which they could not yet attack Hitler directly in Europe.[70] In this way, air power may have helped sustain civilian support for the war and belief in ultimate victory. It also inflicted unprecedented human and material damage upon civilian society.

Hitler, more than any other individual in modern history, dem-

66. Milward, *War, Economy, and Society*, p. 74.

67. Sir Charles Webster and Noble Frankland, *The Strategic Air Offensive against Germany, 1939–1945*, vol. 3, *Victory* (London, 1961), pp. 287–289.

68. British Bomber Command lost about 56,000 men during the whole war, compared to more than 20,000 British soldiers killed *on the first day* of the Somme offensive in 1916. Ibid., p. 286; Keegan, *Face of Battle*, p. 255.

69. Michael Walzer, *Just and Unjust Wars: A Moral Argument with Historical Illustrations* (New York, 1977), p. 256.

70. "The initial attacks of Bomber Command up to the spring of 1942 scarcely caused the Germans much inconvenience, though it cannot be doubted that they contributed powerfully to the maintenance of British morale in a period when no other directly offensive blows could be struck at Germany." Webster and Frankland, *Strategic Air Offensive*, p. 287.

onstrated the possible extent and the ultimate limit of the role of a single individual in international politics. Despite the experience of the First World War and the limitations upon German resources in the 1930s, which would clearly have dissuaded many other German leaders from preparing for or unleashing another general war in Europe, he managed by careful manipulation of contemporary politics, economics, and military technology to conquer most of western Europe and to bring his armies to the banks of the Volga. Meanwhile, as we shall see, he had also undertaken to implement an extreme version of the principle of nationality on a new and horrifying scale. But he could not prevail in a long-term struggle with economically superior powers, and he could not turn to diplomacy when the military balance turned against him. His opponents in the Second World War not only blamed the war upon Hitler and the Nazi regime but also insisted upon total victory and unconditional surrender. Diplomatic feelers among the warring powers seem to have been considerably less frequent than in the First World War.[71] In the end Hitler brought about not merely the complete defeat of his own nation but the end of an era in European history.

Largely as a result of the war, the European states lost their remaining empires, their military autonomy, and some of their political independence. The war doomed Hitler's dreams of imperialism and left the British and French governments too weak to hold on to their empires as well. In the decades following the war, the Western European nations prospered within a restored world economy thanks largely to the economic help and military protection of the United States. Meanwhile, the Soviet Union, rather than Germany, successfully established an informal empire in Central and Eastern Europe—an empire held together officially by Communist ideology and unofficially by large Soviet occupation forces. European attempts to realize the turn-of-the-century dream of imperialism—the dream of European world empires capable of competing with Russia and the United States—had culminated in another *reductio ad absurdum*. In Europe, at least the economic re-

71. Some evidence has emerged of Soviet interest in a separate peace during 1943, but it is equivocal. Hitler himself certainly never undertook a major peace initiative. See Wojtech Mastny, *Russia's Road to the Cold War: Diplomacy, Warfare, and the Politics of Communism, 1941–1945* (New York, 1979), pp. 81–84.

quirements of military power in the twentieth century had brought the era of autonomous military power and the rational use of force for political goals to an end.[72]

Extermination and Transfer: The Nationalities Question and the Second World War

During the Second World War the Nazi regime both pursued an extreme imperialist program to achieve economic self-sufficiency and took even more drastic measures to achieve its preferred solution of the question of European nationalities. Various Nazi agencies used new police powers to begin reordering Europe's population through forced migration and extermination. After the Nazis' defeat in 1945, the victorious Allies also used drastic measures to redraw the ethnic map of Europe.

The Final Solution of the Jewish question—the extermination of between five and six million European Jews, mostly in gas chambers—is of course the most infamous aspect of Nazi nationalities policy. The origins of the Final Solution have become the subject of a bitter and continuing historical debate, focusing upon the role of Hitler and the degree to which policy arose from ideology or from circumstances.[1] Here I shall try to shed new light upon the debate by examining it within the framework of twentieth-century European international politics.

The nationalities question lay at the heart of National Socialist ideology from the beginning. Hitler believed, and never tired of repeating, that the essence of human history lay in the struggle of different races for living space. As already noted, the acquisition of sufficient space involved the conquest of much of Europe and the establishment of a German territorial and economic unit comparable to the United States. Nazi ideology also called for the elimination of a variety of racially, politically, and socially undesirable elements from the German national community, and the resettling of much of Europe with Germans. Before the seizure of power,

72. A point made effectively with respect to Germany by Michael Geyer, *Aufrüstung oder Sicherheit*, pp. 489–505.

1. Summaries of the debate include Richard Breitman, "Auschwitz and the Archives," *Central European History*, 15, nos. 3–4 (September–December 1985): 365–383; Saul Friedländer, "Introduction," in Gerald Fleming, *Hitler and the Final Solution* (Berkeley, 1983), pp. vii–xxxviii.

Hitler spoke of removing much of the population of eastern Europe and replacing it with Germans. Many of these plans, of course, had roots in the late nineteenth and early twentieth centuries, and in the war aims of the imperial government in the First World War.[2]

The existence of these aspects of Nazi ideology, however, in no way guaranteed that they would be implemented. Imperialism before 1914 provides an excellent example of an ideology which governments never tried to implement in any thoroughgoing fashion, largely because it did not reflect economic reality.[3] Similarly, the presence of certain groups in German society—including gypsies, homosexuals, Jews, Marxists, the deformed, the antisocial, and the mentally ill—reflected historical, social, and biological reality, and their elimination could not be undertaken within the customary framework of a modern state. The clearing and resettlement of vast areas of eastern Europe also lay outside the framework of modern international politics, although the Turks had expelled and exterminated large populations during and after the First World War.

The Nazi regime, like the Stalinist regime in the Soviet Union, eventually attempted to solve some of the contradictions between its ideology and reality by transforming reality. This required considerable political and institutional innovation. While Hitler in the early stages of his rule appeared to play the mediating role characteristic of modern heads of government—especially in reconciling the claims of traditional and National Socialist institutions—several truly revolutionary Nazi organizations, especially the SS and police organizations, gradually secured more and more independent power and began to use it to transform German society during the 1930s. This process accelerated after 1939, as most of Europe became available for the realization of Nazi ideology.

Hitler's personal role in this process was limited but critical. His own stature and his propaganda, as Hans Mommsen has argued, legitimized National Socialist ideology and the pursuit of its specific goals by subordinates. He seems, indeed, to have played relatively little role in the *design* of policy toward undesirable ele-

---

2. Nolte, *Three Faces of Fascism*, 507–534, contains a fine summary of the fundamentals of Hitler's ideology. For Hitler's 1932 remarks, see Kaiser, *Economic Diplomacy*, pp. 60–61.

3. See above, pp. 301–303.

ments, including Jews and foreign nationalities. Yet he allowed subordinates such as Himmler and Heydrich to work toward the implementation of ideological goals which he undoubtedly shared, culminating in the Final Solution of the Jewish Question. The executors of Nazi policy—like Hitler himself—were generally men whose social origins would not have destined them for political power in imperial or Weimar Germany, but who had seized the extraordinary opportunities offered by the Nazi movement and the collapse of traditional authority.[4] They all shared the same fundamental goals for German society and the German people—ideas which had been widespread at least since the Wilhelminian period, but which no one had actually tried to implement before. The collapse of existing authority—first in 1918, and then in 1933— gave them their opportunity.

Nazi racial policy—like Nazi economic policy—was driven by self-fulfilling prophecies. We have seen that in economics, the decision to rearm as rapidly as possible during the 1930s increasingly made it impossible for the Germans to live by participating in world trade and helped precipitate the war of conquest which Hitler had declared to be essential from the beginning. In the same way, initial steps in German racial and nationalities policy—such as plans to expel Poles and Jews from provinces annexed from Poland in 1939, and the decision to confine Polish Jews to ghettos— destroyed existing social and economic life, without replacing it with a viable alternative. This in turn encouraged the application of even more radical measures.

The emergence of Nazi racial and population policies paralleled the growth of the power of the SS and police agencies, which exploited Nazi ideology to build up enormous power. From the time of its inception, National Socialist ideology—like the other radical nationalist ideologies that preceded it—focused upon the unification, purification, and protection of the German national community, *as defined by the ideology itself.*[5] Before their seizure of power, the Nazis argued ceaselessly that Germany had fallen into the hands of foreign, antinational elements—including Socialists,

4. As noted by Martin Broszat, "Soziale Motivation und Führer-Bindung des Nationalsozialismus," in Michalka, ed., *Nationalsozialistische Außenpolitik*, pp. 92–116 (see also *Vierteljahreshefte für Zeitgeschichte*, 18, 1970: 392–409).

5. This is quite clear from numerous provisions of the original party program of February 24, 1920—see for example points 4–6, 18, and 23 in Noakes and Pridham, eds., *Documents on Nazism*, p. 38–39.

Communists, and Jews—who must be purged from national life by any means necessary. Before 1933, the SA acted out this belief in violent clashes with Socialists and Communists and individual terrorist actions against Jews. After the seizure of power, a great many different agencies, eventually including the SA, the Gauleiters of the Nazi party itself, the Schutzstaffel or SS, the Security Service (Sicherheitsdienst or SD), the Reich Main Security Office (Reichsicherheitshauptamt, or RSHA), Himmler's Reich Commissariat for the Strengthening of Germandom (Reichskommissariat für die Festigung des deutschen Volkstums, or RKFdV), the Four Year Plan, the Führer Chancellery, the Government-General of Poland, and the various *Reichskommissariats* that ruled the occupied territory, all fought for the right to watch, arrest, incarcerate, expel, murder, and dispossess the enemies of the regime.[6] Indeed, the competition among these various agencies for men, money, authority, and mission became an essential aspect of politics under the Nazis. And just as the struggle for money, honors, and political power under Napoleon encouraged the further expansion of his empire, the struggle for authority over the enemies of the Reich encouraged the creation of new categories of enemies and the extension of the struggle beyond the frontiers of Germany.[7]

To understand the Final Solution it is also essential to note that even before the seizure of power, Hitler had endorsed the murder of enemies by Nazi party members as legitimate political action. This happened most dramatically in the summer of 1932, after nine members of the SA and SS were brought to trial for the brutal murder of an unemployed Polish worker, Konrad Pietzuch, in the Silesian village of Potempa. At their trial they defended their act as part of a struggle between German and un-German interests, and Hitler—as well as Göring and Röhm—publicly declared his "unbounded loyalty" to the condemned men.[8] After the seizure of

6. Broszat, "Soziale Motivation," pp. 110–111, argues that after the seizure of power Hitler and the Nazis emphasized these "negative" aspects of their ideology rather than making any attempts to realize its utopian elements, and thereby avoided turning the energy of the movement against itself. This may simply reflect a more fundamental truth about modern states: that their destructive power vastly exceeds their creative power.

7. This problem has been discussed by Ronald M. Smelser, "Nazi Dynamics, German Foreign Policy, and Appeasement," in Wolfgang J. Mommsen and Lothar Kettenacker, eds., *The Fascist Challenge and the Policy of Appeasement* (London, 1983), pp. 31–46.

8. Richard Bessel, "The Potempa Murder," *Central European History*, 10, no. 3 (September 1977): pp. 241–254.

power, this view became institutionalized within the SS, whose members regarded themselves as "fighters" or "political soldiers" locked in an eternal struggle for the welfare of Germandom. This struggle, by its very nature, had to take place beyond the bounds of legality, and SS men also had to steel themselves emotionally to perform the difficult tasks before them.[9] Nazi theory and practice, then, legitimized political murder.[10]

A variety of institutional innovations, all introduced within this ideological framework, helped shape Nazi attempts to deal with the nationalities question in eastern Europe during the Second World War. In the months after the Nazi seizure of power the concentration camp emerged as the key institution for dealing with enemies of the regime. Originally established by the SA and the SS, the new camps received thousands of prisoners, most of them political activists from opposition parties, during the months after the seizure of power. Some prisoners died from torture in the concentration camps, and the camp administration successfully asserted its freedom from judicial accountability, confirming once again that proclaimed enemies of National Socialism were subject to murder.[11] Hitler resisted attempts by the state judiciary to disband the concentration camps in the summer of 1933, and after Hitler's purge of the SA in June 1934, the SS took sole responsibility for them. In the meantime, the ambitious SS man Reinhard Heydrich assumed more and more authority over the German political police, becoming head of a new Main Office of the Security Police (Hauptamt Sicherheitspolizei), including both the Security Police (Sicherheitspolizei), the Gestapo, and the SD. In February 1937 Heydrich secured the right to incarcerate a number of distinct categories of undesirables, including political prisoners, antisocial elements (including prostitutes, drifters, and those unwilling to work), habitual criminals, homosexuals, and Jehova's Witnesses. Each of these types of inmates wore a special badge. The camps

9. Hans Buchheim, "Command and Compliance," in Helmut Krausnick, ed., *Anatomy of the SS State* (New York, 1965), pp. 302–359.

10. While I also believe this view of politics fulfilled a critical emotional function for those who held it, this is another issue which simply cannot fully be dealt with within the framework of this book. A promising start has been made by Alice Miller, *For Your Own Good* (2d ed., New York, 1984), pp. 142–147.

11. Heinz Höhne, *The Order of the Death's Head: The Story of the SS* (New York, 1971), pp. 210–211.

also became an independent source of labor for the SS.[12] In 1938 Heydrich formed *Einsatzgrüppen* and *Sonderkommando* from the Sicherheitspolizei and SD and sent them into Austria and Sudetenland to arrest, terrorize, and incarcerate enemies of the Reich, including Socialists, Communists, Jewish leaders, political émigrés, and religious opponents.[13]

Not until after 1938 did Jewish policy become the preserve of the security services. Nazi Jewish policy from 1933 through 1938 focused upon driving the Jews out of the German economy, legally denying them their rights as German citizens, and encouraging them to leave Germany. Economic measures against Jews, from which Nazi party activists had hoped to benefit, fell after 1936 under the control of Hermann Göring in his capacity as head of the Four Year Plan, while legal measures such as the Nuremburg laws were developed by the ministerial bureaucracy. Heydrich's SD managed in 1938 to assume control of Jewish emigration policy, and its Jewish expert Adolf Eichmann opened an office in Vienna after the *Anschluss* to encourage the emigration of Austrian Jews. The *Kristallnacht* of November 9–10, 1938—an outburst of anti-Jewish terrorism provoked by Joseph Goebbels and undertaken by the party apparatus—led to a reconsideration of Jewish policy. The security services sent tens of thousands of German Jews to concentration camps, and Göring appointed Heydrich head of a new Central Office for Jewish Emigration in November 1938.[14] Despite the opposition of the Foreign Office, Eichmann and Heydrich favored Jewish emigration to Palestine. Unfortunately, of course, the British government had restricted entry into Palestine severely, and Western countries would take only small numbers of Jewish refugees.

Meanwhile, other elements of the Nazi regime moved slowly toward the implementation of a series of widespread ideas, well known in Germany since the 1890s, regarding the possible sterili-

---

12. Martin Broszat, "The Concentration Camps, 1933–45," in Krausnick, ed., *Anatomy of the SS State*, pp. 399–452.

13. Helmut Krausnick and Hans-Heinrich Wilhelm, *Die Truppe des Weltanschauungskrieges: Die Einsatzgrüppen der Sicherheitspolizei und der SD 1938–42*, part 1 (Stuttgart, 1981), pp. 19–31.

14. The best studies of prewar Jewish policy are Uwe Dietrich Adam, *Judenpolitik im Dritten Reich* (Dusseldorf, 1972), and Karl Schleunes, *The Twisted Road to Auschwitz: Nazi Policy toward German Jews, 1933–39* (Urbana, 1970).

zation or extermination of mental incompetents, chronically diseased persons, and the aged and infirm. Several books had argued that the state had the right to take the lives of those who could contribute nothing to society, and some doctors and jurists had endorsed these ideas. Sterilization had become an accepted practice for some mental incompetents before 1933, just as it had in a number of American states.[15] Hitler spoke privately of the possibility of large-scale euthanasia during the 1930s, and from 1936 to 1939 many inmates of private institutions for the infirm, aged, disabled, and mentally ill were transferred to state institutions. Sometime in late 1938 or early 1939, the Führer Chancellery—a small office, headed by SS member Phillip Bouhler, which handled petitions to Hitler from around Germany—received a request for the "euthanasia" of a blind, deformed newborn child. Hitler personally approved the killing, and the Führer Chancellery began planning an extensive program to deal with such children.[16]

Nazi population and extermination policy entered an entirely new phase on September 1, 1939, when the attack upon Poland began. That month the SD sent new *Einsatzgrüppen* into Poland with a new mission: the shooting of the entire Polish leadership class, including the aristocracy, intelligentsia, priests, politicians, and civil servants, as well as anyone who showed the slightest signs of resistance to the German occupation. Although no exact figures are available, the *Einsatzgrüppen* seem to have shot tens of thousands of people in the last months of 1939. The order, according to Heydrich, came directly from Hitler, but Heydrich apparently did not have permission to reveal this to other German authorities.[17] Hitler and Heydrich both indicated that they were implementing a well thought-out strategy: the elimination of the Polish leadership class as a means of turning Poland into a vast pool of ignorant slave labor.[18] On September 27, 1939, a decree created the RSHA, headed by Heydrich, which combined the SD with the Security Police and Gestapo. Within months, Heydrich and

15. Ernst Klee, *"Euthanasie" im NS-Staat: Die "Vernichtung lebensunwerten Lebens"* (Frankfurt, 1983), pp. 31–43; Klaus Doerner, "Nationalsozialismus und Lebensbvernichtung," *Vierteljahreshefte für Zeitgeschichte*, 15, no. 1 (January 1967): 121–152.

16. Klee, *"Euthanasie" im NS-Staat*, pp. 66–81.

17. Helmut Krausnick, "Hitler und die Morde in Polen," *Vierteljahreshefte für Zeitgeschichte*, 11, no. 2 (April 1963): 196–209.

18. Krausnick, *Die Truppe des Weltanshauungskrieges*, pp. 32–106; Martin Broszat, *Nationalsozialistische Polenpolitik, 1939–1945* (Stuttgart, 1961), pp. 20–48.

Himmler each disposed of a separate hierarchy of security forces within occupied Poland.[19]

Around the same time, Hitler issued an October decree, back-dated to September 1, 1939, authorizing the murder of thousands of Germans with mental and physical impairments in new euthanasia centers. The Führer Chancellery organized Aktion T4 to carry out these murders and built killing centers, complete with gas chambers, with the help of the technical institute of the RSHA. Gassings began in January 1940, and approximately 70,000 people died before August 1941, when Hitler officially stopped the action. Many doctors cooperated in the action, but it aroused powerful opposition in the Catholic church.[20] An RSHA *Sonderkommando* under Herbert Lange carried out the murder of inmates of mental institutions in East Prussia and the annexed parts of Poland during the winter and spring of 1940, using mobile gas vans also developed by the Führer Chancellery and the technical institute of the RSHA.[21]

Population policy also took giant steps forward in the first few months of the war. Hitler himself had endorsed the old Pan-German idea of evacuation for the inhabitants of the east to make room for German settlement as early as 1928, and by 1937 he was discussing the expulsion of millions of people from conquered territory. The implementation of such policies began immediately after the conquest of Poland.[22] Heydrich received orders from Hitler to create Jewish ghettos in Poland and deport all Jews from the Reich into a special reservation near Lublin. Complaints from the military postponed this step, but another SS agency—the Rasse- und Siedlungsamt (RuSA) of the RKFdV—revived plans similar to those of the High Command during the First World War. Himmler, who had originally been a farmer himself, was a devoted adherent of the idea that Germans must return to the land, and the RKFdV, which he headed, was designed to create a new German peasant aristocracy in conquered eastern territories. Germany had now

19. Höhne, *Order of the Death's Head,* pp. 345–346.

20. Klee, *"Euthanasie" im NS-Staat,* pp. 76–343.

21. Christopher R. Browning, "The Development and Production of the Nazi Gas Vans," in *Fateful Months: Essays on the Emergence of the Final Solution* (New York, 1985), pp. 58–59.

22. Höhne, *Order of the Death's Head,* pp. 334–336. In the Hossbach Conference Hitler spoke of the "compulsory emigration of 2 million people from Czechoslovakia and a million people from Austria." *Documents on German Foreign Policy,* D, I, no. 19.

annexed a huge strip of Poland, and the RKFdV revived the 1914–1918 idea of deporting all Poles and Jews from the annexed territory into occupied Poland (the Government-General) and resettling Germans from the Baltic states—now occupied by the Soviet Union—in the new territories. Himmler gave Heydrich and the RSHA the task of deporting the Poles and Jews.[23]

Despite an enormously complicated struggle among various state and party bureaucracies, perhaps 1 million Jews and Poles were expelled from the annexed territories by mid-1941, and about 200,000 Germans were resettled. Because of the resistance of the Nazi Gauleiters in the new areas, however, many of the Germans from the Baltic states wound up in camps in the old Reich.[24] Meanwhile, Polish Jews were herded into ghettos beginning in the spring of 1940.[25]

By mid-1940, then, Himmler and Heydrich—with the full approval of Hitler—had embarked upon a nationalities policy (or as they would have put it, a racial policy) of staggering proportions. Millions of Poles, Jews, and gypsies would be deported from annexed areas into the Government-General, the Polish intelligentsia would be liquidated, and the remainder of the population would serve as a pool of illiterate slave labor. Himmler, who believed that race, rather than official nationality, was the true basis of human community, wrote in May 1940 that while Poles with sufficient German racial characteristics might be brought into the Reich, the rest of the Poles would not even be taught to read, but would instead be given enough education to learn to count to five hundred and understand that obedience to the Germans was the will of God.[26] Hundreds of thousands of Germans from eastern Europe

23. Höhne, *Order of the Death's Head*, pp. 351–352.

24. Robert L. Koehl, *RKFDV—German Resettlement and Population Policy, 1939–1945: A History of the Reich Commission for the Strengthening of Germandom* (Cambridge, Mass., 1957), pp. 51–88. Earlier, in 1939, Himmler's SS subordinate Ulrich Greifelt had begun resettling Germans from the South Tyrol. Hans Frank, governor-general of occupied Poland, protested the use of his territory as a dumping ground for Jews, gypsies, and other undesirables. The conflicts involved not only Heydrich and Frank but also Göring, who tried to seize all confiscated wealth for the Four Year Plan; the Gauleiters of the annexed Polish provinces, who wanted the wealth for themselves; and local ethnic Germans, who wanted it too.

25. Adam, *Judenpolitik im Dritten Reich*, pp. 250–255; Hilberg, *The Destruction of the European Jews*, 3 vols. (rev. ed., New York, 1985), I, 188–234.

26. Helmut Krausnick, ed., "Denkschrift Himmlers über die Behandlung der Fremdvölkischen im Osten (Mai 1940)," *Vierteljahreshefte für Zeitgeschichte*, 5, no.2 (April 1957): 194–198.

would resettle the annexed areas, and the Jews would eventually be deported from Europe. German occupation authorities actually implemented some of these plans within the Government-General closing all schools above the elementary level.[27]

Although Himmler, Heydrich, and the Führer Chancellery were already putting whole classes of undesirable persons to death by tens of thousands (and using the euphemism *Sonderbehandlung*, or special treatment, to describe this process), no one seems to have proposed killing the several million Jews who had now come under Nazi rule, and Himmler's May 1940 memorandum on Poland had specifically rejected "out of inner conviction the Bolshevik method of extermination of a whole people as un-German and impossible."[28] Instead, a variety of sources make quite clear that both Hitler and the RSHA leadership (which included Adolf Eichmann, the Jewish specialist of that office) planned to deport Europe's Jews to Madagascar after the end of the war—an idea discussed both in Germany and in Poland during the late 1930s.[29] Here Jewish policy shows a rather striking parallel with economic policy: in each case, the early stages of German expansion had aggravated the problem it was designed to solve. Just as the annexation of Austria and Czechoslovakia had increased the demand for imported raw materials and foodstuffs, expansion into Austria, Czechoslovakia, and above all, Poland, had vastly increased the Jewish population within the Reich. In addition, the formation of closed Jewish ghettos in Poland cut the Jewish population off from the economy and helped start epidemics of disease, while attempts to move the population of the annexed territories into Poland made matters worse. Both developments helped lead to the adoption of more radical solutions: the conquest of the Soviet Union to create a self-sufficient economic unit, and the extermination of the Jews.

The planning for the invasion of Russia led to further innovations in Nazi policy. Months before the invasion of the Soviet Union, Hitler had decided that this war would be a *Vernichtungskrieg*, or war of annihilation, designed to eliminate the Bolshevik

27. Ihor Kamenetsky, *Secret Nazi Plans for Eastern Europe: A Study of Lebensraum Policies* (New Haven, 1961), pp. 107–112. Similar policies were implemented in the Ukraine, and to a lesser extent among the Bohemian Czechs.

28. Krausnick, "Denleschrift Himmlers." Himmler may have been trying to discredit proposals for mass murder made by someone else.

29. Adam, *Judenpolitik im Dritten Reich*, pp. 255–257.

ideology entirely.[30] In the spring of 1941 Heydrich formed new *Einsatzgrüppen* and ordered them to shoot Communist party and Soviet government cadres and to provoke pogroms against Jews. But the *Einsatzgrüppen* victims were only a small fraction of the casualties the Nazi authorities expected. Civilian and military planners anticipated that millions of Soviet citizens would starve to death as a result of German expropriation of their food supplies; various remarks indicate that Soviet prisoners of war would be shot or starved to death, as more than a million eventually were; and in July 1941, when the war appeared to be won, Hitler spoke freely of plans to raze Moscow and Leningrad to the ground and allow their population to die on the spot.[31] The murder and expulsion of much of the existing population, followed by resettlement with Germans and other Aryans, had emerged as the preferred Nazi solution to the nationalities question in eastern Europe.

In light of all these plans for mass murder, it hardly seems surprising that Nazi authorities in the summer of 1941 abandoned the idea of resettling the Jewish population of central and eastern Europe—either in Madagascar or in eastern Russia—and adopted instead the solution of extermination. The existing record does not include evidence of a single, specific decision, but rather suggests a series of more or less independent steps. Initially, sometime around the June 22 date of the invasion of the Soviet Union, Heydrich seems to have made it clear that he expected the *Einsatzgrüppen* to shoot *all* the Soviet Jews, as well as Soviet gypsies and the mentally impaired.[32] The *Einsatzgrüppen* actually killed several hundred thousand Jews, gypsies, and mental patients during the second half of 1941, mostly by shooting, but also in mobile gas vans.[33] On July 31, Heydrich received from Göring the authorization to prepare for the "total solution of the Jewish question."[34]

30. Hillgrüber, *Hitlers Strategie*, pp. 516–532.

31. Browning, "The Decision Concerning the Final Solution," in *Fateful Months*, pp. 28–29; Hillgrüber, *Hitlers Strategie*, p. 539.

32. The timing of the order to shoot the Jews is a controversial point; see Browning, "Decision Concerning the Final Solution," pp. 16–20, who argues quite convincingly that the *Einsatzgrüppen* assumed this task at the latest within a few weeks of the attack, and that some of their leaders pursued it from the beginning.

33. See Donald Kenrick and Grattan Puxon, *The Destiny of Europe's Gypsies* (Sussex, 1972), pp. 142–150, and Klee *"Euthanasie" im NS-Staat*, pp. 367–379.

34. Klee, *"Euthanasie" im NS-Staat*, p. 21. The question of why Göring gave the authorization has not definitively been cleared up. Göring had emerged during the late 1930s as the principal figure in charge of Jewish affairs, largely because they then focused

During the same month, Gauleiter Arthur Greiser and other Nazi authorities in annexed Wartheland, where the establishment of the Lodz ghetto had cut Jews off from their means of support and caused widespread epidemics, also raised the question of extermination.[35] As one SS participant noted, since the Jews could no longer be fed, "It should be considered seriously if it would not be the most humane solution to dispose of the Jews, insofar as they are not capable of work, through a quick-acting agent. In any case it would be more pleasant than to let them starve."[36] Sometime that autumn Greiser actually asked Himmler and Heydrich for trained executioners to deal with his district's Jews, and Himmler and Heydrich dispatched Herbert Lange's *Sonderkommando*, which had already exterminated the mentally ill in the region. Lange arrived in late October or early November with gas vans, built the Kulmhof death camp, and eventually gassed more than 152,000 Jews.[37]

In the spring of 1941, some Nazi authorities also discussed plans for the deportation of German Jews to an unspecified reserve within the Soviet Union. But when in August 1941 the Jews of several of Germany's largest cities were deported, they were sent to the ghetto of Lodz, where Greiser was preparing the extermination of the Jews of the Wartheland. More German Jews sent to Minsk and Riga were shot by *Einsatzgrüppen* in November. And the new *Reichskommissar Ostland*, Hinrich Lohse—the ruler of occupied White Russia and much of the Baltic states—contacted Viktor Brack, a leading figure in the euthanasia program of the Führer Chancellery, to secure gassing facilities for Jews within his domain.[38] In October occupation authorities in Serbia, which the Germans had conquered earlier in the year, also discussed the dis-

---

upon economic questions, and as we have seen, he had given Heydrich the authorization to form the Central Office for Jewish Emigration in 1938. Presumably Heydrich needed his authorization to proceed with the deportation of the Reich Jews. Eichmann once claimed to have drafted the document for Göring's signature himself; Hilberg, *Destruction of the European Jews*, II, 401; Browning, "Decision Concerning the Final Solution," pp. 21–22.

35. Hilberg, *Destruction of the European Jews*, pp. 234–239, 259–269, discusses conditions in the ghettos.

36. Browning, "Introduction," in *Fateful Months*, pp. 3–4.

37. Browning, "Nazi Gas Vans," pp. 62–65; Browning, "Decision Concerning the Final Solution," pp. 30–31; Höhne, *Order of the Death's Head*, pp. 422–423.

38. Adam, *Judenpolitik im Dritten Reich*, pp. 308–313.

patch of local Jews to somewhere in Russia, where they would be exterminated.[39] In late November Heydrich called the Wansee Conference to inform all interested authorities of the planned extermination of the Jews.[40] It seems, then, that by the late summer of 1941 deportation meant not deportation and resettlement, but rather deportation and murder.

In October 1941, when Hitler officially halted the euthanasia program, much of the staff of Office T4 of the Führer Chancellery was relieved of its euthanasia duties and began building death camps for Jews. While Lange built the Kulmhof camp, Christian Wirth, a major figure in the euthanasia program, began the Belzec extermination camp near Lublin, in November 1941. It began operating in March 1942, and other men from T4 built death camps at Sobibor and Treblinka in the spring and summer of that year. These new camps reported both to the Führer Chancellery and to Himmler's Inspectorate of Concentration Camps.[41] Auschwitz, which had already been built as an all-purpose concentration camp for annexed and occupied Poland in 1940, also acquired a gas chamber and began participating in the extermination program as well. Gas chambers soon became standard equipment at all SS concentration camps, but until the end of the war a distinction persisted between camps like Auschwitz, where able-bodied prisoners might continue to work, and pure death camps like Treblinka and Sobibor, where virtually every inmate was exterminated upon arrival.[42]

We do not know whether it was Hitler, Himmler, Heydrich, or an even lower-ranking official who originally suggested the mur-

---

39. Browning, "Decision Concerning the Final Solution," p. 27.

40. Hilberg, *Destruction of the European Jews*, II, 403. The conference did not take place until January 1942.

41. According to well-known testimony, Himmler, upset by the sight of an *Einsatzgrüppen* execution in the fall of 1941, argued that "a better method had to be found." It may be significant that the construction of the death camps, under the authority of Himmler's Inspectorate of Concentration Camps, transferred the extermination mission from Heydrich's bailiwick, the RSHA, to his own. Although the memoirs of Himmler's doctor, Felix Kersten, suggest some jealousy between Himmler and Heydrich, it is not clear whether this rivalry accelerated the extermination process. Felix Kersten, *The Kersten Memoirs, 1940–45* (London, 1956), pp. 90–99.

42. Browning, "Decision Concerning the Final Solution," pp. 30–31; Hilberg, *Destruction of the European Jews*, III, 894–916. Klee, *"Euthanasie" im NS-Staat*, pp. 334–379, describes the shift of personnel but stresses that the so-called euthanasia program did not really come to an end in August 1941.

der of all the Jews of Europe, but the history of extermination policy suggests how the National Socialists arrived at this plan. From the beginning, Hitler had focused attention upon the problem of real and presumed enemies of National Socialism and had established murder as an acceptable means of dealing with them. After 1933—and especially after the beginning of the Second World War—various Nazi agencies zealously moved to carry out his plans in the most extreme fashion possible. At least three separate agencies—the *Einsatzgrüppen* of Heydrich's RSHA, the Führer Chancellery, and the Inspectorate of Concentration Camps participated in the extermination of Jews, and others such as Greiser, Gauleiter of the Wartheland, took independent initiatives as well. No written evidence directly ties Hitler to the Final Solution, but we know that he was fully aware of the decisions to shoot thousands of people in Poland, to gas thousands of German mentally ill and aged persons, and to shoot the entire Soviet leadership in the course of the war against Russia. Indeed, Hitler seems to have taken the lead in the planning for the Russian atrocities and was closely informed of the *Einsatzgrüppen* activities.[43] We have no reason to doubt that he was fully aware of the decision to exterminate the Jews of Europe as well. The decision grew out of the momentum Hitler had unleashed by defining revolutionary political objectives and encouraging the proliferation of bureaucracies to achieve them. Indeed, what seems to have happened in 1941 is that various Nazi agencies—the SS concentration camps, the *Einsatzgrüppen*, and section T4 of the Führer Chancellery—each of whom up until then had been killing specific groups of victims with specific technologies, began to share their assigned victims and their particular ways of killing them.

The subsequent implementation of the Final Solution—carried out with the help of the German Foreign Office, the military authorities in certain territories occupied by Germany, and governments of nations allied to Germany—killed approximately five million European Jews. According to the most authoritative survey, only tiny minorities of Jews living in 1939 in greater Germany, Greece, the Netherlands, Poland, the Soviet Union, and Yugoslavia survived; roughly half of Jews living in Belgium, Hungary, Norway, and Rumania escaped; and relatively smaller fractions of the

---

43. Fleming, *Hitler and the Final Solution*, pp. 73–74.

Jews of Bulgaria, France, and Italy died. Lower casualties reflected both better opportunities for escape and the resistance of local governments.[44]

The extermination of the Jews was not simply the product of Nazi anti-Semitism but rather one element in a more far-reaching attempt to solve the nationalities question in eastern Europe according to the Nazis' racist and imperialist ideology. Nazi plans for the movement and extermination of peoples did not stop with the Jews. The gypsies, who had long been defined as dangerous racial elements by Nazi ideology and had been followed closely by the RSHA, were also designated for extermination sometime in 1942, and more than 200,000 were eventually murdered.[45] In addition, far more sweeping measures would apparently have been undertaken against the Slavs of eastern Europe had the German campaign in the Soviet Union been successful. The RSHA outlined such measures in the *Generalplan Ost*, written sometime in late 1941 and circulated for comment early the next year. The contents of the plan may be inferred from the comments of Erhard Wetzel, of the new Ministry for the East, headed by Alfred Rosenberg.[46] The plan foresaw the deportation of more than two-thirds of the 45 million inhabitants of occupied Poland and European Russia to Siberia, the deportation of perhaps half the Czechs, and the resettlement of 10 million Germans in the emptied territory. Wetzel, who seems to have viewed himself as a moderate, argued in his comments that a somewhat higher proportion of Poles might be regarded as suitable for Germanization. Significantly, Wetzel himself strongly opposed the complete extermination of the Poles or Great Russians but noted that other authorities were arguing for such steps.[47] Recognizing that an insufficient number of Germans might be available for resettlement, Wetzel suggested that the Nazis

44. Hilberg, *Destruction of the European Jews*, III, 1048, gives these figures. Volume 2 describes events in each country in considerable detail.

45. Donald Kenrick and Grattan Puxon, *The Destiny of Europe's Gypsies* (Sussex, 1972), pp. 76–184.

46. See Helmut Heiber, "Der Generalplan Ost," *Vierteljahreshefte für Zeitgeschichte*, 6, no. 3 (July 1958): 281–292.

47. Hilberg, *Destruction of the European Jews*, III, 99–1002, presents some additional evidence of interest in the extermination of the Poles, especially those in territories incorporated into the Reich. As it was, Nazi terrorism took the lives of an estimated 3 million Poles, in addition to 3 million Polish Jews; see Jan Gross, *Polish Society under German Occupation: The Generalgouvernement, 1939–1944* (Princeton, 1979).

might have to make use of other Nordics from Holland, Denmark, Scandinavia, and even England as well. Various German authorities also planned the deportation of many Lithuanians and Czechs, once again with the proviso that racially valuable elements would be maintained.[48] The RuSA of the RKFdV carried out colonization projects involving tens of thousands of Germans in the Government-General and the Ukraine,[49] but the war prevented any full implementation of the *Generalplan Ost*.

The Nazi solution to the nationalities question—including the extermination of the Jews and gypsies and the planned extermination and movement of tens of millions of other peoples—reflected both Nazi ideology, which defined categories of enemies and undesirables and legitimized murder as a means of dealing with them, and the internal dynamics of the Nazi regime, which encouraged various agencies to assume these tasks to expand their own power and influence. Yet neither the exclusivist nationalism behind these beliefs, nor the means adopted to implement them, were unique to the Nazis. As early as 1915, the Turkish government had already resorted to genocide against the Armenians to realize these principles, and we have seen that Europe in the interwar period had failed to develop an alternative set of beliefs and institutions which would enable different nationalities to live together within the same state. Population transfers were also implemented by several other governments in the era of the Second World War.

Thus, the German government apparently encouraged population transfers among the states of southeastern Europe who cooperated militarily in the German war against the Soviet Union. After the Vienna Award of August 30, 1940, had partitioned Transylvania between Hungary and Rumania, approximately 219,000 Rumanians and 160,000 Magyars exercised an option to repatriate into their national state. Bulgaria and Rumania also exchanged between 60,000 and 100,000 of their conationals from the Dobrudja after a treaty of September 7, 1940, gave the southern Dobrudja to Bulgaria. Somewhat smaller population transfers occurred among Hungary, Croatia, Serbia, and Bulgaria after the German conquest and partition of Yugoslavia in the spring of 1941. The largest single

48. Norman Rich, *Hitler's War Aims: The Establishment of the New Order*, vol. 2 (New York, 1974), pp. 45–50, 358–359.
49. Kamanetsky, *Secret Nazi Plans*, pp. 49–72.

population transfer in German-dominated Europe, however, involved more than 1 million Germans who left the Baltic states, occupied Poland, the South Tyrol, and various parts of the Soviet Union, including territories annexed by the Soviets from Rumania. Although Nazi agencies planned to resettle these Germans in the annexed Polish provinces, the Government-General, and other parts of the Soviet Union, relatively few of them actually found new homes, and many of them spent virtually the whole war in concentration camps in Germany.[50]

Transfers in eastern Europe also took place outside the German sphere. Immediately after the outbreak of the war the Polish government had deported 50,000 ethnic Germans from their homes near the frontier and shot several thousand of them.[51] The Soviet Union under Stalin had already carried out the deportation and death of millions of people.[52] As already noted, after war began the Soviets exchanged Germans from the Baltic states and eastern Poland during the 1939–1941 period, and received a considerably smaller number of White Russians and Ukrainians in return. After their victory over Finland in March 1940, they allowed several hundred thousand Finns to leave the territory they annexed in the peace treaty. More than half of these Finns returned to their homes after Finnish victories in the renewed war that began with the German-Finnish attack upon the Soviet Union and returned to Finland once again when the Soviets regained the territory. The Soviets also took drastic steps designed, apparently, to eliminate the elements of the middle and upper classes in the Baltic states and annexed areas of Poland whom they regarded as dangerous to Soviet rule. These steps included the murder of 14,500 captive Polish officers at Katyn and elsewhere in 1940 and the deportation of perhaps 143,000 politicians, army officers, academics and others from the Baltic states beginning in the fall of that year.[53] A few months

---

50. Joseph B. Schechtman, *European Population Transfers, 1939–1945* (New York, 1946), *passim*, including summary tables, pp. 482–487; Koehl, *RKFDV*, pp. 210–223.

51. Broszat, *Nationalsozialistische Polenpolitik*, p. 47.

52. Robert Conquest, *The Harvest of Sorrow: Soviet Collectivization and the Terror-Famine* (New York, 1986), even argues—not entirely convincingly—that Stalin had adopted mass murder through starvation as a solution to an important nationality problem as early as 1930, when he allowed millions of Ukrainians to starve to death as a result of the collectivization of agriculture and the collection of grain.

53. Schechtman, *European Population Transfers*, pp. 367–399; Louis FitzGibbon, *Katyn* (London, 1971), p. 180; Georg von Rauch, *The Baltic States, The Years of Independence: Estonia, Latvia, Lithuania, 1917–1940* (London, 1974), p. 228.

after the German attack in 1941, the Soviets abolished the autonomous region of the Volga Germans and deported several hundred thousand of them to Siberia. They also eventually deported the Crimean Tatars, who were occupied by the Germans, and several smaller minority groups from the Caucasus.[54]

But the most massive movements of population took place at the end of the war, after the Allied leaders had agreed to the restoration of Czechoslovakia and to large Soviet and Polish annexations of German territory. As early as 1941–42, British Foreign Office officials agreed that these territorial changes might also require huge transfers of population.[55] The expulsion of Germans from East Prussia and the eastern part of Germany began with the Soviet invasion of these territories, when millions of Germans began to flee. The Soviets and the new Communist Polish government began wholesale expulsions of Germans in the first half of 1945. And although the British and American governments made some efforts to moderate this process, they endorsed the expulsion of Germans from these territories in principle at Potsdam, as well as the expulsion of German minorities in Czechoslovakia and Hungary. Despite some British and American attempts to halt the transfers pending further international agreements, Soviet, Polish, Czechoslovakian, and Hungarian authorities all proceeded to expel their German population. According to West German statistics, almost 12 million Germans were expelled from the eastern territories, including about 7 million from territory lost to Poland and the Soviet Union, almost 3 million from Czechoslovakia, and almost 2 million from Hungary, Rumania, and Yugoslavia.[56] The Allies, in short, had endorsed an extreme solution of the question of German minorities, agreeing in effect that no non-German state should have to tolerate large numbers of Germans within their midst.

The creation of the state of Israel in 1948 and the emigration of approximately half a million surviving European Jews largely completed the disappearance of the Jews from central and eastern Eu-

---

54. Robert Conquest, *The Soviet Deportation of Nationalities* (London, 1960), pp. 10–71. See also Ingeborg Fleischauer, "Unternehmen Barbarossa und die Zwangsumsiedlung der Deutschen in der UdSSR," *Vierteljahreshefte für Zeitgeschichte*, 30, no. 2 (April 1932): 299–321.

55. Lothar Kettenacker, *Krieg zur friedenssicherung: Die Deutschlandplanung der britischen Regierung während der zweiten Weltkrieger* (Göttingen, 1989), pp. 441–446.

56. Alfred de Zayas, *Nemesis at Potsdam: The Anglo-Americans and the Expulsion of the Germans* (rev. ed., London, 1977), pp. xxv, 60–102. An additional 2 million expelled Germans are listed as missing or dead.

rope.[57] As a result of all these murders and transfers during the Second World War, minorities, who in the 1930s made up 25 percent of the population of seven eastern European states, comprised only 7 percent of the population of these states by 1970.[58]

The enormous power of the image of a homogeneous national community—a power which emerged during the nineteenth century, when nationality gradually supplanted dynastic legitimacy as the organizing principle of the European community—led in the twentieth century to the greatest tragedies in European history. Before and during the First World War, the peoples of the multinational empires of central and eastern Europe increasingly aspired to create their own national states; before, during, and after the Second World War, Central and Eastern European governments became increasingly intolerant of their minority populations, and eventually decided, in various ways, to eliminate them. Postwar developments in Northern Ireland, Belgium, Canada, Poland, Czechoslovakia, and Rumania—not to mention bitter conflicts in much of the third world—suggest that nationality conflicts remain the most difficult of all the issues with which modern political systems must deal. The experience of the two world wars testifies to the unprecedented power of the national idea, but suggests that the spread of this essential feature of modern politics has been a catastrophe for European civilization.

The Origins of Totalitarianism

Europe in the first half of the twentieth century experienced the collapse of dynastic monarchy in virtually the entire Continent, the emergence of new states, the triumph of new ideologies, and most dramatically of all, the emergence in Russia and Germany of totalitarian regimes that sought to transform their societies—and in the National Socialist case, the whole of Europe—according to their ideology. Since the Second World War, a vast historiography has discussed the role of class interests, domestic institutions, and intellectual traditions in bringing totalitarianism to power. One cannot for one moment question the importance of research into the sources of the intellectual and emotional appeal of Bolshevism

---

57. Abram Leon Sachar, *A History of the Jews* (5th ed., New York, 1965), pp. 453–454.
58. Horak et al., *Eastern European National Minorities*, pp. 2–4.

and National Socialism, their techniques of political mobilization, and their relationship to classes and interest groups. At the same time, the rise to power of both these totalitarian regimes and the implementation of National Socialism must also be understood within the context of European international politics. It was above all the failure of the Russian and German empires to meet the demands of the First World War that destroyed traditional authority and gave the totalitarian regimes their opportunity. In addition, as we have seen, the Nazis in practice focused upon the implementation of two widespread goals in contemporary European international politics: the creation of a self-sufficient economic unit and of a fully homogeneous national community based upon common ethnic or racial origin.

War, indeed, rather than the consequences of industrialization, has proven to be the supreme test of modern political systems and the source of almost every major modern European revolution. The political impact of war emerged during the nineteenth century, when wars created the new kingdom of Italy and the German empire, toppled the French Second Empire, and forced the Austrian empire to transform itself into Austria-Hungary. Russia's first large-scale revolution broke out in 1905 as a result of the Russo-Japanese War. Then, in the First World War, all the major European nations took the field on behalf of imperialism and nationalism, the two major issues in contemporary international politics. They did so even though imperialism had not made a vital contribution to their economic prosperity, and although the map of Europe could not possibly be redrawn along strictly national lines. The war left all its participants poorer than when they began it and left a host of national claims unfulfilled. Worst of all, the governments involved found that only a decisive victory would satisfy their peoples. Logic decreed that they could not all win, and the state of the military art made it almost impossible for any of them to do so.

Failure in war, rather than nationalist or class-based revolutionary movements, destroyed the empires of central and eastern Europe. While the Russian and Austro-Hungarian empires certainly faced internal threats before 1914—threats with both a class and a national basis—they maintained their power as long as they remained at peace. War encouraged their enemies to endorse national claims against them, while inability to win victories progressively undermined the confidence of their peoples. The collapse of the Russian empire in 1917 resulted directly from its performance in the war, and the fall of Kerensky's provisional government owed more than a little to its attempts to continue it. The Bolsheviks took advantage of an almost complete collapse of existing authority to attempt the transformation of their society according to revolutionary principles.

Imperial Germany also collapsed as a result of the First World War. German society and Germany's political structure were both far stronger even in 1918 than those of Russia, and the fall of the empire did not in the first instance bring a revolutionary movement to power. But the experience of Versailles, inflation, and depression—all three, in varying degrees, results of the First World War—discredited the Weimar republic in its turn, allowing Hitler and the Nazis to garner the electoral support of about 40 percent of the German people and to secure legal power in January 1933. Hitler's foreign policies may have had relatively little to do with his accession to power, although his almost immediate adoption of an independent course in foreign policy undoubtedly helped him consolidate his power in the early years of his rule. But it was the short- and long-term consequences of the First World War that gave him, like Lenin, the opportunity to get within sight of political power, by discrediting traditional authority and creating a vacuum.

Once in power, Hitler and the Nazis focused increasingly upon the actual implementation of extreme programs of economic imperialism and nationalism which had begun to emerge during the First World War. National Socialism tried to overcome the two fundamental contradictions around which, as we have seen, the international conflicts of the first half of the twentieth century revolved. The first contradiction reflected the consequences of the commercial and industrial revolutions. National European economies had become parts of a single, worldwide economic structure, within which no individual member enjoyed complete economic independence or control over worldwide economic forces. European governments before 1914 frequently endorsed imperialism as a means of maintaining economic independence, but in practice they did very little to impede the growth of the world economy. National Socialism, by contrast, committed itself to a break with the world economy and sought to establish a self-contained, independent economic unit that could wage war on a world scale.

The experience of the First World War had made it much more difficult for the other major European states to cope with Hitler's demands. Politically, economically, and military, the French, British, and Soviet governments had relatively little confidence in their ability to resist him. This diffidence, as we have seen, enabled him to overcome the weaknesses in his own position during the years 1938–1941, during which he became too strong to be defeated by a coalition of European powers. Hitler's attempt to escape the consequences of the industrial revolution—consequences which included the relegation of the European nations to the status of second-rank powers—lay at the heart of the origins of the Second World War, just as a belief in the importance of imperialism had earlier led Germany into the First World War.

The second, more difficult contradiction between European ideology and reality juxtaposed the principle of nationality with the multinational demographic structure of central and eastern Europe. Even after the destruction of the empires of central and eastern Europe, the principle of nation-states based upon a community of peoples of common language, religion, and ethnic origin consigned millions of Europeans to the status of inferior citizens, since the map of Europe simply could not be divided into homogeneous national units. Attempts both before and after the First World War to accommodate the claims of different nationalities within the same state generally failed, and by the 1930s many European minorities were as far as ever from recognition as full members of their national communities. Under Hitler, the Nazis explicitly set themselves the goal of *creating* a homogeneous national community, if need be by population transfer and extermination. The Soviet Union and the states of eastern Europe adopted similar policies at the end of the Second World War, and the question of national minorities was largely solved, not politically or culturally, but forcibly.

Despite the uniquely destructive *effects* of Stalinism and National Socialism, both of them drew upon widespread—though hardly universal—beliefs in European politics.[1] Moreover, their attempts to implement their ideologies reflected the two beliefs which François Furet identified as the bedrock of revolutionary consciousness: that all misfortunes can be solved politically, and that since

---

1. As argued by Arendt, *Origins of Totalitarianism, passim.*

everything can be known and changed, there is a perfect fit of action, knowledge, and morality.[2] Although Nazi practice was in many ways unique, the fundamental principles of Nazism drew upon beliefs that had influenced European international politics at least since the late nineteenth century. Since the 1880s European politicians had frequently endorsed the idea that industrial powers needed a large, protected economic hinterland to secure their economic future, and other powers had taken important steps to implement this idea during the 1930s. European political leaders, intellectuals, political activists, and revolutionaries of virtually every identifiable ethnic origin had adopted and attempted to implement the idea that European states should be composed of ethnically, linguistically, or racially homogeneous populations since the late nineteenth century. In practice, moreover, several governments had discussed and carried out population transfer and extermination to achieve this goal during the First World War.[3]

Because neither one of these beliefs had a real foundation in fact, their influence, culminating in the Nazis' attempts to implement them, tends to confirm David Hume's belief that reason is merely the slave of the passions. Imperialism and nationalism fired the European imagination not because they corresponded to reality, or even because they could easily be achieved. The secret of their appeal lies buried in the emotional development of nineteenth- and twentieth-century Western man, who has customarily proclaimed rational justifications for his particularly irrational passions. The ideas for which National Socialism murdered millions and changed the course of European history were common European ideas, and the tragedy of National Socialism is therefore a European tragedy as well as a purely German one.

2. Furet, *Interpreting the French Revolution,* p. 25.

3. Arendt, *Origins of Totalitarianism,* pp. 185–221, also argued effectively that the treatment of Africans by Europeans in the late nineteenth century foreshadowed the Nazis' extermination of European peoples.

Conclusion

European War: The Historical Problem

The history of these four periods of general European conflict, in which governments undertook and continued wars for political purposes, confirms Clausewitz's view of war as the continuation of politics by other means.[1] Clausewitz's famous dictum, however, carries with it a further implication which history does not support: that war has consistently *enabled* governments to realize their political goals. Writing in the aftermath of the great age of rationalism in political theory and international politics, Clausewitz easily adopted this premise, and most subsequent historians of international conflict have done the same. Yet our four cases—especially the first and the last—show that prolonged, general war frequently reflects the inability of statesmen to use war as an instrument of politics within the contemporary political, economic, and social context.

Thus, the wars of the years 1559–1659 stemmed from two related sources: the European aristocracy's attempts to retain its independent authority, backed up if need be by force, and the European princes' attempts to impose theirs. These wars may have served the needs of the aristocracy, but they rarely helped the state. The leading factions of the French civil wars generally won a reconfirmation of their privileges after each rising, culminating in the payoffs they secured from Henry IV, and a new generation

1. See the excellent commentary in Bernard Brodie, *War and Politics* (New York, 1973), pp. 8–11, 440–453—a work which raises many of the same issues as this one, although generally in the context of American foreign policy since 1945.

even managed to secure similar treatment at the end of the Fronde. The Dutch magnates who led the revolt against the Spaniards eventually established their own independence, and the English aristocracy and gentry preserved their standing against the monarchy. For monarchs and their favorites, however, war in this period was generally disastrous. Philip II, Olivares, Ferdinand II, and Richelieu and Mazarin, who began wars to strengthen their authority, eventually weakened it instead, owing to their inability to bring wars to a successful conclusion or finance them out of existing resources. Armies were another obstacle to the effective use of war for political reasons during this period, since they frequently observed no loyalty to anyone but themselves and mutinied when their employers could not pay them.

Louis XIV and his fellow monarchs, by contrast, used war in the service of politics more successfully than any other generation of modern European political leaders. Louis in particular did so because he defined the political goals of war in highly subjective terms. The major professed goal of his wars—the glory of the king—served him well because of its inherent flexibility. Whenever a campaign met an indecisive or inglorious end, the king might restore his luster by opening a new front, arranging a new coalition, or making peace. While Louis frequently entertained grandiose schemes such as securing his election as Holy Roman Emperor, or securing the whole Spanish empire for his house, he never irrevocably committed his prestige to attaining them. His fellow princes exercised the same latitude in defining their goals and also abandoned dreams of total victory when they could not fulfill them. Ultimately respecting only their own interests, they entered and left wars at their pleasure, frequently changed sides, and, in the case of smaller states, did what they could to profit from conflicts among larger powers. Their participation in war generally strengthened their authority, and the authority of European states grew steadily during the late seventeenth and eighteenth centuries.

The gradual encroachment of reason upon glory as the main justification for war during the late eighteenth century eventually overturned both the existing international equilibrium and the prevailing principles of dynastic and historic legitimacy. The idea of reason enabled the European powers to claim territory purely and simply on the grounds of utility, and therefore to legitimize in principle any territorial acquisition. Monarchs also relied upon reason to remove the remaining privileges of their nobility, towns, and church. When the French revolutionary wars came to an end in 1802, all the major states, and the minor German princes as well, had made important territorial gains, and many had reduced the privileges of their political rivals at home. Napoleon's attempts to use rationalism to establish his authority throughout Europe and to replace much of Europe's ruling elite, however, ended in failure. European resources could not support his wars and his attempts to endow a new ruling elite, and the extent of his aims eventually made it impossible for him to realize them diplomatically or militarily.

For the most part, the political utility of European war has declined dramatically in the industrial era, both because of its enormous cost and because of the difficulty of making meaningful gains. European governments in this era sometimes derived political benefits from wars fought outside Europe, and in the nineteenth century short wars fought on behalf of nationalism also brought governments major territorial gains, but in the twentieth century general war proved to be even more politically disastrous than in the sixteenth and seventeenth centuries. Twentieth-century war made unprecedented political demands upon governments. Governments now claimed to fight on behalf of their whole peoples, and their peoples seemed to insist upon a decisive victory which they could not achieve. No European government won a decisive victory in either of the two world wars. While failure to achieve victory brought down governments, defeat destroyed whole regimes and the social structures which supported them. The First World War remains the critical political event of the twentieth century precisely because it destroyed the legitimacy of the German, Austro-Hungarian, and Russian empires, and thereby opened up opportunities for the growth of totalitarian regimes designed to transform reality according to abstract principles. Democracy and nationalism had threatened these empires before 1914, but their governments had survived those threats as long as peace prevailed. War destroyed the central and eastern European empires, whose traditional legitimacy could not survive defeat. The resulting political confusion, increased in Germany by the economic consequences of the First World War, led eventually to the Second. Politically that war repeated the pattern of the First.

Defeated governments collapsed entirely, and even the political leadership in victorious countries drew no immediate political benefits from the war.[2]

War has rarely brought any real benefit to the people of Europe. While the Second World War performed the essential service of destroying the Nazi regime, which might have destroyed European civilization altogether, the Nazi regime itself was a consequence of an earlier war. European governments have benefited from war in eras in which they could achieve their stated aims. This has become more rather than less difficult during the twentieth century. Modern societies demand that wars be fought to a brilliantly successful conclusion, and wartime governments have become hostages to realities far beyond their control. Curiously enough, political systems based upon the glory of individual monarchs have handled international politics more flexibly than systems claiming to represent the interests of their whole society. War has been harder to begin, but also much harder to end, in the era of democracy.

European War: The Historiographical Problem

The idea of a community of states—that is, of well-defined, distinct bodies of men, exercising legitimate authority within a specific domain, disposing of a monopoly of force, and enjoying the right to make war and peace—lies behind the whole idea of international conflict. Overall, historical treatments of European war have suffered from an excessive idealization of the state, an overestimation of its powers, and a penchant for exaggerating the wisdom of its acts. This tendency takes the specific form of presuming that every great war involves great stakes, both for governments and peoples, and that historical outcomes have been in some sense useful and preferable to other possible outcomes. The roots of these intellectual tendencies go back to the beginnings of Western civilization.

Efforts to give the state a specific ethical mission, and to measure existing states against a theoretical ideal, seem to have received

---

2. Thus both Churchill and De Gaulle fell from power within about a year of the end of the war, even though both eventually returned under entirely different circumstances.

their greatest impetus from Plato. Much later the political theorists of the Middle Ages measured state action against the dictates of Christian thought, and Enlightenment thinkers put forth reason and the natural laws which they claimed to derive from it as the measure of a good state, designed to promote happiness. Early in the nineteenth century Hegel turned the state into the embodiment of progress, a tradition expanded, in different ways, by the Marxism which grew out of Hegelian philosophy.[3] Shortly thereafter Leopold von Ranke placed the state at the center of modern history, ascribed to it the role of developing and embodying the national genius of each individual European people, and measured its effectiveness largely according to the military power which it could deploy.[4]

Ranke also helped enshrine the idea of the balance of power in modern European history—"the guardian spirit [Genius] which always protects Europe from domination by any one-sided and violent tendency, which always meets pressure on the one side with resistance on the other, and . . . has happily preserved the freedom and separate existence of each state."[5] Since no particular state ever has subjugated all of Europe, this principle has provided the dramatic framework for most treatments of general wars, whose authors tell the story of how Europe resisted threatened conquest. Here I have argued essentially the opposite: that each era of conflict reflected a *common* state of political development among the different European peoples, that the balance among them reflected a balance of their resources, and that the limitations of contemporary military technology, which in most periods militated against the achievement of decisive victories, guaranteed a balance more effectively than anything else. What this view lacks in heroic inspiration, it gains in accuracy.

Ranke, at least, gave each of the major powers a particular and worthy role in maintaining the balance. His successors among the

3. See Cassirer, *Myth of the State*, for an excellent discussion of all these developments. With respect to Marxism, I am suggesting simply that Marx regarded the state as the embodiment of existing society, whereas Lenin turned it into the agency of revolutionary activity.

4. These tendencies are all evident in Ranke, "The Great Powers," in Theodore H. Von Laue, *Leopold Ranke: The Formative Years* (Princeton, 1950), pp. 181–218. See also Leonard Krieger, *Ranke: The Meaning of History* (Chicago, 1977), pp. 238–239, and Meinecke, *Machiavellism*, pp. 377–391.

5. Ranke, "Great Powers," p. 189.

Prussian school of historians, led by Heinrich von Treitschke, abandoned his approach and assigned a primary value to the growth of their own national state, and therefore to the rise of the Prussian state that had created the new Germany. The same spirit informed numerous nineteenth- and early twentieth-century French students of the Napoleonic wars, who focused on France's failure to secure the so-called natural frontiers.[6] The war guilt controversy after the First World War spurred the publication of a great deal more literature devoted to the cause of one or another European state.

More skeptical attitudes toward international conflict have always been common among the people of Europe and have been powerfully expressed by novelists.[7] Such attitudes are more rare among historians. Writing in the 1850s, Tocqueville, one of the greatest of European historians, took a highly skeptical attitude toward the growth of European (and especially French) state power in the seventeenth and eighteenth centuries, arguing that the state had tended to reduce liberty among the people and drained the vitality from French political life. Fifty years later, a number of penetrating and generally skeptical works on the diplomacy of the Napoleonic era appeared, suggesting that a long period of peace stimulates a more broad-based, critical attitude within the historical profession.[8] Shortly before, in 1894, Henry Adams, then president of the American Historical Association, had warned his colleagues that a new and more scientific history was almost certain to draw conclusions offensive to property, the church, or the state.[9] The critical spirit did not in general survive the First World War, and most of the enormous literature published on the origins of the war in the 1920s and 1930s concentrated upon defending or refuting the war guilt clause of the treaty

6. These included such apparently dissimilar figures as Adolphe Thiers, Albert Sorel, Edouard Driault, and Georges Lefèbvre; see Geyl, *Napoleon, For and Against*, pp. 235–350.

7. Examples drawn from several different periods include Hans Jacob Christoph von Grimmelhausen, *Simplicissimus the Vagabond*; Tobias Smollett, *Roderick Random*; Erich-Maria Remarque, *All Quiet on the Western Front*; and Joseph Heller, *Catch-22*.

8. These include books by the Frenchman Raymond Guyot, the Englishman J. Holland Rose, and the American Robert Lord, which I cited frequently in the third chapter.

9. Henry Adams, "The Tendency of History," in George Hochfield, ed., *The Great Secession Winter of 1860–61 and Other Essays* (New York, 1958), pp. 415–423.

of Versailles. But the greatest of all works on the subject, Albertini's *The Origins of the War of 1914*, dealt with all the great powers in an impartially critical spirit and ended with the statement that the outbreak of war in 1914 reflected the general ineptitude of European diplomacy.[10]

Across the Atlantic, the United States in 1787 had adopted a constitution based quite specifically upon suspicion of state power. A minimalist conception of the state, together with a profound suspicion of military and naval establishments and a distaste for European power politics, characterized American political life for most of the nineteenth century. This did not of course prevent the United States from fighting expansionist wars, from taking part in the imperialist scramble in the 1890s, or even from entering the First World War, but an anti-imperialist tradition remained strong well into the 1930s. The Second World War and its aftermath, however, enshrined various aspects of the myth of state power within the United States. The defeat of the Nazis and the Japanese and the subsequent economic revival, for which governments naturally took a great deal of the credit, seemed to confirm the utility of military power and the state's ability to promote prosperity. The climate of the cold war, in which western governments made very large peacetime demands upon their peoples for the purpose of meeting a proclaimed Communist threat, had the same effect, and the traditional anti-imperialist attitude was almost extinct by the 1950s.[11] Throughout the world states have continued to claim the right and the capacity to act for the common good, both domestically and internationally. So strong was this tendency that the original critique of the cold war, undertaken in the 1960s by American revisionist historians, accepted the idea of an all-powerful state, while arguing that the American government had used its power for essentially malevolent purposes.

The rationalist model of state behavior underwent a brilliant attack almost twenty years ago in Graham Allison's *Essence of Deci-*

---

10. Albertini, *Origins of the War of 1914*, III, 702.

11. Interestingly enough, perhaps the greatest classic of the anti-imperialist tradition—Charles A. Beard, *President Roosevelt and the Coming of the War, 1941: A Study in Appearances and Realities* (New Haven, 1948)—appeared after the *Second* World War. So out of step was it with prevailing opinion, however, that it has never received anywhere near the attention it deserves.

sion, which put forth some alternative explanations of government policy in crisis.[12] I have taken a similar approach here while dealing with a much broader range of historical problems. A true history of politics requires an understanding of the ways in which the broader political context influences the actions of individual statesmen; the impossibility, in many instances, of controlling events; and the frequency with which actions have unintended consequences. Each of these facts of political life threatens the myth of the state so dear to most politicians and many historians. Yet these facts themselves are not nearly so frightening as our persistent failure to acknowledge them.

12. Graham Allison, *Essence of Decision: Explaining the Cuban Missile Crisis* (Boston, 1971).

Afterword, 2000

Since 1945 Europe has lived through a new era in international politics—the Cold War—and is now about ten years into the post–Cold War period. Since neither era included a general war in Europe, neither deserves a full treatment within this book. Nonetheless, both may be compared with the four periods I have treated in detail here to suggest why the Cold War did not result in a major conflict despite its profound ideological antagonisms, and to identify the possible sources of conflict in the new era.

The international politics of the Cold War in Europe grew directly out of the era of the two world wars but showed some new features as well. To begin with, both the United States and the Soviet Union proclaimed foreign policy goals of extraordinary scope. Their official ideologies made even the dreams of Napoleon look relatively restrained. After the proclamation of the Truman Doctrine in 1947, the government of the United States seemed committed to the maintenance of non-Communist regimes throughout the world, without reference to their particular strategic importance. The Eisenhower administration in the 1950s quietly decided to fight local wars—and if need be a world war—almost anywhere that Communism tried to expand.[1] At times American politicians suggested that the security of the United States depended on the disappearance of Communism. Meanwhile, the Soviet Union claimed to be assisting the entire world in a transition from capitalism to socialism and Communism. Both powers, in short, put themselves forward as the opposing models

---

1. See David Kaiser, *American Tragedy: Kennedy, Johnson, and the Origins of the Vietnam War* (Cambridge, Mass., 2000), chap. 1.

between which the rest of the world must choose. But since they were quite unable to put these fantastic goals into practice, they, like the European imperialists of the late nineteenth century, faced the difficult political problem of reconciling these goals with reality.

In the early decades of the Cold War, the two powers generally solved this problem by failing to acknowledge unpleasant facts. The United States and some of its allies refused to recognize the governments of Communist China and East Germany for decades after they had clearly established themselves, preferring to deny their right to exist, and the Soviets initially took a similar position toward West Germany. Not until the Helsinki Final Act of 1975 did both sides officially accept the post-1945 European territorial settlement. Much of the Cold War, moreover, rested upon a principle that had initially emerged during the First World War: that negotiation with an adversary was possible only from a position of commanding strength.

The atmosphere of the Cold War, combined with the advent of strategic nuclear weapons, enabled the military establishments of the United States and the Soviet Union to command an unprecedented share of their nations' peacetime gross national product. With their social and political systems supposedly threatened with destruction at any moment and with the whole world theoretically at stake in the competition between them, the two governments built up the largest military forces in peacetime history. Yet general war never came. Growing evidence suggests that neither side ever seriously considered a military attack upon the other's position in Europe, much less upon its home territory.[2] Their caution undoubtedly owed much to their awareness of the potential effects of nuclear weapons, but it also reflected their lack of any real interest in changing the situation in Europe as it had evolved after 1945.[3] With the help of nuclear weapons, Moscow and Washington seem to have learned the lesson that had eluded European governments in the first half of the twentieth century: that it is almost impossible for modern states and societies to benefit from all-out war.

2. See, for example, Vladislav Zubok and Constantine Pleshakov, *Inside the Kremlin's Cold War: From Stalin to Khrushchev* (Cambridge, Mass., 1996); and especially Marc Trachtenberg, *A Constructed Peace: The Making of the European Settlement, 1945–1963* (Princeton, 1999).

3. The first book to emphasize this was Anton W. Deporte, *Europe between the Superpowers: The Enduring Balance* (New Haven, 1978).

Outside Europe—and especially within the territories that liberated themselves from European colonialism after 1945—the United States and the Soviet Union pursued informal imperialism on a grand scale. Going well beyond the views of late nineteenth-century Europeans, they each adopted the position that the disappearance of any friendly third-world government meant a defeat and a danger to themselves, while any opportunity to extend their sphere of influence had to be taken. But they rarely deployed military force to shore up their friends or defeat their enemies, preferring to employ economic and military aid, political subversion, and covert action to score points in a continuing and inconclusive competition. The United States deployed combat troops to protect friendly regimes twice, in South Korea and South Vietnam, and the Soviet Union did the same in Afghanistan.

The experience of the United States in Korea and Vietnam paralleled the European experience of the First World War. The public expected victory. Victory in these two conflicts was defined quite differently, but in neither case could the government that began the war achieve it, and Presidents Truman and Johnson suffered the fate of Asquith and Bethmann Hollweg as a result. Neither one dared to run for re-election, and the electorate turned dramatically against their party. In both cases a reluctance to accept the difficulty of achieving victory persisted long after the war. Although the Soviet government did not have to deal directly with public opinion in Afghanistan, their involvement was also a failure, and their decision to conclude the conflict after eight years helped signal a fundamental change in their regime. Together, Vietnam and Afghanistan revealed military power to be a most ineffective means of maintaining weak, friendly third-world governments.

The demise of Communism in 1989–1991 ushered in the post–Cold War era. The historical debate over whether the Soviet collapse owed more to international or to domestic influences will require decades to resolve, but that it destroyed one era of European international politics and began another cannot be disputed. Now, after nearly a decade, one may distinguish certain critical aspects of the new era and the ways in which it has already threatened and will probably continue to threaten the peace of Europe.

One is a revived nationalism in Eastern Europe. The end of the Soviet empire revealed that the nationalities conflicts that played such an important role in the era of the two world wars had continued to fester under Communist rule, and within just a few years they had led to yet another application of the principle of self-determination on an even more sweeping scale. Slovakia, Slovenia, Croatia, Bosnia, Macedonia, Belarus, and Ukraine have become independent for the first time, and the Baltic states have been restored.[4] The territory of pre-1914 Austria-Hungary, parceled out among seven new states after the First World War, now includes a total of ten. War has broken out between the former Yugoslavia (now inhabited mainly by Serbs) and Croatia and Bosnia, and a new war took place in 1999 in Kosovo. The NATO alliance intervened carefully in the Bosnia war and, more massively, albeit only from the air, in Kosovo. Another series of nationality conflicts has broken out in the Caucasus regions of the former Soviet Union, leading to a large and indecisive war in Chechnya and a new conflict in Dagestan. Communist rule, it is clear, kept these political struggles under wraps for forty-five to seventy years, but the inhabitants of Eastern Europe have yet to discover an institutional structure that would allow different ethnic, linguistic, and religious groups to live together in peace. Hungary and Rumania signed a new Basic Treaty in 1996 promising to respect the rights of their respective national minorities and specifically pledging to grant them the human rights promised by the United Nations charter and other European treaties, but their example has not yet been widely imitated.[5]

Yet the renewed outbreak of conflict and war in Eastern Europe has never seriously threatened to unleash a broader European conflict because of the enormous political transformations in Western Europe. Six European nations—France, Italy, West Germany, and the Benelux countries—formed the European Economic Community (EC) in 1957, and the Community (now the EC) has expanded and moved toward full economic union during the last forty years, almost completely renouncing the economic imperialism that did so much to bring about the two world wars. They also show no signs of abandoning the American-led NATO alliance, despite the disappearance of the Communist threat, or of reopening territorial quarrels. Germany renounced its old borders once and for all in the course of its reunification. The right-wing parties that have tried to challenge the growing power of supranational institutions have not yet been able to affect this long-term trend.

4. Ukraine, of course, had briefly been independent in the immediate aftermath of the First World War.

5. For the treaty see 36 *International Legal Materials* 340 (1997).

Thus, although the political differences between Western and Eastern Europe that played such an important role in the origins and course of the two world wars have if anything become more substantial, they have not threatened similar consequences because of the reorientation of Western European international politics. NATO, the European Community, and other international institutions have tried to stop the new Balkan wars, and even intervened directly in two of them, but no individual state has taken advantage of these conflicts to risk a wider war for its own purposes, as Germany did in 1914 and then again under Hitler. Nor does any nation show signs of doing so in the near or medium-term future. The NATO countries also cooperated to defend the common interests of the Western world in the Persian Gulf War against Iraq.

How, then, shall the continuing problems in Eastern and Southeastern Europe be resolved? The recent inclusion of Poland, the Czech Republic, and Hungary in NATO, and the continuing discussions of their eventual membership in the EC, suggest that the institutions of Western Europe might steadily advance further to the East, eventually integrating the whole continent into a multinational economic, political, and military structure linked closely with the United States. Should this occur, it would clearly solve, at least for the time being, the problem of European international politics in the modern era that has been the subject of this book. Yet whether it will occur turns on historical questions of the broadest possible character.

Viewed as a whole, the last three centuries have witnessed a gradual expansion of democracy and capitalism, as foretold in the first half of the nineteenth century by two great European thinkers, Tocqueville and Marx. So fundamental are their comments on the direction of Western history that they deserve once more to be quoted. Writing in 1835, Tocqueville argued that democracy, by which he mainly meant social and political equality, was certain to sweep over the Christian world. "The gradual progress of equality is something fated," he wrote. "The main features of this progress are the following: it is universal and permanent, it is daily passing beyond human control, and every event and every man helps it along."[6] Thirteen years later Karl Marx and Friedrich Engels described the spread of capitalism in even more prophetic terms. "The bourgeoisie,"

---

6. Alexis de Tocqueville, *Democracy in America*, trans. J. P. Mayer (New York, 1964), p. 5.

they wrote, "by the rapid improvement of all instruments of production, by the immensely facilitated means of communication,

> draws all, even the most barbarian, nations into civilization. The cheap prices of its commodities are the heavy artillery with which it batters down all Chinese walls, with which it forces the barbarians' intensely obstinate hatred of foreigners to capitulate. It compels all nations, on pain of extinction, to adopt the bourgeois mode of production . . . In one word, it creates a world after its own image.[7]

The history of the last 150 years suggests that both democracy in the narrower Tocquevillian sense and bourgeois capitalism as described by Marx and Engels are destined sooner or later to encompass the entire globe. Communism, it seems, was merely a long and costly detour from this more natural path, and Marx and Engels miscalculated both the time that the spread of bourgeois capitalism would take and what would come after it. The spread of these new economic and political institutions, however, has been a very uneven and temporarily reversible process, and not only in Russia, China, and other countries that have come under Communist rule. Moreover, while democracy in the sense of social and political equality has continued to spread apace, elections and representative institutions have not reached nearly as much of the globe. Thus, while the world in 50 or 100 years will probably be both more democratic and more capitalist than it is today, the process is unlikely to be either smooth or linear.

As a result, it remains very unclear exactly what European, NATO, or United Nations military forces can do to speed up or defend the progress of democracy, capitalism, and human rights in many parts of the world, including Eastern Europe and the former Soviet Union. The admission of Eastern European states into the European Community has already been delayed, perhaps indefinitely. Certainly NATO has not discovered any means of settling nationality conflicts in Southeastern Europe more justly. Although a NATO occupation force has now kept the peace in Bosnia for several years, after Serbs had already carried out substantial ethnic cleansing, the return of the state to some kind of normal political life is not in sight. In Kosovo, NATO bombing induced the Yugoslav government to withdraw its troops and allow for the return of a large portion of the Kosovar Albanian refugees. It seems, however, that the long-term

---

7. Karl Marx and Friedrich Engels, "Manifesto of the Communist Party," ed. Robert Tucker, *The Marx-Engels Reader* (New York, 1972), p. 339.

result of NATO's intervention will be to remove the Serbs, rather than the Albanians, from the province—a solution parallel to the solution of nationality conflicts involving Germans in 1945, and one that will not provide a very useful or inspiring example for solving other nationality conflicts.

The official policy of the United States—clearly more than ever the leader of the NATO alliance—assumes that the spread of democracy can and should be a continuing, linear, and irreversible process. Such an assumption, combined in much of the world with the absence of any obvious military competitor, can easily tempt the United States and its European allies to intervene in a host of violent domestic political struggles or to try to topple murderous regimes. Yet whether military action can deal with such problems at a reasonable cost remains very unclear. Intervention in the former Soviet Union, moreover, would raise a host of very serious dangers, all the more so because of the presence within Russia of thousands of nuclear weapons.

And thus, although the Western world may not have been so united in its way of life, its beliefs, and its basic institutions since at least the late Middle Ages, both the purposes for which it will deploy military power in the immediate future and the success it will achieve suddenly have become, once again, very open questions. For the moment the NATO alliance faces no immediate military threat to its security, but any large-scale use of force to affect the political and economic development of Eastern Europe or other parts of the world could easily prove as futile and as costly as the efforts to increase royal power in the late sixteenth and early seventeenth centuries. And thus, while the shape of the new era in European and world affairs is only slowly emerging, the maintenance of peace and the pace of progress will still depend largely upon politicians' skill at mediating between imagination and reality—the task of politics in every era, continually changing according to circumstances, yet remaining essentially the same.

Index